ALLEGORIES OF HISTORY

ALLEGORIES OF HISTORY

Literary Historiography after Hegel

TIMOTHY BAHTI

THE JOHNS HOPKINS UNIVERSITY PRESS

Baltimore and London

This book has been brought to publication with the generous assistance of the Horace H. Rackham School of Graduate Studies and the Office of the Vice President for Research, The University of Michigan.

The Johns Hopkins University Press
701 West 40th Street
Baltimore, Maryland 21211-2190
The Johns Hopkins Press Ltd., London

Library of Congress Cataloging-in-Publication Data

Bahti, Timothy, 1952–
    Allegories of history : literary historiography after Hegel / Timothy Bahti.
        p.   cm.
    Includes bibliographical references and index.
    ISBN 0-8018-4342-1 (alk. paper)
    1. Literature and history.   2. History—Philosophy.   3. Historiography—
History.   4. Germany—Historiography—History.   5. German literature—
History and criticism.   I. Title.
PN50.B36   1992
907'.2—dc20   91-41130

Paul de Man *in memoriam*
Jim Siegel *per amicitiam*

Contents

vii

Preface

I began writing a part of this study in 1978 and first came to conceive it as a book in the early 1980s. As I have worked on it, changes have of course occurred in the context of American literary-theoretical scholarship. Various renewed appeals to kinds of historical study have come under various names: the "new historicism," the "new history," the call to "always historicize." Much interest and work have also been directed toward the institutional status and structures of literary studies, in the present as well as in the preceding century or two. My work had its conception and orientation—however unclear both initially were—independent of either the revived cachet of rehistoricizing or the archeological inquiries into the institutions of criticism and theory. My attention in this book to these contemporary developments has been more epiphenomenal than essential, and I have tried to avoid discussions that might, in their polemics, distract from the scholarly issues at hand, which I understand to be the constructions and deconstructions that underwrite the discourse of history per se. I have added a few remarks in a brief afterword.

Several readings of twentieth-century Germanic literary historians and theorists were first written, it now seems to me, in an attempt to respond to the intrinsic interest and difficulty of their problems. As I learned more about their conceptual and discursive contexts, I realized that eighteenth- and nineteenth-century German philosophical and institutional texts were inscribed in their own work and that these earlier writings had to be studied both to help to understand the later achievements and failures and as a possible contribution to present-day research that reconsiders literary history and literary reading. Thus what is here part one first emerged as the backdrop and stage for part two, which was already playing out its own dynamic. Then with Hegel it took on its own interest, as did the Benjamin chapters in part two.

My research and writing have been assisted by many people and institutions for a long time. Research support from Dean John D'Arms and the University of Michigan's Horace H. Rackham School of Grad-

ix

uate Studies and from Associate Vice President Hemalata Dandekar and the Office of the Vice President for Research has been generous and timely. A fellowship at the Woodrow Wilson International Center for Scholars in the fall of 1984 allowed me to do much of the research for the first part of the project, and I express my gratitude to the Wilson Center's director then, James Billington, to its Program Secretaries Ann C. Sheffield (History, Culture, and Society) and Seymour Drescher (Western Europe), and to its staff and especially to my research assistant, Jane Garnett. My colleagues Robert L. Kyes and Stuart Y. McDougal have been crucially supportive in the years of finishing this work. My editor, Eric Halpern, has been committed and patient in equally generous and necessary measures.

My teachers at Yale University, Jacques Derrida, John Freccero, and Geoffrey Hartman, informed much of my thinking and reading in the topics of this book during graduate school and in years since. A number of friends have been especially encouraging in their suggestions and support, and I wish to thank Ellen Burt, Cynthia Chase, Rodolphe Gasché, Jerry Graff, Werner Hamacher, Christiaan Hart Nibbrig, Richard Klein, Jim Porter, and Alan Waters.

Paul de Man taught me what I know about reading, and this work would not have been possible without his challenging teaching and the rigorous example of his writing. Jim Siegel's generosity with his conversation and writings and his excitement for Hegel and Benjamin have sustained my reading and thinking for all the years I have worked on this book. It is dedicated to them.

Claviers–Ann Arbor,
April 1991

PART ONE

I

History Enters the University: Philosophy and History to the University of Berlin

I n 1959 the *Historische Zeitschrift* celebrated its hundredth anniversary. The journal had been founded and edited by Ranke's student Heinrich von Sybel. Its contributors had included Ranke as well as such other distinguished nineteenth-century German historians as Georg Waitz, Johann Gustav Droysen, and Theodor Mommsen. It was briefly edited by the most widely read German historian of the century, Heinrich von Treitschke, and then for forty years by the most honored German historian of the first part of this century, Friedrich Meinecke. It was, in short, the emblem for German historical studies, which discipline was taken, in 1959 as it still is today, to represent one of the highest achievements of nineteenth-century German intellectual life. To mark its centenary, then, the journal commissioned an issue devoted to "the history of historiography in the German-speaking countries." Included in the volume was a monograph-length contribution, "The German Universities and the Study of History." In this piece, Josef Engel, after painstakingly and subtly tracing the developments of the university study of history from the fourteenth century onward, found himself in his chronicle near the end of that great century of German historical writing and penned the following paragraphs:

> The idealist concept of Wissenschaft unleashed German research upon all areas of study and worked for the whole world like a yeast for immeasurably expansive research. It also included the demand that all Wissenschaften expand knowledge and progress within knowledge. But the knowledge that was supposed to be newly acquired was taken to be attainable, both as objectively valid and as real knowledge. However long the process of achieving knowledge might stretch into the future, the concept of knowledge—as that which was to be expanded, confirmed,

and perfected—nonetheless demanded that it be possible to complete such knowledge and fix it once and for all. An endpoint characterized by pure and real knowledge was at least strived toward and therefore also held to be attainable.

This was the ethos with which newly autonomous scholarly and scientific research made its triumphant march into the [nineteenth] century. It was still valid when, for example, Schopenhauer (in "Über die Universitäts-Philosophie" from *Parerga und Paralipomena*, published in 1851) denied philosophy the character of a Wissenschaft and declared that its representation in the university was an absurdity. The irritated pride of the rejected Berlin *Privatdozent* was less decisive for this judgment than his insight—dictated by the rigorously idealist concept of Wissenschaft—that philosophy within a university dependent upon the state would be Wissenschaft "that is yet to be found"; that furthermore, even if one disregarded this independence, philosophy in the university could only make "philosophy" into an "applied" one; and that finally, so long as the "ever wider expansion of every kind of historical, physical, and even philosophical knowledge" continued, philosophy in the university would necessarily be able to contain only "allegorical truth" in relation to the state of knowledge at the moment.

With Schopenhauer a change was announced that was continued by historians under the sign of that "historicism" which had become suspect because of this very change. We mean the feeling that all scholarly and scientific work is in principle undecidable, a feeling that broke out at the end of the nineteenth century and even included the natural sciences (as Max Planck's remark on the impossibility of a "presuppositionless" science indicates). Philosophy at this time was limping along behind these scholarly and scientific developments and, after its collapse in the second third of the century, was only slowly once again beginning to reflect upon its task. When it did, it gave expression to this same feeling in Heidegger's phrase about "the hiddenness of being" (*die Verborgenheit des Seins*)—without, however, providing any help to the Wissenschaften that had already noticed this somewhat earlier.

Goethe's saying that "world-history [*Weltgeschichte*] must be rewritten from time to time" (to Sartorius, 4 February 1811) was composed out of skepticism toward the character of Wissenschaft and as a devaluing judgment about the scholarly and scientific character of universal history (*Universalgeschichte*). Now, at the end of the century, this saying was seen by the discipline of history as a summons and as an exact expression of its own special scholarly and scientific character and was elevated to become a leitmotif of its own work. Ranke and the older phase of historical studies could still cover up this thought, which disqualified ultimate historical knowledge, through their recourse to the claim of the immediacy of every epoch before God and in their belief in the imperishable force of moral energies directed toward the ethical sphere that were at hand in every

4

epoch in a different manner; and thus they were able to preserve the scholarly and scientific character of history as a discipline duty-bound to objectivity. Or, like Mommsen, it rescued itself on the island of the "major industry" of the discovery of historical sources, regulated only by formal accuracy to the works. The new historical thinking, on the other hand, which had relieved itself of its older universalist-moralistic and idealist grounds, either sought to trace out the existence of laws that were immanent in historical occurrences (as Lamprecht did) or understood epochs as wholes bound together through specific continuities. Thus the question regarding the possibility of knowledge about them seemed to be solved simply through Dilthey's concept of understanding—a concept fundamentally fuzzy, taking off from the universality of human homogeneity and yet thoroughly steeped in the subjectivity of lived experience. As a consequence of this concept, the "bogey man" of a logical separation of two kinds of knowledge necessarily had to be postulated, that of the natural sciences on one side and the human sciences on the other. Despite great outward confidence, from the 1880s onward the historians lost the essentially common content of their work. And in addition to their own disputes, they saw themselves exposed to attacks from the outside that blamed them for the relativizing of knowledge and accused them of yet many more sins against the spirit of "Wissen"-schaft.[1]

I have presented these paragraphs, with their ample complexity, at the beginning of this study because in the very difficulty they recount and contain they succinctly pose the problems that underlie this study as well. The quoted paragraphs are written by a historian of historiography and of the disciplinary institution of historical Wissenschaft, and they attempt to describe a crisis in the philosophical underpinnings of the practices of that historiography and that institution. The present work, written by a student of literature, is a study of literary historiography in its relations to German idealism, Hegel, and the *Geschichtsphilosophie* (philosophy of history) and practices of historiography that issue from them. Historically, Engel's account of his subject at that nineteenth-century juncture that we have just read may be taken to be accurate—in its broad contours if not in its many missing details. It corresponds roughly to that development in intellectual attitudes that is now known, after Troeltsch's title of 1922, as "the crisis of historicism."[2] This large "crisis" includes such forbidding names as Schopenhauer, Nietzsche, and finally Heidegger, and it involves the persuasive demonstration (persuasive at least within German intellectual circles of the time, and to many since) that instead of simply having man and all things human *in* history (historicism's fundamental tenet), one has historicism within man as a particular form of his "will to power," man

5

within historicity, and both within temporality—whether this tempo-rality is then construed as an eternal return or the "thrownness" of being.

Engel's problems underlie the present study, or form its backdrop. For the present study, on twentieth-century literary historiography in the wake of Hegel, finds its objects of investigation displayed against the background of general historiography in the modern university. The literary-historical writers whom I treat each stood in direct and mani-festly conscious relations to the modern problems of history, of how to think about it and how to write it. Whether Erich Auerbach, Georg Lukács, or Walter Benjamin, they were at once heirs to the Hegelian and nineteenth-century historicist traditions, and alternately bewil-dered questioners and determined critics of this German historical thinking. To the extent that the writers and writings this study ad-dresses are situated against the backdrop of the "crisis of historicism," it has seemed useful to me to reconstruct, not the century-long unfold-ing, criticisms, and decay of German historicism—a highly specialized and well-worked subject that offers a number of worthy studies, includ-ing some in English[3]—but rather its initial institutionalization: its phil-osophical "legitimation," one might call it, which led to the early prac-tical development of historical studies (including the history of modern languages and literatures) in the nineteenth-century German university. For although the late Nietzsche and (at least until recently) the mature Marx may be held by many, and with much justification, to be the en-during German thinkers of history from that century, it was in the uni-versity and in the very idea of scholarly and scientific knowledge (Wis-senschaft) that history came into its own as a modern way of thinking and writing, and here we are closer to Hegel and his *university* heri-tage—which includes Ranke, many literary historians, and the early Nietzsche—than to Marxism or the late Nietzsche. I might add that just as our contemporary theoretical debates about literary study are almost exclusively "universitarian," the discipline of the study of mod-ern literatures, in which these debates take place, is itself a consequence of the institutionalization of history per se within the German univer-sity: modern literary studies remain to this day what they became in the early nineteenth century, an institutional adjunct to modern historical study and thought, and this goes a long way toward explaining the re-cently renewed appeals that the study of literature return, after some alleged "theoretical" wandering, to "history."[4]

Thus, preceding the main analytic and critical parts of this book—the studies of several of Hegel's confrontations with history and those of several Germanic literary historians writing their histories or theories of histories——I have seen fit to introduce an expository part, an exposition of the university's philosophic justification and implementation of history as being an object and locus of knowledge at all. This exposition divides into several sections. First I sketch the development of "history" as a disciplinary discourse in the German universities from the late-medieval trivium to the "modern" *Philosophische Fakultät* at the beginning of the nineteenth century. Then there is the relation between idealist philosophy's rhetoric about Wissenschaft in the university and proto-historicist rhetoric about the specific Wissenschaft of historical studies. Here the discussion necessarily focuses on several philosophers' writings on university study, including some of those oriented toward the founding of the University of Berlin, the most idealized university in its inception and the most prestigious and emulated university in the world by the end of the century, above all as regards the study of history. It is from this perspective that we can then turn to the figure of Hegel, whose position in German philosophy and the German university nineteenth-century German historians, especially Ranke and then German literary historians, may be said to have "followed," to have been at once "after" and, despite themselves, "according to."

For one textual event or writer to follow, to come after, another is a literal historical fact; for the same text or writer to be discursively "according to" a preceding one is a representation and an interpretation.[5] The German *nach*, like the French *après/d'après*, captures this double sense in a single word. History, as Hegel and others have noted, is also a double word, naming the events and their representation and interpretation, the history that happened or was made and the history that is done by thought and writing. We have already seen in passing Schopenhauer refer to philosophy's mere "allegorical truth" with reference to an ever-expanding field of knowledge, including historical knowledge. If history in its first sense is not only very, very large when it refers to the past that has already passed but ever-expanding when it includes the awareness that each passing moment enlarges this history, could history in its second sense—its representation, its knowledge—ever have more than an "allegorical truth" vis-à-vis the unfixed and enlarging dimensions of its literal basis? It was Schopenhauer who also offered, in *Die Welt als Wille und Vorstellung* (2:444), a motto for history: *Eadem, sed aliter*, "the same, but otherwise." Might this be understood not only as a world-weary reflection of the "plus ça change, plus ça reste la même chose" variety (or of Kafka's elliptical entry in his diary on 5 January 1912: "Uniformity. History") but as an insight into allegory as well? In these opening pages of a study that announces "Allegories of History: Literary Historiography after Hegel"—with this "after" now understood in its double sense—I would conclude with an introductory remark about allegory and history.

History is put together and comes apart as allegory. There is a "sameness, but otherwise" to this aspect of history: a sameness that insists that history be literal in its attachment to—indeed, in its first sense, as its wishful identity with—what really happened; an otherwise that adds the other of interpretation and meaning as the level at which history as understanding attempts to occur. To signal the otherness built into the two senses of the term "history"—each sense is the other of the other, the literal sense only uttered from the perspective of the interpretive one, the interpretive one unutterable except as a representation of the literal one—is to signal allegory, *allos-agoreuein*, "to speak otherwise." "Allegory" here is not a dismissive or pejorative term, nor one of approbation. It is an analytic term of a certain expansiveness and flexibility, naming an aspect of figurative rhetoric, a kind of writing and discourse, and also a structure of reading. It will be the burden of proof of this book to demonstrate the allegorical structures—"the same, but otherwise"—of the conception of history and of the practices of historiography, first in Schelling and Fichte, then in Hegel, and then in the individual literary-theoretical and literary-historical works of our modern authors. The point here may be left as follows: History is put together as literal signs for meanings of a past that survives, if at all, as those very signs; but the meanings would survive—live on—and re-present a meaningfulness beyond the literal passages of time that the signs mark, and this is allegory as construction, an allegorical construction of the doubled thing that is history. And history comes apart as meanings that negate both the literal character of their signs—that temporality which constitutes them as historical—and the very meaningfulness that would be constituted in a difference from that literalism of history. This is allegory as deconstruction, an allegory that emerges from reading history as and how it is written. Neither the one nor the other, the putting together or the coming apart, is *the* allegory of history. For any allegory is always allegories, speaking otherwise.

A narrative of the development of historical studies in the German universities repeats history, and in at least two senses. It tells the story of a story, of a "historical development," and since it is a story that historians have at times had reason to be interested in, it can scarcely be retold without relating parts of their versions of it. In what follows I will be relying extensively on the published research of other scholars.[6] But I also mean to recount their findings in such a way that some of the implicit assumptions that have conventionally guided such scholarship might be opened for critical questioning. For while Josef Engel is shrewder than many in the way he understands the rise of historical studies to be also the increasing unfolding of its problems, the traditional way of treating this topic has been to see it as the triumph of history over the pre- and nonhistorical. Thus Herbert Butterfield may be taken as representative when he writes that "it would appear that in this field [the history of historiography] the primary object of study has always been the development of a more technical form of scholarship, the rise of a more scientific history, and the progress in the critical treatment of sources."[7] The language used here—"development," "more technical," "rise," "more scientific," "progress," "critical treatment"— implies the improvement over time of historical thinking and writing as a scientific and scholarly activity, and to the extent that inquiries into the history of historiography are usually carried out by professional, disciplinary historians, this conceptual and terminological bias should scarcely surprise us. My purpose, however, in retelling their story— along with the employment of many of their terms—is to highlight the appearance of history in the university as a scientific and scholarly activity per se and thus to display the means and grounds by which the university intellectually justified this kind of study.

The late-medieval German universities (the first was founded in Heidelberg in 1385, and ten more were instituted before the end of the fifteenth century) were not dominated by a single faculty, as the University of Paris was by theology, or as the universities in Bologna and Salerno were by law and medicine, respectively. Theology was, to be sure, considered the highest, or "queen," science, but not to the exclusion of the other faculties, and four faculties were held in a hierarchy that characteristically not only placed theology at the top (at least theoretically) but had the *facultas artium* at the bottom. The three higher faculties constituted professional schools, or, as they are called in German, *Erziehungsinstitute*, pedagogic institutes for training in a particular professional domain, while the lower arts faculty served the role of a *propaedeuticum* for the other three—a role it retained until the late seventeenth century, when improved secondary schools allowed many students to enter the professional faculties directly. Within the arts faculty, studies were themselves hierarchically organized according to the scholastic-Aristotelian division by which formal and logical training in the trivium was the prerequisite for study of the quadrivium (arithmetic, music, geometry, and astronomy), although scholasticism had progressively enhanced the status of Aristotelian logic within the arts, so that the quadrivium was effectively rendered more trivial than the trivium. At least in theory, however, the *artes* were a *propaedeuticum* for the three higher faculties and held their own *propaedeuticum*—the trivium—within themselves.

Under the pressure of Italian-inspired humanists (the plural "humanists" should be retained in order to distinguish this development from early nineteenth-century German "humanism"), the late-fifteenth- and sixteenth-century German arts faculties faced a challenge to their formal-logical training in the trivium. This development is often somewhat simplistically understood as the Renaissance humanists' introduction of historical and philological material—classical as opposed to post-classical or medieval Latin; Greek; and ancient Roman and Greek poets and orators—into the university curricula and thus as the immediate initiation of historical studies therein. But this understanding is both wrong as regards the immediate impact of the humanists and misleading as to the actual introduction of history into the university. The challenge to the arts faculties was not an argument for history but rather one for the moral *content* of the *artes*. It must be admitted that ethics had been included in the trivium in preceding centuries, in a curious relationship with grammar as well as with rhetoric, but under the dominance of logic in the scholastic system its status was nonetheless marginalized. Now the pressure was for the content of the *artes*, as opposed to formal-logical training in them: the arts were to yield the teaching of virtue by way of worldly wisdom. This meant an expansion of the *propaedeuticum* of the trivium into a form that would better suit the moral, content-oriented goal, and it specifically meant the inclusion not only of logic, grammar, and rhetoric but also of poetry, ethics, and, indeed, history. Thus the trivium became the *studia humanitatis*, and history found its place in the arts faculty as a particular *ars*.

But to say this much is already to *re*simplify and misrepresent the matter, for this development of the "humanities" was less an introduction of two or three new "arts" into the faculty than it was an expansion of one art—rhetoric—to include two or three other things. History and poetry were included within a branching out of the *ars rhetorica*. Viewed from a perspective that is Continental and not exclusively Germanic, this was not so much progress as regress, for in the less Aristotelian organization of the Italian and other European arts faculties, history had already been included, if only as an *appendentia artium*, then nevertheless as a glorified appendix. As Engel writes,

> The Ciceronian *historia magistra vitae* runs through medieval writings on the theory of knowledge; indeed, sometimes history even appears as the crown of the trivium [Hugo of St. Victor, *PL* 176, 185C] and almost synonymous with ethics [cf. John of Salisbury's image of *historia* as *omnium artium imago*], that is, with the purpose of basic education by way of

the seven *artes liberales*—and especially the trivium—which Thierry of Chartres had spoken of as a *synodus ad cultum humanitatis*.[8]

From this perspective, the introduction of history into the German arts faculties was not the establishment of a "high road," an elevated study parallel to the other arts, much less its promotion as the common meaning of those arts. History was at best one art among others, and actually one art within another, included as a kind of writing, along with poetry, within rhetoric, just as oratory or eloquence had already been included there. These kinds of language use—today we would call them "discourse"—together constituted the stuff, the material, from which virtue or morality could be learned.

The oft-touted rise of textual criticism and source study in "the Renaissance" is relevant here only to the extent that historical writing, poetry, and eloquence—once they were conceived as representing worldly wisdom, which could in its turn be used in the service of an education toward morality—demanded their establishment in reliable and, what was equally important, numerous editions (sufficiently numerous to make up a "humanistic" education). It was a question not of determining a historical truth about the past but of using a moral truth drawn from a past text for present purposes, and establishing enough such texts-of-truth-and-virtue to enable a viable educational program. Just as the *humaniora* within the German university did not lead to their own study in any practical or intellectual sense but rather continued in their propaedeutic service to the "higher" faculties, so was history present not as an object of study in its own right but only as historiography, as one kind of writing among others (collectively called *eloquentia*), all of which could be studied and taught as the verbal embodiment of moral wisdom. Thus, if Eugenio Garin could write of the Italian Renaissance humanist Speron Speroni's *Dialogo delle lingue* (1552) that "he reduced history to a description of the particular and described the particular as *truth*, reported by the historian with the help of rhetorical artistry,"[9] it is much more the case in German universities of this time that history is "reduced" to the communication of the *generally* true in the sense of the *exemplary*, whereby the rhetorical term "exemplar" *(exemplum)* also indicates that the historiographer is viewed not merely as using rhetoric but as one rhetorician among others (poets, orators), with all of rhetoric providing the *exempla* for wise and virtuous action. Thus the first so-called chair for history in a German university, the *lectura historica* established at Mainz in 1504, indicates only a division of labor in the teaching of virtue through wisdom, wherein its occupant would teach only ancient historians, and not ancient poets and orators as well; and indeed, the first occupant, Bernhard Schöfferlin, could write in introduction to his translation of Livy that "for what would most of all serve as wisdom for a worldly man, there is nothing more useful and fruitful than diligently reading histories and ancient stories."[10]

If it is a commonly held assumption that the Reformation, and the Lutheran reform of Protestant universities that came with it, changed all this, this is as much an oversimplification as was the opinion regarding historical philology imported from the Renaissance. The tendency toward a self-justifying, lay study of the *humaniora,* which may have been immanent to the humanists' reforms of the arts faculties (namely, morality as the goal of the *artes*), was suppressed by Luther's reinforcement of theology as the crowning faculty of the universities. The *facultas artium* retained its scholastic-cum-humanist form: Hebrew was added to the Latin and Greek already studied under "grammar," "logic" was maintained even if cleansed of some of its scholasticism, and "rhetoric" continued in its tripartite form as oratory, poetry, and historiography, and all of these arts were directed toward the training of preachers, that is, as a *propaedeuticum* for theology as the *scientia sacra.*

In practice, which is to say in the person of Melancthon and his effects upon the Protestant universities from 1518 onward, moral education received an increasingly prominent role in the arts faculties, and while he continued, in his *Encomium eloquentiae,* to assign historiography, together with oratory and poetry, to eloquence as its area of study, "history" also appears as that which gathers together "omnium humanorum officiorum exempla" and thus as a domain that subsumes the material of eloquence, if not exactly as a potentially independent area of study. (Melancthon also allowed that "omne artium genus ex historia manare," and his student Viktorin Strigel, in *Oratio de historia* [1551], presented "history" as the comprehensive term for the *studia humanitatis,* and as an independent unit of study comparable to theology, physics, and astronomy.)[11] Nonetheless, the actual *study* of history, as opposed to its quasi-theoretical characterization, remained in the service of moral teaching, and in the hands of teachers of rhetoric. As for the Catholic universities at this time, reformed in the second half of the sixteenth century by the Jesuits, their *ratio studiorum* of 1599 also had history in the service of moral education, if only indirectly and cautiously, that is, as providing, along with poetry and oratory, the *eruditio* necessary for the proper utilization of rhetoric in formal and intellectual training on behalf of *prudentia.* In both kinds of sectarian universities, in other words, history remained linked to rhetoric and in the service of the moral education of Christian men. It was only in a later consequence of the Reformation, when "history" changed from being a part of the arts faculty's general *propaedeuticum* to become what in German is called a *Hilfswissenschaft*, an auxiliary study, first to theology and then to law, that the theoretical status and methodological practice of history was changed as well.

It is these later developments that have been understood as ultimately having led to the recognition of historical studies as first a necessary, then an autonomous discipline, although the changes were slow to be manifested as such. The general process of "detheologization," or secularization, of science and knowledge, which has been studied by Hans Blumenberg as the "legitimation of curiosity,"[12] had little immediate impact on the German universities, where theology reasserted its dominant role throughout the seventeenth century, above all in the more systematically organized Catholic universities. (This "legitimation," especially regarding the natural sciences, took place, as in England, in the academies rather than in the universities.) On the other hand, the *artes* in general continued gradually to be granted a certain justification of the value of their own study, as theology began to cede to them the teaching of ethics, which it had initially denied the "humanists." With specific regard to history, the Melancthonian reforms alluded to above allowed the study of history—of man as the agent of worldly events— to enter into the widely European practice of "exemplary history," which by the eighteenth century became what George Nadel has called "the empirical part of moral philosophy."[13] But these same reforms also allowed "history" to be used by the theological faculties for the practical, exemplary instruction of their students in ethics, since history could be construed, in a post-Augustinian fashion, as the perpetual self-revealing of God and His church, and its study could therefore be used to help lead one to correct belief. Thus, parallel with a gradually secularized pedagogy of history as ethically exemplary, its study also developed into what Engel characterizes as "a theological Wissenschaft outside of theology," that is, outside of the theological faculty.[14] But not for long. For by the end of the seventeenth century theology had closed back upon itself in the sense that instructors of church history were now included within its own faculty. Generally, then, the century saw "history" transformed from mere preparatory material, one more part of the arts faculty's *propaedeuticum* to theological doctrine, to a *Hilfswissenschaft* within theology. At the same time, the law faculties increasingly took in the "humanistic" methods of textual criticism and source exegesis and thereby similarly began to create a historical *Hilfswissenschaft* of their own.

It would appear that the arts faculty thus lost history to the others, losing its one area or discipline in which investigation, or "research," the uncovering of new information (as opposed to the formal training handed down in grammar, rhetoric, and logic), was being pursued and which therefore might have elevated this faculty above its status as a mere *propaedeuticum*. But several long-term advantages evidently accrued to historical studies from this division—or appropriation—of labor. For one thing, the absorption of church history into the theology faculty freed, to some extent, the arts faculty's study of history for the revision of "profane history." Thus, for example, under pressure from philologists and their attempts to characterize post-classical Latin, the old view of *Universalhistorie* divided into the ages of the Assyrian, the Persian, the Greek, and the Roman world empires—a view derived from the Book of Daniel but associated at this time with Melancthon—gave way to attempts at the reperiodization of human history that is still with us today, namely as "ancient," "medieval," and "modern" (a revision generally attributed to Christopher Cellarius, of the University of Halle, in 1685 but anticipated by Petrarch).[15] This kind of concern with the whole of human history, adopted from the exemplary tradition and from theological history, was to mark German historical studies for the next two centuries, for when they finally became an autonomous *Fach*, or university discipline, its name would be *Universalgeschichte*, a name it retained in some German universities into the 1870s.

On the other hand, the incorporation of historical studies into the law faculties as a new *propaedeuticum* for students of jurisprudence paradoxically gave rise to developments that finally delivered history back into the arts faculties. In the service of the interests of the new, separate territorial states that had been granted their rights vis-à-vis the Reich by the Peace of Westphalia in 1648, the new historical study within jurisprudence was in structure not unlike the earlier treatment of "history" for the purpose of teaching ethics: that is, it was not so much the study of the past as its appropriation for the present; in this case, not so much the history of law as history used to serve the new, contemporary law.[16] But what this meant in practice was the proliferation of "special disciplines" researching and passing on local and not-so-local information: the history of the Reich, statesmanship, chronology, historical geography, diplomacy, genealogy, source study, heraldry, numismatics, and the like.[17] Many of these "disciplines" passed back into the arts faculties, and ultimately into *their* discipline of "history," by a steplike process in which first some of this introductory material was taught by law professors but within the walls of the arts faculty (once again the *artes* as *propaedeuticum* for a "higher" faculty), then an increasing amount of it was "farmed out" to the historians themselves for teaching to the law students (again the *propaedeuticum*), until finally, in Göttingen around the mid-eighteenth century and elsewhere thereafter, much of it was essentially incorporated into the historical *Fach* of the arts faculty as its own disciplinary material. But before this actually happened, an implicit recharacterization of "doing history" had occurred as well. For one thing, such law-oriented historical "special disciplines" taught not only *material* and its legal applications but also methods and techniques for *discovering* it; and this has always been held to be one of the hallmarks of the modern university and its "sciences" (Wissenschaften), namely, the teaching of techniques for scholarly and scientific research or discovery in place of the older passing down of a fixed body of unchanging truth.[18] Furthermore, the material of history was itself recharacterized. It was no longer only a collection of writings for the exemplification of moral behavior or the demonstration of the truth and purity of a religious creed. It had become as well an open-ended body of information for usefully illuminating and altering (or reaffirming) the practical, quotidian world.

The new professorships of "history" that were set up in the German arts faculties to teach these jurisprudential materials and techniques took their place alongside, and not in combination with, the older rhetorical-moral historical professorships still labeled chairs for "history and poetry" or "history and eloquence" or, quite simply, "morals." (It is salutary to recall that the first professorship of history in France was established at the Collège de France in 1769 as a chair for "history and morals," perhaps in this context indicating the impact of Voltaire's study of the same title.) But if there was an immanent tendency toward research in this new historical study, its disciplinary task within the faculty was still that of a *propaedeuticum*, as a *Hilfsdisziplin* for jurisprudence, and thus this kind of historical studies remained as similar to the older rhetorical kind in its pedagogic status and mission as it was dissimilar in its fundamental views of its material. It is all the more surprising, then, that it was at Göttingen, where the law faculty itself taught much of its preparatory material to its own students, that the "modern" disciplinary study of history should have been initiated, methodologically if not yet theoretically.

There may have been several reasons for this, all of them rather local to Göttingen. The first two occupants of the chair for *Universalgeschichte* took over the teaching of those *Hilfswissenschaften* left untaught by the law professors: first genealogy, chronology, and numismatics, then also diplomacy, paleography, heraldry, and geography.[19] The second occupant, Johann Christoph Gatterer, founded in 1766 a *Historisches Institut*—the first such institute, or "department," in Germany— thereby rendering these "disciplines" more autonomous from their jurisprudential application. A generation of historians was being schooled at Göttingen at this same time by classical philologists (e.g., Heyne, the teacher of the Schlegel brothers, Wilhelm von Humboldt, and Karl Lachmann) and Biblical scholars (e.g., Michaelis) in the latest methods of collating manuscripts and recovering a "purified" text through diagnosis of interpolations and corruptions and the discovery of earlier sources; Gatterer himself taught historical methodology (the "Enzyklopädie"), and, in what may be a slightly exaggerated interpretation, it has been suggested that these influences from textual philology set new standards for scholarship and research in the discipline of history and came to embody the model of Wissenschaft in practice before its theoretical articulation a generation or two later.[20] The whole university was watched over, from its founding in 1737 until 1770, by Baron von Münchhausen (first as its *Kurator*, or "trustee," then as prime minister of Saxony), who was partial toward historians, especially "modern" ones. In 1769 August Ludwig von Schlözer was appointed professor of history, and he trained such influential historians or friends of history as Friedrich Rühs, Wilhelm von Humboldt, and Johannes von Müller. Gatterer, Schlözer, and their students decisively influenced the course of what had by then become a pan-European fashion for writings that were variously named *Universalhistorie, Weltgeschichte, Welthistorie,* and *allgemeine Geschichte,* issuing and reissuing multi-tome editions. Finally, since it was a newly founded university with an explicitly mercantile aim—that of attracting as many paying students from as many parts of Germany and Europe as possible—the promotion of new and interesting studies was in its own self-interest, and the "modern" kind of history was one such area of study (learned societies for matters historical had appeared during the century, and it is said that the number of German historical periodicals multiplied from 3 to 131).[21]

What all of this is meant to suggest is the flourishing of what are now considered quintessentially "modern" or at least "proto-modern" methods of historical study and historiography, a flowering that exceeded the propaedeutic service that the study was still supposed to provide as a *Hilfsdisziplin* to the "higher" law faculty. All of this was being done by historians within the arts faculty, without anyone either inside or outside that faculty giving a theoretical justification as to *why* it was being done. That is, there was as yet no articulated university rationale for the lower faculty's pursuit of historical study beyond that of its propaedeutic role in behalf of the higher faculties.[22] Furthermore, in its development of history as a *Fach* Göttingen remained the German exception: at Halle, the only other noteworthy university of this time, the distinguished historically minded professors were the Biblical scholar J. J.

Griesbach, the ecclesiastical historian J. S. Semler, and the classical philologist Friedrich August Wolf. Altogether, this was a low time for German universities, and in 1795, in the very city where fourteen years later a university would be founded expressly on a theoretical program that justified the scholarly and scientific pursuit of knowledge in its own right, the famous Berlin intellectual debating circle called the Mittwochgesellschaft could choose as its topic the question of abolishing the German universities.

In the pages above I have retained the name "arts faculty," even though this lower faculty had been renamed the *facultas philosophiae* at some universities as early as the sixteenth century. The two names were still virtually interchangeable in the early eighteenth century, but then the new one took over throughout Germany. It is time to introduce it into my discussion as well, but not without some preliminary examination, for a considerable amount of argumentative force regarding the status of history within the university comes to hinge upon the claims of "philosophy."

At first the renaming of the *Artistenfakultät* as the *Philosophische Fakultät* seems only to have affirmed the status quo, that is, the dominance of the trivium within it and *its* domination by the study of Aristotelian logic; the new name did not pretend that this faculty was anything more than a *propaedeuticum* for the three higher ones, which role, as we have seen, it maintained up through the eighteenth century. The *Abitur*, or secondary school certificate entitling one to attend university, was introduced in Prussia in 1788, but it was not until 1834, when the *Abiturzwang*—the *requirement* of the certificate—was instituted there, that the philosophy faculty was in practical terms elevated to parity with the other three, that is, when its task was no longer to dispense needed propaedeutic instruction to undereducated secondary school "graduates" wishing to enter the higher faculties. The philosophy faculty was, however, then directed to undertake the training of secondary school teachers—previously the task of the theology faculty, when these teachers received any university training at all—in addition to its newly found scientific and scholarly pursuits. Yet even if the philosophy faculty retained a subordinate position regarding both pedagogic practice and student numbers well into the nineteenth century,[23] the establishment of the University of Berlin upon an explicitly philosophic program, together with earlier such programs by Kant and Schelling, may be taken to indicate a new set of claims and expectations for the university and its relations with knowledge.

To what "philosophic" organization of the earlier German university and its *Philosophische Fakultät* do these later developments contrast themselves? The medieval-scholastic organization of the university may be viewed as a "rational" system, not because it appealed to the eminent rational authority of Aristotle, but because it represented, in Friedrich Paulsen's words, "the desire for an ecclesiastically based world-view that could be established in thought or, at least, justified by reason."[24] Its lower faculty trained one in the forms of language and thought, while only the three higher faculties were called *scientiae* and held to teach the substance of knowledge. (The "humanists" altered nothing in this respect: their *humaniora* offered *eruditio* and *prudentia*, not *scientia*.) Now what this knowledge might, from our perspective, be said to have lacked—even, or especially, in the law and medicine faculties—was a sufficient reason for its reality or actuality as opposed to its possibility or reasonableness; and thus the characteristic format for university "examinations" could be the *disputationes*, which tested plausible or reasonable *usages* of thought, argumentation, and reference to authoritative texts (Aristotle, the Bible, Church fathers, and scholastics) rather than the reality or actuality of the things held to be known. Northrop Frye has written eloquently of the epistemological limitations inherent to this scholasticism:

> Syllogistic reasoning . . . led to nothing genuinely new, because its conclusions were already contained within its premises, and so its march across reality seemed increasingly to be a verbal illusion. Then again, an analogical approach to language appeared to have no criteria for distinguishing existents from non-existents. Grammatically, logically, and syntactically, there is no difference between a lion and a unicorn: the question of actual existence does not enter the ordering of words as such. And if it does not, there can be no real difference between reasoning and rationalizing, as both procedures order words in the same way. The difference can be established only by criteria external to words, and the first of these criteria has to be that of "things," or objects of nature.[25]

But before we adopt too quickly our "modern" perspective and seize upon this university organization's lack of a place for investigation in the sense of the discovery of the empirical, one might reflect upon Frye's ostensible distinction between reasoning and rationalizing. For it is not clear that there was any felt tension or opposition between rationalizing reality and reasoning about it with the help of empirical investigation, when the university and its organization of knowledge were structured according to the doctrinal position that the truth had been *given* and thus did not need to be found, but only explained, passed on, and policed. If, as Richard Rorty suggests, our contemporary satisfaction with histories of the natural sciences may obtain "because we have, in these areas, clear stories of progress to tell,"[26] then by contrast the older sense of satisfaction with doctrinally given *scientia* would go a long way toward accounting for the absence of any intra-institutional pressure for "progress" toward new historical studies being felt within the university under the scholastic model: there already was a "clear story to tell," and it was that the truth was already there, without need of any progress. And thus, paradoxically, there really *was not* any story to tell, for there was not any intrinsic need for a sense of "movement" within disciplinary or university practices that Heidegger characterizes as the "revision of fundamental concepts," which indicates the very "level" of a Wissenschaft in its capacity for *crisis*.[27]

Jacques Derrida has written, "As far as I know, nobody has ever founded a university *against* reason. So we may reasonably suppose that the University's reason for being has always been reason itself, and some essential connection of reason to being." This remark, with its question of the relation between reason and being, serves to focus an inquiry into changes in the university's self-rationale, and specifically its rationale for reason. Derrida himself focuses on Leibniz's "principle of reason": *nihil est sine ratione;* and in another formulation: *omnis veritatis reddi ratio potest* ("for any truth a reasoned account is possible").[28] "To render reason"—the literal translation of *rationem reddere*—is, in Derrida's interpretation, "to explain effects through their causes, rationally; it is also to ground, to justify, to account for on the basis of principles or roots . . . the response to the call of the principle of reason is thus a response to the Aristotelian requirements, those of metaphysics, of primary philosophy, of the search for 'roots,' 'principles,' and 'causes.'"[29]

Now it is here, in response to the principle of reason, that kinds of reasonable response can be distinguished, including those kinds embodied in different models of the university. Derrida remarks that we do not respond to a *summons* (a summons to *obey*) in the same way as we do to an invitation to question its meaning, origin, possibility, goal, and limits.[30] The scholastic university posed the demand of reason that it "render reasonable," give a reasoned account of, the world within the world-view of an ecclesiastically based doctrine. The truth was given in and by that doctrine—ultimately, in and by its "origin" as Scripture—and reasoning falls into line behind it. In the second, stronger sense of "rendering reason," the response to the principle of reason is to search for *its* principle, to seek to ground or justify reason not in some given, doctrinal "truth" but in its "own," *philosophic* reason or truth. It turns the Aristotelian injunction of metaphysics—to know first principles—toward its own principles and operations, and thereby away from its prior subservience to a given meaning, origin, and limit.

A crucial document of this turn of philosophic reason within the university from obeying a summons to inquiring into its principle is, as Derrida has pointed out, Kant's *Streit der Fakultäten* (1798); Derrida describes this shift as one from "the principle of rendering reason, to reason as the rational faculty—and in the end, to Kant's definition of reason as the faculty of principles."[31] Kant's *Streit* argues for a reversal of the university's hierarchy of "faculties" to accompany the change in the role of reason's reasoning—from rationalizing to inquiring—sketched above. With considerable rhetorical effect, Kant retains throughout the received designations of the "higher" and "lower" university faculties even as he reevaluates their claims and merits. The "lower" faculty has "only to care for the interest of Wissenschaft" (note that Kant says nothing about a propaedeutic interest or function), while the "higher" faculties have governmentally mandated interests of *doctrine (Lehre)* as their responsibilities.[32] And what is this "wissenschaftliche Interesse" of the "lower" philosophic faculty? Kant immediately elaborates: "i.e., the truth, . . . where reason must be entitled to speak openly . . . but reason, according to its nature, is free, and accepts no commands to hold something for [being] true (no *crede* but rather only a free *credo*)." In the interest of truth, which is the interest of Wissenschaft, reason must speak freely, and not in response to any imposed doctrine, command, creed, or canon. Kant concludes this passage in his argument with the politely sarcastic remark that the "higher" faculties are so called because they have the power to command, even if they remain servants of a regime, while the "lower" faculty is so designated because it is powerless to command—while nonetheless the one that is free. Later in his text Kant will continue his irony by remarking, in an echo of the Biblical prophecy, that under such a view of the university as he has just unfolded, "the last shall be first (the lower faculty the higher one), not in terms of having power, to be sure, but nonetheless in the counseling of those who have power (the regime)."[33]

This elevation of the "lower" university faculty is the elevation of the faculty of reason to the point of self-empowerment, from which it might then descend into an inquiry into, and in the service of, its own interests, "i.e., the truth." This may, for my purposes, be called the sufficient beginning of the doctrine of "pure Wissenschaft" within the German university, and specifically within its philosophy faculty: recall Kant's use of "only" *(nur)* with reference to Wissenschaft. After Kant has pointed out that the doctrines that the so-called "higher" faculties serve derive from various "scriptures" or "scripts" (*Schriften*, which he also specifies as norms, statutes, legal codes, canons, authorities)—thus theology's doctrine derives not from reason but from the Bible; law's, not from natural law but from state law; medicine's, not from the physics of the body but from medical code—he distinguishes the "lower" faculty's relation to doctrine as one of autonomy: "it concerns itself only with doctrines that will not be taken as a plumb-line at the command of a superior." [34] But if freedom from submission to a "higher" and exterior authority is taken to characterize the philosophy faculty, why should it be a question of doctrine (or doctrines) at all? Because the exteriority of authority, be it that of a regime or that of a doctrine "founded" upon Scripture, has been internalized, so that the submission of the principle of rendering reason to its *own* principle of inquiring into its grounds, laws, and reason becomes the new and immanent "doctrine" of the philosophy faculty. Autonomy of reason—"academic freedom"—means that it submits to no law or principle other than that of its own discovery or making: "Now one calls the faculty [*Vermögen*] of judging autonomously, i.e., freely (in accord with principles of thinking in general), reason. Thus the philosophy faculty [*Fakultät*], because it must stand for the *truth* of the doctrines that it should accept or also just make room for, will to that extent have to be thought as standing free and solely under the legislation of reason, not that of the government." [35]

There is a threefold argument here. Reason is the capacity for free judgment, for judgment according to its own principles, without exteriority. Its interest—what it stands for—is truth, rather than derived or received doctrine, and therefore its only acceptable "doctrine" of truth is the internalized, now immanent authority of self-judgment. And so the new doctrine becomes one of the autonomous decision and legislation—"the legislation of reason"—of truth by reason: this is what "will have to be thought" by reason's capacity for free judgment.

Kant's powerful argumentation would free philosophy, both its university faculty and its faculty or ability of reason, from its subservient position before other faculties, powers, and their doctrines, and for its own empowerment as legislator and judge. It gives itself its own laws for its procedures and inquiries (as Kant had established elsewhere, above all in his *Critique of Pure Reason*), and it judges accordingly. Once the autonomy of reason as a faculty—again, in both senses of the term: a university and a mental faculty—has been established, the domain of its power becomes crucial. Kant writes quite explicitly that the philosophy faculty "controls" the other three, "higher" ones (and then slyly adds: "and thereby becomes useful to them"), "for everything depends upon *truth* (the essential and first condition of erudition altogether)."

After dividing the philosophy faculty into the "department of *historical knowledge*" and the "department of *pure rational knowledge*," which includes mathematics, "pure philosophy," and the metaphysics of nature and morals, Kant concludes that "it therefore extends itself over all parts of human knowledge (consequently also historically over the higher faculties)." He immediately adds that the philosophy faculty "does not make all [parts of human knowledge] (namely, the particular doctrines or commandments of the higher faculties) into its own content, but rather into the object of its examination and critique, with a view toward the advantage of the Wissenschaften. The philosophy faculty can thus lay claim to all doctrines, in order to submit their truth to examination."[36]

This universalizing model of the philosophical faculty, which would have it include "all human knowledge" within its investigative purview and judgmental prerogative, has reason as its means and truth as its end. The mission is global and also foundational: the philosophy faculty must "be mindful that everything that, so to speak, is set up as a fundamental principle [*Grundsatz*], be true."[37] While Kant is here speaking of the "truth" of particular doctrines taught in the so-called higher faculties, which doctrines might derive from historical, rational, or "aesthetic" (i.e., in this usage, emotional) sources, it is clear that the doctrine of the philosophy faculty's own *Grundsatz*, its radical principle of reason, is held to be unimpeachably, because rationally, true. What is less clear here is the articulation between reason's foundationalism (all truth) and Wissenschaft's global imperialism (all human knowledge),[38] and this difficulty is not immediately obviated by the distinction quoted above between knowledge as an object of critique and knowledge as a "content." My specific interest is in the articulation between the philosophy faculty's claims for philosophic truth (its priority and absoluteness) and its projects for scientific and scholarly knowledge of matters historical (history as an object, form, and "department" of Wissenschaft). Here, the difficulty is apparent in the breadth of Kant's use of *historisch:* it conflates human historical matters such as philology with what we would think of as natural empirical matters, while it also addresses the relation, by way of derivation, between a source, or origin, and a particular outcome, or precipitate. His schematic division of the philosophic faculty into departments of "historical knowledge" and "pure rational knowledge" is of a piece with the Kantian program that all merely historical knowledge—"das historische," objectively or subjectively construed as cognition *ex datis* rather than *ex principiis*—should be brought toward rational inquiry and critical judgment. But there is here a still malarticulated relation of *das historische*, the empirically given and/or factually known, to critical reason: the reasoned character of what might qualify as Wissenschaft and truth is left in an unclarified relation to that body of a posteriori constructions collectively called "das historische" by Kant.[39] A resolution of this difficulty will be attempted by the next generation of German idealist philosophers, and it will appear under the terminological category of "becoming" (Werden).

Whatever its difficulties, Kant's *Streit der Fakultäten* appears as the earliest idealist model for a university in which philosophy would be the crowning, or "queen," faculty, with Wissenschaft, as knowledge of truth, as its mission in lieu of its former propaedeutic tasks. (Kant is fully aware that this university has yet to exist, and he also asserts that because of the regulative relation of truth to doctrine, the "strife" between the philosophy faculty and the others is unceasing.)[40] Although the text had limited institutional influence—for example, it is mentioned only a couple of times in passing in the programmatic writings generated by the call for the founding of the University of Berlin—this accident of history need not diminish its exemplary value as regards both the ambition of its claims and the unresolved character of its inner rationale, especially that rationale which would relate absolute truth to the specifics of historical knowledge.

This orientation and its adherent difficulty of resolving absolutes and particulars might be compared with the contemporary situation of the territorially oriented law faculties, which is where I left off my historical narrative to turn to the larger question of university organization and rationale. On the one hand, there was the longstanding seventeenth- and eighteenth-century fascination with natural law in which historical particulars were adduced for purposes of corroboration and exemplification in the service of an "absolutizing" philosophy of law—not unlike the appropriation of historical instances by "exemplary history," which has been characterized as "the empirical part of moral philosophy." But on the other hand, there had developed the cultivation of the *jus gentium* and the accompanying historical research into discrete particulars: a handling of history that contrasts with its subordinate service to ratiocination about binding universals. Kant's text seems to straddle both tendencies, for he makes considerable claims for the binding and universal authority of reason's judgments, while nonetheless also allowing for the expansive inclusion of "all human knowledge," and not just an exemplary selection thereof, within the philosophy faculty.

The relation between the theory of philosophy's guiding and judging role vis-à-vis Wissenschaft and the practice of the Wissenschaft of history remained a practical as well as a theoretical problem. The relative status or hierarchical position of the university faculties might be a topic for programmatic reformulations à la Kant, but there was the corresponding problem of how a growing belief in and practice of uncovering knowledge and truth could be fitted into a university structure that denied the philosophy faculty the right of entry into the domain of "science" or true knowledge. For while members of the "higher" law faculty might not shrink from stooping into the lower faculty in order to teach their necessary historical "special disciplines" there, a philosopher in his own faculty might still have to try to gain access to a higher one in order to be able to teach "knowledge" instead of propaedeutics— say, to teach natural law in the law faculty or metaphysics in the theology faculty.[41] As the necessity and then (as in the example of Göttingen) the autonomy of research into historical factuality were increasingly recognized, there remained the need for a systematic, structural legitimation of its *truth,* and hence of its knowledge-worthiness, on the part of the university. Kant did a good deal more in his *Streit* for philosophy and its faculty than for history and its place therein. What was needed, to paraphrase Paulsen's remarks on the scholastic organization of the university, was a philosophically based world-view that could be established in thought and justified by reason in such a way that it would presuppose and therefore legitimate its verification and documentation through the scientific and scholarly study of reality. The belief in the rationality of reality, as embodied in the university, is a constant throughout the scholastic, the enlightenment, and the coming idealist universities; indeed, the idea of a university cannot be conceived without such a belief: "nobody has ever founded a university *against* reason." The innovation is that reality not only be rationalized, and that thought not only be judged by reason as to its truth, but that reality, including things historical, be thought and investigated so that it might yield and manifest *its* reason and truth.

It would not surprise a Rortyan pragmatist, a Hegelian idealist, or a neutral observer between the two that concrete practices sometimes run ahead of their theoretical conceptualization and legitimation. I suggested above that this is an aspect of what was happening with the study of history at Göttingen in the late eighteenth century and mentioned the influence exerted there upon the European historiographical practices of *Universalhistorie* and *Weltgeschichte.* This is an arcane topic in the history of historiography, and it need not concern us at great length. But its general reorientation at this time sets the stage for a text by Schiller that we shall examine in detail, and so a few remarks on "universal history" will bring forth a version of the problem of the relation of philosophy and history, which we have just seen both raised and skirted in the Kant text.

A widely known, thirty-eight-volume *Universal History from the Earliest Account of Time to the Present* was published in England from 1736 to 1765 and was rapidly translated into Dutch and German. The German translation, in thirty volumes, came out in Halle from 1744 to 1767 under the direction of the theologian and ecclesiastical historian Sigmund Jacob Baumgarten and his student Johann Salomo Semler; the Göttingen historian Schlözer then added a *Fortsetzung* volume of *Allgemeine nordische Geschichte* in 1771. As this additional title suggests, the "English model" of universal history was that of the aggregate, or compendium, a large and ever larger collection of detailed histories of states, localities, and also churches; Gatterer published in Göttingen in 1761 a *Handbuch der Universalhistorie nach ihrem gesamten Umfange von Erschaffung der Welt bis zum Ursprunge der meisten heutigen Reiche und Staaten*, which title similarly tells it all: "universal history according to its whole expanse from the creation of the world up to the origin of most of today's empires and states." But somewhere along the way of this migration and translation of English universal history, the model changed; the English version, now associated with the older "polyhistory," was criticized in favor of what was named—curious choice— "pragmatic history."[42] The choice of the term "pragmatic" was evidently meant to contrast this kind of universal history not only with the English version but also with "philosophical history," that is, universal history written by philosophers. If English universal history was primarily additive or cumulative, this new kind was to stress inherent connections rather than distinctions, peoples in their relations rather than separations, thus leading to a common history of mankind; but if, on the other hand, philosophical history was felt to have oversimplified or overschematized history, this new kind would respect the recorded facts by beginning with them and letting the schema issue therefrom.

The "philosophical" kind of history apparently represented both a model and a threat; Schlözer could write admiringly that it was philosophical history that was "perpetually connecting results with their causes" and that he would write "the history of mankind, a new sort of history, hitherto only written by philosophers."[43] What kind would this be? He wrote that "the task of the historian is to put [the facts] together to form a unity [Einheit]."[44] How will this be done? By putting together (*zusammenstellen*) what is found together: *Zusammenhänge*, "connections," either diachronic or synchronic.[45] In Gatterer's version, "the chief concern of the pragmatic historian is the search for the occasioning circumstances and causes of noteworthy events and to develop as well as possible the whole system of causes and effects, of means and intentions, no matter how confused they may at first seem." But this "whole system" marks a limiting threshold:

> The *highest level of the pragmatic* in history would be the representation of the universal connection of things in the world [*die Vorstellung des allgemeinen Zusammenhangs der Dinge in der Welt*] (*Nexus rerum universalis*). For no event in the world is, so to speak, *insular*. Everything hangs together with something else, occasions something else, produces something else, is itself occasioned, is itself produced, and then occasions and produces once again. The events . . . are all intertwined in one another and bound together. That one man could attain this highest level of the pragmatic will not be expected by any rational person.[46]

The "systematic" character of this universal history, then, is at once an assumption borrowed from "philosophy"—from a sense of rendering reasoned explanation to relations of causes and effects, with the concomitant assumption (recall Leibniz's principle) that there are no such relations that need remain unreasoned and unreasonable—and an impossibility for the historian's representational skills and labors. The "unity" of which Schlözer spoke is assumed to have been given or present in the past but may not be regiven or re-presented by even the most industrious historian. If the system is not the *end* of historical inquiry but rather its beginning, enabling assumption, then the task is rather to portray to the extent possible the "inner relation of events" (synchronically) and the "relation between causes and effects" (diachronically) and so to "think oneself into the spirit of the events," an "ideal present" of "intuitive understanding" (*anschauende Erkenntnis*) that might reproduce, however partially, "a whole that once existed."[47]

The dilemma, then, is to reproduce unity in the face of an assumed unity of "system" that is itself unreproducible. The means, as Gatterer already knew, would be *narrative*. The philosopher Louis O. Mink recognizes the same point when he calls universal history "an ideal that never became an achievement, but one that served as a regulative principle of thought about the past," and credits it with "the presupposition that past actuality is an untold story." In an excellent summary, he makes these points about universal history:

> Universal History was not the idea that there is a particular plot in the movement of history but the assumption that underlay all proposals to display one sort of plot or another. . . . it was the claim that the ensemble of human events belongs to a single story. . . . the idea of Universal History specifies that there is a single central subject or theme in the unfold-

ing of the plot of history. . . . Finally, Universal History did not deny the great diversity of human events, customs, and institutions; but it did regard this variety as the permutations of a single and unchanging set of human capacities and possibilities, differentiated only by the effects of geography, climate, race, and other natural contingencies.[48]

What these remarks bring out is the extent to which claims of the "single story," "single subject," and "single set of human capacities"— what Schlözer called "unity," and Gatterer, "the universal connection of the things in the world"—are, as it were, the *promise* held out but also held back by the past. It can be told that this is what history (the past) tells, but it cannot be truly told by history (the discourse). Mink's use of the Kantian "regulative principle" to describe this is probably as good as any choice of term, for in Kant's own "universal history," the *Idee zu einer allgemeinen Geschichte in weltbürgerlicher Absicht* (Idea for a Universal History on a Cosmopolitan Plan) of 1784—which I will not treat here, if only because it concerns the future more than the past— the "hidden plan of nature" that men should act rationally, which he adduced as such a "single theme" of world history, was admitted to be just such a regulative but unknowable idea (hence the "hidden"), what Mink calls "a hypothesis which enables one to ask the right questions but which should be regarded as heuristic rather than as true."[49]

How would a story be told that not only claimed to tell "all" of world history—for this is the ambition of universal history—but also—for this, too, is universal history—had to tell or at least show its dénouement in a non-knowing rather than a "true" knowledge? We may get an answer by way of a close examination of a late-eighteenth-century text on universal history that displays the uncomfortable relation between history and philosophy we glimpsed in Kant's *Streit* and have just reviewed in universal history's ambivalent appeal to "connections" of "causes and effects." The text is Friedrich Schiller's "Was heisst und zu welchem Ende studiert man Universalgeschichte?" (What Is Universal History and Why Does One Study It?), his inaugural lecture at the University of Jena in 1789 as, of all things, professor of philosophy. Schiller knew something of Kant—perhaps more of Kant than he did of history—but our interest here lies not in determining his lecture's precise degree of Kantianism but in observing his version of that more general problem of relating historical study and knowledge to philosophic judgment and truth. The text does more than argue, in Mink's summary, that the universal historian "explains the whole contemporary world by discerning those chains of events that have led up to the present, and displaying them as a single and coherent whole,"[50] and its explicit ambivalences and even contradictions display an exemplary version of the historical-philosophic *(geschichtsphilosophisch)* impasse of its time.

Schiller's essay creates a windshield-wiper effect as it moves back and forth between its "sides" of historical study and philosophic interpretation. It is loose, grandiloquent, hortatory, all of which characteristics befit an orally delivered inaugural lecture by someone who, while an honored writer, is a bit out of his depth in this discussion of Wissenschaft. Schiller begins by seeming to appeal to the familiar tradition of exemplary history: "objects of instruction" and "excellent models for imitation" are offered to the observer by "the great, wide field of universal history" (he indifferently uses such names as *Universalgeschichte, allgemeine Geschichte, allgemeine Weltgeschichte,* and simply *Weltgeschichte*).[51] But in the same breath he inserts the claim that universal history also offers "the philosopher such important conclusions," and it is this aspect that he then picks up and extends a few paragraphs later. His vehicle for this first contrast of history and philosophy is one of caricature: he opposes the *Brotgelehrte,* the merely money-earning "bread-and-butter scholar," to the "philosophic mind." The former's work yields "piecework": "everything he does seems fragmentary [*als Bruchstück*]"; "he feels himself cut off, torn away from the interdependence of things, because he has failed to connect his activity to the great whole of the world" (423). But lest this last charge be taken as one of pedantry and ivory-tower isolation alone, Schiller's contrasting portrait of the "philosopher" places the accent not on an academic world–real world dichotomy but on the part-whole distinction.

> How entirely differently does the philosophic mind conduct himself! . . . [he] strives to expand his field, and to restore its connection with the others. . . . What the bread-and-butter scholar severs, the philosophic spirit joins together . . . everything converges together, and his active drive toward harmony cannot remain satisfied with fragments. All his efforts are directed toward the perfection [*Vollendung*] of his knowledge [*Wissen*]; his noble impatience cannot rest until all of his concepts have ordered themselves into a harmonious whole. (424)

One notes here the rather conventional claims for the ordering and holistic ambitions of the philosopher, with special emphasis on the synthesizing or harmonizing power, which yields, as it were, a whole greater than the sum of its parts. But if the call for "perfection of knowledge" seems to denote an idealist concept of Wissenschaft, it also signals an ambivalence. Schiller continues the same paragraph first with this addition: "Perhaps [new discoveries] fill a gap which had disfigured the developing whole of his concepts [*das werdende Ganze seiner Be-*

griffe], or fit the last, still missing stone into his edifice of ideas, and complete it." This sentence sustains the notion of the possibility and desirability of complete and perfect *(vollendete)* knowledge as part of the "philosophic spirit," but the next sentences seem paradoxically to counter with a yet more perfect flexibility within *incompleteness:*

> But on the other hand, should [the new discoveries] demolish it . . . yet *the truth is ever more dear to him than his system,* and he will gladly exchange the old, deficient model for a new and more beautiful one. Indeed, if no external blow shakes his edifice of ideas, then he himself, compelled by a ceaselessly operating drive for improvement, is the first to take it apart out of dissatisfaction, in order to put it back together again more perfectly [*vollkommener*]. Through ever new and ever more beautiful forms of thought the philosophic spirit progresses toward greater excellence, while the bread-and-butter scholar, in eternal paralysis of spirit, guards the unproductive monotony of his scholasticism. (424)

The tension and indeed the contradiction within this sketch of the "philosopher" seem more compelling than its transparent contrast with that of the dry-as-dust pedant. The drive toward the perfection of knowledge attributed to the philosopher aims at completion, even if only asymptotically, but this sense for completion—which would be "the truth"—is then made dependent upon and must yield before a dynamic, and therefore unstable, sense of its growth and development. It is not only that new particulars might come to light and need a place within the whole; "the edifice of ideas" gives way before an *immanent* drive for ever more perfect improvement.

What has not been solved by Schiller in this opening portrait is the relation between the "developing whole" of philosophic knowledge and the objects of this knowledge, on the one hand, and the terms of its completeness, on the other. And here it is not incidental that his topic is the study of history. If philosophy were to be condemned to undo ceaselessly its constructions of knowledge, even if in the name of "improvement," then it would appear to be essentially as fragmentary as mere partial knowledge of partial objects. But if it were to pretend to attain completion and perfection, it would resist "new discoveries," be a mere "system" of ratiocinations, and so also approximate its counterpart in their shared "scholasticism." What has yet to be correlated is the movement of Wissenschaft, the production and achievement of knowledge, with some similar movement or dynamic within its objects of knowledge. Rather than a Sisyphean construction and dismantling of edifices of ideas or systems, matched by ever more new discoveries of and amongst ever more historical particulars, what is implicitly called for is the strict integration of the "developing whole" *(das werdende Ganze)* of philosophic-conceptual knowledge with the development—the immanently directional character, the *Werden* or becoming—inherent in its objects of knowledge: in the real, historical world. The alternative to this teleology shared by Wissenschaft and history, and to be combined in historical Wissenschaft, is in Schiller's opening contrast not a complacent sense of progressive, asymptotic "improvement" of knowledge but rather a necessarily circular invention and reinvention of versions of knowledge under the mantle of a "truth" that never reveals itself.

A second version of Schiller's dilemma regarding the status of philosophic knowledge appears when he turns to the specific concept of universal history. He begins with what was by his time a conventional historical-anthropological view of "primitive societies": discoveries by European travelers are said to "show us societies arrayed around us at the most varied levels of formation [*Bildung*], as an adult might be surrounded by children of different ages, and reminded by their example of what he himself once was and whence he started" (426). This convention, which one recognizes from Lessing's notion of the "Erziehung des Menschengeschlechts" or Kant's version of enlightenment as the progress of mankind from childhood to adulthood, is adopted by Schiller not only out of smugness (although there is a considerable amount of that) but to repose a problem of knowledge and understanding. The judgment of the contemporary situation is not felt by him to be his problem, at least not at this moment, still two months before the beginning of the French Revolution; as a wooden if highly optimistic follower of Kant, Schiller can believe that "all thoughtful minds are joined today in a union of world citizenry, and all the light of the century can now illuminate the spirit of a new Galileo and Erasmus . . . man has come to conform to laws . . . where compulsory duties upon man leave off, morality takes over" (428). But what, then, of the "reminder" of earlier "levels of development" just mentioned? Beyond its function in an invocation of a philosophic view of mankind's enlightenment toward free morality, the appeal to the "primitive" is an injunction for historical explanation.

> Who would suppose that in the refined European of the eighteenth century one glimpses only a more advanced brother of the recently discovered Canadian [Indian] and of the ancient Celt? All these skills, artistic instincts, experiences, all these creations of reason have been implanted and developed in man in a matter of a few thousand years. . . . What brought that one to life? What elicited this one? What conditions did man traverse until he ascended from *that* extreme to *this* one, from being an

unsociable cavedweller to being a mentally gifted thinker and a cultivated [*gebildeten*] man of the world? Universal world-history answers these questions. (429)

Over and above the adoption of a philosophic model of reason's liberation and enlightenment, or a political-philosophic stance regarding the shared heritage of humanity among all peoples, Schiller's call here—like that of Schlözer and Gatterer we glanced at above—is for historical explanation of what is otherwise a theory of reason still faced with bewildering and apparently intractable facts of difference. In the next paragraph, he specifically invites an explanation of diachronic differences within the same people and region and, correspondingly, of synchronic differences across different regions.

But let us notice that Schiller's appeal to world-historical explanation links the "levels of formation [*Bildung*]" of mankind to "advancement" and "development" toward his contemporary "cultivated" (literally, "formed" or "imaged," *gebildet*) man. His implicit model of historical explanation includes a teleology of the object of study—the universal study of man—toward the vehicle, perspective, and moment of its knowledge and understanding: the Wissenschaft, the scholarly practice of universal history as a mode of knowledge. The assumption of perfection and completion on the part of the "philosophic mind" addressed above is therefore taken up in this initial version of Schiller's position on historical knowledge.

Schiller's focus is upon the coexplanatory burden being placed upon historical "development" and universal-historical knowledge: the former leads toward the latter; the latter explains the former and would therefore include a reasoned account of how the former led up to the latter. "Even the fact that we find ourselves together here at this moment, at this level of national culture . . . is perhaps the result of all prior events in the world: the *whole* of world-history at least would be needed to explain this single moment" (430). Such a perspective might appear both dizzyingly presumptuous and daunting enough to induce skepticism in someone unwilling to know the whole of world history to explain one present moment. But Schiller finds the same correlation between historical development and implied historical explanation in more modest slices of time as well: "Would Greece have borne a Thucydides . . . , or Rome a Horace . . . if these two states had not been elevated to those heights of political well-being which in fact they achieved? In a word—if their *entire* history had not preceded them?" (432). And yet the more weight Schiller comes to place upon the relation between the totality of historical events and the explanatory power necessarily contained within them, the more his model begins to creak under the pressure.

An insight into a collapsing model of historical understanding can first be glimpsed in his characterization of the kind of explanatory model he has implied: "Thus there extends from the present moment to the beginnings of the human race a long chain of events which interlock as cause and effect" (432). The image of the chain highlights the assumption of unbroken continuity—and Schiller immediately adds that no man could know all this in its entirety, for some events are undocumented, others unreliably documented, documents are lost or corrupted, and so forth. But more significant is the introduction of the cause-and-effect imagery that has been latent throughout his remarks, as it was explicit in the remarks by Schlözer and Gatterer. Schiller repeatedly begins his characterizations of universal-historical knowledge from the present moment backward, as in the last sentence quoted above, or from an earlier moment (the birth of Thucydides) backward, in other words, from effect back to cause. Within the limitations established by the availability of "evidence" for a causal explanation,

> the universal historian picks out those [events] which have had an essential, undeniable, and easily discernible influence upon the *contemporary* state of the world and the condition of the generation now alive. It is thus the relation of a historical fact to the *contemporary* constitution of the world to which attention must be paid in assembling materials for world-history. World-history thus proceeds upon a principle that directly contrasts with the beginning of the world. The real series of events descends from the origin of things to their most recent ordering; the universal historian ascends from the most recent state of the world up to the origin of things. (433–34)

In effect, the historian's "principle" is that effects precede causes, in the sense that the effects, in their current or at least later state, epistemologically determine the notion of their causes by providing criteria for the latter's selection and relevance.

But this metalepsis (the inversion of cause and effect) is not—not just yet—a problem for Schiller. The supposition of historical development as a continuous chain of causes and effects is merely being matched, as if in mirror symmetry, by a corresponding account of historical explanation as a "chain" of effects and causes. But what has been crucially introduced here is an implicit remodeling of the mechanistic, cause-and-effect imagery for an understanding of historical "development." History may still be assumed to proceed from cause to effect, but this is not what history as scholarship studies and comes to know. History as it is known or "done" (as opposed to its instantiation or being "made") comes to know the mental enactment of a certain causality from out of a present (or earlier) state construed as an effect or set of effects; it then reenacts the "development" of the history from cause to effect that it—the historical study—has just constituted.

> If [the historian] ascends in his thoughts from the current year and century to the one just past and notes there among the events offered those which comprise the explanation of the ones that followed next; if in this way he has proceeded step by step to the beginning, not of the world . . . but to the beginning of historical remains; then he can return along the path he has made and, guided by the facts he has marked out, descend easily and without obstruction from the beginning of historical remains down to the most recent times. (434)

In Schiller's deft switch from a mechanistic, cause-and-effect model of history as development to a rational, effect-and-cause model of historical explanation as the reenactment of an "original" world-historical process, he has accommodated the fragmentary state of evidence and documentation through the introduction of the criteria of present relevance and reconstructive explanatory power, and he has also elevated history from mechanistic necessity to the freedom of rationality, or reasoning's freedom. The historical process is rendered rational—known—when reason slides smoothly back down the tracks it has just laid. This would be the historical Wissenschaft that could come into its own by providing a reasoned and teleological explanation of how historical development developed up (or down) to the moment of its historical understanding.

But this is where the problem of the "perfect" and "complete" state of such knowledge and Wissenschaft becomes fully apparent. Schiller still needs a mechanistic model for the "original" course of history, and this includes the assumption of a continuous chain of causes and effects: "uniform, necessary and determined [is] the way in which changes in the world develop out of each other." But links are missing for the rational understanding of this course: "in history [the changes] fit together only in a disconnected and fortuitous way. There is thus a remarkable incongruity between the course of the *world* and the course of *world-history*" (434). The burden of reinstating historical continuity and totality—the scholarly counterparts to the "philosophic" drive toward completion and perfection—falls back upon philosophic understanding: "So our world-history would become nothing but an aggregate of fragments [*Bruchstücken*] and never be worthy of the name of a Wissenschaft. But now philosophic understanding comes to its aid, and in joining these fragments together by artificial [*künstliche*] links, elevates the aggregate to a system, to a rationally coherent whole" (435).

The very accusation lodged against the pedantic "bread-and-butter scholar," that he is confined to piling up fragmentary knowledge, has reappeared vis-à-vis the universal historian, and the same countermove has also reappeared: a drive toward totalization, toward a reasoned whole, toward a system. But just as the initial introduction of this countermove brought on immediate doubts about the sufficient finality and perfection of any such "systematic" construction of knowledge, the appeal here also contains a question mark regarding the status of the rational coherence introduced by "philosophic understanding": its "artificiality." In the transition from a narrative reconstruction of the causality of past events (from effects to causes and back to effects) to a systematic and rational understanding of the process, more is apparently at stake than mere mirror symmetry. A process that is still founded upon a mechanistic, physical model—causes and effects— must yield to a rational understanding of humanity and its universal history, and so Schiller would claim "the uniformity and immutable unity [*Einheit*] of physical laws and human nature" (435). But this "unity," evidently the systematic and rationally totalizing contribution on the part of "philosophic understanding," is precisely the "artificial link" that would turn fragmentary evidence of linked causes and effects into a whole, continuous, and rational chain of explanation and understanding. That Schiller suspects this artificiality of being just that is evidenced in his next sentence's immediate characterization of this correlation between physical laws and human nature as "the method of inference by analogy": the "unity" of the two spheres—those of causality and rationality—is an artificial one, itself inferred from the artful practice of analogizing one thing (rational explanation) with another (causal description and narration).

The "method" that would render historical observation and reconstruction rational and coherent, and thus make universal history "worthy of the name of Wissenschaft," now ironically turns in Schiller's closing paragraphs into a nearly parodistic reprise of his initial portrait of the "philosophic mind" ceaselessly building and rebuilding its "systematic understanding" toward some deferred and unrevealed truth.

> The philosophic spirit cannot linger for long among the material of world-history before a new impulse is activated within him which strives for harmony—which irresistibly urges him to assimilate everything around him to his own rational nature and to raise every phenomenon which comes to him up to the highest efficacy [*Wirkung*] he knows—up to *thoughts*. Thus the more often and the more successfully he renews the

attempt to connect the past with the present, the more disposed he will be to put what he sees as the interconnection of cause and effect into an interrelation of means and ends. (435)

The last sentence indicates Schiller's—the universal historian's—burden: to transform reconstructed causality, as a manner of historical observation assumed by inference from mechanistic laws of nature, into reasoned human explanation of a *teleology*, which leads from means to ends or purposes. The causality that "explains" by description (or narrative reconstruction or reenactment) a relation between events as that of a cause to an effect is not the same as a teleology, which explains the reasoned relation between a means and the enactment of an intention, goal, or end; Nietzsche will come to argue this point repeatedly. Here, Schiller is at once encouraging the "philosophic spirit" to transform and elevate the apparently mechanical into the realm of human reasoning with its regard for intentions and purposes and subtly deflating the confidence and finality with which philosophic reasoning could offer such an understanding.

> One phenomenon after another begins to withdraw from the realm of blind chance, of lawless freedom, and to align itself as a fitting link into an harmonious totality (which, to be sure, is present only in [the philosopher's] conception). Soon it is difficult for him to persuade himself that this sequence of phenomena, which in his conception [*Vorstellung*] took on so much regularity and purpose, is denied these properties in reality: it is hard for him to restore to the blind rule of necessity what had begun to acquire such a clear form under the borrowed light of reason. (435-36)

Even as Schiller depicts, in a Kantian fashion, the elevation of human phenomena out of the realm of necessity, out of "blind"—that is, unenlightened—obedience to rules or laws of chance (hence, "freedom" only in appearance, "lawless freedom" rather than rationally decided obedience to and freedom within laws of practical reason), he characterizes the achieved understanding, not as reason, let alone as truth, but as mere imaginative and conceptual presentation (*Vorstellung*). His accent is on the sheer "borrowed" character of such a "philosophizing" *Vorstellung* of history, and specifically on its *unreal* status with respect to the actual "properties" of historical reality.

It is a short step from such an orientation to the conclusion that the "philosopher of history" builds castles in the sky, then "reads them into" the history he was ostensibly trying to understand or render reasonable.

35

Thus he derives this harmony from out of himself, and transplants it from himself to the order of things, that is, he imports a rational goal into the course of the world and a teleological principle into world-history . . . but as long as important connecting links are still missing in the sequence of world [historical] changes, as long as fate still withholds the final explanation of so many events, he will declare the question *undecided*, and that opinion wins which offers greater satisfaction to the understanding and greater bliss to the heart. (436)

Instead of effectively transforming world history's "blind chance" of causal "necessity" (this is not a contradictory formulation in the Kantian vocabulary) into a rational explanation of inherent teleology—the movement from means to ends, and also the very teleology adumbrated in Schiller's initial sketch of human history as that which leads up to its historical understanding—Schiller has portrayed the "philosophic mind" transporting its own rationality and harmony into historical reality and unsuccessfully compensating for or covering up the still-fragmentary, still-undecided state of the world-historical process.

Schiller's circuitous itinerary in his lecture suggested a path from fragmentary knowledge of historical events, developments, and changes to their totalization within coherent philosophic understanding: first by way of the mechanistic assumption that past leads to present as if by causality, then by the doubly teleological assumption that the past leads to *present understanding* by way of the intellectual transformation of a mechanistic or natural-physical *rule* into the rational, immanently teleological *law* of human reason's self-understanding. But this series of attempted transformations hinged on several weak joints, not only the fragmentary state of historical evidence or documentation but, what is more important, the merely analogical inference between world events as rule-governed and world-historical understanding as self-governed by the law of reason. There was also the damaging imputation, not that reason reads history backwards to reconstruct its narrative (what else could it do with history?), but that it reads *itself into* history to "construct"—as if out of thin air—its understanding of "rational purpose" and a "teleological principle" at work in historical developments. The teleological completion and perfection toward which "philosophic understanding" strives at each point in Schiller's essay is still self-consuming at its end, as finality is withheld by fate; and so universal history lapses back, in the last sentence quoted above, into *Unwissenschaftlichkeit*, into unscholarly and unscientific appreciation: mere opinion *(Meinung)* satisfying and pleasing certain faculties of understanding and disposition.

As history—the past—verges into the destiny of a fate still withholding itself, and as this fate verges into a last judgment that would provide "the final understanding of so many events," so does the teleology of historical understanding disappear into a vanishing point of deferral on the one hand, of faith on the other. Schiller encourages his youthful audience to buck up and keep the faith: "merely the tranquil prospect of this—if only potential—goal ought to give to the inquirer's diligence an invigorating stimulus as well as an agreeable relaxation." One ought to work collaboratively and asymptotically toward a conjunction of historical understanding with historical unfolding "if he sees himself on the way, or even just guiding a later successor toward solving the problem of the constitution of the world" (436). But Schiller nonetheless both falls back upon a version of exemplary history and withdraws from human understanding the terms and conditions for judging the judgment it might make about historical meaning. Universal history will be "attractive," it will provide "salutary enthusiasm," "it will wean your spirit from the vulgar and trivial view of moral matters, and . . . improve upon the rash decisions of the moment and the narrow judgment of self-interest" (436–37). For its own part, "history alone remains on the scene continuously, an immortal citizen of all nations and ages," while man—initially portrayed as the telos and outcome of all history in the manifestation of his powers of historical understanding—"transforms himself and departs from the stage; his opinions change and depart with him" (437). History's fulfillment in historical understanding has given way to history's onward march through time, and to understanding's degradation or demotion to mere passing opinion, however self-satisfying or provisionally instructive.

History may, in a kind of secularized providentialism (for all universal history is a form of secularized providential history), still be immanently teleological rather than open-ended; it may still tend toward last judgments and the revelation of truth—"she experiences the ultimate fate of all things" (437). But this implies that there has been a powerful reversal of positions from Schiller's opening gambit. If there history had been the object of study, and the universal historian the judge as well as the result of this history, here, in Schiller's penultimate paragraph, history has assumed the mantle or judge's robe of truth, and man the historian has no clothes:

> By analyzing the subtle mechanism through which the quiet hand of nature has, ever since the beginning of the world, developed human powers according to plan, and indicating precisely how this great plan of nature has been served within each epoch, she restores the true standard of happiness and merit, which the reigning delusion of each century falsifies in a different manner. (437)

"She," history; and not "he," the historian or the philosopher. History, initially portrayed as a fragmented object of knowledge, not only becomes full and fulfills its plan but also becomes the agency of whatever "knowledge" (if it can still be so called) it might contain: "she" is the analyst or interpreter, and "human powers" are not reason's supreme judgment but the double object of both nature's plan and history's Olympian observation and judgment. The philosophic historian, first touted as the end-product of and ultimate perspective upon historical events and developments, now slides downward from his pretensions toward perfected or completed truth to provisional opinions, to "reigning delusions" and falsehood. *Sic transit gloria.*

The transition from necessity to freedom is the Kantian—and idealist—project in its broadest terms. In Schiller's subscription to it here, the transition was cast as one from fact to reason: from historical facts to the teleological unfolding of their intrinsic rationale or reasonableness, which teleology included above all the telos of the manifestation of the "philosophic" faculty for judging and understanding this process of development. The "completion" of the process would imply the "perfection" of its outcome—the emergence of universal history as the philosophic and no longer fragmentary Wissenschaft of historical study—and vice versa. And thus, a decade in advance of Kant's model for the philosophy faculty containing all truth and all historical knowledge within its self-legislating and self-judging domain, Schiller projected an idealist relation between historical events and developments (all the objects of study) and the manifestation of the perspective for their true and perfect knowledge. But if Kant, in his *Streit,* came to leave the relation between philosophic judgment and historical knowledge unarticulated, Schiller here was unable to deliver on the promise of the totality of historical events and relations necessarily dovetailing with the "developing whole" of their philosophic understanding. History as event and process remains an incomprehensible, unjudgeable sphere of necessity (even if the necessity of a secularized "divine rule" or providentialism), while human judgment's claims deteriorate from those of systematic truth and rational understanding to ones of satisfactory opinion and passing delusion. An integration of the *Werden,* the becoming of the historical world, with the *Werden* of its scholarly study and philosophic judgment—which would make history a fitting object and means for philosophic knowledge, and historical study "worthy of the name of a Wissenschaft"—has yet to be achieved.

Schiller went on to write a *History of the Thirty Years' War* (published in two parts in 1791 and 1793), but he taught history only through

1790, after which his teaching at Jena was of aesthetics in 1792 and 1793. He then wrote some of the most influential aesthetic theory of his generation, and it may be suggested that the unresolved tension between a historical past and a future philosophic judgment is displaced onto these aesthetic writings, with the tension retained and reworked in their various teleological principles and synthetic efforts. But only a decade after Schiller's teaching, another professor of philosophy at Jena would address the same problems of historical development and knowledge, in their relations to philosophic judgment and truth and within the specific context of a discussion of the university as the site of Wissenschaft.

F. W. J. Schelling's *Vorlesungen über die Methode des akademischen Studiums* were delivered in 1802 and printed in 1803 (and reprinted in 1813 and 1830). They lend themselves readily to the same situation in which Kant's and Schiller's texts were located. Kant claimed—indeed, demanded—the *reasonableness* of truth and Wissenschaft within the philosophic faculty, and within a whole university "controlled" by its philosophic faculty, and yet this reasoned character of truth was left in an unclarified relation to that body of a posteriori constructions collectively called by him "das historische." Schiller's appeal for universal history foundered on his anxieties regarding the relations between historical knowledge and philosophic truth. His efforts were to argue for a transition from causal constructions of history (as mechanistic causality yielding a historical hermeneutics of effects leading back to the discovery of their causes) to a humanly reasoned construction of means in relation to ends, which ends would include the telos of history's true meaning; but these efforts finally left historical meaning and understanding deferred upon a providential last judgment. Schelling displays none of this anxiety about the priority of philosophy vis-à-vis particular Wissenschaften and their objects of study, and he also lends considerable clarity to the special relation of history to philosophic knowledge and truth.

Schelling's assurance regarding the priority of philosophy manifests itself as a series of deductions of all particular *(besondere)* Wissenschaften from the "absolute Wissenschaft" which is philosophy: of the part from the organic whole, of the particular from the universal and absolute and the all-encompassing.[52] Viewed genetically, knowledge would, according to Schelling, depart from God as its "birth-place," and so, just as *philo-sophia* is the striving or love for that original, one wisdom, all individual kinds and disciplines of knowledge depart from and relate back to that one "absolute Wissenschaft" of philosophy (548). His specific arguments about the relations of one or another kind of knowledge to philosophy will, then, depend on his characterization of philosophy's relation to the "absolute" of wisdom or truth.

The idea of the absolute is the idea of absolutely unconditioned knowledge in itself, which Schelling calls the *Urwissen*. Knowledge of this first, unconditioned knowledge, because it would be in a state of departure or distinction from the absolute's original one-ness, is constituted as a mimetic relation with its original, whereas the absolute *Urwissen* itself is posed as the identity—not yet a mimetic relation, according to Schelling—between the truly ideal and the truly real, with the possibility of reciprocal motion or exchange between the two "sides" (Schelling calls this "absorption," *aufgehen*, of the real into the ideal; "transposition," *umsetzen*, of the ideal into the real) (545). But the mimetic relation between philosophy as absolute Wissenschaft and the absolute of *Urwissen* itself inherently aspires toward the condition of identity posited within the *Urwissen*, and so the relation between "original" and "copy" would move ever more closely toward identification. Thus Schelling can speak of knowledge-in-itself as a "prototype" or "original image" (*Urbild*) for human knowledge, which is itself the imaged (*eingebildet*) copy (*Abbild*) or reflection (*Reflex*) of that prototypical knowledge (*jenes vorbildlichen Wissens*) (546–47), and yet to the extent that philosophy as absolute Wissenschaft would "copy" that absolute knowledge-in-itself which is the *Urwissen*, the distinction between "copy" and "original" would have to collapse toward a state of identity. In his fourth lecture, "On the Study of the Pure Sciences of Reason" (which include, above all, philosophy), Schelling comes to characterize the place of this "collapse into identity" as "the Wissenschaften in which . . . knowledge as the reflecting element collapses together [*zusammenfallt*] with the *Urwissen* as the reflected element" (578). The absolute mode of knowledge is "that one which would have the *Urwissen* immediately and in itself [*unmittelbar und an sich selbst*] as ground and object, . . . which outside of this would have no other prototype [*Urbild*]," and this is philosophy (584–85). Unlike mathematics, which Schelling also counts among the "pure sciences of reason" but which has only (visually) *reflected* forms of ideas, only "disparate appearances" of the *Urwissen*, philosophy operates by way of "unmediated rational or intellectual intuition, which is straightforwardly identical with its object, the *Urwissen* itself" (585).

This, then, is the perspective from which Schelling can promote philosophy as the absolute Wissenschaft, anterior and superior to all particular Wissenschaften: it is capable of thinking, intellectually, the very relation of ideas (as thoughts of knowledge) to being, which relation, when one of identity, is the condition of *Urwissen*, absolute truth as the absolute adequacy of idea to being, of the ideal to the real (545–46). Philosophy thus would be "the unmediated representation [*Darstellung*] and Wissenschaft of the *Urwissen* itself" (610). This power of philosophy to identify and identify with or equal the *Urwissen* is the power of reason, which has, however, a wider range of functions than merely the ideal matching or adequation of knowledge to the *Urwissen* in its realm of the ideal. For if nature, being, reality, or the realm of the finite is taken by Schelling as only one "side," aspect, or appearance of the same, one, universal *Urwissen* (its other "side" being knowledge, the ideal, infinity, etc.), then the contribution of human reason to this absolute relation between the real and the ideal is a singular and far-reaching one: it is a "supplement" *(Ergänzung)* to the world of appearances; it should "express [*ausdrücken*] the image [*Bild*] of [real] divine nature as it is in itself, that is, in the realm of the ideal" (548). In other words, Schelling has human reason "re-idealizing" nature or reality in the "light" of reason as it takes the "image," the manifest appearance, of nature and "expresses" it in ideal terms or in terms of knowledge. Just as the absolute is, for Schelling, the reciprocal relation of ideal and real (absorption and transposition), and so nature can be, considered absolutely, "the image of the divine transformation of ideality into reality," this nature-as-transformation can be matched by human reason as the capacity to retransform back into the ideal, or to re-idealize: "the transformation of the latter [reality] into the former [ideality] appears through light and appears completed [*vollendet*] through reason" (549). The traditional topos of the Book of Nature—nature or reality as God's creation and expression—is joined to the tradition of reason as enlightenment or the lending of light to dark matters; in Schelling's hands, reason is granted the "supplementary" capacity of "expressing" the image of reality back into its "original" ideal terms: as knowledge. Reasoned knowledge is the supplementary completion (note the *vollenden*) of reality.

It is this doctrine of knowledge and Wissenschaft, embodied in ideal terms in the absolute Wissenschaft of philosophy, that thus has a mission in the form of the particular, nonphilosophic Wissenschaften of the real. If, in the phrase quoted above, philosophy is the "unmediated representation and Wissenschaft of the *Urwissen*," Schelling adds that "*all other* knowledge is the *real* representation of the *Urwissen*, distinguished from [philosophy] by the element of the concrete" (610). For if the relation between the *Urbild* of the absolute and the "imaged copy" of philosophy as absolute Wissenschaft is supposed to occur in a strictly "unmediated," ideal dimension—that of pure reason—the relation of the

Urbild to other kinds of knowledge is conditioned by the former's "Einbildung ins Konkrete," through which it "forms the whole of knowledge" (578). And it is here that Schelling comes to discuss history, initially in a broadly generalized fashion.

Nature, or being, was said to be the image of the ideal in terms of the real, as knowledge was construed as the appearance of the real in terms of the ideal: this is the internal relation of ideal and real within the absolute as one of identity. Now, part of the "real world" includes time, and so Schelling, in his seventh lecture, characterizes a part of knowledge of this reality as historical knowledge.

> Now it can generally be seen that the becoming-real of an idea [*das reell-Werden einer Idee*] in constant progress—so that the particular is never appropriate to it, but the whole is—expresses itself as history [*sich als Geschichte ausdrucke*]. History is neither that which is purely regulated by reason, that which is subordinated to the concept, nor is it the purely lawless, but rather that which combines necessity within the whole with the appearance of freedom within the particular. *Real* knowledge, since it is the successive revelation of the *Urwissen*, thus necessarily has a historical side to it [*eine historische Seite*], and insofar as all history [*Geschichte*] aims at the realization of an exterior organism as the expression of ideas [*als Ausdrucks von Ideen*], Wissenschaft also necessarily strives to give itself objective appearance and exterior existence. (610)

In this rich passage, our attention should be directed less to the image of perpetual progress, or to the part-whole relation (the one an Enlightenment commonplace, the other a constant in historical hermeneutics), than to the repeated appearance of "expression." For the particular relation of philosophic reason to reality was characterized in the first lecture as the *expression* of the "image" of reality back into "what it is in itself," namely, back into the ideal, and this would be "absolute Wissenschaft." Here, history (*Geschichte*) is characterized as the self-*expression* of "the becoming-real of an idea." The same thought is then repeated: all history, qua realization (or "becoming-real") in or by way of exterior forms, may be construed as "expression of ideas." *Geschichte* here may be understood as natural history together with world history: it is reality considered under the condition of temporality, *tout court*, for Schelling's purpose in this lecture is to distinguish philosophy as "absolute Wissenschaft" from all other kinds of science and scholarship as what he calls the "positive Wissenschaften." The determining distinction is that of temporality: what he called "the *real* representation of the *Urwissen*" (as opposed to its "unmediated," or ideal, representation, which is philosophy) occurs in the medium and condition of time, and it is this that the terms *reell-Werden* and *Realisierung* capture. "History," then, in the materiality of its temporal processes or activities, is understood as the *expression*—the articulation or the appearance of and in signs—of ideas.

What is crucial is the characterization of reality under its temporal condition as the real, material *expression* of ideas in *time*. This "exterior," or outward, manifestation is to be matched, Schelling says, by a Wissenschaft of "objective appearance [*Erscheinung*] and exterior existence," and this would be the "historical side" to *Urwissen:* "history" as historical study or historical Wissenschaft. Schelling describes this in the immediately following sentence: "This exterior appearance can only be the imprint [or impression, *Abdruck*] of the inner organism of the *Urwissen* itself, and thus of philosophy, only that it represents in a separated manner [*nur dass sie getrennt darstellt*] what in the *Urwissen* and likewise in philosophy is one, single thing" (610). A triangular or quadrangular relation between *Urwissen,* philosophy, and the "exteriorized" form of historical Wissenschaft can now be brought to light. If history *(Geschichte)* is the real expression in time of those original ideas of the *Urwissen* which otherwise find their "copy" in the ideal, atemporal form of philosophy as absolute Wissenschaft, then the corresponding historical Wissenschaft would seem to "copy" this real, temporal "expression." This would be a quadrangular relationship: historical study "copies" the "realization" of ideas in history as philosophy "copies" the ideas-in-themselves of the absolute; and it would also appear to involve a parallel mimeticism, with *Abdruck*, "impression," matching or copying *Ausdruck*, "expression." And yet Schelling says that this historical Wissenschaft "can only be the imprint . . . of the *Urwissen* itself, and thus of philosophy." A four-cornered relationship appears to collapse into a triangular one, with the "imprint" of outward, real manifestation in time reducing to the "imprint" or copy of interior, ideal organization and knowledge: to the copy of *Urwissen* and of philosophy.

What is being dealt with, and in a way that still displays its difficulty, is the relation of time to the epistemological structure of expression-of-ideas and its reception as "copy" or "imprint," including the anteriority and priority of this structure in philosophy's relation to the *Urwissen*. If the relation of historical Wissenschaft, as knowledge of exterior, or outward, manifestation of ideas, to its object *Geschichte* is supposed to be strictly mimetic—one of original and copy—then the element of temporality appears to drop away, to be dispensable, and this historical knowledge could be characterized as the copy or imprint of the original itself, *Urwissen*, and of its initial, "identical" copying as absolute Wissenschaft or philosophy. But here the final clause of the above sentence by Schelling should be recalled: "only that [historical Wissenschaft] represents in a separated manner what in [the others] is one, single thing." That is, the mimetic relation in this, *historical* case preserves—reproduces—the temporal aspect as and in the condition of "separation," the condition of the element of Wissen and Wissenschaft being in a disparate and multiple state. Thus, in this initial and idealized introduction of historical Wissenschaft, the character of "historical" knowledge may be reduced to being a copy of "original" philosophic knowledge of the original *Urwissen* itself, and yet the element of temporality is reintroduced and preserved as well.

Historical study and scholarship can then most accurately be portrayed, according to Schelling's formulation, as a twofold set of copies or reproductions. The "historical side" of Wissenschaft's relation to *Urwissen* would be the reception and reproduction of the latter's "expression" of its ideas in temporal reality ("becoming-real," "realization"). Or—in the additional sentence—it would be the imprint or copy, the re-presentation, of philosophy's initial and absolute, ideal copying of *Urwissen*, which copying is itself characterized as a rational expression *(Ausdruck)* on the part of man's reason. The second set or version of copies—a copying of *Urwissen* by philosophy and then an "imprint" of this in historical Wissenschaft—is actually, given the retention of the temporal aspect and the resultant "separated" *(getrennt)* state, a version of the first: "expression" of ideas in time and in the world still has to be matched by its "imprint" in reasoned knowledge, but this imprint or copy will, in its "separated" form, bear the marks of its "original"'s temporal character as *expression*. The "expression" itself is not a mimetic copy of an original *Urwissen* but its *articulation outward:* its material spacing into time and the world. And so the reception and reproduction of this expression, were it to be in a mimetic relation to *its* original, could not be a static or, better, unified impression but rather must sustain this character of expression in its own aspect of separation in and across time: as articulation. Thus the reasonable, knowledgeable *(wissenschaftlich)* response to the real manifestation of *Urwissen* in time and in the world will be a re-expression of expression: the latter's reception as "impression," and its reproduction as articulation. To anticipate Schelling's final and more specific characterization of "historical Wissenschaft," this could be narrative transcription or representation of the original *Werden*, or it could be an interpretive, rationally comprehending transformation of "original" into "copy," but in either case the identifying mimetic relation of knowledge to object of knowledge—history—must preserve and reproduce the temporal mode of the latter's character as expression and articulation.

44

In his tenth lecture, Schelling comes to speak of history as historical Wissenschaft—"Historie"—in a manner closer to the conventional modern and more concrete understandings of historical studies or the historical discipline. After brushing aside both the mere chronicling of events and the pragmatic ("exemplary") appropriation and transmission of empirical evidence for didactic or political (ultimately subjective) purposes (637–39), he characterizes "true history" as follows:

> true history [die wahre Historie] rests upon a synthesis of the given and real element with the ideal, but not by way of philosophy—for it rather annuls [aufhebt] the reality and is thoroughly ideal—for history should be thoroughly in reality and yet at the same time ideal. This is nowhere possible but in art, which allows the real to subsist [bestehen] altogether, as the [theatrical] stage represents real events or stories [Geschichten], but in a completion and unity [Vollendung und Einheit] through which they become the expression [Ausdruck] of the highest ideas. It is thus art through which history [Historie], insofar as it is the Wissenschaft of the real as such, is at once elevated [erhoben] above the real to the higher realm of the ideal, upon which Wissenschaft stands; and the third and absolute standpoint of history is therefore that of historical art [historischen Kunst]. (639–40)

What aligns this passage with the call for an "exterior," or outward, Wissenschaft of Geschichte in the seventh lecture is the identification here of "true history" (Historie) as "the expression of . . . ideas." Geschichte as "object of study" and Historie as the appropriate mode and means of knowledge—a true Wissenschaft—are matched, mimetically, as expression to expression. The mediation of the first expression, as that of ideas on the part of, or issuing from, the Urwissen, with the second one is said to occur artfully, by way of Kunst, and here closer attention must be granted.

If historical studies were simply to re-express an expression of ideas in the form of a re-idealization, this would cancel (aufhebt) the very component of "realization" or "becoming-real" that is the property of such an expression of ideas in reality—what the seventh lecture identified as their "separation" into and across time. Thus Schelling here rejects the sheer "philosophic" appropriation of history—just as he had earlier said that history is not "subordinated to the concept"—and insists upon a coexistence of ideal and real in historical knowledge, even as history itself (Geschichte) is the expression, or extrusion, of ideal elements—ideas—into the realm of the real. But as he is rejecting a philosophic Aufhebung of the element of the real, his alternative suggests a proto-Hegelian formulation of the problem that Hegel will express,

45

very nearly contemporarily with this text, in *his* use of *aufheben:* to preserve, to allow to subsist *(bestehen lassen)*, while at the same time to transform by elevation *(erheben)*. Specifically, Schelling attributes this kind of procedure to art, which in his example of "the stage"—dramatic art—"represents" the real, but in such a "completion and unity" that the real becomes "the expression of the highest ideas."

Now, the operative term here in Schelling's formulation of the historical-scholarly *(wissenschaftlich)* re-expression of history, in his representation of historical representation, is *Geschichten,* "histories" or "stories." *Geschichte,* in a traditional usage that reappears, incidentally, in Ranke's texts, was used to designate the actual realization of ideal elements in reality and in time ("the becoming-real of an idea . . . expresses itself as *Geschichte*"), while *Historie* was used to indicate the scholarly "matching" of this manifestation on the part of Wissenschaft (its "historische Seite"). Here, *Geschichte* returns as the means of historical re-expression and representation. The term collapses the distinction and oppositional tension between *Geschichte* as what occurs in reality and in time and *Historie* as what aims back at the ideal realm ("upon which Wissenschaft stands") by making itself mean both things, and to say it means both is to say that *Geschichten* here are allegorical, that is, both literal and figural. Literally, they are the "real events" *(reale Begebenheiten),* the acts and evidence of history as that which happens—*Geschichte* as *das Geschehene*—but as narrated, retold, or represented, they are the narrative "histories" or stories by which the "events" become the vehicles, signs, or means of expression of "higher ideas": they are an expression or articulation of meanings. Thus they are literally what they are—events—but also figuratively allegorical signs of higher meaning.

The double meaning of *Geschichte*—the real occurrences represented as their meaningful narration—whereby *Geschichte* becomes *Historie* through the preservation and elevation of *Geschichte* as events into narrative, is appropriately understood as allegorical, since Schelling in the eighth lecture introduced the concept of allegory to designate a "world-historical" distinction between the Greek and the Christian religions, a distinction that he held to be responsible for the very introduction of a historical consciousness. There, Schelling posited that for Greek religion the universe is viewed as nature, while for Christianity it is viewed as history (617). More specifically, Greek gods are embodied in the finite, and thus nature or the finite becomes the *symbol* of the infinite—the symbol, for Schelling, being the impression of the infinite into the finite, which he also characterizes elsewhere as the "unity of the infinite and the finite *still existing before separation*" ("ungetrennte,

46

noch vor der Trennung bestehende Einheit des Unendlichen und End-
lichen")[53]—whereas with the appearance of Christianity the finite is
said by Schelling to be only an *allegory* for the infinite, with nature not
the abiding embodiment but only the fleeting appearance of the infinite,
not eternal but *historical* (618)—the allegorical, for Schelling, being the
expression of the finite into the infinite. Schelling's prime and founding
instance here, in a manner comparable to but ultimately quite different
from Hegel's theological writings of the late 1790s, is the figure of
Christ: nature and natural existence not as an appropriate and abiding
embodiment of the ideal (the symbolic, "Greek" mode) but rather as
the transitional embodiment of the true infinite in the finite and the
sacrificing of that very mode of existence in a return to the realm of the
infinite—Christ's allegorical character as "in der Zeit vergängliche Erscheinung" ("appearance transitory in time") (622), as a temporalized
sign, or signifying temporality.

But Christ, before he can figure Christianity, is the figure for the post-
Greek, for the expression of finitude into infinity, and the specific character of expression here is that it occurs in and into time as departure
and distinction from an otherwise spatialized embodiment of the infinite in the finite. As Schelling put it in his *Philosophie der Kunst*, "where
the unity is separated, there is the finite posited as finite, and only thus
is the tendency [*Richtung*] from finite to infinite possible, thus the unity
of the finite with the infinite. . . . [Thus is] the finite . . . posited as
allegory of the infinite."[54] The post-Greek is the post-symbolic, and so
Christ figures allegory as the temporal expression of—the historical articulation out of and away from—a mimetic reflection that collapsed
toward identity when it was conceived as "before" time in the sense of
without time. Expression—recall Schelling's formulation—is *supplementary* in that it accounts for time as the scene and condition of departure and distinction; as such, time is or must be made supplementary of
the "moment," state, or condition from which it is the very departure.
In rhetorical terms, allegory supplements symbol; in "historical"
terms, Christianity supplements the Greek experience; in conceptual
terms, the beginning—of time, expressed as history—supplements the
origin. Allegory, as the expression of a difference from and within what
otherwise would be unexpressed (and unexpressible?) "unmediated
representation," marks the point and becomes the sign where philosophy yields and is supplemented by its own allegory, history. Philosophy
either grants existence and meaning to history or is expressed by and in
history.

In Schelling's tenth lecture, the allegorical structure of the historical
representation of *Geschichte* by way of *Geschichten* can now be more pre-

cisely appreciated as what is in fact a twofold or double structure of allegory. The very condition of possibility for a "scientific and scholarly" (*wissenschaftlich*) consideration of history as real events in time is that they be considered as meaningful, that is, that they signify something other than their sheer facticity, the mere fact of their occurrence. This condition is granted in the positing of history as the "becoming-real" of ideas: as their expression. This may be called a first allegory of history: truth, or at least meaningfulness, expresses and articulates itself as history (*Geschichte*). The doubly allegorical procedure of historical Wissenschaft is then as follows: "Real events" are received and "copied" or represented as verbal, narrative constructions—one real, literal set of things, namely, the events, is transformed and refigured into the higher, rational mode of their re-expression—and then this "level" or aspect of "impression"-as-narrative-re-expression is taken (back) as the representation or signification, the expression, of an ideal or "higher" meaning. This may be called a second allegory of history: history as events must be retrospectively received and interpreted—imprinted, and read—and then written and expressed as meaningful, even as true study, as a *wissenschaftlich* story or narrative. But even as this formulation would have, in the "second" allegory, history read before being written, so the real point is that the second allegory means the first. One sequence in Schelling's argument is that *Geschichte*, in the sense of events, yields by way of *Historie*, in the sense of historical studies, *Geschichte* as *Geschichten*, or historical narratives. But the so-called second allegory in Schelling's argument describes this sequence: historical narratives, by way of the discourse of historical studies, yield *Geschichte* as events. The study of history—its *wissenschaftlich* study toward its truth—is supplementary to its origin in history. In each case, the procedure is allegorical in the strict sense of *allos-agoreuein*, "speaking otherwise": the ideal realm of the *Urwissen* expresses itself in time as real events; these events are received and transformed from their condition of being literally real events to being figurative signs or expressions, a narrative representation of their articulation. This representation—a *Geschichte*, or story, to the extent that the narrative presupposes completion—is then figuratively the expression of its "higher" meaning.

When Schelling adds some sentences in his tenth lecture to the passage quoted above, he elaborates this twofold allegorical transformation implied in the double meaning of *Geschichte*. He writes that "the sequence [of events] itself must not be empirical, but rather must only be comprehensible from out of a higher order of things. Only then does history [*Geschichte*] receive its completion [*Vollendung*] for reason, when the empirical causes . . . are used as the tools and means of appearance

[*Mittel der Erscheinung*] of a higher necessity" (640). Schelling could scarcely be more explicit. If history-as-events were merely reproduced or recorded as a chronological-empirical sequence, this would not be knowledge or Wissenschaft, but only a confinement in the realm of the materially real. To comprehend history "from out of a higher order" is both to posit it as issuing from an ideal realm and to comprehend or understand it from out of the higher realm of reason; otherwise, one would have mere subjective-pragmatic understanding, unsatisfying to the absolute claims of reason. The "completion" and perfection of history occurs through its transformation from the realm of empirical causality—reminiscent of Schiller's attempt to overcome a causal construction of history—into a relation of means and ends: the same empirical events become, qua allegorical signification, the "means of appearance"—the signs—of a "higher necessity," the "necessity" of reason to render reasonable the real phenomena of events in time that otherwise would appear merely "lawless." The events of history, as what occurs *(das Geschehene)*, are "allowed to subsist" or are preserved, as *signs*, even as they are used, transformed, and "elevated" as the "means of appearance" of their higher meaning: the expression of ideas.

It is true that Schelling, throughout these lectures, is noticeably tempted to reduce history's scholarly and scientific expression, *its* Wissenschaft, to the absolute Wissenschaft of philosophy. And he does not always succeed in resisting such a collapse of the ideal-in-the-real into the ideal *tout court;* in one such instance, he writes: "The opposition that is commonly made between history [*Historie*] and philosophy exists only so long as history is comprehended as a series of contingent events or as mere empirical necessity. . . . History [*Geschichte*], too, issues from an eternal unity and has its roots in the absolute just as nature or any other object of knowledge does" (621). History (*Geschichte*) threatens to reduce, through its *wissenschaftlich* elevation as *Historie*, to philosophy to the extent that history is removed from its empirical domain and returned, like every other "object of knowledge" for Schelling's Wissenschaft, to its source in the absolute. And as this very phrasing indicates, the danger of reducing the Wissenschaft of history to the absolute Wissenschaft of philosophy has its counterpart in the danger of deducing history from and by philosophy because of its ostensible source in the same, one absolute, or *Urwissen*. In the former case, the reduction threatens to cancel the real, manifest, temporal character of history as that which becomes real in the world and in time and to transfer it into the pure ideal realm of philosophic knowledge. In the latter case, history would be prematurely, as it were, deduced from and re-idealized back into the realm of ideas, at the cost of the very appear-

ance—what Schelling called "the appearance of freedom in the particular"—in reality and in time that constitutes it as history. In the first
case, Wissenschaften of particular objects of knowledge becoming the
absolute Wissenschaft of philosophy would be, to paraphrase Hegel's
critique of Schelling, comparable to the night in which all cows are
black, because no cow is discernible. In the second case, the possibility
of the deduction of historical "knowledge" and truth from out of philosophy, since both—together with all other "objects of knowledge"—
have their "roots" in the absolute, leaves Schelling open to the accusation that is later made, however loosely, against all of German idealism
and its "philosophies of history": that they treat history, the a posteriori
par excellence, on a priori grounds and therefore mistreat it.

Despite these temptations and dangers, however, Schelling's formulation of the Wissenschaft of history in his *Lectures on the Method of
Academic Study* is central for the developing scientific and scholarly
study of history within the "idealist" German university. Its importance
lies not in its claims for reason (Kant had promoted these) nor in its
ambitions for philosophic judgment of historical events and chains of
events (Schiller had advanced these, even if unsuccessfully and ultimately in bad faith). Its importance is in its specifically allegorical
construction of the problem: that one and the same thing—history as
Geschichte—may be both retained in its empirical, material, and temporal form as events and "elevated" into a mode of appearance and manifestation *(Erscheinung)* as narrative articulation, or "story" *(Geschichte)*. This much of Schelling's allegory of history is little different
from traditional Christian providential or salvation history *(Heilsge-
schichte)* as itself patently allegorical. But then the additional specification is that instead of the "allegory" being illuminated by faith and,
ultimately, a last judgment, this narrative is then comprehensible by
reason and indeed *is* reason's "illumination" and expression of real objects of knowledge *into and as knowledge*—as their higher, "ideal" meaning. The very allegorical treatment and transformation of historical
objects of study is what both grants them their meaningful, knowledge-
worthy status and preserves them in their empirical aspects as the signs
or vehicles of their meanings. And if this allegorical embodiment only
awaits its transition into and its "completion" in reason, then this attitude nonetheless is consistent with the essential characteristic of the historical phenomenon, namely, that it is in transit, that it is that which is
temporally phenomenal, which arises, transpires, and passes away.

The allegory of history—the view of history as a literal unfolding of
events that yield to their allegorical understanding by reason—is, I sub-

mit, the bedrock foundation for the "modern" scientific and scholarly study of history. It allows historical events to be not only empirically, factually evident—that which happens or occurs, "one damned thing after another"—nor only available to one or another subjective, pragmatic appropriation and arrangement (whereby it might be useful to compare this instance with that situation or possibility and thus perhaps "learn" something practical or instrumental from history). Rather, it allows historical events to be the manifestation or expressions of a significance that human reason, on its own terms, might illuminate and come to know as knowledge; and in order to qualify as knowledge (*Wissen*), history must be "raised" to the stakes of Wissenschaft. This is the ambition of modern historiography, and its stakes, for Schelling as for the subsequent German idealists, are always the ones of truth. History, in its allegory, is the temporal unfolding and reasonable appropriation of its knowable truth.

The founding of an institution of higher learning in Berlin is discussed in the early 1800s, but only in the wake of the Prussian defeat by Napoleon at Jena in 1806, and as a part of the subsequent "Prussian reform movement," do these discussions take on a special and increasingly concrete focus, leading to the university's founding in 1809 and its opening in 1810. The historical-political circumstances of these institutional developments have received considerable documentation and interpretation.[55] But the discussion and foundation of the University of Berlin are also parts of another set of circumstances, historical-political as well but more explicitly *discursive:* not the military defeat and occupation and the administrative reform of the Prussian state but the discourse of philosophy in late eighteenth- and early-nineteenth-century Germany—its status and role in the university and its relations to a discourse of Wissenschaft in general, of historical Wissenschaft in particular. These university discussions of philosophy and history occur amidst many immanent, institutional developments and determinants and are accompanied, of course, by as many external and even accidental factors. I have rehearsed some of these factors—mostly immanent ones, sometimes with a glance at their social and historical occasions—in the earlier sections. I will now focus on an idealist continuation of these discourses of university study and thought as it emerges in the discussion and foundation of the University of Berlin. What distinguishes this idealist discourse, and marks it *as* idealist, is that unlike the varied and occasional character of most of the earlier versions of the debate (including Kant's and Schelling's contributions), this discussion both begins with its ideals and has the model and foundation of a *real-ideal* university as at once its occasion and its outcome, its aim and its end.

The immediate background for the several programmatic writings on the University of Berlin is one of broad organizational issues. The late eighteenth century was, as I have noted in passing, a low point for German universities regarding their student enrollments and perceived social efficacy, to the degree where a respected debating society could discuss abolishing them altogether, and the first tentative proposals for an institution of higher learning in Berlin eschew the model of the university. Thus J. J. Engel, an influential Berlin enlightenment figure and member of the royal circle, could in 1801 and 1802 discuss an "allegemeine Lehranstalt" for the city as a union of three or more independent and practical faculties; and Julius von Massow, minister of justice but also with responsibility for higher education, could advocate the elimination of universities and their replacement by autonomous professional academies. When at this same time K. F. Beyme, chief of staff of the royal cabinet, argued against von Massow's plan, he nonetheless also formulated his proposals in opposition to the universities: the universities could, in the provinces, be directed toward training for state service, while Berlin should have an "allgemeine Lehranstalt"—not a university—as a pure academic institute.[56] Von Massow and Beyme may have held opposite or inverted views of the practical-professional or intellectual-academic character of the institution that should exist in Berlin, but they shared the sense that it should *not* be organized as a university.

In his lectures, Schelling himself had left an unpromising formulation for the organization of the university. On the one hand, he could speak approvingly in the third lecture of "the coherence of all the Wissenschaften among themselves, and the objectivity which this inner, organic unity has received through the exterior organization of the university" (577), and it is this position that orients the progression of his subsequent lectures from the priority of the "Wissenschaften of pure reason" to their relation to the "positive Wissenschaften." But when he returns to questions of university organization, he presents a surprisingly pre-Kantian view. To be sure, he still portrays the "Objektivität" of particular Wissenschaften from the perspective of the undivided "inner organism" of the *Urwissen* and of philosophy: "the exterior schematism of [the positive Wissenschaften's] division and unification must be sketched according to the image of philosophy's inner *typos*." But what this means is that three "positive Wissenschaften" are said to correspond to three versions of philosophy's inner relationship of the ideal and the real: one that objectively represents "the real and ideal world as one" ("the immediate Wissenschaft of the absolute and divine essence," which is theology); one that outwardly represents the *real* side of philosophy, "the absolute expressed in the real" (the Wissenschaft of nature and of the organism, which is medicine); and one that objectifies the *ideal* side of philosophy, "the absolute expressed in the ideal" (the Wissenschaft of history as that of "the development of the constitution," and thus the Wissenschaft of law, or jurisprudence). Then, with a critical aside at Kant's *Streit* (said to be "one-sided"), Schelling reintroduces a hierarchy among these three Wissenschaften, which are *faculties* insofar as they attain a "real objective existence" through and in the state: theology must be the highest, since it is the objectification of the innermost core of philosophy (the real-ideal union), and then law is ranked above medicine "insofar as the ideal is the higher potentiality of the real." But as for a philosophy faculty, there is none: Schelling opines "that there simply is not and cannot be one, and the very simple proof of this is that that which is everything, for that reason cannot be anything in particular [*das, was alles ist, eben deswegen nichts insbesondere sein kann*]." Philosophy is objectified in the three "positive Wissenschaften" of theology, law, and medicine, but nowhere in its totality. "The true objectivity of philosophy in its totality" could only be art *(Kunst)*, but since the faculties issue from the state as "knowledge having become objective," and since philosophy is owed "unconditional freedom" by the state (see his fifth lecture, on the relation of philosophy to the state), there can no more be a "faculty of the arts" than there could be a philosophy faculty. There are only "free interrelations" among the arts, and thus Schelling reintroduces the older *collegium artium* as the truer form for philosophy within the university (612–14).

The surprising thing, then, is that Schelling preserves the hierarchy of the three "higher" faculties within the organization of the university even as he dissolves the claims—advanced, say, by Kant—for philosophy to be another and even higher faculty within it; and he does all this from the perspective of the absolute priority of philosophy as Wissenschaft. While it might appear that he is suddenly overwhelmed by false modesty with regard to philosophy—since it is everything, it cannot be anything in particular—Schelling is also preserving the Kantian distinction between the "applied," or "dogmatic," faculties as agencies of the state and philosophy as unconditionally free. The paradox is that philosophy is the absolute center of the university as an organization of Wissenschaft and yet a vanishing point with respect to its institutional status: philosophy is everywhere, its "faculty" or objectification nowhere. The empowerment of philosophy as the apotheosis of Wissenschaft—absolute knowing of the absolute as "original knowledge" (*Ur-wissen*)—is at once the idealist program for the university par excellence and an idealization of philosophy that, by its very idealization, still rubs against the grain of the university's organization. The status of philosophy and the philosophy faculty within the university has yet to be adequately articulated, even though the character of the university as the institutional organ and organization of Wissenschaft is already in view.

The several programmatic idealist writings on the university (or other academic institute) to be established in Berlin were a response to Wilhelm von Humboldt's request put to Friedrich August Wolf, Johann Gottlieb Fichte, and Friedrich Schleiermacher when Humboldt was directing plans for the institution's founding. (Schleiermacher himself headed the *Einrichtungskommission,* which called the new faculty to Berlin and administered the university's foundation, in 1808–9.) Wolf's response apparently was not completed, and it has not survived in other than fragmentary form, although Humboldt at one point foresaw the philologist heading the *Einrichtungskommission;* Wolf did become a member of the original university faculty.[57] Schleiermacher's *Gelegentliche Gedanken über Universitäten in deutschem Sinn* (Occasional Thoughts on Universities in a German Sense), 1808, is a well-known document on the liberal definition of the university, its self-governance, and its pedagogic mission. Schleiermacher is eloquent in making Wissenschaft the university's "essence" (*Wesen*), which he also understands as the introduction of students to "the idea of Wissenschaft," attending to "the unity and holism [*Allheit*] of knowledge, so that they learn to become conscious in each kind of thinking of the basic laws of Wissenschaft, and thereby gradually cultivate in themselves their own faculty [*Vermögen*] of researching, discovering and representing."[58] Here he appeals to "the actual name" of a university (from *uni-versum*), which is not a mere "gathering" of multiple knowledges but the place where "the totality [*Gesamtheit*] of knowledge is to be represented, in that one brings the principles and, as it were, the groundplan of all knowing [*Grundriss alles Wissens*] to view." Philosophy would be at the center of this idea of Wissenschaft—he sometimes uses "philosophic spirit" and "scholarly and scientific spirit" interchangeably—and "pure philosophy, speculation," is that "universal" on which "all particular knowing rests; there is no capacity for scholarly and scientific production without the speculative spirit." Accordingly, "it is universally acknowledged for the university that philosophic instruction is the foundation [*Grundlage*] of all that is done there." But apart from some further, by-now familiar attributions of foundational and universal power to philosophy with respect to Wissenschaft, Schleiermacher's document has little to say to our interests, especially since it has virtually nothing to say about history as a university Wissenschaft.[59] So, too, Humboldt's own memorandum to the king, "Über die innere und äussere Organisation der höheren wissenschaftlichen Anstalten in Berlin" (1809–10), which he formulated after receiving the suggestions he had solicited from the others and which survives only in part, is notably sketchy about the particular Wissenschaften. While it proposes a radically idealist model of Wissenschaft, which I have analyzed elsewhere,[60] it has nothing to say about history, which is surprising since Humboldt is also the author of the later, better-known essay "On the Task of the Historian" (1821).

The remaining idealist proposal for the university is Fichte's *Deducirter Plan einer zu Berlin zu errichtenden höheren Lehranstalt* (A Plan Deduced for a Higher Teaching Institution to be Constructed at Berlin) of 1807.[61] Fichte had been, after Jena, in Berlin from 1799 to 1805 and was then briefly "professor for speculative philosophy" at Erlangen; when he returned to Berlin, his *Reden an die deutsche Nation,* held at the Prussian Academy of Wissenschaften in 1807–8, achieved considerable popularity. He was to become the University of Berlin's first philosopher, its first dean, and its first elected rector, and after his death in 1816 it was his chair that Hegel was called to fill. Despite this apparent welcome in Berlin and its university, his plan for the new institution, following upon one written the previous year for Erlangen's reorganization, met with no practical success at all.[62] But my point here is not to tell a story about the (failed) institutional realization of Fichte's model but to analyze its model for the philosophic realization of a story.

When I say that Fichte's *Plan Deduced* had no practical success, I mean that when the University of Berlin took on its actual institutional shape, its inspiration came from Schleiermacher's model, and not Fichte's. A faculty senate, deans, a rector, student autonomy—these were Schleiermacher's ideas, whereas Fichte had the silly idea of professors' wearing uniforms that would designate their specializations, and his plan stood for (as he ultimately resigned as rector in a dispute over) faculty control over student discipline. But this is anecdotage. The rhetoric of Wissenschaft in the university—what becomes known, with the University of Berlin, as the *Wissenschaftsuniversität*—and of the centrality of philosophy therein, is nowhere stronger than in Fichte's text, and his articulation of history to philosophy advances even upon Schelling's, so that the *distinction* of the Wissenschaft of history is established at the same time that it would be philosophically "legitimated."

Fichte deduces the university logically and genetically from philosophy. Knowing *(Wissen)* is primarily knowing the art of using knowing ("die Kunst, das Wissen zu gebrauchen"), for if knowing is not "permeated [*durchdrungen*] with clear and free consciousness," it is only a mechanical and repetitive mental activity, whereas understanding (*Verstand*) is "the free activity of comprehending." The employment of understanding in learning must in turn be learned, or "elevated to clear consciousness"; "the art of learning as such is to be learned."[63] The "higher teaching institution" is thus "a school in the art of the scholarly and scientific [*wissenschaftlich*] employment of understanding" (5). From these assumptions and definitions, Fichte "constructs" (*errichten*) a university on the notion of *permeation by consciousness,* a form, in other words, of enlightenment. "The art of Wissenschaft," which is what the university teaches, is to be "permeated [*durchdrungen*] with clear consciousness . . . , to the point of knowledge [*Erkenntnis*] of the universal, as well as in the specific individual determinations that it takes on in particulars." The university's "essence" is "the art of forming the scholarly and scientific artists themselves [*die Kunst, den wissenschaftlichen Künstler selber zu bilden*]," and this "presupposes a Wissenschaft of the scholarly and scientific art [*eine Wissenschaft der wissenschaftlichen Kunst*]" (11). This Wissenschaft is philosophy.

Fichte describes the education of a student and the "enlightenment" of a specific discipline or Wissenschaft as equivalently an introduction—of and by philosophy—into the "art of Wissenschaft" whereby "one clearly understands *what* one is doing, and *how* one does it." A student may possess a particular "talent," thus a particular "natural gift," but he is limited to its practice and purview; he needs "to permeate [*durchdringen*] this standpoint with the concept, and so be able to make a free art out of a mere natural gift." Similarly, "the spirit of each' specific Wissenschaft is a limited and limiting spirit," and before it is practiced, it must be "understood, i.e., the kind and manner of mental activity it demands must be known, and so the universal *concept* of its art must itself precede the *practice* of this art." "Now," Fichte continues,

> that which grasps in a scholarly and scientific manner [*wissenschaftlich*] *all* mental activity—including as well all specific and further determined expressions of the same—is philosophy; accordingly, it is from the philosophic formation of art [*von philosophischer Kunstbildung aus*] that the specific Wissenschaften must be given their art, and that which in them previously was mere natural gift, dependent on good fortune, must be raised to a reflected ability and practice; the spirit of philosophy would be the one that first understands itself, and then, within itself, understands all the other spirits. (16)

The specific "art" (Fichte means *Kunst* as close to *techne*, as in *ars interpretandi*) of the specific Wissenschaft would be "a further determination

[*Bestimmung*] and individual application of [the philosophic artist's] universal philosophic art." Accordingly—and alluding to the traditional "priority" of logic in the trivium—"all higher scholarly and scientific education must issue [*ausgehen*] from philosophy, and at universities, the philosophy lectures must be heard first and by all" (16). Correspondingly, "the first and exclusive condition of possibility for constructing a scientific and scholarly school of art [*Kunstschule*]" is a philosopher who practices the art of philosophizing and who, in teaching his students this art, would have them use it to "permeate [*durchdrängen*] the positive material [*positiven Stoff*] of the specific Wissenschaften, which is provided to them from elsewhere" (17). In a final repetition of the terminology of these claims, Fichte says that "with this developed philosophic spirit as the pure form of knowing, *the whole scholarly and scientific material [gesamte wissenschaftliche Stoff] must in its organic unity* be grasped and permeated [*durchdrungen*] at the higher teaching institution, so that one might know exactly what belongs to it or not, and thus the strict boundary between Wissenschaft and non-Wissenschaft be drawn" (19).

If to know philosophy is to know "the pure form of knowing" (and "*all* mental activity in a scholarly and scientific manner"), and to know in a scholarly and scientific manner—as opposed to by sheer talent or luck—is to know "the universal *concept*" of an "art" before and above its practice, then it is consistent that Fichte can deduce, in a parallel fashion, the *education* of the students, the *development* of a university, and the *permeation* of the specific disciplines *with consciousness*, all from the Wissenschaft of philosophy. "Permeating" the "positive material" of the specific disciplines, like the "further determination" of their "arts," is an "application" of philosophy. It is this prioritizing of philosophy— no surprise, coming from a philosopher—that has given Fichte the mixed image of being both a promoter of the Wissenschafts-university and a demoter of the autonomy of specific disciplines, or Wissenschaften. Part of his ruse is to take philosophy's earlier position as part of the *propaedeuticum* and invert it from chronological priority in university studies into logical priority as a foundation, or *Grundlage* (which term we have seen Schleiermacher use as well), whence other disciplines "issue" (*ausgehen*) and receive its "application" (*Anwendung*). As the historian of history in the German university Josef Engel puts it, "The [older university's] merely temporal sequence of pre-studies [*Vorstudium*] and Wissenschaft . . . is reinterpreted into an essential, inner connection of ground and consequence."[64] But this same achievement is then feared or resented as a belittling of all other disciplines as mere extensions, applications, or deductions of philosophy—or worse.

Fichte himself argues in his *Plan Deduced* that the Berlin "higher learning institution" ought to have none of the traditional "higher" faculties, since medicine, he claims, is exclusively practice, not Wissenschaft, while theology—if it is not either the hocus-pocus of God's will inaccessible without revelation or the teaching of the Scriptures as mere vehicles for popular instruction—is absorbable into philology and history: it would be, in the manner of Lessing's "Erziehung des Menschengeschlechts," "the *history of the development of religious concepts among men*," and when practiced outside of a theology faculty, it would have the advantage of freer judgments regarding authorship and canon-history than is the case with prejudgmental church history (26). As for law, jurisprudence is either practical or, in its scholarly and scientific aspect, reliant upon history. But here, Fichte's specifications both help explain the resentments against his prioritizing of philosophy and anticipate his further remarks about the Wissenschaft of history.

"The scholarly and scientific material [*Stoff*] of *jurisprudence* is a chapter from out of history . . . It should be *a history of the development and progressive shaping [Ausbildung und Fortgestaltung] of the concept of right among men*, which *concept of right* itself—independent of this history, and as *master* and not at all as *servant*—must first already be found through philosophizing" (26). Although Fichte uses *Geschichte* for "history" each time in this passage, it is clear that he means the historical as *das historische*, the a posteriori;[65] and when he says that "the concept" (of right) ought first to be found by philosophy, independent of the a posteriori history, he lays himself open to the charge that the *Stoff* of another Wissenschaft can be deduced a priori from the Wissenschaft of philosophy and its concepts—in fact, the historian of the University of Berlin, Max Lenz, paraphrases Fichte's last sentence here as, "But what law should be is known strictly a priori [*Was aber Gesetz sein soll, wird schlechthin a priori erkannt*]."[66] And other historians as distinguished as Ranke will hold against idealist philosophy (sometimes naming Hegel when it would more justifiably appear to be Fichte) its ostensible deduction of history from concepts a priori.[67]

If here it seems that Fichte, like Schelling before him, is equivocating with respect to history's subordination or nonsubordination to philosophy's concept, his continuation to this brief passage on jurisprudence points the way toward his more complex thoughts on history. The "practical" aspect of law will, in fact, involve a changed attitude toward history:

> The office of judge, and legislation as well, are the practical application *of history;* and so jurisprudence's first encyclopaedia is the encyclopaedia of

history, in that this is the ground [*Boden*] on which it and the scholarly and scientific employment of understanding in it [*der wissenschaftliche Verstandesgebrauch in ihr*] rest, and the practice of the same [jurisprudence and understanding] in their greatest power is actually the art of bringing forth a history—and to be sure, a more gratifying one than the former [*eigentlich die Kunst ist, eine Geschichte, und zwar eine erfreulichere, als die bisherige, hervorzubringen*]. (26)

The "practice" (*Ausübung*) of jurisprudence—will it be to change *history* in the future, and for the better, or to rewrite or retell *history* (*Geschichte* as the narrative form of *das Geschehene*) of the past, and in a more gratifying manner? And could the second alternative *be the same as* the first? "To bring forth a history," especially in the context of jurisprudence as the *application (Anwendung)* of history, certainly sounds like *making* history. But Fichte is talking every bit as much about books (encyclopaedias, for starters). Whatever is ostensibly "deductive" or "a priori" about his view of the concept in history, history also is available for reshaping *in history*.

How might, for Fichte, the Wissenschaft of history take its genesis, in his Wissenschafts-university, from philosophy and its "foundation" or "ground"? The material (*Stoff*) of history, like its students, comes to the university from outside; before entering, the students are already to have received "a general image of the transformations of the human race through the major events of the ruling peoples, alongside an image of the general shape of the surface of the earth [*Oberfläche des Erdbodens*] as the stage [*Schauplatze*] of these transformations" (10). But its permeation by consciousness in the mode of understanding remains reserved for the university, and hence for philosophy: "the indication, how one is supposed to *understand* the whole of human history, should probably best fall to the philosopher" (21). This burden of understanding already raises the dignity of historical material above the stuff of mere *eruditio*, and as a goal, understanding orients the otherwise nonteleological character of sheer "transformations" (*Umwandlungen*). Toward the end of the *Plan Deduced*, in his most extended discussion of history, Fichte reflects on the projected change in the "art" of doing history at the Wissenschafts-university: formerly, its task was "*to find* that clear concept and the hard data that give an overview of events under its direction"; now, he imagines, this is found and recorded in books the students can read. What remains is "another task, doubtless the following: to elaborate further those data, and to connect them, and thus increasingly to permeate with the grounding concept [*durch den Grundbegriff zu durchdringen*] the formerly not-yet permeated material

59

of the facts [*des bisher noch nicht durchdrungenen Stoffes der Facta*]" (62). From "the surface of the earth" as the stage of human history to its permeation or "penetration" (*durchdringen*) by a deeper, more profound "grounding concept," Fichte's Wissenschaft of history would find or give a foundation to sheer surface appearances. What is the "grounding concept" for historical Wissenschaft?

Fichte's preceding paragraph is extraordinary, and in it an answer lies buried. Universal history (*Universalgeschichte*) is not an "accidental" (*Zufälliges*) art that can be dispensed with; rather, it has

> to reply to a definite [*bestimmte*] question pressing upon [*aufdringende*] the human species, and to do so according to definite [*bestimmten*] articles of inquiry that likewise already are present in the human mind; as, for example, how [*wie*] our species [*Geschlecht*] gradually raised itself to a human mode of living, to lawfulness, to wisdom, to religion, and to whatever else the educational development into true man [*die Ausbildung zum wahren Menschen*] may consist in. (62)

This recalls very precisely Schiller's charge to the "philosophic" historian to explain how history led up to "our" contemporary level of *Bildung*—but with several crucial additions. The question pressing upon (*aufdringend*) one corresponds to the permeating (*durchdringend*) task of the philosopher, just as this "definite" (*bestimmte*) pressing question corresponds to "definite" articles of inquiry already at hand in the human mind, displaying an implicit doctrine of *Bestimmung*, or determination, between mind's disposition and its operation. And what all of these are oriented toward—the pressing, the permeating, the definite question and articles—is not just any development but that of the *true*: "die Ausbildung zum wahren Menschen." The correspondence and coherence of the question of the story of man (*Universalgeschichte* as a universal story, a story of the universal), the task of the philosopher, and their mutual *Bestimmung* would be scholarly and scientific truth. Universal history has to answer a question put to it by, and determined by, man's mind; the question presses toward the answer as the answering presses toward and permeates the material; and the telos of the history of the species having "raised itself . . . to true man" would be met, in truth, by the teleology of truly knowing *how* (*wie*) this happened: *Geschichte* as the narrative of what happened would become and be *Geschichte* as the true knowing, or Wissenschaft, of what and how it happened.

How this is to be done involves a story of the ground, a procedure of allegory, and indeed an allegory of the ground. To begin with, Fichte declares that as such inquiries yield results, the material (*Stoff*) of history will have to be recharacterized, or more precisely—recalling one sense of the claim about a revised history of law—that a different histor-ical narrative *(Geschichte)* will have to be brought forth:

> One would then also see that the previously marked-out epochs according to the rise or decline of great empires, according to battles and peace treaties, the lists of rulers and the like, were only provisional auxiliary means [*provisorische Hilfsmittel*], intended for a mode of thinking that is affected only through the motion of external sense [*die nur durch die Er-schütterung des äusseren Sinnes berührt wird*]—in order nevertheless to sup-port and preserve [*erhalten*] the sphere of that better yield [*bessern Aus-beute*]. (62)

At this juncture, "that better yield" is still unclear, but what is clear is that a certain way of writing history is being linked to a certain earlier *university* practice of doing history and that both of these are now being uncovered in their new and previously hidden meaning—in other words, as allegory. When historiography according to world empires, wars, or princes is called a "provisional auxiliary means" for another way of writing history, it is being compared to the role of history in the earlier, pre-Wissenschafts-university as a *propaedeuticum* for higher study, or an "auxiliary discipline" *(Hilfswissenschaft)* for such higher Wissenschaften. This earlier *historical practice of history in the university* is now to give way to its philosophic "permeation" and overcoming in the Wissenschafts-university but is still a "means" of providing the ma-terial, the *stuff,* for its philosophic enlightenment (as the students are to bring their "general image" of universal history with them to the uni-versity). So, too, the earlier kind of historical *narrative* is to be overcome (it is "only provisional") but is also still justified in the service it pro-vided, which was to "support and preserve" a sphere that only now will become accessible.

The "mode of thinking" that characterizes both the older way of doing history in the university and the older narrative writing of history is said to rely on "the motion of external sense." This obscure phrase that sounds of eighteenth-century empirical psychology is, in fact, the cue to Fichte's allegory of history here. A deeper meaning—that "sphere of that better yield"—was supported and preserved in or be-neath the external *Sinn* (both sensuous sense and its dimension of mean-ingful sense). Fichte continues:

> And one would refer only to those epochs of history that more inwardly join or adapt to the interest of the human curiosity for knowledge [*inniger an das Interesse der menschlichen Wissbegier sich anschmiegenden*], which now in any event would draw forth with them those first, less significant ones as well [*jene ersten weniger bedeutenden mit sich fortführen*], so that the

61

portrait [*Gemälde*] might receive its complete life [*vollkommenes Leben*] right down to the real soil [*bis auf den wirklichen Boden herab*]. (62)

Now, a reperiodized history more closely matches the "interest of knowledge" that is the interest of Wissenschaft (recall Kant's similar phrase about the "scholarly and scientific [*wissenschaftliche*] interest" of the philosophy faculty, "i.e., . . . the truth"), and the specification that such reperiodization "more inwardly" matches the interest contrasts this new narrative with the older one, which only "moved the external sense." Outside gives way to inside, sense to its inner meaning, the husk to its kernel, and yet the latter, reperiodized epochs will continue to "lead forth with them" (*fortführen*) the earlier, now less-significant ones, just as they first "supported and preserved" the "more inward" and "better yield" that is now being uncovered. The literal supported and preserved the allegorical "sphere"; the allegorical will continue to draw the literal but now "less significant" narrative along with it. Together, the two narratives (the two periodizations of history) will yield the "portrait" of history its "complete life."

But "right down to the real soil"? What could this possibly mean? I have resisted translating *Boden* as "ground(s)," and for reasons that now will become clear. Fichte's discussion of universal history (itself an example of "the progressive development of the scholarly and scientific art") now gives an example:

> One would, for example, no longer say: under so-and-so's rule the plow was invented, but rather inversely: when the plow was invented, so-and-so ruled, whose life perhaps had influence on the further events of the plow, of which latter history it is here alone our concern [*auf welches letzteren Geschichte es hier doch allein ankommt*]. The art of history would thereby doubtless have progressed, in that one now first rightly knew what one was to be asking after in the same, and what one was to be looking at in it; it would be permeated with a clear concept [*mit einem klaren Begriffe durchdrungen*]. (62)

Instead of "under so-and-so's rule the plow was invented," "when the plow was invented, so-and-so ruled," and *now* one is supposed to know "what one was to be asking after" in history—a plow?! Could Fichte's point be at once as remotely trivial as his inversion appears, and as obscure as the claim that *now* we know what history and its knowledge are all about? No, the point of this plow is not trivial, nor need it remain obscure.

In his paragraph to this point, Fichte has been explicitly recharacterizing history's narrative as he goes along. If history is supposed to tell a progressive, developmental story toward "true man," it will move beyond a *chronicling* of empires, wars, rulers, and the like, with their—at best—flux or alternation (rise and fall, war and peace), to a history of progress, such as the invention of a tool of agriculture. But just as one periodization supported and preserved another potential one within or beneath its "external sense," which latter one can then draw forth the former one with it, so counting by kings and naming the invention of the plow can be reversed into recounting the progress of the plow and naming the king: one narrative, first mistakenly but nonetheless helpfully read for its apparently self-sufficient meaning or reference (to empires, wars, rulers, etc.), is now revealed and understood allegorically as having been only literal, only "exterior" and "provisional," and yet nonetheless the way of supporting and preserving the more inner, more interesting level of meaning that now comes into its own—but not altogether into its own, for it draws with it that first narrative counting of reigns of kings. So, too, throughout Fichte's account here, exterior *markings*—the periods marked out *(abgesteckt),* the motion (or "irritation," *Erschütterung)* of the "exterior sense," the former propaedeutic and auxiliary services of history—become the signs, or "means" *(Mitteln),* for reading the inner meaning, but thereby the spatial mode— outside/inside—becomes a *temporal* one as well, for the exterior signs at once tell the story of their temporal passage into "history" (a prior, now historical way of doing and writing history) and are preserved as such signs in Fichte's (re)telling of history as its overcoming of its previous mode, and with the help of that very mode. The signs of the past become the signs of passage, and the signs of passage pass into or give way to its allegorical reading as its coming-to-knowledge.

But in this allegory of history, one is not left only with the inner content (once maintained by its now-"provisional" means) now carrying with it its outer means or signs, as if the two parts—literal and allegorical—might, like the two directions to Fichte's example (king-plow, plow-king), make up the "complete picture." For what about the "real ground" and the permeating concept *(Begriff)?* One dimension or aspect of history that Fichte's allegory is uncovering here is that of its evidentiary structure: that events and their dates are not the sufficient *stuff* of history (while they may be of chronicle) but only the evidence— the signs—for a "real" meaning to be written as narrative and read with comprehension. So events and their dates mean more or less in relation to other more or less significant events and dates. Here, it is not the king and his dates that *mean;* at most they *signify* an adjacency (an "auxiliary" status of, at most, "influence") to the *meaning* of the story of the plow, which can be variously characterized as a progressive story versus a cyclical one, a one-time event versus a static human condition of rulers and ruled, a technological history versus a military-political one, and so on. But were this account of Fichte's "discovery" to stop here, it would risk retrivializing his example of the plow and the "complete portrait."

For the plow is beneath the king in history's conventional (or previous) hierarchy but above the king in our "later" interest of human curiosity for knowledge, and it is introduced by Fichte as an example of how the latter kind of history keeps the former kind with it "so that the portrait might receive its complete life down to the real soil." Not only that the story of the plow would keep that of the king with it ("when the plow was invented, so-and-so ruled"), but that that of the king always already kept—"supported and preserved"—the plow in *its* soil ("under so-and-so's rule the plow was invented"). The "real soil" is wherever the plow is. The *point* of the plow, however, is to turn up something *beneath it*. Beneath the empires, wars, and rulers are the "more inward" historical periodizations, narratives, and meanings, and beneath the plow in the real soil that turns up there, there turns up a further finding in turn: the "clear concept." To invent *(erfinden)* the plow is to find *(finden)* something beneath it and its point: what it unearths from the real soil of kings *and* plows, empires, wars, rulers *and* technology, is something deeper than soil: the *ground* of history in philosophy's concept, the foundation, or *Grundlage*, of the Wissenschaft of history.

This scarcely pronounceable word *Pflug* then means, from its literal letters downward, not only a rewriting of the narrative and a rereading of the meaning of history but its allegory as its Wissenschaft: with this sign of invention, one finds its meaning in its knowing. History means its passage from exterior to inner, from artificial surface to real soil, and then to the light of the concept underneath it—from narrative to Wissenschaft. "Mit einem klaren Begriffe durchdrungen" could also be translated as "penetrated with a clear concept," as if pierced with the point of a plow. The plow becomes the figure—the literal sign for the allegorical meaning—for Wissenschaft, as the meaning of rewriting the narratives of history becomes the claim that they mean that they lead to—point to and yield, or uncover—its knowledge. History—the plow—means its philosophic knowing: that it can be known as Wissenschaft. Now the scholarly and scientific study of history can begin, as "one now first rightly knows what one is to be asking after in the same, and what one was to be looking at in it." *Geschichte* as what happened means *Geschichte* as what is told in a story, which means *Geschichte* as what is done as a Wissenschaft in the university.

Few philosophers become historians—although Hegel was one—and fewer historians become philosophers—although Nietzsche was one. When the University of Berlin opened with a faculty of twenty-four full professors, twelve in its *Philosophische Fakultät*, there was the one philosopher, Fichte; two great philologists, Friedrich August Wolf and August Boeckh; the historically minded professor of *Kameralistik*, Friedrich Christian Rühs (this discipline later became political science and political economy)—but no professor of history. Schleiermacher was in the theology faculty, where his colleague Wilhelm de Wette taught historical theology, and the great historian of Roman law, Friedrich von Savigny, was in the law faculty. Barthold Niebuhr, who taught Roman history in the philosophy faculty from its opening until he became Prussian ambassador to Rome in 1815, was never a full professor or *Ordinarius*. Josef Engel writes that at just this time, "despite the remarkable significance attributed to historical study [*Historie*] in all the programs for the university, the Wissenschaft of history still did not possess *in concreto* any systematically grounded unequivocal [*systematisch begründeten eindeutig*] object."[68]

Engel's language is exact. Fichte may have "grounded" the object of the Wissenschaft of history, but it will remain to Hegel to do so "systematically," and even then the object will never be "unequivocal," *eindeutig*, but doubly signifying—*zweideutig*, or "ambiguous"—in its two aspects of letter and spirit, literal and allegorical, historical event and historical meaning, *Geschichte* and *Geschichte*. In Fichte, in his words, all the unicity remains on the side of philosophy: "unity [*Einheit*] and the view of the matter from out of One viewpoint [*aus Einem Gesichtspunkte*] is the character of philosophy" (21). For the historians, any *one* particular thing is in danger from this oneness; Engel recounts the fear that "the [historical] particular [*Einzelne*] not be interpreted from out of the higher philosophic concept of the unity of events [*Begriff der Einheit des Geschehens*]."[69]

Within two decades there would be not one but several historians in Berlin's philosophy faculty: the historian Friedrich von Raumer in 1819, the comparative philologist Franz Bopp in 1821,[70] the first professor of German literature (*Deutsche Philologie*) in the world, the former classical philologist Karl Lachmann in 1825, and by this same year two "associate professors" (*Extraordinarien*) of history, Leopold Ranke and Johann Gustav Droysen. By this time as well, there would be Hegel as

Fichte's successor and—to rejoin the narrative at the point where the present study began—the philosophy *Privatdozent* Schopenhauer, lamenting both philosophy and history in the university.

Hegel's achievement was a systematic entwining of philosophy and history such that the philosophy of history and the history of philosophy equivalently taught the development of history toward freedom, of philosophy toward truth, and of both toward their Wissenschaften. This was celebrated by his students and followers but resisted by many more. After his death in 1831, an adulatory funeral, and the pious collecting and editing in the 1830s of all his lectures, the Hegelian "two decades" at Berlin were visibly over. When in 1841 King Friedrich Wilhelm IV replaces Altenstein with Eichhorn at the *Kultusministerium*, to run the university and to resist "*Hegelschen Pantheismus*," and Eichhorn calls Schelling—by now a conservative Christian—to the chair of philosophy, Soren Kierkegaard, Jakob Burckhardt, and Friedrich Engels are in the audience for the inaugural lecture and it seems a different, post-Hegelian time. Max Lenz writes of this as "the unphilosophic age" *(das unphilosophische Zeitalter):* "after the death of the master, the historical principle [came] ever more strongly to the forefront of the *Geisteswissenschaften*, and in it they found a unity [*Einheit*] such as philosophy had never been able to offer them. This was now the universal tendency [*allgemeine Zug*] of the time. . . . The unphilosophic age had arrived."[71]

With history, not philosophy, now offering "unity" and the "universal," we are already *after Hegel* in our narrative, which began, after all, with the collapse of unity and universality in German historiography and the Wissenschaft of history by the end of the century. The historian from whom I drew, Josef Engel, claims that "none of the scholarly and scientific historians of the nineteenth century, breathing with full lungs the new scholarly and scientific air, could withdraw from the fascination of Hegelian philosophy. . . . And in the muted or audible opposition from the historians, at first concerned about their methodological position as a Wissenschaft more intuitively than systematically and fully conscious, the dependence upon idealist philosophy and its perfecter Hegel remains traceable."[72] While it seems true that the historiography and historical methods of Droysen or Ranke owe much more to Hegel than is commonly acknowledged, to establish this in a scholarly manner would be another story, another study.[73] So, too, would be the telling of the story of German historical narratives in this century, of their decline from idealism and universalism to *Realpolitik* and nationalism. By the end of the century, its most popular academic and official historian, Heinrich von Treitschke, could write in the year of his death, nationalistically and proto-racially, that a sufficient goal of history as a Wissenschaft was "to awaken in our race [*Geschlechte*] a thinking consciousness of its becoming [*eine denkendes Bewusstsein seines Werdens*]."[74]

Here we are long *after* Hegel, but in the language of "thinking consciousness" and *Werden*, it "remains traceable" that we are also still *according to* Hegel. As I turn now to Hegel, it will be not to prepare a tracing of his tracing in nineteenth-century German literary or other historiography but to find what is already "after and according to" an allegory of history in Hegel's own attempt at a systematic philosophic Wissenschaft of history, which doubled allegory of coming after a past and rereading and rewriting "according to" it will then be traceable in twentieth-century literary historiography after Hegel. To look for this in Hegel will be, it turns out, to return to the point of Fichte's plow: to find what historical Wissenschaft turns up in its soil, even if this be bones and broken statues.

2

History and Hegel:
An Introduction

To present Hegel as the figure of the fulfillment of the modern university's Wissenschaft of history is perhaps surprising, even paradoxical. The surprise is not the identification of Hegel with the modern university, specifically with the University of Berlin.[1] Hegel's identification of truth and absolute knowledge with scholarly and scientific study (Wissenschaft), and of Wissenschaft with encyclopaedic forms and divisions, is well known, and such a version and entitlement of Wissenschaft correspond broadly with the claims for university knowledge and the philosophy faculty's divisions of study as I have been tracing them in the philosophic writings preceding and leading up to the founding of the University of Berlin. There is also the implicit identification of the embodied forms of objective knowledge that a Hegelian encyclopaedia is, and the objective form of freedom that the state is—an identification that suggests, then, the *state university* as the objective embodiment of encyclopaedic Wissenschaft; this association of Hegel and the Prussian state university has been long held and often fruitfully reexamined.[2]

The surprise—and paradox—is rather the presentation of Hegel as a figure of *historical* Wissenschaft. Perhaps no one would be more reluctant to admit such a claim, or more suspicious of its consequences, than a historian, and this reluctance and suspicion have a long pedigree, beginning with some of the historians who were Hegel's contemporaries at the University of Berlin. Hegel a historian? Did he not always seek to overcome history for the sake of and from the vantage point of philosophy? Is it not the historical given, the factuality of history and its particulars, that is imperiled at every turn by the Hegelian sublation of fact toward concept, of appearance toward philosophic truth—as well as by his ruthless "Desto schlimmer für die Tatsachen"? We are here on the threshold of decades of misunderstandings, anxieties, clichés, and downright prejudices. Only a combination of wide-angle overviews and detailed examinations or reexaminations will allow us to approach an understanding of Hegel as *the* figure of historical Wissenschaft.

Hegel's work—not all of it (not, for example, the prespeculative "theological" and early philosophical writings), but the bulk of it—may for our purposes be divided into three, roughly chronological parts. (It should go without saying that my purposes here are not Hegelian and that this division or even the notion of its possibility would not be accepted by some Hegelians.) There is the *Phenomenology*, which studies the modes of *"appearing* [or 'phenomenal'] knowledge" in a narrative and roughly chronological-historical manner, leading up to and terminating with the standpoint of the text's authorial voice, that of absolute knowledge. We shall examine the *Phenomenology*'s terminal point in the next chapter; here, it is sufficient to quote no less a Hegel scholar than Alexandre Kojève, saying of this point that "l'introduction de l'Histoire dans la philosophie est pour Hegel sa découverte principale et décisive."[3] There is then the *encyclopaedic* work in the strict sense, which Hegel began to write in 1808 and continued revising until 1831: the *Wissenschaft der Logik* and the *Encyclopaedia of Philosophical Wissenschaften*, a non-narrative (or at least minimally narrative) and nonphenomenal mode of philosophical knowledge and discourse that is already announced in the famous preface to the *Phenomenology* (written after the work itself, in 1807).[4] Its authoritative and succinct statement on the *philosophic* overcoming of history and narrative that it understands itself to be may be found in the second part of the *Wissenschaft der Logik*, "On the Concept in General": "Philosophy should not be any narrative of that which happened [*keine Erzählung dessen . . . was geschieht*] but rather a knowledge of that which is *true* in it, and furthermore, from out of the true, it should comprehend [*begreifen*] what in narrative appears as a mere occurrence [*was in der Erzählung als ein blosses Geschehn erscheint*]."[5] And then there are the many late works, beginning with versions of the *Philosophy of Right* (which he first gave as lectures during his first semester at Berlin in 1818 and first published in 1820), which return to the narrative, chronological mode but from the vantage point of the achieved encyclopaedic vision, which retell histories of morals and laws and states, of art, of religion, of philosophy, and indeed of world history from the achieved perspective of absolute knowledge.

It is this third "part" of Hegel's writings—mostly lectures given over the last dozen or so years of his life, and most of them given or repeated during his tenure as professor at the University of Berlin—that would principally concern the scholar of "Hegel the historian," and so they shall in part concern us here, both in some of the details of the lectures on world history and on aesthetics, for example, and in their larger, paradigmatic status as narrative, historical modes of philosophizing on the "far side" of philosophic Wissenschaft as absolute knowledge. But before entering into a detailed and sustained discussion of Hegel on and in history and historical Wissenschaft as I understand these matters, we would do well to return schematically to some of the points about history as a matter for Wissenschaft, and as a mode thereof, that have emerged in the foregoing examinations of idealist philosophy and its programmatic statements on history as an object and a kind of scholarly and scientific study.

Historical *facts* are what Louis O. Mink calls "evidence of the occurrence in real space and time of what [history] describes," and as just such facts they remain "contingent and discontinuous."[6] Such facts can have a variously positive status, and as such, they can be objects of knowledge: as events under a description, facts always already are objects of knowledge. If all we know of history is facts—of events that happened in the past—then all we have of "history" in this mode is *chronicle,* the proverbial "one damned thing after another." History in this limited sense would be the doubled term for the past event (of which there is the minimal "fact," or belief, that it occurred) and some knowledge thereof (factual "historical knowledge"—although some, Mink among them, would deny that such a mere chronological series of bits of factual knowledge deserves the appellation "historical knowledge"), the *res gestas* and the *historia rerum gestarum;* Mink gives "the population of Romania in 1930" as such a fact of knowledge, and even "a series of events across their contingent relations" would still only be factual historical knowledge.[7] It is important to note here that the "doubled" character of history in this delimited mode is one of minimal identification, or identity: the fact is that the event(s) happened, and the knowledge is just the assured declaration (identification, or proposition of identity) of that fact.

To raise the question of *meaning* with reference to the facts and their knowledge is to escape the bounds of historical facts and their "historical" knowledge in the mode of mere chronicle. Strictly speaking, the only "meaning" of the knowledge of a fact could be that it is true (or false) in the sense of "accurate": the meaning of our historical knowledge of the fact of Romania's population in 1930 could only be that that knowledge is accurate, or inaccurate, or somewhere in between, just as the only meaning of the identifying proposition "The cat is on the mat" is that it corresponds, or does not correspond, to the fact that the cat is (or is not) on the mat. This is not what we mean when we speak of historical meaning, and so we must distinguish historical meaning and its *understanding* (or comprehension) from historical facts and their knowledge. The fact is that the Holocaust happened. We may know one grisly fact after another, in a wider or narrower time frame, in the manner of a chronicle and a chronology. But to know to count to 6 million (or to 5.1 million) is not to know anything of the Holocaust's meaning, not to understand anything. One could count to 6 million and not understand a thing about death.

What does it mean that the French Revolution happened when and as it did, or that Baudelaire influenced Mallarmé? These are properly *historical* questions, not of knowledge of facts—they presuppose both the facts of the events and identifying knowledge thereof—but of meaning. Here, "history" names a doubled structure of a different sort than the identifying event-knowledge model of chronicling and chronological history. Rather, history is the knowable and known series of events as facts *and* the dimension of their meaningfulness insofar as this is held to be comprehensible or understandable—or, to describe this second aspect differently, insofar as it is constructed by a narrative. As Mink puts it with customary but no less admirable clarity: "Narrative form makes events and actions intelligible as belonging to a structure of meanings. . . . Individual statements about the past may be true or false, but a narrative is more than a conjunction of statements, and insofar as it is more it does not reduplicate a complex past but constructs one."[8] "History" without *this* dimension of meaningfulness would be, quite precisely, meaningless: it would be to know facts and to insist at the same instant on their insignificance, to know that events happened in the past, to have quite specific knowledge of them, and to know nothing more. To know what they *mean* is to know that history has another dimension: that it can be explained, or can explain or explicate, unfold itself; that it can convey or be made to convey a meaning; that it can be understood or comprehended—that history, however small a slice of it, leads up to something and that *this* is its meaning.

Now, a great deal will hinge upon different models of historical *meaning* and of historical *understanding*, and that is where we are at this stage in the present study. For a subjective or a pragmatic understanding of history's meaning (recall Schiller's or Schelling's use of these terms) is, and was, one set of possibilities—one possibility for the modeling of rhetoricians, another for the formation of military and political leaders—and the claim for a scientific and scholarly (*wissenschaftlich*) understanding of it, another. The latter, which is our concern, also does not merely claim positive knowledge of the facts of past events; it is not mere chronicle, in however new and "scientific" or disciplinary a form. Rather, it claims, indeed as its first, enabling postulate, that history is meaningful, that it is *worthy* of *wissenschaftlich* understanding—that it itself is, in its factual, eventful occurrence, the coming into being of the material stuff of or condition for true knowledge, where this "true knowledge" is no longer correspondential accuracy of propositions with facts but the discursive form of scholarly truth. History is true: this is the idealist, *wissenschaftlich* claim in its most radical form. It is not just true that history happened, nor that we know or can know this fact, these numerous, virtually infinite facts. It is rather that history as the transient occurrences of human being (history as the temporally past and passing) is an articulation, the meaning of which can be understood as moments of truthful, and not just factual, status. A lie can be a fact but never a truth, except as the identifying metapropositional truth that it *is* a lie. But in the "second" model of historical meaning and understanding I have been outlining, history can never lie except insofar as it remains lying at the merely factual level; rather, history always tells a truth awaiting its understanding, and *this*—its status as such discursive telling doubled with its comprehensibility—would be its meaning.

A brief discussion of these several senses of history using the language of theories or models of truth may further clarify the issue and conclude this schematic introduction to the detailed analysis of Hegel on history. To be able to speak of history in the strictly chroniclelike, chronological manner of human events occurring in (past) time, a kind of doubled model of "correspondence," of twofold implication, is necessary. We say it is a fact that the American Declaration of Independence was written in 1776 and imply not only that an event happened at that time but that knowledge thereof—*this* factual knowledge, that the event happened—is possible. The correspondence between the event and the time, on the one hand, and the event and the later, retrospective or "historical" factual knowledge of it, on the other, is a doubled one, but each side or aspect implies—or corresponds to—the other; one could not state one side of the correspondence (event to past time, event to knowledge of the "fact") without implying and enacting the other. This apparently trivial point is in fact fundamental, especially the coimplication of historical knowledge at this factual level with the belief that certain events happened historically, at specific past times. The single, overarching correspondence between events, past time, and present knowledge (or "knowability") is the necessary condition under which disciplinary or professional disagreement, as well as the broader ideological and cultural disagreement about what the facts of history are, then takes place. That is, for there to be history *at all*, there must be in place a consensual understanding or agreement, however tacit or unclear, that "history" as something we talk about is that which corresponds to events in the past. We may introduce here Richard Rorty's pragmatic-sociological distinction between knowledge and opinion: "On this view, to say that something is a matter of opinion is just to say that deviance from the current consensus on that topic is compatible with membership in some relevant community. To say that it is knowledge is to say that deviance is incompatible."[9] The consensus of a discourse of history and about history is that knowledge today (any present) can be of facts that correspond—as minimal descriptions—to events in the past, and this cannot be a mere "matter of opinion" for there to be a discourse of history but is rather a binding feature of the possible *knowledge* of history by historians or those who would talk of history. However much both ideologues and professional historians must know and remember that so much hinges upon establishing— and, in turn, disputing—these facts, the one undeniable assumption must be that some such knowledge of the past events must be believed in for there to be history. Otherwise, there is no difference between history and storytelling of the entirely fabulatory kind, or between history and lying about the past. At this minimal level of a model or theory of history and historical discourse, a correspondence theory of truth operates with the sanction of a consensus theory: factual knowledge ought to and often is held to correspond to events in the past, and there is a cultural and disciplinary consensus that both acknowledges this and polices the claims of correspondence. (Thus, the claim that the Declaration of Independence was signed in 1775 will be called an error, and the claim that the document was a progressive one, or a regressive one designed for the continued oppression of the working class, will be debated *historically* precisely to the extent that it refers to and relies upon the various facts of the event's occurrence, not because it may be jazzy or politically advantageous or novel to do so.)

With this last parenthetic remark, we are already on the threshold of the second "level" of our discussion of history. Here, the possibility (however minimal and guarded) and the necessity (as a condition of the discursive genre and the discipline it founds) of historical *knowledge* is brought into possible correspondence with history's *meaning and understanding*. The question is no longer, Did this event or these events occur? (Or, as the above paragraph implies, its equivalent: Do we or can we know the facts of such occurrence?) Rather, the questions are, What does that event or sequence of events mean? and What is our understanding of them? Although I shall argue here shortly that even on this level there is still a correspondence model that, together with an adjunct or auxiliary consensus model, informs our senses of the possible "truth" of historical meaning and understanding, several distinctly different positions on this matter must first be provisionally introduced.

A strictly positivist approach to the problem of historical meaning and understanding, coming as it does from the analytical philosophy of science (Hempel, Popper),[10] focuses on the utility and scope of "explanation" as what is intended by historical meaning and understanding. What a historical event "means" is that it marks the occurrence of human being in time according to a law or explanatory pattern that necessitates such occurrence. To "explain" something retrospectively (historically) is to predict it retrospectively, to explain why it had to happen. (This is part of what Friedrich Schlegel means when he writes in *Athenäum* fragment no. 80 that "The historian is a backwards-turned prophet.")[11] This is the event's meaning—it had to happen, it is the law—and our understanding. Note that this says more than merely that the event *did* happen (mere "factual" historical knowledge in the discussion above): it additionally says that the event happened in connection with antecedent and contemporary events in the manner of a law-governed connection. Describing this view—from which he dissents—Mink writes that "it is only as an instance of a law-governed type that an event or action can be truly understood."[12] In this positivist model, attributions of historical meaning to events would be measured against the event's explanatory value, and claims of historical understanding would be measured against their approximation of explanatory (deductive and predictive) models.

Now it will readily be apparent that this notion of history's meaning and understanding, however out of fashion it is with professional historians and scholars of historiography, is but a version of the same correspondence model we saw at the first "level," and furthermore, I will argue that it is only a strongly (some would say tendentiously) stated version of a correspondence model that nonpositivist historians believe in as well. The correspondence between the events as they happened in the past (let us, in shorthand, call them "the facts," for there are no events in this arena that are not under some discursive description that makes them "factual") and their possible meaning and understanding qua explanation according to a rule or law is of a kind with the correspondence between events of any sort in the natural world and true, that is, scientific, knowledge of nature. This kind of knowledge is not just factual knowledge that something occurred, or that something exists, but knowledge of why it is or was so and why this must be the case. It is this second aspect of knowledge that I have been calling "meaning and understanding," and in the case of the positivist model of historical or natural events and their knowledge, the knowledge corresponds to the necessity, answers to the "why-ness" of the facts. Thus, water in a certain set of circumstances "means" a gaseous compound, while in another set of circumstances it "means" a crystalline structure, and to *know* this is to understand why it must necessarily be the case. To know that political instability and incompetence in a certain historical set of circumstances means (and meant) revolution is similarly to understand that bit of history. In each case, the correspondence is between facts, knowledge, and the clarifying or explanatory power of the latter with respect to the necessity of the former.

If we turn to the altogether different—some would say more modern or liberal—model of nonpositivist historical meaning and understanding, the field might first appear to be wide open for any and all characterizations of what the "facts" mean and how they might be understood. But in fact, the range of meaning and understanding at any given moment of the cultural and disciplinary paradigm (in Stanley Fish's literary-theoretical terminology, the "interpretive community")[13] is considerably narrow, and the hallmark of claims for meaning and understanding remains that they are held to correspond to the facts in the sense of being built upon and out of them. That there obtains a consensus—again, however tacit or unclear—about what history might mean and how it might be understood is everywhere apparent in the continuing utility of the term to distinguish facts from myths, legends, apocrypha, propagandistic fictions and lies and in the distinction of the discipline of history from that of folklore, as well as the distinction of the discipline from the local or national organizations of storytellers, comedians, and the like. Many historians would be in danger of being put out of business if they were to deny that the claims of historical meaning and understanding have an autonomy relative to our or someone else's wishes, dreams, fantasies, and abusive misrepresentations of the past.

But thus far I have claimed only that historical meaning and understanding must minimally correspond to the alleged facts of the past and that there must be a consensus that this is so for there to be a broadly cultural and narrowly disciplinary or professional discourse of history. The particular governance or policing of such correspondence can take two forms, a weak one and a strong one. I distinguish them thus because the first is so easily satisfied, the second somewhat more painstakingly. The weak form of correspondence is that claims of history's meaning and understanding merely fall within the boundaries of the consensus of what is history and what is not (and is rather myth or propaganda or the like). Thus, for a U.S. president (or historian) to state that American history teaches the expansion of civil liberties would correspond narrowly enough to the facts, however arguable it or its counterthesis (the restriction of civil liberties in American history) might then be among historians, while for the same person to state that American history teaches the rightful supremacy of its white citizens over its black ones would be held to correspond not to "history" but rather to racist propaganda. So, too, no one historian (perhaps not even the discipline or culture of historical discourse) might be willing to assign *a* meaning or understanding to the Holocaust, but the boundaries for discussion of such meaning and understanding are nonetheless consensually in place: that the Holocaust might mean that European Jews deserved extermination is as unthinkable as history as is the other extreme, to claim that the Holocaust was a joke by Hitler and some lieutenants that got out of hand, and both are ruled out as historical meaning and understanding as readily as would be the counterhistorical claim about the facts that the Holocaust never happened. Thus, claims about historical meaning and understanding must correspond to the consensus of cultural and disciplinary discourses of history, which consensus is formed and informed by previous and prevailing practices of an alleged correspondence between historical discourse and the facts of past events—a circle, to be sure.

The stronger form of policing a correspondence between meaning and knowledge, understanding and facts, is operative in claims that such attributions of meaning and judgments of understanding can progress or regress, can be variously closer to or farther from the mark. This, then, is a kind of consensus about asymptotic correspondence: no one historian, no one school of historical inquiry, no one moment of historical understanding, may definitively "get it right" as far as discovering the meaning and arriving at an understanding of history (or any slice thereof) is concerned, but each and every such moment may nonetheless be judged according to its relative proximity to a standard of correct correspondence as this is understood by the culture and discipline at the moment in question. I call this asymptotic correspondence because the criterion of judgment is still the correspondence between meaning, understanding, and the facts, while the measure of the judgment is "de-absolutized" with respect to particular judgments (no one may get it right) but still held absolute as a benchmark that all may variously approach or fall short of (thus preserving all the distinctions between good history, bad history, and what is not history at all).

Against this backdrop of correspondence and consensus models of historical truth—and it should be clear that I believe each correspondence model implies a consensus one, and vice versa—I should now like to present a provisional and entirely abstract version of Hegel's model of historical truth, which I will identify as a *coherence* model. Let me recall that all models of historical knowledge insist upon a minimal correspondence to minimal facts (of historical events); otherwise, one is not talking history. The models sketched thus far, then, differ among themselves to the degree that they narrow the range of possible meaningfulness and understanding to an explanatory characterization of those facts (the events under description) as they are alleged to have occurred (answering to the questions of "why" and "how" with reference to the "what" that is the facts of the events), or broaden the same range into a wider consensus of interesting questions that may be asked and interpretations that may be offered of those facts (answering, we might say, the additional question "So what?"). With Hegel, the "facts" are not so much at issue as they are uninteresting—they are there, as we shall see Hegel put in his lectures on the *Philosophy of History*, "as they should be." History happens, is what happened, and there's no gainsaying that, not even by Hegel. All of the matter of historical knowledge is displaced upon the questions of meaning and understanding, and here there is neither the positivist approximation of historical understanding to natural scientific knowledge nor the more liberal expansion of historical understanding to varieties of cultural and disciplinary attribution of meaningfulness to historical events. Rather, historical meaning and understanding are determined by the coherence that thought might render between history as historical knowledge of the facts and its meaning for philosophic understanding, and this coherence, it alone, would be absolute knowledge of history, that is, true history. The "truth" here is not that of a correspondential accuracy but that of a truth that can be thought to happen in history. As Paul de Man put it, "The truth is all around us; for Hegel who, in this respect, is as much of an empiricist as Locke or Hume, the truth is what happens, but how can we be certain to recognize the truth when it occurs?"[14]

Hegel does not shy away from this absolute question. Nor, it should be added immediately, is this advocacy of coherence by any means unique to Hegel. Mink, for example—far more Kantian than Hegelian in most philosophic matters—presents a somewhat similar notion of "comprehension" that would accord essentially with the claim for coherence between historical events in their factuality and the understanding of their meaning when he writes of "the act of understanding in which actions and events, although represented as occurring in the order of time, can be surveyed as it were in a single glance as bound together in an order of significance, a representation of the *totum simul*" (that this sentence concludes with "a representation of the *totum simul* which we can never more than partially achieve" is an indication of his non-Hegelianism and of his final allegiance to what I referred to as the modern, liberal school of historical interpretation).[15] But Hegel's specification of *philosophical* understanding as contributing coherence to history or any other scholarly and scientific (*wissenschaftlich*) study is both an aspect of what we have already seen in some of the German idealist writings on history at this time and crucial to our introductory remarks here. His sense of knowledge, grounded in a dialectic of determinate negation, does not allow it to be measured by *correspondence* to the facts alone; knowledge, as a product of thinking, will negate and overcome the sheer facticity of events, will dissolve—in order to reconstitute— the apparently built-in facts of what happened, what it meant then, in the past, what it appeared as, and so on. So, too, does this kind of knowledge distinguish itself from a relatively free-floating, ever-changing paradigm of cultural or disciplinary *consensus* of what history might mean, of what it might be understood to be; the Wissenschaft of history will be governed by the protocols of philosophy, and they are those of truth, not those of *doxa* or opinion (which is what any consensus "theory of truth" ultimately comes down to). History happened; the events were there and remain factually available in variously descriptive and discursive, that is, *narrative* modes. Now what do they mean? They mean their coherence, which is to say that they cohere—add up and hang together—within their adherence to a manner of thinking, a mode of philosophy. This larger coherence, which makes history coherent in our colloquial sense of that term—which makes it comprehensible—is the understanding or comprehending of history by thought: its grasping or conceiving in and by the concept. Hegel's philosophy of history—it will come as no surprise to anyone who has heard something of Hegel—arises out of a reading of historical events and facts (it is "*of* history" in this strong genitive sense) and is at the same time a philosophizing of history, a philosophical appropriation, or *Aneignung*, of that which, as historical events, or *Ereignisse*, was not yet proper to philosophy but foreign to it.

This is "Hegelianism," as Hegel sometimes articulates it and as much teaching and hearsay of "Hegel" has passed it on, in and out of school. In the two chapters that follow, I will examine several versions, from several Hegel texts, of this Hegelian model of history, leading an inquiry into what does and does not fit within its self-understanding of history comprehended from the far side of absolute knowledge and asking as well what the allegory of history is for Hegel at the end of history's "legitimized" entry into the philosophy faculty. What is his version of an allegorical structure of history, where and how do levels of the historical letter and spirit cohere or detach, and what does it mean—with respect to allegory—to read Hegel reading history?

3

Historical Anthropophagy and Its Passing: Hegel's *Absolutes Wissen*

The fellow demands time to be digested.
—Engels on Hegel

Ainquiry into Hegel on history may begin under the sign of digestion, for Hegel, at the end of the *Phenomenology of Spirit*, will apparently suffer no indigestion: absolute knowing would digest absolutely. That this is the end (the goal, not the last point chronologically) of a series of staged reflections upon digestion in Hegel may be touched on only in passing in a treatment of Hegel's problem of history and its overcoming. That it is also the point at which the motif of digestion leads to the structure of Hegel's "historical anthropophagy" is of greater interest and import. The issue is pertinent because the end and product of the *Phenomenology* is, I shall argue, "history as we know it"—history in the sense of doing and knowing history, history as a "scholarly and scientific study," a Wissenschaft—and this is produced by digesting human history. Hegelian scholarly *(wissenschaftlich)* history eats or cannibalizes humanity; hence, "historical anthropophagy."

Our first inquiry can begin by retracing some of the features of this ending to the *Phenomenology*, to bring out thereby its problematic of digestion in its relation to history, before turning to the structure of the problem of digestion in Hegel and then returning to the *Phenomenology*. Here, we must first begin a bit before the ending, recalling the position at which the work has arrived: absolute self-consciousness as spirit *(Geist)* in the mode of the concept, hence also in the mode of Wissenschaft. "Spirit, therefore, having won the concept, unfolds its existence and movement in this ether of its life and is *Wissenschaft*."[1] This movement presents itself as determinate concepts, not as shapes of consciousness; as a logical and not a phenomenal discourse. But "to each abstract moment of Wissenschaft there corresponds a shape of phenomenal [*erscheinenden*] spirit as such. . . . To know the pure concepts of Wissenschaft in this form of shapes of consciousness constitutes the side of their reality." Thus "Wissenschaft contains within itself this necessity of externalizing [or, as Hyppolite translates it, "alienating"][2] the form of the pure concept, and the passage of the concept over into *conscious-ness.*" On the one hand, this is absolute Wissenschaft's return to the beginning of the *Phenomenology,* for spirit's immediate identity with self (as the self-knowing spirit, grasping its concept) is, in its difference— the difference within the identity of any two "things"—"the *certainty of immediacy,* or *sensuous consciousness*—the beginning from which we started," that is, the first chapter of the *Phenomenology,* on conscious-ness as sense-certainty. And this "return" to phenomenology also antic-ipates the integration of logic with the philosophy of spirit in the later *Encyclopaedia of Philosophical Wissenschaften.*

But on the other hand, the appeal to the "reality" of the pure con-cepts of Wissenschaft refers to a dimension of these concepts that in-deed *refers,* and beyond the necessary self-reference of self-certainty ("this is this," or "now is now"). To the extent that the "externalization" spoken of by Hegel expresses a connection of spirit's self-certainty to an object, the object is still dependent, not yet fully free, and this external-ization is still, as it were, somewhat internalized—internal to spirit as consciousness. The reality to which Hegel appeals is real, "out there," as objects for any and all real scientific and scholarly knowledge. This reality is what happens—and now we come to the very last paragraphs of the *Phenomenology* (see the appendix to this chapter)—and spirit's relation to it is one of *sacrifice,* externalization or alienation into *"free contingent happening,"* observing *(anschauend)* its being as space or na-ture and its self as time or history.

As nature, this mode of spirit's externalization is "its living immedi-ate becoming"; just that, the existence and the ongoing subsistence *(Bestehen)* of nature, which always presents objects for possible knowl-edge, including the objects that are ourselves and that we present to ourselves as the being(s) of the human subject. But as history, external-ization (into time) is a knowing and self-mediating movement. The ap-parently immediate reinstating of knowing and mediation is predicated by—and thus *mediate,* mediated by—time, the fact that *this* externali-zation is into and within time. The relation between *Geschehen* and *Ge-schichte* is one between *Geschehen* and *das was geschehen ist; Geschichte* is necessarily *nach Geschehen,* it is retrospective, and thus reflective, *nach-denkend.* Thus, externalization or alienation from conceptual spirit into time is at once, as history, the externalization of externalization, which we may understand as turning, not the inside out, but the outside in: the negation of its—externalization's own—negativity. And thus, exter-

nalizing spirit into time is also returning it as and into history as a becoming or vehicle of knowing and mediation.

All this is preparatory to the next sentence, which with its mention of
digestion interests us especially. What we are given to witness in this
presentation of the procession of history is first a slow (*träge*, sluggish
or inert) movement and succession of spirits; then a quasi-static, mu-
seumlike gallery of two-dimensional images, in which we might imagine we are the ones who are slowly moving; and then the reintegration
of these two versions whereby each image or spirit observes itself so
fully endowed (*ausgestattet*) as to be stuffed (*satt*), microcosmically or
monadically embodying all of spirit's wealth, and therefore moves, now
as both object and subject, so slowly because the self (recall that this is
the self that spirit observes itself as in time) "has to penetrate and digest
this entire wealth of its substance." The next sentence paraphrases what
we would "understand" to be "meant" here: that externalization, externalizing or negating itself, has become withdrawal or internalization
(*Insichgehen*), that this is the famous Hegelian *Erinnerung* whereby existence or shape for consciousness becomes inner conceptualization,
and that all this is spirit's "fulfillment of perfectly knowing what it is."
But why, in the sentence we have just been attending to, "digestion"?
And why, since this is specifically *human* history (for Hegel does not
here conceive of nature as also being or having *natural history*, as in ge-
ology or evolutionary biology or—as we shall see much later—Benjamin's special use of the term), does the mention of penetration and
digestion necessarily suggest that spirit must eat of the human historical
shapes: that it must commit anthropophagy?

To broach these questions, and then to return to the remainder of the
ending of the *Phenomenology*, in order better to understand what Hegelian history as *Er-Innerung* might mean, we must detour, however
rapidly, through some of Hegel's treatments of cannibalism and digestion. These treatments are in, respectively, the *Philosophy of History* and
the *Encyclopaedia of Philosophical Wissenschaften*, of which both are
texts posterior to the *Phenomenology* chronologically but in which the
discussions of cannibalism and digestion are still conceptually and discursively below the structure and interest they achieve in the passage we
have just been looking at. The discussion in the *Philosophy of History*
presents a happy symmetry with the ending of the *Phenomenology:* if
there there is explicit mention of digestion with only the hint of the
meal that must precede it, in the *Philosophy of History* there is the explicit mention of cannibalism but no mention or trace of digestion. The
mention occurs in the introduction, and with reference to Africa. The
whole point of mentioning Africa at all is to drop it, "to leave Africa"—

I quote Hegel—"not to mention it again. For it is no historical part of the world, it has no movement or development to exhibit."[3] Hegel re-emphasizes the nonhistorical character, which is not even *pre*historical, when a few lines later he continues, "What we properly understand by Africa, is the unhistorical [*das Geschichtslose*] and the unopened, which is still thoroughly involved in the natural spirit, and which had to be presented here only on the threshold of world history" (129; 99).

We will return to this "unhistorical" character, on the threshold of history, presently. How has he reached this emphatic statement to conclude his introduction of the (non)topic of Africa? He has done so via some ten pages on Africa's natural condition, in which he seems especially fascinated by reports of its violence and cruelty: "outbreaks of terrible hordes . . . [which] display the most thoughtless inhumanity and the most disgusting brutality," murders of kings and children and wives, "plunder and carnage run[ning] wild," slavery—and cannibalism (121–29; 92–99). The discussion of cannibalism follows immediately upon discussions of magic, fetishism, and worshipping of the dead, which are themselves introduced by these foreboding sentences:

> The peculiarly African character is difficult to comprehend, because in reference to it we must quite give up that which accompanies each of our notions, [namely,] the category of universality. [Here] the characteristic point is that [his] consciousness has not yet attained to the intuition of any fixed objectivity, such as, for example, God, or law . . . the knowledge of an absolute being that would be an other, a higher [one] vis-à-vis the self, is entirely lacking. [This] represents the natural man in his thoroughly wild and untamed state; one must abstract from all reverence and morality—from that which we call feeling—if one would rightly comprehend him: there is nothing consonant with humanity to be found in this character. (121–22; 93)[4]

Hegel has not begun this way just to tell us about magic and fetishism and the worship of the dead. These display the common feature of man believing not in a god but rather in his own power over the elements, the supernatural, the dead; there is here no objective relation with an independent other, "but as the objectivity is nothing other than the individual arbitrariness bringing itself to self-observation, this arbitrariness remains master of its image" (123; 94). What this undialectical elevation of man entails is that

> since man is posited as the highest, it follows that he has no respect [*keine Achtung*] for himself, for only with the consciousness of a higher being does man achieve a standpoint which guarantees him a true respect. For if arbitrariness is the absolute, the only fixed objectivity that is intuited,

then spirit can not know of any universality at this stage. [Africans] thus possess this perfect *contempt* [*vollkommene Verachtung*] of men. (124; 95)

It is this very Kantian passage of "no respect" for a higher being or principle leading to "disrespect" for oneself that is the real point of the portentous earlier remarks; and there is yet more hyperbolic prelude to what is really upsetting Hegel: "The undervaluing of man reaches the incredible [*Die Wertlosigkeit der Menschen geht ins Unglaubliche*]" (124; 95). What is unbelievable, what we would have to give up all thought and feeling for humanity to understand and would still find virtually incomprehensible, is that "it is looked upon as something quite customary and acceptable to eat human flesh" (124; 95). Cannibalism is here at the limit of human understanding, an end of the human subject in its nonobjectivity, its lack of any relation to an objective other, a mere threshold of history.

Hegel says further of this "Menschenfleisch zu essen" that "to devour [*verzehren*] man is altogether coherent with the African principle; for the sensuous [*sinnlichen*] black man, human flesh is only the sensuous, flesh and just flesh [*Fleisch überhaupt*]," and apart from a few lurid details and the repetition of *verzehren* and the use of *fressen* (125; 95), this is all he says. There is no mention whatsoever of the digestion of what is eaten. What we may draw from this brief but elaborately and melodramatically staged mention of cannibalism is that Hegel's virtual limit of comprehension, his step toward the incomprehensible and thus the unbelievable, is at once the threshold of digestion and of history. Man's eating of himself, his sensuous relation to his sensuous flesh, is the uncomprehended, scarcely conceivable (*unbegreiflich*) version of his nonobjectified relation to the world. The absence of any mention of digestion, of any treatment of how this nonrelated self-consumption would or could assimilate itself, once eaten, marks the same limit that Hegel's effort (and failure) at comprehending the nonhistorical does.[5] What Hegel withholds when, in his opening remarks to this section on Africa, he calls it "the land of children [*das Kinderland*], which on the far side of the day of self-conscious history is concealed in the black color of night" (120; 91), is not only history in the face of Africa's "humanity" but also digestion in the face of its anthropophagy.

Let us hold on to this curious mention of a "far side" (*jenseits*) of self-conscious history, for we might rather have expected a "near side" (*diesseits*) of what is *before* history; this image will return to us when we return to the end of the *Phenomenology*. If we now turn very briefly to the second discussion of these matters, that in the *Encyclopaedia of Philosophical Wissenschaften*, we find a second symmetry of sorts: where in the *Philosophy of History* there was cannibalism without digestion, here there is digestion without cannibalism. The systematic treatment of digestion here, as part of the analysis of the "animal organism" and of what Hegel more specifically calls "assimilation," must be reduced in our current consideration.[6] Digestion, as *"mediating* reproduction" (440; 360), is oppositional: "This system of living movement is the opposite of that of the outer organism; it is the *power* [*Kraft*] of digestion—the power of overcoming [*überwinden*] the outer organism" (448; 367). This overcoming entails a conversion *(Umschlagen)* of outer into inner that is not a matching of like to like—what Hegel could have said of African cannibalism, as he did of its fetishism or worshipping of the dead—but rather "in the living being [in assimilation] we have a subject which preserves itself and negates the specific quality of the other [*die Eigentümlichkeit des Anderen negiert*] . . . as *mediation*, assimilation is *digestion*—opposition of the subject to the external" (479, 480; 393–95). We may now better understand why any mention of digestion was missing from Hegel's discussion of African cannibalism. Here, with digestion, we have positing *(setzen)* as opposition *(Entgegensetzung)*, the subject against the other or external, which it then negates, not through possession or seizure alone, but through conversion or mediation. There, in Africa, the "outer" was posited as the same as the inner: nature under man's power and at his disposition, man as other merely like man as self, flesh or sensuousness as just such flesh or sensuousness.

But in a Hegelian mediation, the other determines and redefines the self as it mediates and digests the other. "But this *involvement* with the outer world . . . has likewise the determination of *externality over against the universality* and *simple* self-relation of the living being . . . the object and the negative over against the subjectivity of the organism, which the latter has to overcome and digest. . . . the return-into-self is the negation of its outward-directed activity" (480–81; 395). The double structure of what Hegel calls digestion is, then, both opposition to something external and opposition to self insofar as this self is involved in such opposition outwardly directed; overcoming the former, through (its) ingestion and digestion, means overcoming the latter self-opposition through returning inward and reproducing oneself. From this self-division the external is made into or recognized as inner, as what the subject or self is *an sich,* in itself. As Hegel puts it, "The organism has to conquer [*überwinden*] this its own process, this entanglement [*Verwickeltsein*] with the external [thing]. . . . by the negation of its other it has posited itself as subjectivity, as real being-for-self [*reales Fürsichsein*]" (491; 404).

But there is this further consequence: "This self-relation is immedi-

ately diremption and division of itself, and the constitution of subjectivity [is] immediately a repelling [*Abstossen*] of the organism from itself.
Thus the differentiation does not take place only within the organism
itself, but rather it is to produce itself as something external to itself"
(491; 404).

This last production-as-externalization is not the point at which we
saw Hegel begin, with an initial orientation of the organism toward
something external that it would ingest and consume, and with it we
may conclude our attention to digestion in the *Encyclopaedia*. This is
the step of the by-product or leftover of digestion, what Hegel calls abstract, formal repulsion. Excretion is "the conclusion of the process of
assimilation" (492; 404), and Hegel comments upon this in a curiously
epistemological yet readily familiar language: "Excrement [means]
nothing other than this, that the organism, recognizing its error [*seinen
Irrtum erkennend*], gets rid of [*wegwirft*] its entanglement with external
things" (492; 405).

Just as truth lives from error in Hegel, so does the organism. Hegel
wants the "error" of the organism to be *its* error, the excrement to be *its*,
and not some merely, and still, external matter. Hegel tries to convince
himself and us that excrement is not undigested "surplus matter" but
assimilated material together with the added organic material of digestion (such as bile) and concludes that "in truth . . . the activity of the
organism is purposive; for it consists precisely in getting rid of the
means after the end has been attained [*nach erreichtem Zwecke das Mittel
wegzuwerfen*]. . . . [Excretions] are therefore nothing else but the organism's own process which it discards in material shape" (493; 406).

With this treatment of digestion, including its by-product or discard,
we can begin our return to the end of the *Phenomenology*. The whole
process of digestion is conceptually, for Hegel, the self-assimilation and
self-mediation of the organism as its "last stage" of animality, but it is
materially the producing and ridding of excrement, the means toward
the former end. What drops away from digestion here is this excrement,
although it is the organism's, the process's material or means and shape.
This disjunction between the process and the shape is the mark of its—
the organism's—still nonintegrated stage, a mediating and self-
mediating that, while conceived by spirit, does not consciously comprehend itself as such but can only be so comprehended by an Other that
is spirit; this is why Hegel, in his discussion of assimilation, could call
it "das bewusstlose Begreifen" (485; 399). The conscious comprehending of this unconscious comprehension is not only the difference between spirit and the natural organism but also that between history at
its end and history at the threshold of its beginning. Of nature, Hegel

wrote that "in [it] we thus do not see the universal arise; that is, the universal of nature has no history. Wissenschaft, constitution, etc., have, in contrast, a history, for they are the universal in the spirit."[7] And this recalls to us the status of cannibalism in Africa. What drops out of the organism in digestion is *its* material shape, excrement as the sign of its self-mediating process, which is itself, via this sign, reconceived as comprehension (however unconscious). And the difference between the temporality of digestion producing excrement and that of excrement producing, or being assimilated as, comprehension is the difference between natural time, which does not produce or know the universal, and history, which is *of* the universal. So, too, what falls out of cannibalism is not consumption but assimilation or digestion, not time but history, not Africa but Africa as a sign—as a sign of any signified, of any comprehensibility that would be other or more than its incomprehensibility.

Neither African cannibalism nor organic digestion knows history, nor is either known by history, comprehended within it. Cannibalism does not know—in Hegel's text—any digestion; it is not even unconscious comprehension but rather an other, an alien to comprehension. And digestion does not *know*—explicitly—any self-consumption, except *textually*, in the trace of the process whereby the process consumes its means but also leaves them behind as the leftover traces of this, its self-consumption.[8] If we line up African cannibalism, organic digestion, and absolute knowing as history, the *Gesamtprozess* looks like this: cannibalism is nonhistory and nondigestion, digestion is prehistory and precannibalism, absolute knowing is history as cannibalism. Let us return to the text of the end of the *Phenomenology* to attempt to understand this schema.

When shape (*Gestalt*) is remembered, or *erinnert*—this is where we left off in the text when we turned to the other texts and themes—the clue given us by the preceding appearance of the term *verdauen* allows us to understand this "giving over of shape to remembering and internalizing" as the *conscious*, *comprehending* counterpart to digestion's "giving up" or discarding of *its* shape as mere *means*. Rather than being left behind as mere traces of a process, mere leftover means, the shapes of consciousness—as the stuff of human history, phenomenologically construed, which would include, in and as its prehistory, shapes of *un*conscious comprehension such as digestion and its excrement—are reinternalized as signs for remembering. Withdrawn into itself in this internalized remembering, which is also the withdrawal of the shapes of history from themselves, consciousness is in what Hegel calls "the night of its self-consciousness" the exact counterpart to what he called Africa:

"on the far side of the day of self-conscious history in the black color of night." But "in this night" the "vanished existence," the withdrawal of shapes of history from themselves and into consciousness, is preserved, and precisely in a sublated, new form "reborn out of knowing" as signs—"a new world and a new shape of spirit." This is "history as we know it," history as we ·"do it" when we are scholarly and scientific (*wissenschaftlich*) historians, and not history as what *was done, was geschehen ist*, what has become "historical."

Doing history as Wissenschaft, as "historical Wissenschaft" (as opposed to *Naturwissenschaft*), is what spirit now does: as if "all that preceded were lost," in a momentarily "false" consciousness of "immediacy" with "this new world and shape," spirit learns to read history, "the higher form of the substance" that was *das Geschehene*. It starts not at the beginning, at nonhistory or prehistory, but at "a higher level," at history as having been penetrated, digested, internalized, remembered—turned into narrative, "a succession in which one spirit relieved another of its charge and each took over the realm of the world from its predecessor." The end, or "goal," of this narrative, this syntagm, is the "revelation of the depth [of spirit], and this is the *absolute concept*," the paradigm; if Jakobsonian poetics is the paradigmatic axis projected into the syntagmatic axis ("The poetic function projects the principle of equivalence from the axis of selection into the axis of combination"),[9] Hegelian history is the projection-qua-introjection of the syntagmatic axis into the paradigmatic one. Thus, pursuit of the linear "succession"—history as we know it—leads to opening up, or "revealing," the "depth" of history as neither we nor spirit have yet known it: namely, as spirit knowing itself, and no longer in the mode of phenomenal shapes, not even in the series of historical signifiers, but as concept and absolute Wissenschaft. The first extension out into the shapes of time, which is the extension (back) out into historical shapes, and the *Insichgehen*, or withdrawal, of self and shapes into depth in remembering (*Erinnerung*) are both sublated as their (re-)externalization in and as *time*, now a nonlinear, nonnarrative, nonhistorical time. This goal—absolute or pure Wissenschaft, "spirit that knows itself as spirit"—is, in terms that, here and in the next chapter, still have to become closer than Hegel's remoteness from us, the depth of an allegory of history as an allegory of reading: revealing the meaning of history as its elevation and overcoming in and into meaning.[10]

But Hegel still has this "goal"—we are still following Hegel's text, nearing its end—linked to its path, its end (*Zweck*) linked to its means: "*This goal* . . . has for its path the remembering of the spirits as they are in themselves and as they accomplish the organization of their realm." The latter organization, which is as they are "comprehended," is Hegel's phenomenology, at once the book we are finishing to read and the works being announced here, which will rewrite and reread it: the "Philosophy of Spirit" in the *Encyclopaedia*, and the *Philosophy of History*. But the "path" that is "the remembering of the spirits as they are in themselves [*wie sie an ihnen selbst sind*]" is the ongoing Wissenschaft of history, historical Wissenschaft—including literary history. This anticipates Ranke's famous "wie es eigentlich gewesen,"[11] which, although it exceeds the bounds of this study, should not pass unremarked, for I believe Ranke echoes Hegel here, whether intentionally or against his very intentions.[12] This "remembering of the spirits as they are in themselves" means we are still reading, still internalizing from shape to sign, from means to end—still digesting. We are still, to the extent that their digestion is not complete, preserving them—the shapes of human history—with a trace of their externality, their oppositional status, "their free existence appearing in the form of contingency," which is the earlier "form of *free contingent happening*." But if *this*, history as what happened and happens, could ever be comprehended together with "the *science of knowing in the sphere of appearance*," with what today we would call a *theory* of history, we would have "comprehended history, . . . the remembering, the internalizing and the Golgotha of absolute spirit, the actuality, truth and certainty of his throne."

Let us recall how this paragraph, with its first mention of the famous *Erinnerung*, of giving over the shape of spirit to remembering, called this a "[sinking] in the night of its self-consciousness." On the far side of this sinking into the dark, deep night is, then, the sublation of obscure depth into revealed truth. But this is also the place of a skull, Golgotha (*gulgoleth*). Where did this skull come from? It comes, I submit, from where it was "concealed on the far side of the day of self-conscious history in the black color of night," from a place Hegel could only call "Africa" and a process he could only call "Menschenfleisch zu essen." On the far side of the day of self-conscious history, itself following the "night of its self-consciousness," there is revealed not only "truth" but its means or vehicle, what was repressed or concealed heretofore: the "digestion" of the human body in spirit's self-knowing, anthropophagy having become philosophical anthropology through *historical* anthropophagy. This Golgotha is of course, allegorically, Calvary, the place of giving up the body for the spirit. But it is also, quite literally, as its literal sign, the place of a skull (*Schädelstätte*).[13]

Where did this skull come from? Surely it was not ingested, digested, and excreted. One thinks of Kliban's cartoon: never eat anything bigger than your head.[14] If it was not ingested and digested, perhaps it was spit out, if this were any more imaginable. One recalls that Hegel, in the discussion of digestion in the *Encyclopaedia*, associates the "highest and lowest parts of animal organization [as] intimately connected: just as speech and kissing, on the one hand, and eating, drinking and spitting (*Ausspucken*), on the other, are combined in the mouth" (492; 404). He recalls here the passage in his *Phenomenology* where he notes that the organs of excretion and the genitals are combined by nature in the living being.[15] Despite all this recalling or recollection, we still do not know where this skull comes from. Because strictly speaking, quite literally, it could no more have been partially ingested and then spit out (*ausgespuckt*) than it could have been fully ingested and then passed or excreted. It is as if it were gnawed clean and left to dry, between the dark night and the clear, revealed day, between a nonhistorical moment that knows no consciousness (no comprehension either)—the historical unconscious, it may be[16]—and the "far side of self-conscious history" that knows only self-consciousness. But this is all fantasy, what Hegel would call "picture thinking" (*Vorstellung*) or mere *Pissen* ("pissing around"), compared with absolute *Wissen*. The allegory or philosophic discourse of this text refuses to "know" how this shape came to be there, on the "far side" of "getting rid of the means after the end has been reached . . . discarding [the process] in material shape." It is left over, from out of "Africa."

Left over to be read, that is. Or less read than remarked. We re-mark once again that the "far side of the day of self-conscious history," which is how Hegel referred to Africa, is the far side of the day of self-conscious history that followed *Er-Innerung* sunk in the night of self-consciousness, now "remembered" not as cannibalism—inconceivable (*unbegreiflich*)!—but as absolute knowing, which is also, I have argued, historical anthropophagy. But this is to remain within a "reading" that is still allegorical, the allegoresis of Hegelian sublation. So we re-mark as well that the *Schädelstätte*, Golgotha, is "both" sublation or allegory—trading the body for the spirit, while promising thereby resurrection of the body—*and* the literal place of the skull, the material leftover, left over. To read the literal skull as meaningful is to allegorize it. Thus it becomes, in the very last lines, the chalice from which spirit drinks its "own" infinitude: a container—of material shape—for the contained; in other words, a sign. But simply to re-mark it as the leftover, not ingested nor digested nor excreted, is to refuse to read it as anything more or less than dead stuff. For Hegel, this would be not to read at all, or—the same thing—to claim to *know* something unreadable. This is what provoked his violence and contempt in the *Phenome-*

nology's section on "Phrenology," namely, the supposed position that the skull, as spirit's externality, was knowable "not as an organ, nor as language and sign, but as a *dead thing*"; "what in truth is being said may be expressed here as saying that *the being of spirit is a bone*," and this is "the disgracefulness of unconceptual crude thought [*Schmächlichkeit des begrifflosen nackten Gedankens*] which takes a bone for the reality of self-consciousness." [17]

Unread and unburied, the bony skull haunts like an anti-spirit the spirited reading of signs that internalizes and digests, remembers and appropriates, paradoxically at once incorporating and spiritualizing. [18] As one says in French, "On tombe sur un os," and perhaps with the rise of history as a Wissenschaft on such a bone, the historian falls as well. Scholarly reading of the past would rest with satisfaction upon a hidden cannibalism. "We," like Hegel, would surreptitiously cannibalize when we "do" history as a Wissenschaft, turning dead marks into spiritual means to knowledge. Marks in texts become narratives of history, literary history in both senses that we are coming to give to this phrase (the history of literature; history as allegory). But far from serving an exclusive production of spirit—or in today's less-exalted versions, the production of historical interpretations, of history as our monographs and our knowledges—a re-marking of the mark "of" history (for it is not innocently, in an objective genitive, "of" history, any more than "Africa" or the skull were) would allow for a different inflection of Hegel's allegory of history. This would be to seek out the moments in his corpus that are the scene of the production and reduction of his history as that which allows spirit or meaning to be read, and to read itself. This would be to see the appearance, like that of the skull that shows up at the end of the *Phenomenology* from a strange dark night of (un)consciousness, the appearance of a minimal stuff or material of "history": the leftovers, neither excrement nor expectorant nor even necessarily bones, but the dead stuff, the marks. For even the skull is always already a marked mark, a mark that leads to prosopopeia, to giving a face to this skull, to giving a face to *Geist*, to personification: a production of spirit. But the mark—what marks it? What could be on a still un-re-marked "near side" of this allegory?

Appendix: From the end of Hegel's
Phänomenologie des Geistes

... Das Wissen kennt nicht nur sich, sondern auch das Negative seiner selbst oder seine Grenze. Seine Grenze wissen heisst, sich aufzuopfern wissen.

Diese Aufopferung ist die Entäusserung, in welcher der Geist sein Werden zum Geiste in der Form des *freien zufälligen Geschehens* darstellt, sein reines *Selbst* als die *Zeit* ausser ihm und ebenso sein *Sein* als Raum anschauend. Dieses sein letzteres Werden, die *Natur,* ist sein lebendiges unmittelbares Werden; sie, der entäusserte Geist, ist in ihrem Dasein nichts als diese ewige Entäusserung ihres *Bestehens* und die Bewegung, die das *Subjekt* herstellt.

Die andere Seite aber seines Werdens, die *Geschichte,* ist das *wissende,* sich *vermittelnde* Werden—der an die Zeit entäusserte Geist; aber diese Entäusserung ist ebenso die Entäusserung ihrer selbst; das Negative ist das Negative seiner selbst. Dies Werden stellt eine träge Bewegung und Aufeinanderfolge von Geistern dar, eine Galerie von Bildern, deren jedes, mit dem vollständigen Reichtume des Geistes ausgestattet, eben darum sich so träge bewegt, weil das Selbst diesen ganzen Reichtum seiner Substanz zu durchdringen und zu verdauen hat. Indem seine Vollendung darin besteht, das, was *er ist,* seine Substanz, vollkommen zu *wissen,* so ist dies Wissen sein *Insichgehen,* in welchem er sein Dasein verlässt und seine Gestalt der Erinnerung übergibt. In seinem Insichgehen ist er in der Nacht seines Selbstbewusstseins versunken, sein verschwundenes Dasein aber ist in ihr aufbewahrt; und dies aufgehobene Dasein—das vorige, aber aus dem Wissen neugeborene—ist das neue Dasein, eine neue Welt und Geistesgestalt. In ihr hat er ebenso unbefangen von vorn bei ihrer Unmittelbarkeit anzufangen und sich von ihr auf wieder grosszuziehen, als ob alles Vorhergehende für ihn verloren wäre und er aus der Erfahrung der früheren Geister nichts gelernt hätte. Aber die *Er-Innerung* hat sie aufbewahrt und ist das Innere und die in der Tat höhere Form der Substanz. Wenn also dieser Geist seine Bildung, von sich nur auszugehen scheinend, wieder von vorn anfängt, so ist es zugleich auf einer höheren Stufe, dass er anfängt. Das Geisterreich, das auf diese Weise sich in dem Dasein gebildet, macht eine Aufeinanderfolge aus, worin einer den anderen ablöste und jeder das Reich der Welt von dem vorhergehenden übernahm. Ihr Ziel ist die Offenbarung der Tiefe, und diese ist *der absolute Begriff;* diese Offenbarung ist hiermit das Aufheben seiner Tiefe oder seine *Ausdehnung,* die Negativität dieses insichseienden Ich, welche seine Entäusserung oder Substanz ist,—und seine *Zeit,* dass diese Entäusserung sich an ihr selbst entäussert und so in ihrer Ausdehnung ebenso in ihrer Tiefe, dem Selbst ist. *Das Ziel,* das absolute Wissen, oder der sich als Geist wissende Geist hat zu seinem Wege die Erinnerung der Geister, wie sie an ihnen selbst sind und die Organisation ihres Reichs vollbringen. Ihre Aufbewahrung nach der Seite ihres freien, in der Form der Zufälligkeit erscheinenden Daseins ist die Geschichte, nach der Seite ihrer begriffenen Organisation aber die *Wissenschaft des erscheinenden Wissens;* beide zusammen, die begriffene Geschichte, bilden die Erinnerung und die Schädelstätte des absoluten Geistes, die Wirklichkeit, Wahrheit und Gewissheit seines Throns, ohne den er das leblose Einsame wäre; nur—

aus dem Kelche dieses Geisterreiches
schäumt ihm seine Unendlichkeit.

. . . Knowing knows not only itself but also the negative of itself, or its limit. To know one's limit is to know how to sacrifice oneself. This sacrifice is the externalization in which spirit displays its becoming spirit in the form of *free contingent happening*, intuiting its pure *self* as *time* outside of it, and equally its *being* as space. This its last becoming, *nature*, is its living immediate becoming; it [nature], the externalized spirit, is in its existence nothing but this eternal externalization of its *continuing existence* and the movement which reinstates the *subject*.

But the other side of its becoming, *history*, is a *knowing*, self-*mediating* becoming—spirit externalized into time; but this externalization is equally the externalization of itself; the negative is the negative of itself. This becoming presents a slow movement and succession of spirits, a gallery of images, each of which, endowed with the complete wealth of spirit, moves thus slowly just because the self has to penetrate and digest this entire wealth of its substance. As its fulfillment consists in perfectly *knowing* what *it is*, [in knowing] its substance, this knowing is its *withdrawal into itself*, in which it abandons its existence and gives its shape over to remembering. In its withdrawal into itself, it is sunk in the night of its self-consciousness, but in this night its vanished existence is preserved; and this sublated existence—the former one, but now reborn out of knowing—is the new existence, a new world and a new shape of spirit. In the immediacy of this new world and shape, spirit has to start afresh to bring itself once again to maturity as if, for it, all that preceded were lost and it had learned nothing from the experience of the earlier spirits. But *remembering*, the *internalizing* [of that experience], has preserved it and is the inner being and in fact the higher form of the substance. So although this spirit starts afresh and seemingly from its own resources to form and educate itself, it is at the same time on a higher level that it starts. The realm of spirits which is formed in this way within existence constitutes a succession in which one spirit relieved another of its charge and each took over the realm of the world from its predecessor. Their goal is the revelation of the depth [of spirit], and this is *the absolute concept;* this revelation is therefore the sublation of its depth, or its *extension*, the negativity of this withdrawn "I," which [negativity] is its externalization or substance—and [this revelation is also] its [the concept's] *time*, in that this externalization is in its own self externalized, and just as it is in its extension, so it is equally in its depth, in the self. *The goal*, absolute knowing, or spirit that knows itself as spirit, has for its path the remembering of the spirits as they are in themselves and as they accomplish the organization of their realm. Their preservation, regarded from the side of their free existence appearing in the form of contingency, is history, but regarded from the side of their comprehended organization, it is the *science of knowing in the sphere of appearance;* the two together, comprehended history, form the remembering, the internalizing and the Golgotha of absolute spirit, the actuality, truth and certainty of his throne, without which he would be the lifeless solitary; only

> *from the chalice of this realm of spirits*
> *foams forth for him his own infinitude.*

4

Mournful Anthropomorphism and Its Passing: Hegel's *Aesthetics*

*And he smelled it more precisely than many people
could see it, for his perception was after the fact and
thus of a higher order: an essence, a spirit of what
had been, something undisturbed by the everyday
accidents of the moment, like noise, glare, or the
nauseating press of living human beings.
That scented soul, that ethereal oil was in fact the
best thing about matter, the only reason for his interest
in it. The rest of the stupid stuff—the blossoms, leaves,
rind, fruit, color, beauty, vitality, and all those other
useless qualities were of no concern to him. They were
mere husk and ballast, to be disposed of.*
—Patrick Süskind, *Perfume*

The narrative conclusion of Hegel's *phenomenology* of consciousness and its announcement of the Wissenschaft of "conceptually grasped history [*die begriffene Geschichte*]" leave history less between a rock and a hard place than between a bone and the hard knowledge of absolute consciousness. Such an either/or is like those that litter Hegel's terrain as he assimilates and overcomes their oppositions, but even when "relieved" (*aufgehoben*) of their oppositionality, they may still serve to define the place and procedures of his mode of knowledge.[1] The *Geschichte* of Hegel's *Phenomenology of Spirit*, which means both its narrative or story and its historical argument about the development of human culture (*Bildung*), takes place within the parameters of a before and an after. Before, as we have seen, is Africa and its anthropophagy, which are before history and about which nothing can be known: they are the nonhistorical and therefore the incomprehensible. After history is absolute consciousness and its Wissenschaft of history: history as we "do" it. In between, and passing from the beginning of history to its end, is digestion. And on that place, marking it and what is passed or otherwise left behind by the transformation of history into its *Wissenschaft*, are the bones.

Hegel's *Lectures on the Philosophy of History* have served to frame an inquiry into the structure of his argument about history, with the end of the *Phenomenology* announcing precisely the end of that argument: the point at which history arrives as a narrative and is overcome in its knowing. But the *Philosophy of History* lectures offer a less inviting avenue for an inquiry into Hegel's actual treatment of historical *material*. Perhaps this claim will come as a surprise, but for those who have read in their often tiresome summaries of historical stages—especially after the brilliance of similar narrative steps in the *Phenomenology*—there will be scant surprise at all.[2] These lectures follow, but in interest fall below, the *Grundlinien der Philosophie des Rechts*, with their sustained argument for the rise of the state as the objective embodiment of freedom. And the lectures that follow the ones on the philosophy of history, especially those on the philosophy of religion and the history of philosophy, may be the site for Hegel's reinvigorated return to an engagement with the problem of narration as what must be overcome by philosophy.[3] Here, we will touch on the *Philosophy of History* lectures only once, symptomatically, before turning to another text on historical materials.

The *Philosophy of History* lectures assume throughout the position at which the *Phenomenology* arrives, where history turns into salvation history. From early in the introduction to the last paragraph, they declare world history to be a theodicy.[4] In the middle of a long paragraph in the middle of the introduction, this idea is stated bluntly: "God rules the world, the content of his rule, the carrying out of his plan is world history." This, however, is neither a purely religious nor a merely historical position but must be a philosophic one as well; the very next sentence continues, "This [plan] is what philosophy wants to grasp," and the paragraph concludes, "For reason is the perception of the divine work" (12:53).[5] But surrounding this central claim that equates history with salvation history and the religious perspective of theodicy with the task of philosophic reason are some puzzling and curiously recalcitrant further sentences. On the one hand, in contrast to subjective "ideals," which, depending on the "impatient" youthfulness or "ripe" age of one's perspectives, can be held to be variously unsatisfied or sufficiently satisfied by the world, "philosophy is supposed to lead to the insight that the real world is as it should be [*dass die wirkliche Welt ist, wie sie sein soll*]." "That which is truthfully good"—in contrast to the subjec-

96

tive ideal of "the good"—"the universal divine reason is also the power to realize itself. This good, this reason is, in its most concrete presentation [*Vorstellung*], God" (12:53).

But if what is, is as it should be—if this is the theodicic justification of "the real world" and its history—the judgment does not occur without negativity. Just as justifications of good—and God—are called for in the face of evil, so here some aspects of what is are not as they should be. As the paragraph in question moves toward its conclusion, a divide is made within "what is." "For only what is carried out from out of [God's plan] has reality; what is not appropriate to it is only rotten, worthless existence [*was ihm nicht gemäss ist, ist nur faule Existenz*]." What would "rot away" would also vanish like a deceptive appearance: "Before the pure light of this divine idea, which is no mere ideal, the appearance that the world is a crazy, foolish occurrence vanishes [*verschwindet der Schein, als ob die Welt ein verücktes, törichtes Geschehen sei*]." In the terms of Hegel's analysis, the "appearance" of mere *Geschehen* falls away—"rots"—as that which is the mere "existence" of an event (or of all events), while the real world-*Geschichte* shines forth as precisely what was real. Thus, Hegel concludes, "philosophy wants to know the content, the reality of the divine idea, and to justify the scorned [*verschmähte*] reality. For reason is the perception of the divine work" (12:53), Now—under the light of philosophy's knowledge—reality is known as reality, not as appearance, and so the term can be used both for the "divine idea" and for what was previously "scorned." What has been opposed and then divided within what is, is on the one hand the *real* ("the real world is as it should be") and on the other, rot, the appearance of craziness and foolishness, the disdained.

What appears contradictory here—but is not—is the tension between events and history. World history is the carrying out of a divine plan, and *only* this has reality; whatever else there might *be*, rots as mere existence, or falls away as the mere appearance of some crazy happening (*Geschehen*). For the real—which is the reasonable, which in turn is the good—to be, the events that merely occur must disappear, or enter into the status of mere appearance. World history *is* on the far side of the (dis)appearance of its occurrence (*Geschehen*). The passage from one to the other—across their divide—is both the narrative unfolding of the "divine plan" and the philosophic knowledge of its meaning as reason.

Now this passage across a divide is also the passage or passing of time from one mode of being (existence) to another, more real one (reality). It is first marked grammatically in Hegel's German by the passage from events as they abstractly happen—the infinitive *geschehen* and its nominalized form *das Geschehen*—to the indicative reality of what happens—the inflection *geschieht* and the nominalized *das, was geschieht* or *die Geschichte.*[6] A reality worthy of philosophic knowledge, and to which philosophy should lead, depends upon a further passage of time, namely, that what *is,* is as it *should be,* that is, past. What is—as it should be—is over, and what is not has rotted away. But this latter still "is" in some form of "existence," perhaps just as rot (or as a "rubbish heap of history"). Not unlike at the end of the *Phenomenology,* this paragraph from the *Philosophy of History* leaves the disappearance of appearance and its replacement by philosophic knowledge—the philosophy of history—with a faint afterimage of a leftover: a trace of rot.

Such language of time passing, the reality of the past, history as knowledge, and what is left behind as what can no longer occur—all this recalls not only the situation at the end of the *Phenomenology* but that of another of Hegel's works. The *Lectures on Aesthetics* are from the late, "return-to-narrative" part of his career (1818–29), but they hold to the argumentative spine of the *Phenomenology:* the appearance of spirit across the story of its modes of appearance, here the sensuous appearances of art. The *Aesthetics*'s own divide would appear to be between the *history* of art—its forms and "stages," from pre-Greek or "Oriental" antiquity to Hegel's own European present—and the Wissenschaft of art's philosophic study and knowing. In this divide, in between history and Wissenschaft, would be the art works themselves. Since they are—as we shall see Hegel claim—both material *and* ideal, they would seem to be a more promising kind of historical *stuff* than the "rotten existence" we have just seen Hegel refer to history as in its passage away from events and into philosophic knowledge. Surely art remains admirable even when it *is* history, while (human) history may be viewed as that "despised reality" in need of justification. And surely it remains more tangible than the historical event *(Geschehen)* in its sheer historicity.

But a turn to the *Aesthetics* meets a popular and still current misunderstanding about its historical stance. And this leads directly into the question we have raised, and left hanging, about the material of history considered from the perspective of its *wissenschaftlich* knowledge. For the popular understanding of the *Aesthetics* holds that Hegel viewed art as, variously, a thing of the past, or at an end, or with at best a diminished and uncertain future: thus, as if thoroughly historical, like the narrative of the *Phenomenology* or the "rotten existence" of history within its justification in the *Philosophy of History.* But if the issue of art's historical character might be understood otherwise, then it may appear less as just another item in a series of Hegel's treatments of the historical past than as a way into thinking the structure of Hegel's *ma-*

terial of history. It is, we shall see, a treatment of material that exposes its historical structure; what can be brought to light is the way in which the artwork belongs to, and is "properly," the passing and passage of time into the past. This is not, in other words, a *historicist* description (or prescription) about "art as a thing of the past" but a philosophic claim about art at any and all times being constituted *of* a structure of temporal passage. Thus, when Paul de Man says that a reading of the *Aesthetics* "should clarify the relationship of art and literature to the dimension of pastness that is a necessary component of any discourse involving history,"[7] he correctly links the *Aesthetics* to all the other historical-narrative parts of Hegel's *oeuvre* and draws one into the central problem of the *Aesthetics* alone: the "pastness" that is *of* the material and the event of art itself.

It first appears that Hegel's *Aesthetics* will examine and indeed participate in an overcoming of pastness. This pastness would furthermore be contrasted negatively with the values and perspective of philosophic thought. A passage very near the beginning of the *Aesthetics* indicates as much in language similar to that just seen in the *Philosophy of History*. Hegel would establish the "worthiness" of art for a scholarly (*wissenschaftlich*) treatment by claiming that "truthful art," in association with religion and philosophy, is only a way "to bring to consciousness and to express the *divine*, the deepest interests of man, the most all-encompassing truths of spirit."[8] What distinguishes art in this company of religion and philosophy is that it "sensuously represents the highest [*das Höchste*]." At first, art, in Hegel's characterization of its collaboration with spirit, is caught within an opposition with which spirit struggles: thought presses upon "a *supersensuous world*" as a "*far side* [*Jenseits*]" of immediate consciousness and present feeling, which themselves are "the *near side* [*Diesseits*], sensuous reality and finitude." But if spirit enters into this "breach" between "near" and "far," Hegel continues, it must also heal it, and it does so in producing "the works of fine art as the first reconciling, mediating span between the merely exterior, sensuous and transient [*Vergänglichen*], and the pure thought; between nature and finite reality, and the unending freedom of conceptual thinking" (13:21). This is the very language of the introduction to the *Philosophy of History*, with "the divine" and "pure thought" on the "far side" of a once-belittled "mere . . . transience," as if on the far side of a now-justified history.

Hegel's next paragraph at once sustains a language of transience and complicates the perspective upon it. Working within a contrast of appearance (*Schein*) and reality, and a critique of the everyday "reality" of appearances and the inner world of feelings, Hegel means to praise art's dimension of appearance: "Only on the far side [*jenseits*] of the immediacy of feeling and of exterior objects is the authentic reality to be found" (13:22). That on the "far side" of which such authentic reality is to be found is further described as "a chaos of accidentalities," "this bad, transient world [*diese schlechte, vergängliche Welt*]," while art's contribution to attaining such a "far side" is put as follows: "For truthfully real is only the being in-and-for-itself, the substantial of nature and the spirit, which, to be sure, gives itself presence and existence [*Dasein*], but which in this existence remains [*bleibt*] the being in-and-for-itself, and only thus is truthfully real. The rule of these universal powers is precisely what art emphasizes and allows to appear" (13:22). The "far side" of the "bad world" of transience is a "present [*Gegenwart*]," but paradoxically a present that "remains in-and-for-itself" and, evidently, does not pass away. This "present" is, to the extent that it is a product of art's activity, at odds with the very world of sensuous transience of which art also partakes.

The *passage* of time—*Vergänglichkeit*—hints that passage is itself a part of how art releases itself or its product from its condition of sensuousness. Hegel repeatedly structures his discussions of art around the imagery of expression; so, on the next page of his *Aesthetics*, he says of "the appearance of art" that "it itself points through and beyond itself [*durch sich hindurchdeutet*] and hints from out of itself [*aus sich hinweist*] toward something spiritual that is supposed to come into presentation [*Vorstellung*] through it [art's appearance]" (13:23). The several prepositions and prefixes translated here as "through," "beyond," "toward," and "out" signify an expression or extrusion outward of something inner, something given presence through a passage through, even a *transit*. Art in Hegel's view is productive—this much is a commonplace—but it is productive of something that appears to counter and overcome the very conditions of its appearance, which are those of passage and transience.[9]

The apparent contradiction is further sharpened by Hegel in the paragraphs that immediately follow, which have given rise to the argument that for Hegel, art not only allows or effects passage but itself passes away. Once again, Hegel's employment of prepositions and prepositional prefixes comes to indicate the strong sense of motion, direction, and passage that occurs in his understanding of art. He begins here by recalling that "art [is not] the highest and most absolute way to bring to spirit's consciousness its truthful interests" and that "only a certain sphere and level of truth is capable of being represented in the element of the artwork," namely, "it must lie in its [truth's] own determination to go out to the sensuous [*zu dem Sinnlichen herauszugehen*] and to be able to be adequate to itself in the same" (13:23). The "expression" of truth out into the sensuous medium of art corresponds to a first moment of art as productive; but as several quotations have already suggested, art will also be productive of something precisely on a "far side" of sensuousness. Hegel introduces this dimension in a long passage on a different aspect of art, one that contrasts with the "adequacy" of sensuousness to art's truth:

> By contrast there is a deeper version of the truth in which it is no longer so related to and friendly toward the sensuous that it could be taken up and expressed [*ausgedrückt*] by this material in an appropriate manner. Of this kind is the Christian understanding of the truth, and above all the spirit of our contemporary world, or—more correctly—of our religion and our culture of reason, appears beyond the stage [*über die Stufe hinaus*] at which art makes up [*ausmacht*] the highest way of being conscious of the absolute. The particular kind of art's production and of its works no longer fills our highest need [*füllt . . . nicht mehr aus*]; we are beyond [*wir sind darüber hinaus*] being able to honor works of art as divine and pray to them; the impression they make is of a more reflective and sober kind. . . . Thought and reflection have surpassed [*überflügelt*] the fine arts. (13:23–24)

To follow this long passage is to pass through and beyond art's "expressive" (*ausdrückend*) passageway of spirit in(to) sensuous shape. Art "makes up" and—to follow the imagery of *ex*pression—"makes *out*" a mode of consciousness of "the highest" or "the absolute" character of spirit. But doing so, it also is done with it: *ex*pressing *out*, it passes *beyond* (*über . . . hinaus*) the very stage of this production of expression. Having been the expression of spirit's need for consciousness, and expressing spirit *into* material embodiment, art has filled both its role and its container, as it were, and suddenly "we are beyond" and also "above" (*über*) its "stage."

There is an additional feature to Hegel's narrative here, but there seems to be as well an equally obvious thing that Hegel is *not* saying, despite the frequent impression on the part of his readers that it is otherwise. Hegel is narrating, already in this very early introductory passage, the "progress" of Western culture across some recognizable stages—from Greek culture, mentioned earlier by him, to "the Christian understanding of the truth," to "the spirit of our contemporary world"—at the same time that he is explaining art's constitutive function of raising spirit to self-consciousness through an engagement with sensuous material and forms. The analytic argument about what art is, is of a piece with the narrative argument about how spirit moves: the former, in fact, is the *expression* of the latter; as art presses spirit through and out of itself, it yields a certain story about where spirit is and what has become of it. Art yields history.

But this is not the same as to say that all *Hegel* is saying is that art is *historical*. Spirit is beyond and above a certain engagement with art. This can certainly be expressed historically, as Hegel does in a subsequent sentence: "The beautiful days of Greek art and the golden age of the late Middle Ages are over [*sind vorüber*]" (13:24). Or it can be expressed in terms of a critical characterization of our contemporary perspective: "Our present is, according to its general condition, not favorable to art" (13:25). But neither the historical nor the contemporary reflection on art means that as art yields historical change, it becomes merely historically past. It is this issue that confronts the widespread judgment that Hegel consigns art to a historical past. The sentence in question—one of the most quoted (and misquoted) in the *Aesthetics*—reads: "In all these relations [its no longer satisfying our highest needs, the days of Greece and the Middle Ages being over, our contemporary conditions being unfavorable], art is and remains in the aspect of its highest determination a thing of the past for us [*ist und bleibt die Kunst nach der Seite ihrer höchsten Bestimmung für uns ein Vergangenes*]" (13:25). Contrary to a *historicizing* line of Hegel reception,[10] we should see this claim as rather *about history* and its passage(s).

I shall turn in a moment to the "for us" of the sentence, but first let us look at two other of its parts. "In the aspect of its highest determination" refers to art's role in producing spirit's self-consciousness and specifically recalls Hegel's earlier mention of "the spirit of our religion and culture of reason" being "beyond the stage" of art's rendering the highest service to a becoming conscious of the absolute; clearly, more trivial services may still be rendered by art. A second and more challenging part of the sentence is its central statement that "art is and remains . . . a thing of the past." This is less a prophecy (if it were, Hegel would have used *wird bleiben*, "will remain") than a paradoxical statement of the historical—not historicist—attitude. What *is* past *remains*, or does not pass further, or away. Art, Hegel has claimed, is a productive passage, and now, as it passes into a pastness, it produces a temporal suspension: it is past, and remains past.

While there is admittedly loss in such a passage,[11] there is nonetheless also still the production of a perspective. "What is now aroused in us through art works is—in addition to immediate enjoyment—at the same time our judgment, in that we submit [*unterwerfen*] to our thinking consideration the content, the artwork's means of representation, and the appropriateness and inappropriateness of both" (13:25). To submit, subject, or, literally, "throw down" art before thought is to complete a passage through art and to retain art as an occasion for such productivity. For if art is a means for raising spirit to consciousness, thought itself "precisely makes up [*macht . . . aus*] the innermost essential nature of the spirit" (13:27). And so thought about or, more accurately, "down" upon art is on the "far side" of a passage art itself has helped to produce. Thus, when Hegel speaks of the Wissenschaft, the scholarly study of art as just this "thinking consideration," he *connects* art and thought across time rather than divides them between a historical past and a post-artistic present: "The Wissenschaft of art is thus of far greater need in our time than in the times in which art for itself as art already provided full satisfaction. Art invites us to thinking consideration, and to be sure, not to the goal of calling art forth again [*wieder hervorzurufen*], but rather to knowing in a scholarly way what art is" (13:25–26). To know what art is, is to know how, in helping to express spirit and produce its self-consciousness, it passes over into a past stage that remains in and for knowledge. The "we," here as in the famous earlier sentence, are the scholarly knowers, the knowing scholars: students at Hegel's lectures, scholars in all the art-historical departments (which includes the literature departments) since the University of Berlin.

If art is "for us" a thing of the past, this is so that its knowledge may be one of the future. The artwork is at a threshold or divide, within time and between times, and as a divide it hints at a crisis. In the last pages of the calming and assured introduction to the *Aesthetics* any sense of crisis would be muted, but a curious divide begins to loom nonetheless. On the one hand, scholarly knowing reflects upon art and even begins to reflect it in its structure, but on the other hand, the "surpassing" and "subjecting" of art by thought continues to give off an aura of risk and loss. Thinking's reflection *of* (as opposed to *upon*) art occurs in its reduplication of a structure of expression. We have already seen Hegel characterize art as an expression on the part of spirit; as he puts it in the last paragraphs of the introduction, "art and its works, as having sprung and been produced from out of spirit, are themselves of spiritual kind, even if their representation takes up into itself the appearance of sensuousness and permeates the sensuous with spirit." Spirit is *out* there, expressed into sensuousness (*das Sinnliche mit Geist durchdringt*), but also impressed by sensuousness's appearance (*den Schein der Sinnlichkeit in sich aufnimmt*). Thus Hegel can say that "art already lies nearer to spirit and its thinking than [does] merely exterior, spiritless nature; in art products it [spirit] is only dealing with its own [*hat es . . .*

nur mit dem Seinigen zu tun]" (13:27). The proper element of spirit is exteriorized and alienated in its artistic expression into sensuality but remains for its recognition and reappropriation by the same spirit in the mode of thinking:

> If artworks are not thought and concept, but rather a development of the concept out of itself, an alienation over into the sensuous, then the power of thinking spirit lies in this: to grasp *not only itself alone* in its particular, proper form as thinking, but equally to recognize itself in its *expressive exteriorization* [*Entäusserung*] into feeling and sensuousness, to comprehend itself in its other, in that it transforms the alienated into thought and thus leads [it] back into itself. (13:28)

This remarkable sentence not only rehearses schematically a dialectical movement from self out into otherness and back into self but allows art's expression and the expression of art's scholarly study to be mirror images of one another. That is, spirit's exteriorizing expression *(Entäusserung)* is re-cognized as belonging or proper to interiority, but this knowledge is in turn (re)expressed as the thinking, comprehending, and knowing of Wissenschaft. An initial permeation of sensuousness by spirit in art's expression is answered by a second, reappropriating permeation of art by spirit in thinking: "Since thinking is its [spirit's] essence and concept, it is finally only satisfied when it has permeated [*durchdrungen*] all products of its activity with thought as well, and so only then [*erst*] truly made them its own" (13:28).

Thought as the higher form of spirit thus re-produces art's productivity: each produces a form of spirit for consciousness, with art's expression of spirit into sensuousness being "truly made its [spirit's] own for the first time" when *this* is re-expressed in spirit's *own* medium of thought. It should be evident that such a model of exteriorizing expression and its mirror image—at once reduplicating and inverting—of interiorizing expression follows an idealized model of poetics and hermeneutics. What is expressed in the made *(poiesis)* verbal work may be reproduced in its comprehending absorption into our understanding. That such a symmetrical but reversing relation may not always be without difficulty and either loss or leftover is known not only from recent theoretical work that questions the adequacy of, say, literary hermeneutic to poetics.[12] Other parts of Hegel's *oeuvre* have already suggested the tensions between the interiorized, the digested, and the leftover, or between history as spirit's exteriorization and the concept as its reappropriation. Here the tension may be pursued several steps further along the lines of our inquiry into a temporal *divide*.

For the sentence just quoted included the signs of temporal contrast:

between a "final" satisfaction when spirit's thought "only then" makes art truthfully spiritual and the temporality of art itself. This recalls a similar contrast between "our time" of "the Wissenschaft of art" and "the times in which art for itself as art already granted full satisfaction" (13:25–26). Hegel heightens this contrast yet another time near the end of his introduction when, immediately after the claim of thought "only then truly making art spirit's own," he continues: "But art, far indeed . . . from being the highest form of spirit, receives its authentic verification only [erst] in Wissenschaft." The temporal divide in each of these instances is between the time(s) of art, when spirit participates in an elevating production of its own self-consciousness through its embodiment in sensuous form, and a time that subjects (unterwirft) and looks back and down upon art even as it claims it "truthfully" and as its own. Art becomes and remains "für uns ein Vergangenes," but this mode of remaining is its first (erste) truth. What is it in art that wants spirit to pass through it, that wants itself to pass, to become past, but only (erst) thus to become what it, in truth, is?

A foreshadowing of this temporal dimension of art's "productivity" is elaborated in yet another paragraph of the introduction, where Hegel, as if in a voice not his own,[13] speaks of accusations that might be lodged against the "scholarly thinking consideration" of works of fine art. The accusations are, in effect, of murderous and disfiguring acts:

> The artistically beautiful appears in a form that expressly contrasts with thought, and that it [thought] is obliged to destroy in order to practice its own particular activity. This notion hangs together with the opinion that the real as such—the life of nature and of the spirit—is disfigured and killed through comprehension; that instead of being brought nearer to us through conceptually appropriate thinking, it only becomes thoroughly distant, so that man, in using thinking as a *means* of grasping what is living, rather more kills the *goal* itself. (13:27)

It is the next paragraph that, in response to this view, argues for thinking as "the innermost essential nature of spirit." But here, the language of death and destruction, disfiguration and murder, suggests a darker dimension to the "debate" being carried out in Hegel's mock polyphony. This dimension is that of the *consequences* of time's divides, and not just of the divisions themselves. A structure of before-passage-after, which when dominated by spirit is one of spirit's expression outward, into, and through art, then to be looked down and back upon as a passage/past that remains for scholarly study (Wissenschaft), may be available for a dialectical understanding in which history presents no loss even as time passes. But when the same structure is dominated by, or more correctly, embodied in, the body, then—as Hegel's rhetoric here suggests—the stakes of a temporal division are a matter of life and death, and perhaps of a perspective beyond and looking back down upon the dead. But in this version, what would be the object of "scholarly thinking consideration"? History, yes, but insofar as a scene of death, would it be a corpse, a grave, a relic, or what? And would the attitude or view be one of equanimity, sublimity, or what? What is the attitude of a *reading* of (literary-artistic) history?

It is well known that Hegel retells his introductory story of art as passage in both his narrative of the *stages* of art and that of the *shapes* of art. As we turn to the central, or middle, moment of these narratives—the classical stage, the shape of sculpture—we do so by way of another of Hegel's versions of art as a model of in-betweenness. This version appears in the course of his still-introductory discussion of the status of sensuousness in the artwork ("the sensuous aspect of the artwork should have existence only insofar as it exists for the spirit of man, but not insofar as it itself exists as sensuous for itself" [13:57]—thus, following Kant, not as an object of desire [*Begierde*]). Art must have a sensuous element, but, Hegel says, it "may appear only as the surface and the *appearance* of the sensuous" (13:60). Spirit seeks in art's sensuousness "sensuous presence [*Gegenwart*], which, to be sure, remains sensuous but should just as much be freed from the scaffolding of its sheer materiality." The language of a "present" that "remains" is of course within a *spatial* setting of sensuousness that becomes surface-level appearance, as if lifting off from its supporting materiality, but a temporal anomaly or tension is fleetingly hinted at nonetheless. The next sentences expand upon this peculiar position of art's sensuousness while drawing out the mere implication of its temporal setting: "The artwork stands in the *middle* between immediate sensuousness and ideal thought. It is *not yet* pure thought, but, despite its sensuousness, *no longer* sheer material existence either, such as stones, plants and organic life." The association in Hegel's German between "middle" (*Mitte*) and "(im)mediate" ([*un*]*mittelbaren*) recalls his characterization of art as a medium for spirit's mediation of itself toward its self-consciousness, but it also suggests an *implementation* of art's middle position in(to) a temporal process: "standing in the middle," art steps or moves between— it is a passage. The "not yet" is already a "no longer" as well, and the "no longer" tends toward that which is "not yet." But if art is a passageway, it is also that "present that remains." And so Hegel's sentence continues: "the sensuous in the artwork is itself something ideal, but which—as not being the ideal of thought—is still at the same time as a thing [*zugleich als Ding noch*] outwardly present or at hand" (13:60). The no longer/not yet position-in-passage is here momentarily halted in and as a "not yet no longer"—a "still at the same time [*zugleich . . . noch*].*" The doubled character of art's sensuousness as *both* ideal *and* thingly is presented temporally as a doubled perspective of passage between, and of still the middle position. Middle and medium, passage and a present past, or a present that remains and does not pass: art's sensuous embodiment is a form for a form of time that repeatedly indicates and resists its divisions into the stages of a crisis.

Such indication and resistance—movement toward and an arresting countermovement—may now be explored as, across steps, Hegel comes to describe the classical art form and its acme of sculptural "shape." As the purest version of spirit-in-art, between spirit's inwardness and outward alienation, and between sensuousness's sheer thingliness and mere appearance, Greek sculpture ought to present, not contradiction, hesitation, or uncertainty, but a serene—restful and happy—poise.[14] Indeed, one of Hegel's first sketches of the "classical art form,"[15] in his anticipatory presentation of the three stages of art, previews just such balance and equanimity:

> As the dissolution of this doubled lack [of the symbolic art form, with the only-abstract relation of the idea to its shape and its consequent faulty or abstract correspondence of meaning to shape], the classical art form is the free, adequate imaging [*Einbildung*] of the idea in the shape properly belonging to the idea according to its concept, with which it [the idea] therefore can come into free and complete accord [*Einklang*]. (13:109)

Hegel's repeating and enfolding language here has idea in accord with itself and its concept, shape informed or impressed by the idea, and both in an echoing concord with one another. This singular moment of adequacy between inner and outer, spiritual and material, content and form, would appear—as the term "complete" suggests—as an ultimate height, and indeed the next sentence combines an exclusive "first" (*erst*) with a realized last or completed end: "Thus the classical form first and alone [*erst*] offers the production and intuition of the completed ideal and presents it as realized" (13:109).

The movement or spanning from no longer to not yet, from first to last, appears realized and thus suspended in this moment. Hegel's next, remarkable paragraph specifies the shape of this art form, which is—still in preview—what this art must look like. It turns out that it must look like us. The "peculiarity" (*Eigentümlichkiet*) of the content of classical art is that it is the "concrete idea and, as such, the concrete spiritual" (13:109). As such, this content needs a shape from amongst nature "that for itself is fitting for [*zukommt*] the spiritual in and for itself" (13:110). Our interest here need be less in the fact (the humanist-ideological fact) of anthropomorphism than in two particular claims Hegel makes for its status as a shape for spirit. When he first announces the human shape—"This shape, which the idea as spiritual, and, indeed, the individually determinate spirituality, has in itself if it is supposed to constitute itself or proceed out into temporal appearance [*wenn sie sich in zeitliche Erscheinung herausmachen soll*], is the *human shape*" (13:110)[16]—the condition of temporal appearance is singled out. One might ask why the human shape is unique for temporal appearance; and while the preceding sentence refers to God's "original invention" of the human shape as suitable for "concrete spirituality" (so that now, Hegel appears to suggest, the "subjective concept" of the spirit of art can just "find" its suitable shape ready-made, as it were, in the human), there may be more to the appropriation of the human body for temporal appearance than merely an appeal to a myth of divine origins. For the second claim Hegel immediately introduces focuses not on human *shape* but specifically on the *body*. After briefly acknowledging that personification and anthropomorphism may be held as a "degradation" of spirituality, he argues that "art, however, insofar as it has to bring the spiritual to intuition in a sensuous manner, must proceed to this anthropomorphism, for the spirit appears sensuously in a sufficient way only in its body" (13:110). The body is suddenly already *its*, and *this* sensuous embodiment is "sufficient" (*genügend*) for, evidently, all that the sensuous appearance of spirit entails. Synecdoche, *pars pro toto*, often appears with a part of the body standing for the whole ("All hands on deck!"); here, the body is a part for the whole of spirit's history of appearances in the form of sensuality.

There is not only synecdochal sufficiency in this bodily anthropomorphism but a curious further qualification of *containment:* it is not so much that the body contains (embodies) the spirit but that the spirit contains—limits—the body. "The human body in its forms counts . . . in the classical art form no longer merely as sensuous existence, but exclusively as the existence and natural shape of spirit, and it must therefore be withdrawn from all the deficiency of the merely sensuous and [from] the contingent finitude [*zufälligen Endlichkeit*] of appearance" (13:110). The "temporal appearance" that qualified spirit in the shape of the body is now recalled as its "accidental finitude," but it is precisely this that must be suppressed or removed. The body is necessary for spirit's temporal appearance, but the finiteness and contingency associated with bodily presence in time are not only unnecessary but altogether dispensable. If body is to be suitable for the spirit, spirit must limit the body, prune it of its very temporal finitude.

Although we may insist upon the *temporal* register associated here with bodily appearance, Hegel adds a further sentence that gives a physical, spatial form to this temporality that is at once necessary and limited: "If the correspondence of meaning and shape is to be perfect, then the spirituality, which makes up the content, must also be of *such* a kind that it is in a position to express itself completely in the natural human shape, without towering beyond and above this expression in the sensuous and bodily [*ohne über diesen Ausdruck im Sinnlichen und Leiblichen hinauszuragen*]" (13:110). To return to the terminology of verbal expression (which Hegel invites by combining "meaning" and "shape" into a single "expression"), the meaning of spirit is not to be in excess of its expressive signifier; it is qualified as being fitted to the limitations of this shape. But the very excess of *spirit* that is being denied is imaged forth in spatial, physical terms: "spirituality . . . must [not] *tower* beyond and above this expression in the sensuous and bodily." What is exceeding the reciprocal containment of spirit in the body and the bodily by the spiritual is here doubly figured as an aspect of temporal appearance and a site or dimension of the bodily. "Contingent finitude" is to be removed from the scene of appearance, but as if in a kind of responsive excess, the threat of a "towering" over and beyond the limitations of the body is raised, which figure of excess suggests more body than spirit can fill, or more *of* the body than spirit's meaningfulness can inform.

Readers of the *Aesthetics* will know already that this looming excess of spirit over body, however bizarrely figured here in bodily terms, is what becomes, in Hegel's narrative, the "defect" (*Mangel*) of the classical art form and, in turn, the distinguishing feature of the succeeding stage of the romantic art form. While this succession will not concern us here, a single feature of Hegel's provisional preview of this historical overcoming must still catch our attention. For it continues the figuration of the spirit in terms of the body that has characterized both the classical form's master trope of anthropomorphism and the hinted threat of spirit's "towering" beyond the body. This feature is that of digestion. Its mention is so fleeting, and its function apparently so restricted to the service of exemplification, that undue attention may be unwarranted. On the other hand, not only is exemplification a far-from-innocent procedure in Hegel's works[17] but when the example is one that receives such extended treatment in the *Encyclopaedia of Philosophical Wissenschaften*, its employment here may be granted an importance that exceeds its local illustrative value.

In introducing the overcoming of classical art by romantic, Hegel contrasts first the Greek "unity of human and divine nature" with the Christian view of "God as spirit," then the identification of the former with the body with the identification of the latter with knowledge:

> Now the higher stage is the *knowledge* [*Wissen*] of this unity, which is *in itself*, such as the classical art form has as its content, perfectly representable in the body. But this raising up of the in-itself into self-conscious knowledge brings about an enormous difference. It is the infinite difference that, for example, separates man from animals. (13:112)

We may interrupt this passage to remark on the extraordinary steps in this series of analogies: the Christian god as spirit is to the Greek god in corporeal form as inner, subjective knowledge is to an only implicit (*an sich*) unity, as man is to animals. The association of the higher, more inward, more ethereal forms with knowledge is, of course, quintessentially Hegelian, and so the final step in Hegel's analogizing should not be surprising:

> Man is animal, but even in his animal functions he does not remain standing as in an in-itself like the animal [*als in einem Ansich stehen wie das Tier*], but becomes conscious of them, knows them and raises them up— such as, for example, the process of digestion—to self-conscious Wissenschaft. Man thereby undoes the barriers of his immediacy, which is in-itself, so that precisely because he *knows* that he is animal, he therefore ceases to be animal and grants himself knowledge of himself as spirit. (13:112)

The "example" of digestion is in fact a doubled one: an example of the body *and* of its overcoming in spiritualization. As the previous chapter's account of the *Encyclopaedia* passages displayed, digestion is for Hegel the assimilation and appropriation of an outer into an inner, and as such a figure for dialectic in general. Here, its emplotment in a narrative protohistory of the transition of art forms has it confront its very "bodily" limit. For the first appearance of the example of digestion is as an "animal function," as if beneath human dignity—as in Hegel's dismissive mention of *Pissen* in the *Phenomenology* (3:262)—or at least still beneath human thought. This animal, that is to say, bodily, function can become an object of science (say, dietetics) as man *thinks* about his digestion: "becomes conscious of it, knows it, and raises it up to self-conscious Wissenschaft." This is the aspect of the example *as* bodily or *of* the body. But the very example of digestion is also *of* the spirit, that is, of the appropriation, interiorization, and assimilation of the outer into the inner—or, in Hegel's context here, of the body by the spirit. So the example of the body is overcome in its exemplification of the spirit: digestion is digested, or "the process of digestion" processes or digests the "merely bodily object" of its knowledge, namely, the animal-like *function* of digestion.

Digestion that is itself *and* is digested is like the spirit that, in classical sculpture, is higher than the body but also combined with it and not "towering" above it. But if there the anomalous figure was of a spirit *not* spatially or bodily exceeding the limits of a bodily figure, here the figure is a temporal paradox spanning what Hegel has called an "enormous difference." For, he says, in raising the object of knowledge to self-conscious Wissenschaft—in digesting digestion—man both is and is not an animal: "precisely because he *knows* that he is an animal, he therefore ceases to be an animal." Between the "is" and the "ceases to be" lies less a contradiction than a passage of time and/as knowledge, and a transformation (digestion) of the body into spirit: "and grants himself knowledge of himself as spirit." "Undoing the barriers" or crossing the limits—of fixed contours to bodily shape, of the division between body and spirit, outer and inner—is a temporal passage between two states or moments of being, but as if without loss or leftover, without so much a disfiguring of the body and its functions as their transfiguration.

Hegel's point here, it should be recalled, is to illustrate the overcoming of the classical art form by the romantic as one that occurs at the very limit of illustration or *Veranschaulichung*. But like his employment of the example of digestion, which as *object* of knowledge becomes absorbed and processed by itself as (the figure of) the *process* of knowledge, so is this same transition between stages of art forms—historical passage—a figuration of the passage of art and its history into the philosophic Wissenschaft of aesthetics. When the art of the sensuous embodiment of spirit *knows* itself, it ceases to be art and becomes self-conscious Wissenschaft. The transition to the romantic art form—history as what happens—(pre)figures the absorption of art (and literary) history into historical knowledge—history as what is done in Wissenschaft. Around the figures and emplotments of embodiment, anthropomorphism, and digestion, history "as we know it" is in the making. At what expense?

If it were to cost us only a paradox or two, it would be a simple expense of spirit indeed. But it emerges that Hegel's more extended analytic exposition of the classical art form will sustain the paradoxes of historical passage into history and the spiritualization of the body within a complex configuration of loss and gain, maintenance and decay. Hegel's frequently effusive praise of classical beauty comes to reveal a structure of historical formation and deformation that is the very occasion and productivity of the *Aesthetics*.

When, at the beginning of the extended treatment of the classical art form in the second part of the *Aesthetics*, Hegel refers in passing to the human form as the "adequate outer appearance" for the ideal of art, in that such objectivity is "purified of the infirmity of finitude [*von den Gebrechen der Endlichkeit gereinigt*]" (14:20), we hear perhaps only a faintly amusing fantasy of benign anthropomorphism. But as the exposition continues with a reprise of the by-now familiar contrast between Christianity's romantic art form and the Greek gods' classical one, the risks of anthropomorphism loom larger, for the Christian Passion contributes pain and division to the notion of a human embodiment of the divine, "whereas in classical art the sensuousness is not killed and dead but also not resurrected into absolute spirituality" (14:24). Sensuousness appears poised to remain between two negatives, two "not yet"'s, as it were: between not yet killed, dead, or canceled and not yet lifted up into a survival or living on. In not (yet) submitting to a death of the body and an afterlife of the spirit, the equipoise of classical art and what Hegel calls its "beautiful religion" are showered with a litany of characterizations as "untroubled harmony of determinate free individuality in its adequate existence, this rest in its reality, this happiness, this satisfaction and grandeur in itself, this eternal serenity and bliss . . . which even in unhappiness and pain do not lose the secure self-repose" (14:24). This effusion is an eloquent extension of Winckelmann's "edle Einfalt und stille Grösse" and of at least one aspect of Weimar classicism. But how, then, may it be reconciled with a very different portrait of the Greek gods scarcely ten pages later? This sketch is one of an agonistic and paradoxical encounter with the mortality of the body, which had just been avoided as the praise showered down.

> Insofar as the gods are supposed to exist as spiritual individuals in bodily shape, this entails on the one hand that the spirit—instead of giving itself a view [*Anschauung*] of its essence in what is merely living and animal— much more views the living being as an indignity, as its misfortune and its death, and on the other hand, that it conquers what is elemental in nature and its own confused representation in it. (14:34–35)

This paradoxical formulation would suggest a kind of confrontation with and overcoming of death—the very "not yet" of the preceding passage. The paradox is contained in the view of the body as both a scene of death and one of victory. What is to be seen or viewed in revising or reviewing an understanding of the perfect embodiment of spirit in a body that is so blissfully at peace, "purified of the infirmity of finitude," yet also a scene of unhappy death and consequent struggle? What Hegel comes to see as he views Greek sculpture otherwise is an appearance of history that cannot be seen, but only *read*. Better read than dead, though.

Hegel's remarkable five pages on the Greek gods as sculpture, "Die neuen Götter des klassischen Ideals," touch on many of the aspects of the *Aesthetics* that we have already glanced at and draw them together toward a not-yet-articulated conclusion. To follow Hegel's staging of this articulation, we must isolate several moments in the "rhythm" of this section's presentation, all the while recalling that Hegel's dialectical argumentation resists the abstract isolation of one part from another and instead already anticipates one's giving way to another. But even such an awareness should not shield us from a sensitivity to the radical contrasts and consequences drawn almost despite Hegel's own argument.

He begins by singling out the gods' "concentrated individuality," which is further described as "the spiritual *substantial* individuality, which . . . rests securely on their own universality as on an eternal and clear foundation" (14:81–82). As this language of "individuality" and "universality" suggests, an immanent contrast is implicit, and Hegel addresses it under the rubric of "character," sometimes in a Kantian language of a sort of "unity of the manifold" ("The manifold [*mannigfaltigen*] aspects and traits which enter through this particularity make up—as reduced to simple unity [*Einheit*] with themselves—the characters of the gods" [14:82]),[18] sometimes while recalling the contrasts that are implied:

> They are not the mere abstractions of spiritual universals and, by this, so-called universal ideals, but rather insofar as they are individuals, they appear as an ideal that in itself has existence, and therefore determinacy, i.e., that, as spirit, has *character*. Without character, no individuality steps forth.

But Hegel's most powerful language here describes an exalted and even hyperbolic overcoming of the very contrast to which one is alerted. So, for example, as the above phrase's mention of "an eternal and clear foundation" might already have hinted, the gods are in a state of tension with temporality, which they nonetheless overcome:

> Only through this [the spiritual *substantial* individuality, resting securely as on an eternal and clear foundation] do the gods appear as the nontran-

sient powers whose untroubled rule comes into view [*zur Anschauung kommt*] not in the particular, in its entanglement with the other and the exterior, but rather in its own unalterability and purity. (14:82)

But as if this hyperbolic language of negation (*unvergänglichen, ungetrübtes, Unwandelbarkeit*) were resolving rather too much of the tension, Hegel also immediately (re)turns to the balancing of contrasts that the gods represent: "In the true ideal, however, this determinacy may not lead to sharp limitation within *one-sidedness* of character, but must equally [*gleichmässig*] appear to be drawn back again into the universality of the divine" (14:82). The balancing between a one-sided "untroubled rule" and "unalterability and purity," on the one hand, and a balance of particularity and universality, on the other, is then struck in the form and language of an oscillation that perhaps recalls Friedrich Schlegel rather more than Kant: "Thus each god is . . . part determined character, part all in all, and hovers in the fully unique middle between [*schwebt in der vollen einigen Mitte zwischen*] mere universality and equally abstract particularity" (14:82).[19] But here Hegel's language of paradoxical synecdoche or partial wholeness—"part all in all"—suggests a *still* unresolved motion in the oscillation or "hovering between." And so his very next sentence continues, as if to conclude decisively: "This gives to the authentic ideal of the classical the infinite security and rest, the untroubled bliss and unlimited freedom" (14:82).

But once again, the hyperbolic negatives—*unendliche, kummerlose, ungehemmte*—call attention to a denial. What is being denied, unsurprisingly, is temporal change; the gods' "infinite security and rest" is precisely against and atop temporality, as this last sentence recalls the earlier "eternal, clear foundation," "the unpassing powers" and "their own unalterability." It is thus that the next step in Hegel's depiction comes as a surprise in adding, within this a- or antitemporal context, that the Greek gods are, after all, corporeal: "Now as beauty in classical art, the divine character determined in itself furthermore appears not only spiritually but also every bit as much externally in its corporeality, in a shape visible to the eye as well as to the spirit" (14:82–83). The corporeality of the gods, in other words, is linked to their visibility—by, indeed, a muted but nonetheless striking redundancy in the phrasing "dem Auge . . . sichtbare Gestalt"—but also, rather more strangely, to their poised "security and rest," "the untroubled bliss and unlimited freedom." One might intuitively understand what it means to see corporeality as "shape visible to the eye," but what does one see in seeing such hyperbolic nontransience, unalterability, security, and rest in the body as well?

Hegel will continue to underscore that one thus sees *spirit* in the body, or better still, in and through the body: "[This beauty's] proper expression is the external shape peculiar to spirit, and to spirit alone, insofar as the inner brings itself to existence in it [the shape] and completely pours itself forth through it" (14:83). Spirit is shaped in(to) bodily shape and pours forth through it. But the verb *hindurchergiessen,* "to pour forth," suggests a rather more excessive or expressive relation of spirit to body than did the earlier *durchdringen,* "to permeate." [20] It nonetheless may not be excessively excessive, if it may be so put, for in that case the universality of classical beauty would appear *sublime*—excessively elevated *(erhaben)*—vis-à-vis its incorporation in a particular. And yet whenever Hegel appears to want it *both* ways, he also tends toward an argument of and for excess. Thus here, for example, in arguing against an excessive or sublime relation of abstract universality to the particular of incorporation, he would have "classical beauty lead spiritual individuality into the midst of its simultaneously natural existence and explicate the inner only in the element of outer appearance" (14:83). The both ways here are precisely "in" and "out": spiritual individuality goes "into" *(hinein)* the natural existence of the external body, and this is then an "unfolding" or "explicating" of the inner outward. The "excess," on the other hand, appears in Hegel's next paragraph, in his own excessive or hyperbolic language about how the outer shape as well as the spiritual "must free itself from every accidentality of outer determinacy, from every dependency upon nature, every sickliness, must be withdrawn from all finitude, from everything transient, from all involvement with the merely sensuous" (14:83). What sort of "outer shape" of spirit's embodiment could this possibly be? It would be one of accord and correspondence between the god's inner spirituality and the human body's outer shape (there are the "both ways" again), but also an *excessive* correspondence or embodiment nonetheless, by virtue of its very perfection. "Only spotless externality, in which every trait of weakness and relativity has been effaced and every spot of arbitrary particularity has been extinguished, corresponds to the spiritual inwardness that is to immerse itself in it and become corporeal in it" (14:84).

An outward body, but a body without any mark: "makellos, jeder Zug . . . verwischt, jeder Flecken . . . ausgelöscht." Hegel's language of an excessively clean surface, or *tabula rasa,* suggests, especially in its terms of erasure *(verwischt, ausgelöscht),* its opposite, that is, a surface or scene about to be (re)marked. A final pair of moments of "having it both ways," and having it excessively so, leads to Hegel's final marking-and-reading the marks of the Greek gods of classical sculpture. "Having it both ways" is a colloquial expression for what in Hegel's rhetoric is a paradox or a benign contradiction. Thus the penultimate of the images we have just glanced at, in which a movement of spirit *into* the body allows the body's appearance to *ex-plicate* spirit outward, is repeated in the claim that in the concrete individuality of the gods, "despite [the spirit's] thorough entry [*Hineingehen*] into the bodily and sensuous shape, there is announced in it its removal or distancing [*Entferntsein*] from all poverty of the finite" (14:84). Entering into the body but already distancing itself from the body's lacks—*any* lacks of finitude—spirit both is and is not there, in the body. In it *and* in excess—in egress—it is both beautiful *and* sublime, or a beauty that in exceeding its bounds of incorporation becomes sublime

> in that the classical ideal steps out into an existence that is its alone—the existence of the spirit itself—its sublimity displays itself blended into beauty and goes over into it immediately, as it were. This necessitates for the shapes of the gods the expression of exaltedness, of classically *beautiful* sublimity. (14:84)[21]

The oxymoron "beautiful sublimity" has the beautiful exceeding its bounds, or the excessive sublime qualified as contained within the beautiful. In either case, the exalted height *(Hoheit)* recalls that "towering" of classical beauty above the body, which "towering" was precisely under the sign of denial or erasure; here, the very exaltedness is about—however momentarily—to be hypostasized as the highest beauty. "An immortal earnestness, an unchangeable rest is enthroned on the brow of the gods, and is poured over their whole shape" (14:84).

The momentary pause of exaltedness upon the very height of the human shape of the gods—their brow as its throne—then tips, falls, and pours over the entire shape, as if enacting or embodying the "pouring forth" *(hindurchergiessen)* of spirit's inwardness through the outer shape. But such tipping and falling disturbs—or contradicts—the claim of "unchangeable rest," if rest pours forth and changes the very shape whose surface it covers. Indeed, what our terminology of rhetorical analysis has isolated in Hegel's language as paradox or oxymoron is identified by Hegel himself in his next sentence as conflict or opposition: "In their beauty they [the gods] thus appear raised [*erhoben*] above their own corporeality, and thereby there arises a conflict [*Widerstreit*] between their blessed exaltedness, which is a spiritual being-within-itself [*Insichsein*], and their beauty, which is external and corporeal" (14:84). Hegel will return to and draw out this "conflict" at and of a height. Here, we may first note that Hegel entangles the "conflict" within a terminological one: not just the now-familiar opposition or tension between inner and outer, spiritual and corporeal, sublime and beautiful, but also, as he continues, one between the ostensible differential singularity of terms themselves. Thus: "The spirit appears wholly immersed [*versenkt*] in its shape"—as if "immersed" meant "poured out into"—"and yet at the same time immersed out of it and only in itself [*aus ihr heraus nur in sich versunken*]"—now as if "poured back out, and back into itself." And then: "It is like the wandering of an immortal god among mortal men" (14:84); the mixing of immortal and mortal—the very feature of the classical shape of the Greek gods and their beautiful anthropomorphism—is now not fixed, "unchangeable" *(unwandelbar)*, but wandering.

The conflict and break that I am suggesting may already be located here in the semantic struggle of Hegel's terms with themselves surprises no one, of course. The one-sidedness of language and meaning is exactly what philosophical, that is, dialectical, thinking and writing overcome in learning and teaching the otherness—other-sidedness—that obtains as well within the apparently single, the isolated, the abstract.[22] Rather, the point in the remainder of this analysis will be to draw out, not the slippage or entanglement of terms, but the appearance of a dimension of Hegel's argument on the far side of that argument's claims. Hegel's major claim, we recall, is for a zenith to his narrative of art's historical unfolding, which high point could be both located in a past moment and form—the Greek gods in classical sculpture—and made to yield present scholarly *(wissenschaftlich)* knowledge; the latter knowledge would be the final "spiritual" overcoming of history's—and art's—passage, which would make both "a thing of the past for us" but also preserve them as precisely such historical Wissenschaft. The stakes in Hegel's argument, then, are less the entanglement than the pairing and coincidence of history and knowledge, event and scholarly afterlife, the body and the spirit here as the classical art form and its meaning. If *these* fall apart, or exceed one another in the form of a "pouring out" like that just glanced at, then Hegel's historical Wissenschaft, the cooperative pairing of narrative and argument, will itself leave either undigested leftovers or unreadable marks.

Paul de Man wrote of a similar *décalage* between codes, or an excess of one that breaks with the claims of another, under the rhetorical term *parabasis:* "a sudden revelation of the discontinuity between two rhetorical codes . . . [which] interrupt[s] the expectations of a given grammatical or rhetorical movement."[23] The literal and more conventional sense of parabasis is that of authorial intrusion in a narrative, which intrusion breaks the spell, fictional or otherwise, that the narrative had cast. At

just this point in the *Aesthetics*, Hegel inserts a parabasis as he introduces his own voice into the scholarly-historical narrative of the Wissenschaft of the artistically beautiful. The rarity of such intrusions is
exceeded by its bizarreness in this particular case. We might have noted
a parabasis very early in the *Aesthetics*, immediately after the famous
claim that "in all these relations art according to the aspect of its highest
determination is and remains for us a thing of the past." There, Hegel
went on to defend a *wissenschaftlich* consideration of art and further to
specify, in his own voice: "I consider philosophizing as altogether insep-
arable from scholarship and scientific activity [*Wissenschaftlichkeit*]"
(13:26). That strong linkage of philosophy and Wissenschaft—
strengthened by the trope of parabasis—would, however, have sur-
prised no one, least of all the students in his philosophy *Vorlesung* or the
readers of the present study of the philosophic argumentation for historical Wissenschaft. Not so unsurprising, though, the parabasis here
in Hegel's discussion of Greek gods and classical sculpture.

Hegel's intervention appears immediately in the wake of the image of
the immortal god "wandering" among mortal men. If this is an image
of radical difference—the immortal among the mortal—it is also one
that, at least in the condition of the conjunction, is now familiar, in that
the gods have long since been attributed human shape. Hegel then suggests that the gods bring forth an "impression" that is, he says, "despite
all difference, similar" to something else. The juxtaposition of difference *and* similarity itself structurally recalls and mimics the "impression" of immortal gods in and amongst the shapes of mortal men; but it
also announces at once an analogy and a contrast that are more striking.
For what Hegel finds "similar despite all difference" is the impression
"that Goethe's bust by Rauch made upon me when I first saw it"
(14:84).

This is probably the bronze version, in Berlin since 1822. We may
already appreciate Hegel's juxtaposition not so much of two different
works of sculpture, as of an immortal among mortals with Goethe
among his contemporaries. But we should also follow what it is that
Hegel draws out of this comparison, and how. "You [*Sie*] have seen it,
too," he continues, so that the parabasic intrusion now extends beyond
Hegel the author into his historical-scholarly narrative, to include the
intersection of his collective (plural) audience, and what *they* might have
seen, with the subject matter of the Greek gods. Hegel now goes on with
what he ("I") and they ("you") have seen: it is "this high brow [*diese
hohe Stirn*], this powerful, commanding nose." This much of Hegel's
ekphrasis recalls the immediately preceding paragraphs: the "high
brow" of Rauch's bust of Goethe recalling the "blessed height" (*Hoheit*)

and the "unchangeable rest enthroned on the brow [*Stirn*] of the gods."
Even as the remainder of this first clause of Hegel's description continues to recall the spiritual mien of the sculpture, oriented toward the
heights ("die geistreiche Stellung des Kopfes, auf die Seite und etwas in
die Höhe den Blick weggewendet"), it also mixes in simultaneously and
cospatially the *human* aspect: "and at the same time the whole fullness
of sensitive [*sinnenden*], friendly humanity [*Menschlichkeit*], and there as
well these developed muscles of the brow." The bust of Goethe, like the
Greek gods in their sculptured shape, is of a divinely high brow as well
as a humanly muscled brow, each in the other. This long descriptive
evocation then pauses to recall that in such human shapes—Goethe's
bust or the sculpted Greek gods—there are embodied, again, the exalted attributes of the divinities: "and in all the animation, the rest,
stillness and exalted character of old age [*die Ruhe, Stille, Hoheit im Alter*]" (14:84).

To this point, Hegel's highly rhetorical verbal act—a parabasis and
an ekphrasis at once—may seem to have recapitulated, or illustrated,
much of his narrative of divine spirits in human shapes and to have
added very little that is new. But there is a further linguistic feature of
Hegel's passage that has been overlooked thus far. It is the deixis of the
locative adjectives "this" and "these" (*diese*), used repeatedly to point to
or show something, as if to the audience of the lectures. To what are
Hegel and his language gesturing—"this high brow," "this powerful,
commanding nose," "these developed muscles of the brow"? The Greek
sculptures are not there, but Rauch's bust of Goethe is supposed to be
standing in for them, by analogy, as it were. But the bust is not there
either, although it might be nearby, somewhere in the corridors of official Berlin. The deictic "this" seems always to be referring to something
that is not there.[24] Or to something that will not stay still, but passes?
Deixis is here the linguistic gesture and mark of the parabasic intrusion
of author (speaker) *and* readership (audience, the *Sie* addressed by the
ich) into the art-historical narrative of the past, the intersection of a
present of speaking and hearing with an already written *past*. But if this
is where "this" is—at an intersection—what does *this* intersection
mark?

The intersection of gods and men, difference and similarity, Rauch's
bust and Greek sculpture, "I" and "you," the philosophical auditorium
and the art-historical narrative, present and past, is also the intersection
of a now with a now. Hegel's long sentence, up to the point that we have
read it, has accented a presence of the bust's "spirit-filled position of the
head" with a simultaneous ("und zugleich") presence of "the whole fullness of sensitive, friendly humanity." This, we might say, is no more

than the co-presence of spirit and the human shape—their coexistence in a single space—in the sculptures of Greek gods, such as Hegel's entire argument has labored to explain and justify. But if, at a single point or mark, two nows intersect in the form of two meanings at a single sign—now this meaning, now that—do we then have just co-presence or coexistence, or is it the more complicated rhetoric of a pun and of allegory?

This point of intersection is the last word that we quoted when Hegel's long sentence was interrupted: *Alter,* in "the rest, stillness, and exalted character of *Alter.*" "Age," in the sense of old age but also, in the context, age in the sense of historical period (*Zeitalter*). Now, this "now" of the age of the Goethe represented in Rauch's bust intersects with a "historical present" or "now" of ancient Greece, which has been represented in Hegel's narrative prior to his parabasis and which the bust now re-presents as well, by a kind of analogy ("in all difference, similar to"). But when the intersection of the two nows, in the "pun" of *Alter,* occurs, it *means* "now . . . now" as "now" and "then." That is, the pun or rhetorical intersection of a contemporaneous present and a historical present, or an (old) age and an age (of old), becomes or means the divergence and separation of sign and meaning in allegory: "now . . . now" comes to mean "now . . . then."

Why should it be of any more than passing interest that in Hegel's parabasis and ekphrasis a now means a then, and a pun becomes allegorical, as the intersection of present and past begin to diverge? Because Hegel's long intervention has only been interrupted, not ended, and its changes of shape and signification have not yet ended, either. Up to the point of its interruption, it has *marked* its "now" in several manners: by the point of the parabasis's intersection with the narrative, by the overlap of terms describing the classical past ("Ruhe, Stille, Hoheit," etc.) with the sculptural object that is ekphrastically present, by the naming of the simultaneity ("und zugleich") of the sensuous ("sinnenden") with the spiritual ("geistreiche"). But now Hegel's sentence will name "now"; it continues, after a semicolon, "and now . . . [*und nun . . .*]." What appears "now"? "And now next to it [*und nun daneben*] the withering of the lips, which fall back into a toothless mouth, the slack of the neck, of the cheeks, whereby the tower of the nose projects still larger, the wall of the brow still higher" (14:84–85). It is as if Rauch's bust of Goethe were changing before Hegel's—and our—eyes, for the lips change from being "well-formed" to "withered," while the nose protrudes "still larger" than its former "powerful, commanding shape," and the brow changes from "high" to "higher."

The power and dilemma posed by Hegel's sentence are concentrated in the words "nun daneben." If "now" is not a stable "now" but precisely the sign of how a temporal sign doubles and diverges into "now" and "then," then where is "next to it"? Is *daneben* the divergent double that similarly haunts the deictic "this" (*diese*), so that "this" always already means something "next to this"? To be sure, the phrase "nun daneben" links the fate of the temporal now with that of the spatial adjacency, but even thus together, they may as a pair signify other and divergent meanings. Clearly, the statue is diverging—parting, changing—from itself; we may say it is aging, drawing out the temporal passage—not a spatializable expanse, but a passage—implied in the momentarily (and now falsely) spatialized *Alter*. But the abruptness of what follows Hegel's semicolon, and of the sheer contiguity of *daneben*, suggests that "drawing out" and "passage" are themselves false renderings of the meaning of Hegel's signs. The juxtaposition of the "rest, stillness and exalted character" of *age* with the changes of *aging* is not a case of continuous "similarity despite all the differences" but one of difference despite all similarities. The toll of transience, of temporality, marks the scene and sculpted shape of its overcoming.

But if this is still a temporal understanding of the "now" (*nun*) becoming the mark of divergence between "now . . . then" and "now . . . now"—the divide of time itself—where is *daneben*? Where are Hegel's devoted listeners expected to glance, or where are we to understand Hegel gesturing or pointing? I want to suggest that *daneben* is written, is in writing, is writing, and nowhere else, and that Hegel is here, "now," reading. To draw *this* understanding out of the passage's nonpassage, its interruptions and contiguities, will involve reading the remaining two pages of Hegel's section "The New Gods of the Classical Ideal."

One of the hardest things to read immediately is the written mark—the punctuation mark of a dash—that separates, in Hegel's prose, the sentence we have been analyzing from the next and, within the next one, its first and second parts. Is *it* the sign meaning *daneben*, and if so, does the dash mean continuity or rather contiguity? For after such a dash ("—"), Hegel continues with, "The power of this fixed shape, which is especially reduced to the unchangeable. . . ." But the very point of what followed "und daneben" signified not a "fixed shape" but an altered and agèd (having aged) one, not the unchangeable but rather the changeable, changed, and changing. It is as if, in Hegel's baffling prose, the dash is undoing, in its separation of sentences, what the "and now next to it" performed in its juxtaposition of the two images of Rauch's bust of Goethe. But then, in a further metamorphosis and comparison, the divergence that the previous sentences have conveyed is reinstated, this time in a redressing and Orientalization of Goethe's shape: " . . . appears [so the sentence continues] in its loose, hanging surrounding like the raised head and shape of the Oriental in his wide turban, but [in his] wobbling overcloak and dragging slippers"; so that the earlier Goethesque juxtaposition-and-divergence of firm and flabby, taut and withered, here recurs as that of fixed and loose, raised upright and "wobbling" down, all the way down to the flat slippers. And then—for the semicolon quoted above is in the text of the lectures, followed by another dash (";—")—Hegel[25] concludes his sentence, his comparison, and his entire parabasis and paragraph with this: "it is the first, powerful, timeless spirit that, in the mask of the mortality that hangs about it, stands ready to let this husk [*Hülle*] fall away, and only still lets it hang loose and freely around itself" (14:85).

The parabasic intersection of authorial intrusion and historical narrative, the contemporary and the ancient examples, has moved from an analogy ("bei aller Verschiedenheit ähnlich") to a pun ("Alter") to an allegory of the signifier aging and peeling away from its meaning, such that here, at last, the very human shape that was to embody divine spirituality attains an oppositional status: that of "mortality hanging around," opposed to "timeless spirit." Aging and allegory have occurred before "our" very eyes, as art—at its anthropomorphic zenith—is about to give up its body, its incorporation, its momentary resistance to transitoriness, for its spirit, its disembodiment, its "far side" of mortality. Hegel's next sentence and next paragraph, when he returns to the explicit theme of the Greek gods as abruptly as he turned away from them and to Rauch's bust of Goethe, sustain this linkage of the passage of time with the passing of the bodily shape: "In a similar way the gods, with respect to this high freedom and spiritual rest, also appear raised above their corporeality, so that they feel their shape, their limbs, amidst all their beauty and perfection, as if they were a superfluous appendage" (14:84). From mortality "hanging around" (*umherhängenden*) to its being felt as a mere appendage or "hang-on" (*Anhang*), the body appears to be falling below the gods, in contrast to the earlier injunction that the spirit *not* be allowed to "tower above" the body. But as if recalling the earlier claim and resisting the latest tendency—as if resisting the *décalage* between narrative argument and the consequences of the parabasis—Hegel returns to a last insistence upon a permeation or interanimation of bodily shape and spirit in the Greek gods:

And yet [*Und dennoch*] the whole shape is ensouled in a lively way [*lebendig beseelt*], identical with spiritual being, without separation, without that sundering of what is fixed in itself and the weaker parts, the spirit not escaping and rising above the body, but rather both *one* solid whole, out of which the being-in-itself of the spirit tranquilly glances [*still herausblickt*] only in wonderful certainty of itself. (14:85)

Hegel's language reaches another stylistic height here, as the contrastive counterclaim of the ensouled bodily shape leads to a litany of claims for "identisch, . . . trennungslos, ohne jenes Auseinander, . . . nicht . . . entgehend und entstiegen, sondern beide *ein* . . . Ganzes." The strength of this hyperbole of nonseparation and nondistinction, as out of place as it is following the previous paragraphs' development of divergence and falling away, may nonetheless distract one from another conspicuous feature of the passage at hand: that spirit "glances out" of the body. It is remarkable because it follows the parabasis that had Hegel seeing Rauch's bust of Goethe ("als ich sie das erstemal sah"), his audience seeing it as well ("Sie haben sie gleichfalls gesehen"), and the bust itself seeming to glance up and away ("das freie Auge . . . die geistreiche Stellung des Kopfes, auf die Seite und etwas in die Höhe den Blick weggewendet"). What is occurring in the alternation of glances in at the sculptures, and out from them?

It will remain for the long paragraph that concludes this section of the *Aesthetics* to respond to the question of the glances, but the recalling of a much earlier passage from the lectures is also necessary for its development. For the image here of the spirit glancing out of its embodiment recalls the first section of the earlier chapter on "Das Kunstschöne oder das Ideal," itself titled "Die schöne Individualität," where it was also a question of the spirit in the body. There, Hegel writes that "the human shape" could be taken as an illustration of how, in the ideal of art's unfolding of the true (*das Wahre*), every part synecdochally "makes this soul, the whole, appear in it" (13:203). The human body at first contradicts this, for its members indicate "only some particular activity and partial impulse," but when Hegel asks "in which particular organ the whole soul appears as soul," he immediately answers, "So we would readily say the eye; for in the eye the soul concentrates itself and not only sees through it, but also is seen in it." This is not only a traditional topos that associates the eye with access to the soul, nor just a familiar dialectical construction in which the subject seeing is viewed as the object seen. For Hegel goes further, in a hyperbole that turns the synecdoche inside out, as it were, to claim not that the eye stands for the body but that in art the body becomes the eye: "Of art it may be claimed that it transforms each shape at all points of the visible surface into an eye, which is the seat of the soul and brings the spirit to appearance" (13:203).[26]

When one looks at the eye of a sculpture, one sees the soul and the soul sees back; indeed, to see sculpture is to see it *as* eye. And to see the eye is to see the appearance of spirit. We recall this earlier passage and its claims in the context of Hegel's argument about the Greek gods in order to begin to make sense of his claim here that the "being-in-itself of spirit tranquilly glances out" of its embodiment in the human shape. We have just noted how this claim resists or contrasts with ("Und den-noch") the divergence of the gods from their shape, as if the latter were a mere "superfluous appendage." What will one's glance at the glancing out glimpse of the tension and divergence at this very point of Hegel's argument? Hegel had begun this whole subsection, with its parabasis and then its retrieval of its argument, by naming a "struggle" (*Wider-streit*) between the gods' "blessed exaltedness which is a spiritual being-in-itself, and their beauty, which is external and corporeal" (14:84). Here, he picks up the thread by continuing that "that above-mentioned struggle is at hand, but nonetheless without coming forth as difference and separation of inner spirituality and its outer element" (14:85). The negative ("das Negative") that lies within is "immanent to this undi-vided *whole*, and expressed on it itself [*an ihm selber ausgedrückt*]." And then there appears another remarkable sentence in this series of remark-able passages. This expression of the negative

> is, within the spiritual exaltedness, the breath and scent of mourning [*Trauer*] which men rich in spirit [*geistreiche Männer*] have felt in the im-ages of the gods of the ancients [*in den Götterbildern der Alten*], even in their beauty perfected to the point of loveliness. (14:85)

"The breath and scent of mourning" is a phrase that doubles and inten-sifies the sense of the transient "within the spiritual exaltedness." For elsewhere Hegel has already contrasted taste and smell with sight and hearing to the effect that the former are "sensuous" as opposed to what he calls "theoretical" senses, that is, objects of taste and smell are nec-essarily *used up*, while those of sight and hearing may remain or re-peat.[27] And so a "breath and scent" here signals what is of transience or passage. So, too—doubled, intensified—that these should be "of mourning," that is, of a reaction to and expression of loss. But to this point where Hegel introduces the term of mourning, there has not been any explicit rendering of loss, only of an expression of negativity. Why mourning, then?

"Men rich in spirit" feel this soupçon of mourning in the face of "im-ages of the gods of the ancients." Whatever else Hegel means by these "men rich in spirit"—for he is presumably alluding to a tradition of the reception of antiquity—he counts himself among them by virtue of his position as *Wissenschaftler* (Wissenschaft being the very site of "wealth of spirit") if not through any further failings of vanity. To have *Hegel* feel mourning is to recall the doublings and intersections that his just-finished parabasis had introduced: Hegel looking (imaginatively) at Rauch's bust of Goethe, as the lectures' audience looked at Hegel, each instance of vision being "illustrative" of a certain view of the sculptures of the Greek gods. But these overlapping or mutually illustrating "views" spanned time and came to signify the passage—the aging—of time; and it is here that "mourning" can come to be sensed, initially in the juxtaposition-and-divergence of a near-pun. For here, most immediately, the "men rich in spirit" are in the face of "the images of the gods of the ancients [*der Alten*]," where *Alten* recalls, in the parabasis, the version of the bust as "in aller Lebendigkeit die Ruhe, Stille, Hoheit im *Alter*," before it gave way to the withering of the lips, the slackening of the neck—to aging. A sculptural image of age *(Alter)* could stand in for those of the ancients *(Alten)*, just as now the ancients can recall the agèd that aged still further ("und nun daneben . . ."). The mourning is generated in the face of the loss—of and by time—seen in the shapes of the bodies, however "restful, still and exalted," or however "beautifully perfected to the point of loveliness."

Mourning is always for the loss of the body, whose "loveliness" *(Lieblichkeit)* here recalls, in a visual pun, its corporeality *(Leiblichkeit)*. Indeed, *Lieblichkeit* "is" *Leiblichkeit*, in the sense that the sign's meaning diverges allegorically from the sign, as beauty means here the aging of the body, the submission of beauty to the very transience of its embodiment. So, too, the aging of the body means the ages of art's embodiment: mourning is here necessarily in relation to history.

It remains to be seen how mourning is also in relation to reading, or how reading appears in the scene of mourning.

> The free, perfect beauty [of the plastic eternal gods] is not able to be satisfied in consenting to a determinate, finite existence; rather its individuality, whether of the spirit or of the shape—although characteristic and determined in itself—only still coincides with itself as at once free universality and spirituality resting in itself [*in sich ruhender Geistigkeit*]. (14:86)[28]

The rest *(Ruhe)* repeatedly identified as a feature of the Greek gods has been slowly transformed from a "mid-point between mere universality and equally abstract particularity" (14:82) to "an unchangeable rest throned upon the brow of the gods" (84), to the view of the gods "raised above their corporeality" (85), to this entire de-corporealization of "spirituality resting in itself": rest has been raised *(erhoben)* above the bodies of the gods to the point of its being raised-and-canceled *(aufge-*

125

hoben) with respect to its determination in or on a body, and yet also preserved (also *aufgehoben*) in its other of "free universality" and pure spirituality. It is this universality that, Hegel then says, some have wanted to address as "coolness" *(Kälte)*, but he immediately adds that the coolness is there only for "the modern fervor within the finite; regarded for themselves, they have warmth and life" (14:86). This rapid switch and contrast of perspectives recalls the parabasis within the historical narrative—"now . . . then" and "now . . . now"—and the juxtaposition-and-divergence of Goethe's *Alter* with the images of the gods of the *Alten*. It should alert us as well to a juxtaposition-and-divergence of meaning with respect to its sign.[29]

Such a juxtaposition and divergence occur following the semicolon that itself closes this claim of the Greek gods' "warmth and life," were they but "regarded for themselves." Who could do this, or rather, what would its perspective be, "regarding [them] for themselves"? For what is *their* perspective? Hegel continues:

> The blessed peace mirrored in their corporeality is essentially an abstracting from the particular, an indifference vis-à-vis the transient [*Vergängliches*], a giving up of the external, a renunciation, not sorrowful or painful, yet a renunciation of the earthly and fleeting, as the spiritual serenity looks down and away beyond [*tief über . . . hinwegblickt*] death, the grave, loss, temporality, and, precisely because it is deep, contains this negative within itself. (14:86)

The mirroring *in* the corporeality is, of course, already one above or *out of* the body: it is, accurate to the precision of Hegel's terms, a reflection that both reproduces and inverts. Thus the peace in the body is a drawing away *(Abstrahieren)* from the body's particularity. And here, in Hegel's new litany of terms attached to giving up—"indifference" and "renunciation," untroubled and painless—a further reproduction-and-inversion appears, for what the gods' peace says goodbye to *(Entsagen)* comes back into its mouth or ex-pression as the negative *(Ent-)* it still contains. Thus to say goodbye to death, the grave, loss, temporality, is to have them all *within* one. Or, in the other of Hegel's image, to look down, away, and beyond these is to have *them* all glance or reflect back.

But even as this long last sentence appears to "contain" the dynamics of mirroring, abstracting, renouncing, and looking away *within* the agency of the gods themselves, Hegel's next sentence reintroduces the perspective of an *other*, outside position. "But the more that seriousness and spiritual freedom step forth in the shapes of the gods, the more that a contrast of this exalted state [*dieser Hoheit*] with determinacy and corporeality may be felt [*lässt sich . . . empfinden*]" (14:86). What was earlier called a "struggle" (*Widerstreit*) between *Hoheit* and the gods' "beauty, which is external and corporeal"—and qualified as a "struggle at hand, nonetheless without [its] stepping forth as difference and separation"—is here this "contrast," which itself is furthermore not just "at hand" for the gods but for an other. For, despite Hegel's passive and impersonal construction ("may be felt"), the contrast itself takes the form of an object for "feeling." *Empfinden* is not only a characteristic of the romantic art form—thus here, the contrast arising in classical art is already being received in a romantic mode—it also recalls "the breath and scent of mourning that men rich in spirit . . . have felt [*empfunden*]." The contrast of the Greek gods with themselves—their *Hoheit* with their *Körperlichkeit*—is felt by an other as mourning.

But just as *empfinden* here recalls the feeling by others of something vis-à-vis the images of the gods, Hegel's very next words re-internalize this feeling-by-others into the gods themselves: "The blessed gods mourn as it were over their blessedness or corporeality." The doubleness of "blessedness or corporeality"—contrast or apposition?—surprises at first, since "blessedness" (*Seligkeit*) has been associated with the gods' "abstraction from particularity," that is, away from their bodies, whereas here it appears linked to that very corporeality. But the linkage is one of contrast, not apposition; "blessedness *or* corporeality," as the object of mourning, indicates a kind of indifference to *which* it is, as long as each is seen in contrast with and detachment from the other. This is the point, it would seem, for the contrast and mutual otherness of the previously perfectly matched inner spirituality and outer embodiment are the occasion for the mourning. But whose mourning? In the first mention of mourning it was "men rich in spirit" who "felt the breath and scent of mourning in the images of the gods of the ancients," while here "the blessed gods mourn." What was characterized just above as a "re-internalization of feeling-by-others" may now be better understood as the gods mourning their own self-displacement, and this self-displacement has itself included the displacement of mourning onto others. Or—here is the dialectical correction—the displacement of mourning onto others *is*, in fact, *their* mourning: as they mourn their "blessedness or corporeality" (the very divergence in this juxtaposition), they give off a breath and scent of mourning to others, which others—"men rich in spirit"—*are* the gods now displaced and transformed by their mourning. Gods that embodied spirit, once they are raised, exalted, or otherwise sublated above that body, are men rich only in spirit: gods become Wissenschaft. The classical art form becomes the romantic one across the modality of feeling mourning and becomes the scholar of art across the raising of spirit.

And what about a raising of a body? Or is the body left behind? Even as spirit separates from the body, rising above it, it still seems to "contain" what it denies, just as "the spiritual cheerfulness" had looked away beyond "death, the grave, loss, temporality" and yet also, "precisely because it is deep, contained this negative within itself." The spirit that contains the mortality, temporality, and sheer loss of transitoriness that it also renounces, the spirit that cancels *and* preserves the body, is the spirit that has become the reader of its letter. For the next sentence, after the semicolon where I have interrupted the quotation, begins: "One reads in their formation the fate that stands before them [*man liest in ihrer Gestaltung das Schicksal, das ihnen bevorsteht*]" (14:86). The impersonality of the "one" is exact to the doubling perspective of the gods who mourn themselves (their loss) and displace this mourning and its very position of elevated spirit onto the "men rich in spirit" who catch a whiff of the mourning.[30] But is Hegel's use of "reads" here casual or otherwise gratuitously colloquial? We may arrive at an answer by considering what it is that is "read," namely, "fate" (*Schicksal*).

The first section of the third chapter, titled "The Dissolution of the Classical Art Form" (we have been in the second chapter, "The Ideal of the Classical Art Form"), is on "Das Schicksal." Hegel's manifest topic here is how the Greek gods, by virtue of their very multiplicity, are at odds with their individuality as a principle of oneness or unification and how they thus conflict with "accidentality" (*Zufälligkeit*) as it is displayed in their struggles with one another and with their circumstances. We may pick up his argument where it most clearly recalls the one we have just left: "Through this finitude immanent to the gods themselves, they get involved in the contradiction of their exalted character [*Hoheit*], their worth [on the one hand], and the beauty of their existence [on the other], through which they are also brought down into the arbitrary and accidental" (14:108). To the extent that the gods, "in authentic sculpture and its individual statues in temples," are represented as "solitary in blessed rest [*in seliger Ruhe*]," they escape this hubbub, but—Hegel continues—"yet they now receive and retain [*doch nun . . . erhalten*] something lifeless, something withdrawn from feeling, and that tranquil trait of mourning that we already touched on above" (14:108). As Hegel explicitly recalls the earlier moment in the lectures, something is also marked as altered. For when is the "now" (*nun*) when the sculptures have "something lifeless" (*etwas Lebloses*), and are they receiving it for a first time (*erhalten*) or preserving it long after (also *erhalten*)? Whatever and whenever this is, it is "withdrawn from feeling," and so we are a step further withdrawn from the displacement of feeling from the gods' feeling of mourning to the "men rich in spirit" feeling the breath and scent of it. Yet even in this lifelessness, they receive and preserve a *trait* of mourning; or perhaps better, in this trait *(Zug)*, they receive and preserve their lifelessness. Their own "life"—the embodiment of spirit in the body—is that of the mark of spirit mourning lifelessness. "This mourning," Hegel continues, "is already that which makes out [*ausmacht*] their fate"; in the doubled moment of receiving and preserving the mark of mourning, their fate is *already* made out, namely, that they are no longer "the altogether adequate expression [of spiritual individuality] in the immediate corporeal and external existence" (14:107), for as spirit is towering, hovering, or otherwise rising above the body, "it [this mourning] shows that something higher stands above them, and that the transition from particularities to their universal unity is necessary" (14:108–9).

We may understand this "tranquil trait of mourning" not only as *signifying* their fate but as constituting it or making it out *(ausmachen)*. Furthermore, they receive and preserve the trait at once, in a split second of "now" that is also the briefest mark between their vitality and their lifelessness. This rehearses the earlier phrasing—precisely recalled by Hegel here ("den wir bereits oben berührt haben")—of "man liest in ihrer Gestaltung das Schicksal, das ihnen bevorsteht," for at the instant that fate stands before them as something they might receive, it is already there, traced in the trait, preserved, as a script to be read. It is not not yet, but not yet no longer, either; it is the "now" of a no longer of the not yet, the very passing of *Vergängliches* and *Zeitlichkeit* that the gods, and classical art, would look away from and yet nonetheless still contain *(enthalten)*.

How does this excursus on fate—Hegel's and our own—help us to understand the "one reading" *(man liest)?* Who is doing what when, here, "one reads"? The "one" who reads—Hegel, or his audience of observers—reads a fate that stands before them; but to the extent that the fate of at once rising above and internalizing or "containing" temporality "stands before them," it is temporality spatialized and made visible: it is writing, the trait. This "fate"—this trait—is composed of mourning, which was "a breath and scent" and is then associated, "now," with "something lifeless, withdrawn from feeling." As breath and scent solidify or sediment into a *trait*, and as it is mourning that is first felt, then the sculptures' contrast of the exalted and the corporeal, and finally the withdrawal from feeling altogether that is represented, it is not just a lifelessness that is setting in and a spirit that is departing. Rather, the sculptures are becoming script as the observers of art ("one") are becoming readers.

To read art is to see it as marked material, marked by the traits of temporality received and maintained. To recall "seeing" art is to re-member Hegel's hyperbolic image of the surface of the shape of art as everywhere an eye, bringing spirit to appearance, to be seen, as well as the later one of the Greek gods' spirit tranquilly looking out of "*one* solid whole*" in wonderful security. From the perspective of reading the trait of *their* mourning, this comes to look otherwise. As if for the first time, it is seen that the sculptures cannot see. At the beginning of the section on the romantic art form, Hegel contrasts it with Greek sculp-tures. What is missing in "those exalted images of the gods," he says, "is the reality of subjectivity being for itself in the knowledge and will [*Wissen und Wollen*] of themselves" (14:131). But what is missing is itself a mark, an external, corporeal one—like the mourning that marked the gods with transience, temporality, and lifelessness even as their spirit was withdrawing. Here, Hegel continues, "this lack shows itself out-wardly in that the expression of the simple soul, the light of the eye, departs from the sculptural shapes [*den Skulpturgestalten der Ausdruck der einfachen Seele, das Licht des Auges abgeht*]" (14:131–32). Once again, something temporal—the "departing"—is marked spatially, cor-poreally; the lack of expression is expressed. "The greatest works of beautiful sculpture are sightless, their inwardness [*Inneres*] does not gaze out of them as self-knowing interiority [*Innerlichkeit*] in this spiri-tual concentration that the eye announces." An eye sees that *these* eyes do *not* see, or to recall Hegel's earlier formulation, it sees that what "tranquilly looks out" is a sightlessness or blindness. "This light of the soul falls outside of itself and belongs to the observer, who is unable to look at the shapes soul to soul, eye to eye" (14:132).

The observer who sees that the sculptures do not see knows what they do not know. *He* has the "knowledge" (*Wissen*) of himself, as "self-knowing interiority," that is denied them by their disjunction of spirit from body. The art-*Wissenschaftler*, who makes knowledge in observing and knowing art, cannot look art eye to eye even as he looks at its eye. It reflects back blindness, and this is *his* insight. He knows that the light is his and that the bodily shape, once "all eyes," is sheer material, marked of a lack. When knowledge returns, in reflection, from material to its inner, spiritual source, one is reading art as, always—one's fate standing before one—the ending of art and the appearing of history. The "negativity" of the Greek sculptures had been at once that over and beyond which they "looked away" (*hinwegblickt*) and that which they contained: death, the grave, loss, temporality. Now, "we see" that they do not look at all, but only, in their blind but marked surface, reflect our looking *and knowing* what our looking eyes mean: the seat of spirit's concentration. To contain negativity now within ourselves (our light, our knowing) is to know the history of art: the death, grave, loss, and temporality of the Greek gods, their bodies, their classical art form.

Like the fate that stands before the sculpted gods for "one"'s reading, the fate of art and history stood inscribed in Hegel's *Aesthetics* as the scene of reading. Already in a first schematic preview of the system of the particular modes of art, negativity that appears as a withdrawal from spatiality and an idealization of materiality as temporality was named "tone" and identified with the art of music. This "beginning ideality of matter" (13:121), to be known by its interiorizing audience as the giving up of outer, corporeal materiality, already announces the narrative argument of Hegel's *Aesthetics*, which is that as art becomes itself, it becomes a narrative to be read and known, the story of its giving up its body to knowledge: donating its body to the cause of Wissenschaft, the advancement of knowledge. Like the sculpture's look, which becomes blind, the musical tone's "beginning ideality of matter" gives way entirely to the audience's—or the observer's—idealization of art as the sheer interiorization of what was outer. This Hegel announces as poetry, the art of sheer writing. Tone becomes, as he puts it,

> the last exterior material of poetry, is in it no longer the toning feeling itself, but a *sign* meaningless in itself. . . . The *tone* thus becomes *word* as sound articulated in itself, the meaning of which is to indicate presentations and thoughts, in that the negative point to which music progresses now steps forth as the perfectly concrete point, as the point of the spirit, as the self-conscious individual. (13:122)

The "point of the soul," all eyes all over the body, is here proleptically announced as the point of the sign—the *punct*uation—as the sheer negative point of spirit. The "sensuous element" of art, which, Hegel says, "was still immediately at one with interiority in music," is here "separated out" *(losgetrennt)* from the content of consciousness; spirit still uses this minimal point of sensuousness as its expression, "but only as a sign worthless and without content for itself [*doch nur als eines für sich wert- und inhaltlosen Zeichens*]." This emptying out of material leads to the point of emptying the sign: "Tone can accordingly just as well also be a sheer letter [*blosser Buchstabe*], for the hearable is, like the visible, sunk down to the sheer indication of spirit" (13:123).

Art loses shape, material, and sensuous embodiment in the sign, which loses its specificity to become "sheer letter." At the end of Hegel's more extended consideration of the transition from music to poetry, in the third part of his *Aesthetics*, as materiality is being left behind, art's "objectivity exchanges its formerly external reality with an internal one, and receives and maintains [*erhält*] an existence only with consciousness itself, as something sheerly spiritually presented and intuited [*als etwas bloss geistig Vorgestelltes und Angeschautes*]." As "spirit thus becomes objective to itself on its own soil," it "has the linguistic element only as means . . . out of which it has returned, as out of a sheer sign, into itself from the beginning [*aus welcher er als aus einem blossen Zeichen von Hause aus in sich zurückgegangen ist*]" (15:229). This remarkable exit from materiality and reentry into itself, which the sign provides for spirit, is there "from the start," as it were: from the start of the *Aesthetics,* from the start of the fate of the Greek gods, from the start of the symbolic art form and its allegory. When Hegel concludes by saying poetry's "artistic embodiment [*Kunstverkörperung*]" is to be grasped "essentially as a departing from real sensuousness and a putting aside of it," it is this, as he adds, "from which art undertakes to free itself." Poetry—the end of art—is merely "that particular art in which art itself at once begins to dissolve itself and receives and maintains [*erhält*] for philosophic cognition its point of transition to religious presentation as such, as well as to the prose of scholarly thought" (15:234). To learn to read poetry—art—is to begin to learn to read Hegel's scholarly prose: art—poetry—receives and maintains the transition to Hegel: its history. The *end* of this history, as Hegel rehearses one final time, is that poetry "goes so far in the negative handling of its sensuous element that it brings that which is the opposite of heavy, spatial material, [namely,] the tone . . . down to a meaningless sign [*zu einem bedeutungslosen Zeichen*]" (15:235).

When spirit, as scholarly knowledge, knows the end of art as, "from the beginning," the sheer meaningless sign or letter—the sign *of* the letter—it knows reading and also allegory. For allegory, from the beginning of Hegel's *Aesthetics,* was also the allegory of sheer language, of "the separation of subject and predicate, of universality and particularity" (13:512). Allegory's "universal personification is empty, the determinate exteriority only a sign that, taken for itself, has no meaning any longer [*nur ein Zeichen, das für sich genommen keine Bedeutung mehr hat*]" (13:513). The sheer, meaningless sign or letter, at the beginning as at the end—"von Hause aus," a no longer "from the beginning" of a not yet—is Hegel's reading of history. Still the mark of *spirit*'s meaning and therefore necessarily readable and rereadable as the passage and detachment and transience of meaning through its temporality, but *un*readable as what it just *(bloss)* is: the material of a sign. Only at the level of sheer thought as the rote memorization and repetition of the signs of the alphabet could this be known;[31] but then it would be unreadable as narrative, namely, the story that leads from symbolic art's allegory, via classical art's Greek gods, to romantic art's poetry as the progressive (narrative) knowing of what the story means from the start. Instead of knowing this *history*, one (thought itself) would remark only the marks of language as their sheer iterability. Poetry repeats allegory, Wissenschaft repeats poetry; the reading of the fate of the Greek gods by "one" knows this as the containing of the negativity of temporality, which looks beyond but still maintains the marks of death, loss, the grave. To read Hegel reading is to see history becoming the *script* it is and to see the unreadability of the sheer level of the letter of that script, because, strictly speaking, the letters are meaningless, and only the allegoresis is meaningful in its denial, its negativity.

Hegel has remained so unreadable and, simultaneously—by his cleverest ruse—so repeatable because he tells us that in studying and knowing history and art (doing their Wissenschaften) we are always already, from the beginning, reading the sheer signs of thought, or reading Hegel. To lose everything and find Hegel, the sheer signs of thought as the marks of his pages, is to confront history in its allegorical otherness— the leftover bones on at once the near side and the far side of "history." The second part of this study examines allegories of history as such post-Hegelian encounters, denials, and reproductions of the script of history left over by Hegel.

PART TWO

5

Auerbach's *Mimesis:* Figural Structure and Historical Narrative

The flourishing of historicism and literary history, first national and then comparative, in the nineteenth and twentieth centuries is widely known. The subject is an enormous one, and to have tried to survey only the nineteenth-century literary historiography that arises in the wake of Hegel would have expanded the size of the present study by at least a volume.[1] I shall have occasion to allude to some of it in what follows. Instead, the focus in this part will be on exemplary twentieth-century literary historians who, writing after Hegel but within the discursive and scholarly and scientific *(wissenschaftlich)* traditions he represents, variously try to reach behind or step beyond him without altogether escaping the shadow that he casts. Indeed, it may be that the most brilliant achievements of modern literary history reduplicate Hegel in his insights into history and its literary and allegorical structures.

To look from Hegel to Auerbach, Lukács, and Benjamin as part of an inquiry into the fundamental structures and operations of literary historiography may seem quaint and even outmoded in the busy context of American literary studies, with its market-driven cycles of novelty and succession. Its debates about literary studies, like most of those that take place in politically heated arenas, have tended to exaggerate the importance of the new and to underestimate the recently past. So for several decades now—ever since the influence of Lévi-Strauss and the achievements of Roland Barthes began to be felt in American literary studies, and then with increasing vehemence since the name "poststructuralism" got coined by academic journalism (whereafter the bogeyman

An earlier version of this chapter first appeared in *After Strange Texts: The Role of Theory in the Study of Literature,* ed. Gregory Jay and David Miller (University: U. of Alabama P., 1985), pp. 124–45.

got sighted everywhere)—the state of literary scholarship has been held to be under attack from many of the latest tendencies in literary theory. The counterattack has come from neoconservatives, neo-Marxists, and most recently, from some of the "new historicists." Interestingly, the danger of literary theory has often been felt to be toward assumptions and practices of literary history within literary scholarship, and the defense of such historical studies sometimes turns the danger into a celebration. History and historiography can be used to describe the problem, name the stakes, and pose the solution. Thus Frederick Crews, in an ill-tempered public pique, could invoke ironically a false "progress" toward literary theory and at the same time deploy the term and notion of historical-scholarly progress as the true method and goal when he complains that a "progress from historically informed interpretation to vapid attitudinizing could stand for the fate of much 'advanced' academic discourse over the past two decades."[2] Thus Frank Lentricchia's response to new developments in literary study, *After the New Criticism,* organizes itself historically, from its title through its contents; it displays a kind of historiography through its "method" of claiming to uncover the new theorists' real sources and thus the real origins of their problems; and it proposes a revamped historical criticism as its alternative, an option proffered, for instance, in the tabloidlike chapter heading "History or the Abyss."[3] One recalls the comedian's rejoinder to the tired threat "Your money or your life!": "Are those my only choices?"

These sorts of mock-dramatic fateful turns or abysmal straits sound very different from the somewhat resigned, somewhat perplexed tone with which Paul de Man begins his *Allegories of Reading:* with the admission that the book "started out as a historical study and ended up as a theory of reading." He allows that this fact may have some punctual significance as evidence of a moment around him, but he resists a genetic-historical account of its origins as well as any prophecy or lament about the future it presages apart from a dry description of some possible scholarly "results": "I had to shift from historical definition to the problematics of reading. This shift, which is typical of my generation, is of more interest in its results than in its causes. It could, in principle, lead to a rhetoric of reading reaching beyond the canonical principles of literary history which still serve, in this book, as the starting point of their own displacement."[4] De Man did not wish to join in polemical disputes about the virtues or the naivetés of the "canonical principles" of literary history, which disputes he believed to be the locus of blindness without much redeeming insight. And although he could express his sense of inevitability about defenses against and backlashes to the attempts at literary theory, he avoided a self-deluding complacency with regard to his knowledge that such "battles of the books" always go on; he felt about these noisy and often mean-spirited debates, I think, as Jacques Derrida does, that "all of this is not very important, but it must be taken seriously."[5]

As we begin our inquiry into Erich Auerbach's writing of literary history, we might take these occasions of apparent struggles between literary theory and literary history and pause to reflect on Auerbach's ambiguous status as an exemplar of what de Man called "the canonical principles of literary history." For one effective way in which the academic arena of promotions and polemics forgets about the value of the recently past is precisely to canonize it, to put it sufficiently high up to avoid closer scrutiny or unwelcome lessons.[6] Auerbach's *Mimesis* is, of course, not forgotten. It is one of the few historically organized works of literary criticism that still deserves and receives wide readership forty-five years after its publication; in other words, it has stood a certain test of time as historical writing. Nor would I wish to claim for our awareness simply that the book stands as a monument to that postwar phenomenon that may be called (now somewhat retrospectively) "NATO humanism" and survives in the countless "Great Books" courses of our curricula: the organization and teaching of a political-cultural view of the West as a continuous and ultimately consistent body of thought and discourse, the hallmarks of which are historical progress, democratic liberalism, a faith in individual man, and a tolerance of multiple gods. In this context, even as the *Western* literary canon is under pressure from the non-Western literatures and cultures for room in the schools, Auerbach's *Mimesis* may continue to do service as an immensely useful—indeed, uncontested—pedagogic tool in the popular dissemination of literary high culture.

Mimesis's exemplary status should be seen to rest primarily on its particular disciplinary or institutional achievements as a sensible and persuasive literary-historical argument. It established a term and concept—that of the "levels of style" and their mimetic power—as an indispensable element, at once thematic and methodological, in our literary-critical vocabulary. Considered thematically, the notion of levels of style is a key cog—apparently (and by his own word) *the* key cog—in Auerbach's machine of historical continuity.[7] He traces the now well-known path from the classical doctrine of strictly distinguishable levels of style to that doctrine's initial disruption by the *sermo humilis* of the New Testament and its story of Christ's incarnation and passion. His narrative then moves on to the theoretical development of *sermo humilis* under Jerome, Augustine, and the exegetical method of figural interpretation; to the combination of mixed styles and figural representation in

Dante; to the further leveling and inmixing of stylistic differences in such figures as Rabelais and Montaigne, Shakespeare and Schiller; until the final destruction of distinct levels of style is achieved, along with the fullest representation of contemporary social reality, by nineteenth-century French realism. But this enormous accomplishment—the historical argument about the mixing and leveling of levels of style for which *Mimesis* is probably best known—is only one side of the book's critical achievement, its thematic side, that is. The other side is the *methodological* employment of style in Auerbach's work: not the historical theme of style as an object of study, then, but the critical practice of *stylistics* as a surprisingly elastic method. One recalls how almost every chapter begins with a stylistic analysis of a brief passage and how Auerbach can then move from the passage to the work in question, from the work to the author, from the author to the period, and from the period to the history of all periods. This method—one might call it a synecdoche turned into metonymy's revenge—offers as powerful and as potentially influential a critical tool qua method as does Auerbach's argument regarding levels of style and representations of reality qua historical themes; and one may remark that in this metonymic elasticity of stylistics, his method represents philology at its most ambitious, implying a methodological continuum that extends from the smallest etymon or morphological unit to the largest dimensions of the histories of languages and literatures.[8]

No one would wish to contest Auerbach's demonstrable achievements; they are what give *Mimesis* its critical value and make it worthy of critical scrutiny in its own right. Its value may appear more greatly enhanced if it is resituated in its German intellectual milieu. Germany is exemplary of the problem of history and theory in the humanities because the so-called crisis or loss of faith in historicism, including literary history, played itself out earlier, more decisively, and against a more desperate background there than elsewhere in the West.[9] Our own non-Germanic perspective may prevent our recognition of this in any but a melodramatic way that plays on the scandal of the last world war. French historians today are perhaps more positivistic, and more self-assured in their positivism, than ever, and literary history has never really been challenged in the French universities. In America, we have many models—psychohistory, cliometrics, the imported demographics of the *longue durée*, and so on—that professional historians employ with confidence, and the "new historicism" seems to have become highly popular in literary-scholarly circles. But since the war years, there has been suspicion inside and outside of professional German historiography (as resurfaced in the recent *Historikerstreit* but predates it by decades),[10] and there have been virtually no outstanding German literary historians or true believers in the efficacy of literary historiography; instead, there have been "work-immanent" interpreters or philologist-essayists, theoretical or Hegelian analysts, hermeneutic promoters or religious brooders on the one hand and more or less vulgar historical materialists on the other. In fact, one can say that the most ambitious literary-historical projects of the last fifty or sixty years by Germans were undertaken in states of exile: Benjamin's unfinished studies of Baudelaire in the nineteenth century—as we shall see in a later chapter—written in Paris and mailed, version by version, to Horkheimer and Adorno in New York; Curtius's *European Literature and the Latin Middle Ages*, written in what he called an "inner exile" within Hitler's Germany; and, of course, Auerbach's *Mimesis*, written in Istanbul, followed by other historical studies written in this country until his death in 1957. Indeed, Auerbach's *Mimesis* stands outside—in exile from—and yet still against its native background of Germany. The country that believed most profoundly and most productively in the centrality of historical thinking in the nineteenth century—the tradition of Hegel, Ranke, and Dilthey—began to lose this heritage at about the same time that it was being most powerfully absorbed into the larger Western context. As literary history flourished in France, England, Italy, and America from the 1860s to the early twentieth century, Germany experienced the general and devastating critique of historicism delivered by Nietzsche's "Use and Abuse of History" and *Genealogy of Morals* and then by Heidegger's *Being and Time*, as well as such specific and interestingly failed attempts at literary *history* as Nietzsche's *Birth of Tragedy*, Lukács's *Theory of the Novel*, and Benjamin's late studies. Auerbach's *Mimesis* appears as at once the counterexample and the survivor of this decline and fall of German historiography.

Auerbach remained devoted to the traditions of Hegel and historicism—which he explicitly linked—and saw his discipline of Romance philology as their heir: he said of *Mimesis* that "it grew out of the motifs and methods of German *Geistesgeschichte* and philology, and would be unthinkable in any other tradition than in that of German romanticism and Hegel."[11] On the other hand, he sought alternative models for rejuvenated historical studies in Vico's *New Science* as well as in Biblical and medieval figural interpretation.[12] These two concerns—both as objects of historical study and as models for historiography—were in turn associated by Auerbach with the Hegelian problem of the sublation (*Aufhebung*) of historical change. The sublation of historical temporality involves the attempted recuperation of change, loss, negation, and sheer difference through their systematic elevation from contingency to

proper, that is, philosophic, meaning. Historical change would be sublated within the philosophic process into the form and concept of its
meaning; most succinctly, the truth of time—time's true meaning—
would manifest itself as the presence of truth, or absolute knowledge. If
Auerbach could occasionally use a Hegelian vocabulary of sublation to
describe some aspects of Vichian history and figural interpretation, his
understanding of *figura* may also be appreciated as a tropological construction of history that can operate without Hegel's philosophic language, if not necessarily at odds with it. From this perspective we may
then turn to Auerbach's *Mimesis* to examine the construction of its history and the figural structure of its narrative.

Auerbach's understanding of figural interpretation begins as a historical and philological thesis about *figura*.[13] *Figura* could not have developed its exegetical and representational meaning and power without
having first extended beyond its service as a philosophic term for the
Latin translation of the Greek *schema* and *typos*. From this, *figura* becomes a rhetorical term for the verbal distinctions between the real and
the apparent or seeming, the straightforward and the stylized, the
model and the copy, the true and the concealing—most basically, the
distinction between the literal and the figurative. Consequently, one
cannot raise the objection that Auerbach's historical understanding of
figural interpretation might have little to do with the theory of *figurative*
language; on the contrary, *figural* in Auerbach's historical sense is
grounded upon *figurative* in our conventional sense. A second crucial
point may be made by juxtaposing several of Auerbach's definitional
remarks on *figura* in the sense of figural Biblical interpretation as it was
developed by Tertullian, Jerome, Augustine, and other early church fathers. On the one hand, the relational understanding of the *figura* as an
event (in the Old Testament and in history more broadly) that is prefigural or prophetic of a spiritual event and meaning (in the New Testament and in Christian or salvation history more broadly) that would
fulfill the figure[14]—this relation between the figure and its fulfillment
must be, Auerbach insists, between two equally real, concrete, historical events. "Real historical figures are to be interpreted spiritually, but
the interpretation points to a carnal, hence historical fulfillment—for
the truth has become history or flesh" (F, 34).

> Figural interpretation establishes a connection between two events or
> persons, the first of which signifies not only itself but also the second,
> while the second encompasses or fulfills the first. . . . Both, being real
> events or figures, are within time, within the stream of historical life.
> Only the understanding of the two persons or events is a spiritual act, but
> this spiritual act deals with concrete events whether past, present, or fu-

ture . . . since promise and fulfillment are real historical events, which either have happened . . . or will happen. (F, 53)

And in a third quotation, this time from the epilogue to *Mimesis*, we read that "an occurrence on earth signifies not only itself but at the same time another, which it predicts or confirms, without prejudice to the power of its concrete reality here and now" (555). Auerbach's main point regarding figural interpretation is precisely that the "figural schema permits both its poles—the figure and its fulfillment—to retain the characteristics of concrete historical reality . . . so that figure and fulfillment—although the one 'signifies' the other—have a significance which is not incompatible with their being real" (195). But if this is his main point, Auerbach must also recognize that the second pole, event, or sign in the relational structure is necessarily privileged over the first. He writes: "The fulfillment is often designated as *veritas* . . . and the figure correspondingly as *umbra* or *imago*"; but against the obvious disjunction and difference thus established between one event or sign as truthful, the other as merely shadow or image (or, in another patristic formulation, as merely *imitatio veritatis*, "the imitation of truth"), Auerbach then immediately adds: "But both shadow and truth are abstract only in reference to the meaning first concealed, then revealed; they are concrete in reference to the things or persons which appear as vehicles of the meaning" (F, 34). Truth and its shadow or foreshadowing are each concretely situated in the real, historical events that are the "vehicles of their meaning," and this despite the implied tension in the concept of *figura* as a relation between two signs both of which are to remain real and historical but the latter of which is to be the truth of the former's mere prefiguration.

The character of this tension may be further indicated by reference to two more aspects of Auerbach's essay "Figura." For one thing, Auerbach makes explicit the tropological, or more precisely, the *figurative*, structure that underwrites this interpretive ambivalence between figural truth and its mere prefiguration:

> Beside the opposition between *figura* and fulfillment or truth there appears another, between *figura* and *historia; historia* or *littera* is the literal sense or the event related; *figura* is the same literal meaning or event in reference to the fulfillment cloaked in it, and this fulfillment is *veritas*, so that *figura* becomes a middle term between *littera-historia* and *veritas*. (F, 47)

In other words, the tension between prefiguration and fulfillment— wherein the latter, as truth, would make the former be less than true, thereby endangering its value as concrete, historical reality—is redupli-cated in, or more accurately, is already implied in, the *figurative* struc-ture of figural interpretation: one event, the *figura*, is historically literal but interpretively figural; the second, fulfilling event, also a historical event, is figuratively the truth *(veritas)* of the *figura*. Thus, there is al-ready a first opposition between literal and figural in the *figura* or pre-figuration itself; this then reappears as an opposition between the *figura* as historical sign and the later figural truth *(veritas)* that "fulfills" it, or that reveals the "true" figurative meaning of that first figure.

The last aspect to which I would call attention in Auerbach's "Fig-ura" essay regards this same point, and helps to move our discussion back toward *Mimesis* and the question of its historiography. Auerbach must repeatedly attempt to explain how the fulfillment of a previous figure can avoid annihilating the value of the former's historical reality; this difficulty is sometimes suspended in his recourse to Hegelian lan-guage, as when he says that the fulfillment "fulfills and annuls [*erfüllt und aufhebt*]" the figure but also is "unveiling and preserving [*enthüllend und bewahrend*]" it (F, 51 and 72). The initial *figura* has the double structure of *littera-historia and* spiritual meaning, although that meaning is not fulfilled until the advent of the *veritas* (say, Moses as a historical figure and as the sign of the Christ to come). Within the *figura*, then, the operation of canceling-and-preserving the literal-historical event in the production of a spiritual sign seems to obey the economy of Hegelian sublation. In the same manner, the *veritas* or fulfillment of this historical *figura* follows the pattern of the Hegelian "conceptual comprehension" *(Begreifen)* of phenomenal and historical experience, and so the *veritas* cancels-and-preserves the historical reality of the previous *figura* in fash-ioning truth through this elevation-and-negation. Yet that initial *figura*, as we have seen, itself displays the double structure of the figurative sign; that is, it is both literal and figurative. What would it mean for the *veritas* to cancel-and-preserve this sublation of the literal into the figu-rative that occurs *within* the very *figura* that the *veritas* fulfills? What is sublated, what is canceled-and-yet-preserved, is precisely this first tro-pological sublation of the historical, the very double structure already at play within the beginning *figura*. Whatever the prior historical event might be, when it is taken to prefigure some later meaning, it becomes doubled (literal and figural), but the later "fulfillment" of the former's prefigural meaning must at once preserve the former's figural charac-ter—as the latter's sign, after all, as its prefiguration—*and* cancel it, render it nothing but a mere *littera*, annihilate it into a non-thing, a dead letter or a corpse. This is, I shall now argue, the structure and operation of *Mimesis:* history, as the historical reality of what happened, including the history of its realistic literary representation, is the *historia et littera* that, rendered figurative in the hands of Auerbach's figural interpretation, must at one and the same time perpetuate or preserve its figural character in a later fulfillment and, *as this very fulfillment,* cancel itself to the extent that it is then merely the dead letter of some other figural meaning of "history."

I take as the operative instances of *Mimesis*'s literary history the chapters on Dante and Flaubert. They are privileged by Auerbach in his epilogue as the two decisive moments, medieval and modern, in realism's overcoming of the doctrine of the levels of style (554–55); but as I shall show, Dante and Flaubert are also, in the exact language and texture of Auerbach's chapters, related to one another as prefiguration and fulfillment.[15] When Dante is said by Auerbach to fulfill the structure of figural *representation* implied in the Christian and medieval concept of *figura,* and thereby to overcome the very concept that prizes the fulfillment over the literal figure, the spiritual truth over the literal historical event or life, he is also seen to carry over the structure of *figura* toward Flaubert, so that Dante prefigures the "real" fulfillment of Western realism in nineteenth-century French realism: Dante becomes the figure for Flaubert's truth. But if the fulfillment of figural interpretation by Dante is supposed to preserve and value the real *historia et littera* of the fulfilled figure, then when Flaubert fulfills the *figura* of Dante, there occurs necessarily the cancellation of Dante's apparent "truth" (now mere prefiguration or *figura*) and the revelation of a different *veritas* behind that "first" truth of Dante's fulfillment. This new *veritas* would be the realization of a lived *historia et littera.* There are, in other words, three figural moments in this story of Auerbach's about Dante and Flaubert: Dante's realism as figural fulfillment, Flaubert's realism as such, and the figural relation between the two.

Readers of the Dante chapter will recall the exquisite stylistic analysis that is so patiently sustained in the initial treatment of the encounter between the Dante-pilgrim and Farinata and Cavalcante in canto 10 of *Inferno* (it is perhaps the best such example of applied stylistics in *Mimesis,* and certainly among the best studies of Dante's style that we have in Dante criticism). After Auerbach recounts the nearly "incomprehensible miracle" and "unimaginable" achievement of Dante's mixing of styles in this passage, and after his discussion accounts more largely for the mixture of the sublime and the trivial or comic that the *Commedia* represents, his discourse turns thematic:

> The *Commedia* . . . [is] a literary work which imitates reality and in which all imaginable spheres of reality appear: past and present, sublime

grandeur and vile vulgarity, history and legend, tragic and comic occurrences, man and nature. . . . Yet, in respect to an attempt at the elevated
style, all these things are not so new and problematic as is Dante's undis-
guised incursion into the realm of a real life neither selected nor preor-
dained by aesthetic criteria. And indeed, it is this contact with real life
which is responsible for all the verbal forms. (189)

Auerbach now begins to argue that the *Commedia*, with its subject of
the *status animarum post mortem*, represents "God's design in active fulfillment," and yet these dead souls, represented as judged for eternity
by God, "produce the impression not that they are dead—though that
is what they are—but alive." "Here," Auerbach continues,

we face the astounding paradox of what is called Dante's realism. Imitation of reality is imitation of the sensory experience of life on earth—
among the most essential characteristics of which would seem to be its
possessing a history, its changing and developing. Whatever degree of
freedom the imitating artist may be granted in his work, he cannot be
allowed to deprive reality of this characteristic, which is its very essence.
But Dante's inhabitants of the three realms lead a "changeless existence."
[Auerbach borrows here a phrase from Hegel's *Ästhetik*, "wechselloses
Dasein," and continues with Hegel as he adds:] Yet into this changeless
existence Dante "plunges the living world of human action and endur-
ance and more especially of individual deeds and destinies." (191)

As Auerbach characterizes it, the existence of the personae is "final and
eternal, but they are not devoid of history. . . . We have left the earthly
sphere behind, . . . and yet we encounter concrete appearance and concrete occurrence" (191). Though not yet named here (as Hegel *is*), the
basis of Auerbach's Dante interpretation is obviously his understanding
of figural interpretation, already foreshadowed in his much earlier book
on Dante and introduced in the last section of his "Figura" essay.[16] The
characters are more themselves, more fulfilled in "reveal[ing] the nature
proper to each," here in their state of eternal judgment than they were
in their real, historical lives: "We behold an intensified image of the
essence of their being, . . . behold it in a purity and distinctness which
could never for one moment have been possible during their lives upon
earth" (192). Auerbach first explains these claims within the context of
the poem's theological thematics: God has judged Farinata and Cavalcante, and "not until He has pronounced that judgment has He fully
perfected it and wholly revealed it to sight." (192). But when Auerbach
then writes of Cavalcante that "it is not likely that in the course of his
earthly existence he ever felt his faith in the spirit of man, his love for
the sweetness of light and for his sons so profoundly, or expressed it so

arrestingly, as now, when it is all in vain" (192–93), this statement is saved from absurdity (a "man" more real in literature than in life?) by two particular facts: that Cavalcante, like Farinata, was indeed a real, historical personage; and that the theological thematics of Dante's poem do indeed confirm Auerbach's judgment that the characters' lives are more fulfilled in God's eternal world than they could have been in their real, earthly, historical lives.

Here, with the examples of human beings represented as more real and more fully themselves after death than in life, thereby retaining "earthly historicity in [the] beyond" as "the basis of God's judgment [and] the absolute realization of a particular earthly personality in the place definitively assigned to it" (193), Auerbach finally and explicitly announces the figural "conception of history" as "the foundation for Dante's realism, this realism projected into changeless eternity" (194): "It is precisely [the] 'full notion of their proper individuality' which the souls attain in Dante's beyond by virtue of God's judgment; and specifically, they attain it as an actual reality, which is in keeping with the figural view. . . . [The dead in Dante represent] the relation of figure fulfilled . . . in reference to their own past life on earth" (196). Auerbach then refers to that feature of the figural conception which I mentioned above, the privileging of the fulfillment as truth over the figure as mere prefiguration: "Both figure and fulfillment possess . . . the character of actual historical events and phenomena. The fulfillment possesses it in greater and more intense measure, for it is, compared with the figure, *forma perfectior.*" "This explains," Auerbach concludes, "the overwhelming realism of Dante's beyond" (197).

But with the phrase "*overwhelming* realism of Dante's beyond," something is set in motion, as if to spill over the bounds of Auerbach's argumentative structure. For the remaining pages now stand this thematic and theologically orthodox understanding on its head as Auerbach goes on to preserve the literal and historical reality *beyond* the realism of its spiritual fulfillment in Dante's depiction of the afterlife. Auerbach asserts that in personae such as Farinata and Cavalcante, "never before has this realism been carried so far; never before . . . has so much art and so much expressive power been employed to produce an almost painfully immediate expression of the earthly reality of human beings" (199). Beyond the thematic and theological justification, then, Auerbach refocuses on Dante's style and its "expressive power."

> Figure surpasses fulfillment, or more properly: the fulfillment serves to bring out the figure in still more impressive relief. . . . What actually moves us is not that God has damned them, but that the one [Farinata] is

unbroken and the other [Cavalcante] mourns so heartrendingly for his son and the sweetness of the light. (200)

In other words, as fulfillment overcomes or surpasses its *figura*'s literal, historical, *real* life, it also preserves and even elevates that *figura* to the point where it surpasses its fulfillment. Auerbach seizes upon this counter-surpassing of the fulfillment (the thematic, theological representation of divine judgment) by the *figura* (the stylistic realism of Dante's representation of the characters' lives in the afterlife) to conclude with three crucial points. First, this "impression" of the realism of life beyond its thematic fulfillment ("the listener is all too occupied by the figure in the fulfillment," he writes) "is so rich and so strong that its manifestations force their way into the listener's soul *independently of any interpretation.*" Second, "the principle, rooted in the divine order, of the indestructibility of the whole historical and individual man turns *against* that order, makes it subservient to its own purposes, and obscures it. The image of man eclipses the image of God. Dante's work made man's Christian-figural being a reality, and destroyed it in the very process of realizing it." Third, as if the previous point were not Hegelian enough in its realization-cum-negation, Auerbach closes the chapter by saying: "In [the] fulfillment, the figure becomes independent. . . . We are given to see, in the realm of timeless being, the history of man's inner life and unfolding [*wir erfahren . . . im zeitlosen Sein das innergeschichtliche Werden*]" (201, 202).

These three closing points of Auerbach's thus expound two kinds of "independence" enacted by a quasi-dialectical *Aufhebung* on the far side of figural representation: the lived, historical realism of that figural representation of an ahistorical, eternal afterlife becomes so powerful as to be "independent of any interpretation"; the *figura* as such consequently becomes "independent" of its spiritual meaning in fulfillment. Both of these effects are brought about by the "dialectic" of figural representation itself: an "obscuring," "eclipsing," or *concealing* of revelation *in* revelation; a "destruction" of fulfilled truth *in* its "realization"; the figure free of fulfillment *in* the fulfillment itself; or the literal and historical— the real—returning *in* its having been turned into the figural and ahistorical or eternal. Auerbach's figural understanding of Dante can therefore be summarized as follows: the historical reality (the past lives of real, historical characters) is made to serve as the *figura* for its fulfillment in divine judgment, but the representation of this fulfillment by its *figura* is so realistic—more real than life, history, reality itself—that the fulfillment becomes in turn a figure whose fulfillment is the realism of, but now *independent of,* the figural representation; the fulfillment of that

historical reality itself in its realism. *Figura* in its Christian, spiritual interpretation thus becomes lived reality "independent of any interpretation."

It should already be clear how this conclusion to Auerbach's chapter on Dante foreshadows his treatment of French realism as the fulfillment of Western literature's development toward the objective representation of contemporary social reality. Briefly, the real, historical world whose representation is promised by Dante's achievement (the realism promised by reality set free) no longer receives its literary representation *within* the domain of figural fulfillment—the spiritual setting of the afterlife in Dante's *Commedia*—but rather is now fulfilled by the realism of the French novelist, a realism not of an afterlife larger and more real than life as *lived* but of the real social-historical lived world itself. No longer would there be a *décalage* between figure and fulfillment; rather, the real, historical world of nineteenth-century France will be both *littera* and *figura* for the novels, the realism of which—like Dante's realism—will now be that literal figure's fulfillment within the very letters of literal figures. Such realistic representation of historical reality is also, then, *Mimesis*'s fulfillment of the *figura* of Dante in Flaubert. Most generally, this unfolding of the "independence" of the *figura* from its fulfillment and from its spiritualist interpretation is, in Auerbach's literary history, the enactment of Western history according to a double-edged structure of secularization. That is, the argument for the historical secularization of literary realism is coextensive with a writing of literary history according to the model of figural representation, the model of *figura* (Dante as medieval figural realism) and fulfillment (Flaubert as modern social-historical realism). Thus, a history of literary secularization is a figural writing of history, a *literary* history with the accent on the adjective, an *allegory* of history as its own literalization.[17]

But the matter is not this simple. The tensions between *figura* and fulfillment are between the literal *figura* (Dante's liberated realism of life) and the figural meaning of literal representation (the letters of French realism made figurative of a higher meaning in Auerbach's interpretive construction of Flaubert's place in history). We need to investigate these tensions more closely now by turning to the chapter on French realism. In striking antithesis to the beginning of the Dante chapter, it begins without a word of stylistic commentary, offering instead several pages of historical information on 1830 and the preceding years as background material necessary for an understanding of a passage extracted from Stendhal's *Le Rouge et le noir*. But this antithesis is not at all surprising; it is rather the first sign of the chapter's figural

relation to the Dante chapter. If there one began and ended with literary *style* as the locus of realism, prior to and finally beyond the poem's thematics of fulfilled judgment, then here one begins with real social-historical detail as the beginning *and* end, *figura* and fulfillment, of the novel's realism. But a second contrast to the Dante chapter is perhaps more genuinely surprising, and it foreshadows things to come. While the Dante chapter began and ended by extolling the passionate and vital expression of the characters' fullest possible lives—"We cannot but admire Farinata and weep with Cavalcante" (200)—here Auerbach begins with a discussion of boredom and negativity:

> No ordinary boredom . . . [no] fortuitous personal dullness, [but] a phenomenon politically and ideologically characteristic of the Restoration period . . . an atmosphere of pure convention, of limitation, of constraint and lack of freedom . . . mendaci[ty] . . . [people] no longer themselves believ[ing] in the thing they present . . . talk[ing] of nothing but the weather . . . unashamed baseness . . . fear . . . pervading boredom. (455–56)

This is all in the first paragraph. What has happened here, where the history of realistic Western literature is to reach its triumphant fulfillment? When, after sections on Stendhal and Balzac, the chapter finally arrives at its treatment of Flaubert, the discussion focuses immediately, for the third time and again in the first paragraph, on Emma Bovary's situation of "mediocrity . . . boredom . . . unrest and despair . . . cheerlessness, unvaryingness, grayness, staleness, airlessness, and inescapability" (483). What has happened to Auerbach's argument? Here his analysis must be followed in precise detail. In remarking upon the selected passage—Emma and her husband at dinner in Tostes ("toute l'amertume de l'existence lui semblait servie sur son assiette")—Auerbach first comments that the reader "sees [directly] only Emma's inner state; he sees what goes on at the meal indirectly, from within her state, in the light of her perception" (483). But if the reader sees through Emma, Auerbach then notes that Emma sees through Charles:

> When Emma looks at him and sees him sitting there eating, he becomes the actual cause of the *elle n'en pouvait plus,* because everything else that arouses her desperation—the gloomy room, the commonplace food, the lack of a tablecloth, the hopelessness of it all—appears to her, and through her to the reader also, as something that is connected with him, that emanates from him, and that would be entirely different if he were different from what he is. (484)

With this reference to Charles as the "actual cause" of what Emma sees, and of what the reader therefore also sees, one must ask whether it is

Auerbach's own voice or his imitation of Flaubert's *style indirect libre*—
that is, of Emma's consciousness—that says all "would be entirely different if he were different from what he is." Is it Emma, in the plot of
the novel, wishing Charles were different so that her life might be different as well? Or is it Auerbach imagining that if Charles were different,
Emma would be, too, and the reader—Auerbach—would see a different world? The question is especially germane, since the suggestion of
a possibly different life that could be available for representation recalls
that larger, fuller, more vital life represented in Farinata and Cavalcante
by Dante.

The next paragraph answers our question, and does so with a sentence I find the most bizarre in all of *Mimesis*. Auerbach begins by re-
capitulating: "We are first given Emma and then the situation through
her," but not in "a simple representation of the content of Emma's consciousness, of *what* she feels *as* she feels it"; rather, "the light which
illuminates the picture proceeds from her, [but] she is yet herself part
of the picture. . . . Here it is not Emma who speaks, but the writer"
(484). Indeed, if the reader gets the scene through Emma, and Emma
gets it through Charles, the reader actually gets both through Flaubert.
Well enough; but then—in contrast to Flaubert's felicitously phrased
expressions, says Auerbach—Emma

> would not be able to sum it all up in this way . . . if she wanted to express
> it, it would not come out like that; she has neither the intelligence nor the
> cold candor of self-accounting necessary for such a formulation. To be
> sure, there is nothing of Flaubert's life in these words, but only Emma's;
> Flaubert does nothing but bestow the power of mature expression upon
> the material which she affords, in its complete subjectivity. (484)

Auerbach's remarks about Emma's lack of self-expression, "intelligence," and "candor" still conform to the critic's conventional thematic
commentary on the representation of a character; but then he speaks of
her "life" and her "subjective material." And now the bizarre sentence:
"If Emma could do this herself, she would no longer be what she is, she
would have outgrown herself and thereby saved herself" (484).

"She would no longer be what she is." She would no longer be
Emma, the unhappy and doomed heroine of Flaubert's novel. Perhaps—surely in part—Auerbach means she would be a different character, less unhappy, less doomed. But who is "she"? "She" is not, as
Farinata or Cavalcante was, a once real and historical person. "She" is
the "real" Emma Bovary who is not. A realistic representation of a fictional character is taken by Auerbach as a person—a "complete subjectivity"—who might have been otherwise than she is, that unhappy fic-

tion. And to be real—"she would no longer be what she is"—would be to develop ("outgrow herself") and to be fulfilled ("save herself").

I can now move rapidly to my conclusion. In Dante, realistic representation translates historical lives into the apotheosis of their actuality, until this fullness of representation saves them from their thematic depiction as dead souls in the afterlife of hell; to recall Auerbach's formulation, they "produce the impression not that they are dead—though that is what they are—but alive" (191). The *figurae* of their thematic fulfillment surpassed and canceled their own spiritual fulfillment and were *refigured* as literal, living, historical figures. Now, with Flaubert, the opposite occurs. The power of the realistic representation of a fictional life set in real, social-historical circumstances appears to Auerbach as the unfulfilled promise of a more spiritually real life that might have been—really, historically, literally. That absent fulfillment would "save" Emma, who is otherwise an inauthentic, unfulfilled, fictional yet realistic *figura*. To adapt Auerbach's phrasing, she produces the impression that she is not fiction—though that is what she is—but real. Her *figura*, as the letters on the pages of *Madame Bovary* producing (signifying, representing) the figure of a real person, would be fulfilled (surpassed, overcome, canceled) in her becoming more (but also less) than she is—in her becoming *disfigured* as a figure (a representation of a reality) and being made literal, historical, real. The move, in other words, from Dante to Flaubert is from real historical life transformed into a literature that is more than a reality to a realistic fictional life transformed into a reality that would be more, should be more, but is not: *plus de réalité*—more, and no more, reality.

Thus, when Auerbach moves, on the next page, to speak of Flaubert's artistic practice, he speaks of "selecting events and translating them into language" as if they were already there, like real, historical lives or a real history, a real past; and he adds: "This is done in the conviction that every event, if one is able to express it purely and completely, interprets itself far better and more completely than any opinion appended to it could do." This exact echo of the claim made for Dante—realism "independent of any interpretation"—is made here in the absence of an authorial judgment: the self-sufficient truth of verbal representation, or what Auerbach calls "a profound faith in the truth of language" (486). But the truth of language here, its *veritas, is* the fulfillment or unveiling of Flaubert's *figure*—Emma—as *letters;* not as a literal, historical being ("a complete subjectivity"), but as *litterae* or letters. The truth of literary realism becomes the revelation of the falseness, the fictionality, of its tropological or figural representation in and through literal letters.

The truth of modern realism is the "no more reality" that disfigures the "more reality" figured in the representation of a person *who is not* except as a *personage* who is "her" letters. It is this truth that surfaces in the final pages of Auerbach's chapter, less as a guilty conscience, perhaps, than as a guilty unconscious. For as his language—in paraphrasing a letter of Flaubert's—still echoes that which he used to praise Dante ("subjects are seen as God sees them, in their true essence" [487]), this truth without interpretation is not that of the plenitude of lived, historical lives but rather that of "a chronic discomfort, which completely rules an entire life. . . . The novel is the representation of an entire human existence which has no issue. . . . Nothing happens, but that nothing has become a heavy, oppressive something" (488). He insists that as with Dante, this interpretation is immanent ("The interpretation of the situation is contained in its description" [489]), but he then goes on, not in praise, but in a final, mounting tirade, full of the negativity we saw in the chapter's first paragraph: Emma and Charles

> have nothing in common, and yet they have nothing of their own, for the sake of which it would be worthwhile to be lonely. For, privately, each of them has a silly, false world, which cannot be reconciled with the reality of his situation, and so they both miss the possibilities life offers them. What is true of these two, applies to almost all the other characters in the novel; each of the many mediocre people who act in it has his own world of mediocre and silly stupidity . . . each is alone, none can understand another, or help another to insight; there is no common world of men, because it could only come into existence if many should find their way to their own proper reality, the reality which is given to the individual—which then would be also the true common reality. . . . [But instead it is] one-sided, ridiculous, painful, and . . . charged with misunderstanding, vanity, futility, falsehood, and stupid hatred. (489)

A "silly, false world" that is not reconcilable with reality and misses life's possibility; stupidity and nothingness, falsehood and misunderstanding, as "what is true" of the characters; and the absence of "true reality" due to the absence of the characters' "own proper reality, the reality given to the individual." This, then, is the fulfillment of Dante's promise of the history of Western realism: representation without reality or so much as the possibility of life; truth as falsehood and nothingness; characters lacking both fulfillment *and* prefiguration of "their own proper reality" except in their figural fulfillment as signifying letters.

Alphabetic characters of inanimate material? Dead letters? *Litterae* as the corpse, the heavy, oppressive nothing of *historia*? When Auerbach attempts to turn, at the end of the paragraph I have been quoting, from his dyspeptic tantrum—"In his book the world consists of pure stupidity, which completely misses true reality, so that the latter should properly not be discoverable in it at all" (489)—he attempts to make this turn with a sudden epiphany: "Yet [true reality] is there; it is in the writer's language, which unmasks the stupidity by pure statement; language, then, has criteria for stupidity and thus also has a part in that reality of the 'intelligent' which otherwise never appears in the book" (489). Auerbach's phrasing here is precisely right even as his meaning is profoundly wrong. The "true reality" that cannot be fulfilled or revealed in realistic representation—for what is revealed is falsehood and nothingness—is nonetheless to be revealed and fulfilled somewhere; but if it is not in the realistic representation, it is not "*in* the writer's language" or "*in* the book" either, as if it were some thematic or semantic representation of meaning to be revealed, fulfilled, and made real in an act of understanding.[18] Rather, it *is* the language and *is* the book: the "true reality" of the letters that unmask—literally, "re-veal"—their representational stupidity and nothingness by their pure statement, as if to say, we are the *littera* and its *figura*, *historia* and its meaning, which now fulfill and reveal the history of our representations of reality by the pure statement of its stupidity and nothingness—its corpse.

And what can we draw from this "exemplary" case of literary history as the literalization of historical letters? The corpse of Flaubert's language is one thing, perhaps the most perfect spine of representational *vraisemblance* in the corpus of Western prose; as for the language of Auerbach's *Mimesis*, we should not bury it but honor it. I have tried to demonstrate how the figural model of interpretation and representation structures and operates upon the historical narrative of Auerbach's study of literary realism. Literally the figural model structures, and is operative within, his narrative of the two-tiered triumph of the representation of lived, historical reality in Dante and Flaubert. But figuratively Auerbach's historiography disfigures the literal narrative and its *figura* by fulfilling them as the letters in a *literary* history, letters that represent the stupidity and nothingness of the real history that thought itself, in this literary mode, to be more real—but is, alas, no more real—than its representation as letters. In its intellectual context, this is a Hegelian allegory: the allegory of historical meaning (as phenomenal appearance) being preserved-and-canceled in its scholarly representation as Wissenschaft, left behind in the uncovering of its truth and yet retained as the mere letter of this significance. Left long enough, the corpse would show its Hegelian bones.

We may understand this as one kind of allegory of history, what may be called the allegory of the *nihilism*—the negativism, the "nothingness," the "stupidity"—of historical meaning, the meaning of historiography being that historical reality is canceled or annihilated in its fulfillment in literature, including those genres called history and literary history. This means that for Auerbach to write and think the historical after Hegel is to enter into allegory, to enact a literary and specifically a rhetorical or tropological mode of discourse. It is fortuitous, not merely accidental, that Auerbach's title and object of study is *mimesis*, for the insight that lies therein is the same one that I have tried to expose within the book's historical narrative: history itself is mimesis, the representation of the dead past, and the figurative structure that appears when history is "done" by a literary scholar is already implied in the rhetorical structure of its ontology, indeed of its name. The term names two notions, ontologically opposed as origin and representation, and the confusion between the two unfolds whenever historical narrative is attempted. "History" is literally the past—*die Geschichte* as what happened, *das Geschehene*—and figuratively its meaning as the history that is thought and written—*die Geschichte* as narrative (*Erzählung*) representing *die Geschichte*. And this history—what we conventionally intend when we use and think the term in either of its senses—must always reduce history as an ontological object into a dead letter, so that it might be "meaningful," the literal sign for an allegorical meaning.

An alternative allegory of history that suggests itself might then be called the allegory of the *eschatology* of historical meaning; in this model, the meaning of historiography would be, not *in* the mimetic representation, but rather the presentation of reality itself, as history, in its very ongoing deferral of fulfillment—reality preserved, that is, as signs to be read, preserved as literature to be read, including history and literary history. But to speak of alternative allegories of history is misleading if it suggests any great choice in the matter; the meaning of this study of Auerbach's historiography, like that of Hegel's, may perhaps be that the letter always grasps, even to the point of throttling, the figure of its own historical life. Rather, the alternation between allegories of history—nihilism or eschatology, dead meaning or meaning deferred—might arrive with the aftermath of Hegelian historiography and be the very structure of history after Hegel. That one pole should be Auerbach's nihilism might be borne in mind the next time the values of literary history, "canonical" or otherwise, would be blithely contrasted to the supposed sins of recent "nihilistic" literary theory.

6

Nietzsche's *Ursprünge*, Lukács's Leaps

Son le leggi d'abisso così rotte?
—Dante, *Purgatorio* 1.46

T o speak of Nietzsche's *Ursprünge*, or origins, does not mean to discuss his sources or his beginnings. *Quellen*, the sources from which a power flows, are what Nietzsche repeatedly cut off. The sources that Nietzsche found, and identified with, at his beginnings—a certain Hellenism, Schopenhauer, Wagner—all were denied, dried up, *Quellen* disqualified; and so does *Quellenforschung* with regard to Nietzsche come up short and become a self-consuming exercise. Sources for Nietzsche become that which does not lead to the outcome that rejects these very sources. So too with beginnings, with *Anfänge* or with *Geburten*. A beginning, especially an organic one, a birth, would yield a genealogy and thereby a heritage and a destiny—the heritage of an ancestry, the destiny of an end, and therefore also a middle, in short, the continuity from birth to destiny, by way of the middle and the *Mittel* of history. A history that unfolds, develops, from origins to beginnings or births to outcomes as inherent goals—this, too, Nietzsche denies. "*Ursprung* and *Zweck*, origin and goal . . . two problems that are, or ought to be, separate" (*Zur Genealogie der Moral*, 2, 12; 2:817).[1]

An *Ursprung* poses another matter. It is not the natural metaphor of a source, nor the organic metaphor of a birth, but a concept and operation that intervene as and so that those powerful metaphors of continuous unfolding (may) become the functioning images they conventionally are. It would be like the "zero" before the counting with fingers begins at "one"; like the radical moment (to be seen again in Lukács) in between a supposed *Grund* or *Boden* and the *radix* or root that would be planted and grown there. It would be like a metaphor for such appearances, growths, development, before they appear as natural or organic images: as such, a model of metaphor in a pre-imagistic function. Our conceptual tradition conventionally insists upon an origin—mythic, ontological, or metaphysical—for beginnings and sources, for the birthplaces for further organic developments, genealogies, growths. Hegel characterizes such an "original" moment before a birth: after a gradual prelude, there appears a break, a leap between such developmental time and a first bolt or *Blitz*—an *Ursprung*, the leap between an origin and a beginning, between "zero" and "one."[2] Hegel's retrospective imagery for the moment when the light dawns and, with a flash, imagery begins—for an origin—responds perhaps to the positing (*setzende*) power of the Book of Genesis's *fiat lux*. Nietzsche also comes to respond to these sources: the *Ursprung* as *Urstrahl*, the lightning bolt of an original thinking and saying, a discourse of origins—first leaps into beginnings, stories, and histories—as a critique of continuities, genealogies, histories.

The theme of Nietzsche's investigation and treatment of *Ursprünge* as a critique of all forms of discourse that begin with beginnings and develop from there is widespread in his *oeuvre* and interwoven with many others. Any beginning that could be chosen would risk misconstruing the problem of the relation between origins and beginnings according to Nietzsche. Chronologically, that is, historically and developmentally—the very forms of thought against which Nietzsche's critique is often directed—one could begin with Nietzsche's critique of truth by way of a critique of its origin in language: his 1873 essay "On Truth and Lie in an Extra-Moral Sense" ("Über Wahrheit und Lüge im aussermoralischen Sinn"). And thus one would also begin with his contemporary work, *The Birth of Tragedy from out of the Spirit of Music (Die Geburt der Tragödie aus dem Geiste der Musik):* a birth from out of an origin. Such a "history" would run from Nietzsche's early works to, say, his critique of origins and history in *The Genealogy of Morals*, where reconstructed origins are used for arguments against received histories, and partial histories for arguments against purported origins. There, "for historical study [*Historie*] of any kind," Nietzsche says that

> the cause of the origination [*Entstehung*] of a thing and its eventual utility, its actual employment and place in a system of goals, lie worlds apart; whatever exists, having somehow come into being, is again and again reinterpreted to new ends, taken over anew, transformed [*umgebildet*] and redirected for a new purpose by some power superior to it . . . the *utility* of any[thing] . . . means nothing with regard to its origination. . . . The "development" [*"Entwicklung"*] of a thing . . . is thus by no means its *progressus* toward an end, even less a logical *progressus*. (2, 12; 2:817–18)

And yet for all his skeptical finesse regarding historical origination, Nietzsche still makes ample use of origination as a structural condition, prior to any histories and determining all: in his argument for a process before particular histories, he claims that a "time-before [*Vorzeit*] is at all times present or may be once again" (2, 9; 2:812).

The goal of this chapter, then, cannot be a historical or otherwise developmental overview of Nietzsche's critical but critically inconsistent views of historicism and histories. Such an overview would have to begin very early, with the second of the *Untimely Meditations (Unzeitgemässe Betrachtungen)*, "The Use and Abuse of History for Life" ("Vom Nutzen und Nachteil der Historie für das Leben")—which proves surprisingly uninteresting³—and end very late, with fragments and aphorisms from *The Will to Power* and the *Nachlass*. In the context of the present study, and the moment it has reached, our interest is less in the history of Nietzsche's critique of history, or the ends and goals of his attempts to put an end to goal-oriented and otherwise "progressive" historicisms, than in his argument about origins in their critical relations to the beginnings of histories, stories, or arguments. But this interest of ours should guard against reverting to another story or history. Just such an evolutionary history of Nietzsche's theme of origins, from its beginnings to its unfolding, would remask the very problem he seeks to *unmask:* the groundless grounding of a beginning, development, and end in an origin so-called, that is, a historical source and destiny. For history, according to Nietzsche, can be *historia abscondita:* history still hidden, obscured, waiting to be "discovered," made original *(Die Fröhliche Wissenschaft,* 34; 2:62). As one of the most powerful theorists of what today is called the history of reception, Nietzsche cautions—especially today, when he would be claimed as the "origin" of so much— against the self-evidential guise of any so-called historical account.

Making nonetheless an initial step toward an origin, Nietzsche's critique of truth by way of its origination in language itself begins with an account of the origin of language. And the language last quoted from the *Genealogy,* that of *Umbilden* and of the reappearances of a moment "before," finds an origin there as well. I shall restrict myself to two sets of paired remarks from the "Truth and Lie" essay.⁴ First: "What is a word? The copying [*Abbildung*] of a sensation of nerves in sound. But to deduce a cause [*Ursache*] outside ourselves from the sensation of nerves is already the result of a false and unjustified application of the principle of foundation or reason [*des Satzes vom Grunde*]" (3:312). A sensation of nerves is the "original," the model for the phonetic copy which is a word, but to construe it as the effect of an original cause is an error. The originating function of the sensation of nerves—a philosophic commonplace from eighteenth-century empiricism—is not itself grounded outside of itself and thus may be a functioning original without a ground, a sufficient cause without inviting a grounding in a deficient principle of ground or reason. Now the paired remarks, from the same paragraph: "A sensation of nerves, first metaphorized or translated [*übertragen*] into an image! First metaphor. The image is reformed in a sound! Second metaphor. And each time a thorough springing over [*vollständiges Überspringen*] of the sphere, right into a totally new and other one" (3:312). Even as Nietzsche's account of the origin of language is dividing, distinguishing discrete moments into a sequence—an origin becoming an epistemological history or etiology—it is also arguing against the validity of such discriminations. The original sequence is no longer simply "sensation of nerves" to "word," but sensation of nerves to image to word—an *Umbildung*—and yet this does not contradict the first version so much as point toward its "origin": the appearance of its origin in imagery, in the intervening imagery, "the first metaphor" of the image of the sensation of nerves. Each metaphor, including the one of the origin of language in sensation, is a "thorough springing over" of the sphere it nonetheless imagistically names, and so the "springing over" and "carrying over" become the very names for the image of origination: *Übertragung, Überspringen, Ursprung*. It is entirely straightforward that only a "totally new and other sphere" names the one it would at once derive and depart from; and so *Ursprung* would be the name that springs away from and out of the process it seeks to designate. Origin is that which springs away from itself and is always elsewhere and "otherwise," "totally new and other."

For the second set of paired remarks from "On Truth and Lie," first this: "We believe we know something about the things themselves, when we speak of trees, colors, snow and flowers, and yet we possess nothing but metaphors of things, which do not at all correspond to the original essentialities [*ursprünglichen Wesenheiten*]" (3:312–13). If it would seem that Nietzsche is here finally making reference to the "things themselves," it should be recalled that such notions are names from images from sensations—"metaphors." These metaphors, normally degraded into their conventional use as words or names, do not correspond to whatever tall or colorful or cold "things" might be out there; this is an obvious implication of Nietzsche's statement. But it also says that metaphors do not correspond to "original essentialities," and these are not essences as properties (*Eigenschaften*), not some essential characteristic such as tree-ness or snow-ness, which might "originally" be accessible to "original" knowledge. Rather, the "original essentialities" to which words, names, and metaphors do not at all correspond are the "essentialities" (of things) that are not to be known except "originally," *ursprünglich*, as the leaping away from and beyond them. Words—even the words "metaphor" and "origin"—name the metaphorical springing out to which they cannot correspond. To name this "ursprüngliche Wesenheit" is original in the sense that it leaps over and away from the sphere of its origination.

And now the paired remarks, still from the same paragraph: "Thus it is not a matter of logic with the 'standing out' [Entstehung] of language; and the whole material in which and with which the man of truth, the researcher, the philosopher, later works and builds—all this stems, if not out of dream-land, then nevertheless not out of the essence of things" (3:313). A logic of either deduction from or induction toward is out of the question here, with the origin of language. And Nietzsche, once again, renames this origination, this time as Entstehung. Entstehung, standing out, is more nearly ek-stasis than Entwicklung or "development." The name for the process of origination is neither logical nor organic. Its departure from and noncorrespondence to an "essence of things" is not a matter of an organic stem or Stamm—Nietzsche is explicit—but one of standing out and apart from: Entstehung as that springing out and apart which is the "essence of the thing" with origination.

What is clear from "On Truth and Lie"'s account of the origin of language is that Nietzsche's Ursprünge do not name a thing, anything substantial, nor an original cause (an Ursache, a cause as a thing). They seek to designate an event, a process that departs from itself, that always exceeds its "original" sphere or condition—a leaping out—and therefore they name themselves, Ursprünge, as that which always escapes and exceeds any "original essentialities."[5] They name, themselves, metaphor—Übertragung, Übersetzen—and are the metaphors of this name. What about yet another metaphor for an origin, then, an origin named Dionysus? The way an origin springs out, tropologically and groundless, is what Nietzsche finds as he tries to track down an origin.

I am referring, of course, to The Birth of Tragedy from out of the Spirit of Music, which seems to name this "spirit" Dionysus. Nietzsche's attempt at a critical-historical argument of a beginning ("birth") from out of an origin ("spirit") is exemplary of the literary-historical and philological effort to trace phenomena—literary genres, languages, "sensations of nerves"—to and from original sources or causes; it offers a paradigm for the assumptions or deep structures of literary history that are with us to this day, such as the tracing of works to and from authors, contemporary conditions, or intellectual currents. Nietzsche retrospectively, in Ecce Homo, glosses this literary-historical dimension of The Birth of Tragedy as something that "smells offensively Hegelian": "An 'idea'—the opposition Dionysian and Apollonian—translated [übersetzt] into the metaphysical; history itself as the development [Entwick-

lung] of this 'idea'; in tragedy this opposition sublimated [*aufgehoben*] into a unity" (2:1108).[6] The literary-historical effort to trace a phenomenon from its origin—here, an idea of fundamental, "original" opposition—to its historical development toward an end as an *Absicht* and *Ziel* is what Nietzsche comes to criticize, and we shall see that it is what is *critical*, that is, in crisis, in a state of decision and dividedness (*krisis* from *krinein*), from its very inception. The original problem is the problem of the positing of an origin: "the opposition Dionysian and Apollonian." We shall necessarily be restricted to a series of Nietzsche's key movements.[7]

Let us recall that *The Birth of Tragedy* attempts to move from a conceptual argument about original drives and sources to a history of the forms of Greek art that preceded and led toward Attic tragedy (cultic rituals, Homer, sculpture, Doric architecture, lyric poetry, and so on). And in the long run it does this well enough for it to be remembered by most readers for just that literary history and the subsequent pages of Wagner *Schwärmerei*, even if it has also been reviled by virtually every classical philologist since its contemporary rejection by Wilamowitz-Moellendorff. But when, on his first page, Nietzsche introduces the Apollonian-Dionysian distinction that would empower his argument, this is already an Apollonian move and position, and Nietzsche is already in trouble: "secret doctrines [*Geheimlehren*]" of aesthetic understanding are being granted the Apollonian "perceptible" (*vernehmbar*) mode of "intensely clear figures [*Gestalten*]" (1:21). There is, then, no initial access to an original moment or opposition except by way of a mode that is already on the far side of the origin: that of phenomenalization as discrimination and individuation, the Apollonian mode par excellence. What is most tellingly described as a *Duplizität*—doubleness and duplicity—between Apollonian and Dionysian before it is then repeatedly recharacterized as a duality (*Zweiheit*), discord (*Zwiespalt*), and opposition (*Gegensatz*)—this "point of departure" is initially always portrayed or represented from the side of appearance and illusion (*Schein*), of "immediate apprehension of form," of images (*Bildern*) and "imagistic powers," of Apollo's "marvelous divine image of the *principium individuationis*": "the full delight and wisdom of 'appearance' [*des 'Scheines'*]" (1; 1:22–24).

Even as Nietzsche must begin at a beginning, already removed imagistically from an origin, his great contribution is his attempt to cut through this imagistic second level: "[to] doubt the forms of knowledge of appearance, when the law of cause or foundation [*der Satz vom Grunde*] . . . seems to suffer an exception," to try to tilt, in other words, toward something or some moment that is pre-Apollonian, to move back toward origins rather than simply to continue with developments (*Entwicklungen*). He makes this effort, while nonetheless also still rehearsing the stages of artistic appearances of and from original drives, first by suggesting that both the Apollonian and the Dionysian are "artistic forces . . . which break out [*hervorbrechen*] of nature itself" (2; 1:25). If their appearance as distinct artistic forms could be grounded in a breaking out of "nature," then their beginnings as phenomenally distinct aesthetic or psychological manifestations—one as dream image or illusion, in Nietzsche's description, the other as intoxication or ecstasy—would be linked to some origin or process of origination. Let us recall Nietzsche's sequential argument here: that there is a barbarian Dionysus or satyr behind the Greek Dionysus and that the Apollonian form comes to offer protection against this primal force—another Apollonian manifestation in the face of a "more original" Dionysian force or drive. But such pacification, Nietzsche insists, while it may offer temporary "reconciliation" (*Versöhnung*) of two opponents, does not solve so much as merely cover up an original breaking out and gap: "Im Grund war die Kluft nicht überbrückt" ("fundamentally the gap was not bridged") (2; 1:27). A process of origination that leads to the containment of that force in distinct modes or forms of artistic production does not "bridge over" a gap but springs over it and carries it over (*Überspringen, Übertragung*). What Nietzsche elaborates as a sustained and reappearing original drive or urge (*Trieb*) behind and beneath any Apollonian "reconciliation" or pacification remains as well *his* drive toward an originating moment before any "Apollonian" distinction between origin and the appearance (*Erscheinung*) of a beginning, between urge or source and manifestation, between ground and image. Thus he asserts that "something never before felt drives itself toward expression, the annihilation of the veil of Maya, oneness [*das Einsein*] as the spirit of the species and of nature itself" (2; 1:28).

This "mysterious *Ur-Eine*" (1; 1:25) would be the origin before origination. "To understand this," Nietzsche writes, "we must demolish [*abtragen*] that artistic construction of *Apollonian culture* stone by stone, as it were, until we glimpse the foundations on which it is grounded" (3; 1:29). He attempts this, we recall, through a doctrine of nature before Olympian gods and art: of sources and grounds before the "transfiguring mirror [*verklärenden Spiegel*]" (3; 1:30) of their divine images and aesthetic imagination. Inverting the customary hierarchy of waking and dreaming—the former as the true, the latter as the illusion—he suggests that our sense of waking, "a perpetual becoming in time, space, and causality, in other words, . . . empirical reality," might actually be "the truly-non-existent," while he adopts as more fundamental "the metaphysical assumption" of "the truly being and original-one [*Ur-Eine*] as the eternally suffering and contradictory [*Widerspruchs-volle*]" (4; 1:32–33). Nietzsche's equation here of the original and the contradictory allows me to move toward the kernel of my remarks on *The Birth of Tragedy*. Nietzsche can derive the Apollonian from such an assumed "origin," considering the Apollonian as the "Vorstellung des Ur-Einen," as "satisfaction of the original desire [*Urbegierde*] for illusion and appearance [*Schein*]," as "the eternally achieved aim [*Ziel*] of the original-one, its redemption through illusion and appearance" (4; 1:33). But as he traces beginnings—*Vorstellungen*, images, appearances—from an origin, this very manifestation of development threatens to contradict the contradictory; it would render the "Ur-Eine als Widerspruchsvolle" into something that becomes, as if in that "Hegelian" manner despised by Nietzsche, one with its other: not contradiction but continuity and resolution, not opposition but unfolding of an aim.

Nietzsche identifies this difficulty quite clearly. The "mirroring back [*Widerspiegelung*] of the eternal and original pain [*ewigen Urschmerzes*], of the sole ground [*einzigen Grund*] of the world," is the "'appearance' [*'Schein'*] here as the reappearance [*Widerschein*] of the eternal contradiction, of the father of things" (4; 1:33). The appearance of original contradiction in a transfiguring reflection or reappearance must be, in other words, an inversion, a contradiction of contradiction: the *Widerspruchsvolle* manifests itself as the appearance that can only represent in an image a departure from and contradiction of its ground. If the origin as "Ur-Eine" is also divided and contradictory (recall Nietzsche's claim of "duplicity" for the Apollonian-Dionysian pair and his use elsewhere of doubleness or *Doppelheit*), then it manifests itself as and in the image of a development as a departure from and contradiction of this "origin": the drive toward resolution. An original oneness of twoness cannot appear as one origin, nor as the two distinct but still related moments of origin and beginning, issue, consequence, or development. Except under the guise of contradiction—a "speaking against" (*Widerspruch*) (of) the *Satz vom Grunde*, which is also known as the law of noncontradiction.

This situation of an origin as contradiction that can only know reappearance or reflection as contrary or inverted appearance (*Widerschein*) is then employed and reworked by Nietzsche in his discussions of the lyric poet and of music. He also, of course, seeks to depart from this contradictory origin of his argument, and it is for this departure—or escape, "coverup," and "redemption"—that the remainder of his *Birth of Tragedy* is perhaps best known: what Nietzsche announces as "births [of the Dionysian and Apollonian] succeeding one another ever anew," a chain of births and rebirths leading toward "the final plan of this becoming and drive [*dieses Werdens und Treibens*]," "the common goal of both drives" (4; 1:35). From beginnings to developments and ends as the becoming *(Werden)* of an original aim *(Ziel):* a history of Greek art from out of a spirit. But before this story is extensively told—toward Attic tragedy and on toward a "rebirth" in Wagnerian opera, the "Hegelian" history that Nietzsche then rejects both in his retrospective preface (1886) and in *Ecce Homo*—he explores again the groundless origin for such births, beginnings, and consequences.

In the example of the lyric poet Archilochus, addressed while it is draped in the developmental-sequential imagery of "seed" *(Keim)*, "Urvater," "originale Natur," and "the first 'subjective' artist" (5; 1:35), Nietzsche asks, What is such a subject? The lyric subject is twice related to and yet twice removed from an origin: he is "become wholly one [*eins*] with the original-one, with its pain and contradiction," and yet does not remain "wholly one" because he "produces a copy [*Abbild*] of this original-one as music." Already divided and contradictory vis-à-vis the origin as contradiction—"wholly one" with it, yet dividing (it) into original and copy—this split reproduces or copies itself "as if in a *similic dream-image*, rendering itself visible through Apollonian dream influence" (5; 1:37). It is as if Nietzsche is trying to have one relation and remove, that of music to origin, be "wholly one" so that *it* could in turn be reproduced as a Dionysian origin for an Apollonian appearance. And this contrary relation of origin to music to image is then exemplified as he immediately contradicts, or speaks against, the relation implied in the formulation "das Abbild dieses Ur-Einen als Musik." He renames it "that reflection without image or concept [*jener bild- und begrifflose Widerschein*] of the original pain in music, with its redemption in appearance": the contrary image of an appearance *(Widerschein)* as an image of a non-image (the *bildlose*) that "redeems" in appearance *(Schein).*

From this contrary origin, neither one nor two but a second version or copy of a contradictory one *(das Ur-Eine als Widerspruchsvolle)*, Nietzsche would then generate a sequence or succession, from one to two: "That reflection," Nietzsche continues, "now begets [*erzeugt*] a second mirroring as a single simile or example": from one to two, and "now" from "two"—a second mirroring—to "one," a "single simile." This single simile is, Nietzsche says, the "Ich":

> The image that now shows him his unity [*Einheit*] with the heart of the world is a dream scene [i.e., Apollonian], which renders sensible [*versinn-*

licht] that original contradiction and original pain, including the original delight of appearance. The "I" of the lyric poet thus sounds out of the abyss of being [*Abgründe des Seins*]: his "subjectivity" . . . is an imagination or imagistic construct [*Einbildung*]. (5; 1:37)

The unity that is imagined—shown in an image—to have issued from a contradiction is a mere dream image; the *Versinnlichung*, or rendering visible, of the original contradiction is, following Nietzsche's logic of transfiguring reflection, a *Verkehrung des Sinns*, a perversion and inversion of the meaning of the origin, as and into the sensuous appearance of unity. From the "abyss of being"—this is an important reformulation by Nietzsche—leaps out the imagined ground of "subjectivity," a *Bild* and *Gleichnis* for that which is *bildlos* and *ungleich*.

Nietzsche does not wish to remain with this contradictory origin of poetic imagery; he wants the "unfolding" *(Entfaltung)* of tragedies and dramatic dithyrambs from this source in lyric poetry (5; 1:37), and so he recharacterizes the "Dionysian musician"—who was first called the maker of an *Abbild* or copy—as a quasi-unified, pre-imagistic origin, as "without any image, nothing but original pain and its original reverberation [*Urwiederklang desselben*]" (5; 1:38). It is this slight but crucial disjunction between *Abbild* and *Urwiederklang* that Nietzsche then explores and disturbs in his interpretation of Schopenhauer and music. To be sure, Nietzsche repeats his new version of the lyric "I" sprung from and yet the same as his origin: "the single, thoroughly truly existent and eternal I, resting on the ground of things, through whose copies [*Abbilder*] the lyric genius sees through to the ground of things" (5; 1:38). This would be a movement from "sounding out of the nonground or abyss of being" to "resting on the ground of things," and from *Abbilder* as departures to *Abbilder* as vehicles of return. Clearly, much hinges for Nietzsche's narrative argument on the possible relations between sounding out and copying.

So when Nietzsche turns to Schopenhauer, he focuses upon the latter's depiction of music and lyric art as what he calls the "marvelous intermixing" of will and pure contemplation: "Who can fail to recognize in this description that the lyric is here characterized as an incompletely achieved art, as if arriving at its goal infrequently and by leaps [*im Sprünge*]." To trace the appearance of an art form from out of a source in the "I"—Schopenhauer's "willing"—is, Nietzsche says, to arrive at an art that appears only in "leaps"—leaps out of an origin. Nietzsche counters that "the subject, the willing individual who furthers his egoistic ends [*Zwecke*], can be thought of only as the opponent, not as the origin [*Ursprung*] of art" (5; 1:40). The drive toward ends (*Zwecke*) cannot be an origin, since it is already post-original because individuated and oriented; and in his subtle but powerful reformulation, Nietzsche has the "I" not as original but nonetheless somehow "originally reverberating" and "leaping out" from a further origin. The first conclusion he draws from this critique is that "our entire knowledge of art is fundamentally [*im Grunde*] a thoroughly illusory one, because we as the knowers are not one and identical with that essence" (5; 1:40). This is a move from "resting on the ground of things" and "seeing through to the ground of things" back to the "ground" as an illusion, as if sounding back out of "the non-ground of being." And yet this critique is made in the name of the ground (*im Grunde*); Nietzsche is also still lingering on a threshold of origination: the state of being "not one and identical with that essence" as nonetheless a copy (*Abbild*) of that "original-one as contradiction."

Lyric poetry, Nietzsche goes on to say, distinguishes itself from Apollonian, Homeric epic poetry in that "the word, the image, the concept seeks an expression analogous to music [*einen der Musik analogen Ausdruck*] and now suffers in itself the power of music." In this formulation, is music an "expression" (*Ausdruck*), so that the lyric's "image" or "concept" might be analogous to it in expression—in, say, its relation to a source—or is it itself the source, a source of power? Nietzsche immediately suggests the latter, for he distinguishes between epic poetry's imitation of "the world of phenomenal appearance [*Erscheinung*] and images" and the imitation of "the world of music." The contrast would redesignate "the world of music" as pre-phenomenal and pre-imagistic, as more "original," a source, for he speaks a moment later of "mere similic presentations [*gleichnisartige . . . Vorstellungen*] born out of music—and not the imitated objects of music—presentations which can in no way instruct us about the *Dionysian* content of music" (6; 1:42). The very relation of images to music—born out of it—also cuts them off from their source. Yet Nietzsche wants and needs a direct and continuous relation between lyric imagery and "the world of music," and so he reappeals—transfers over (*überträgt*)—to Greek folk song as what he calls "the imitation of music": "If, therefore, we may view lyric poetry as the imitative effulgence of music in images and concepts [note the conjunction of visual and musical language], then we can now ask: 'as what does music *appear* in the mirror of "imagisticness" [*Bildlichkeit*] and concepts?' *It appears as will*" (6; 1:43). Music appears as will, just as it also appears in its imagistic and conceptual imitation or mirroring as poetry.

But the will—as opposed to Schopenhauer's egoistic "subjective willing"—also only "appears," as it manifests itself as music. And music,

Nietzsche insists, "cannot possibly be will," just as will cannot be music; one, he says, is aesthetic, the other nonaesthetic. Any "signifying" (Nietzsche's term: *deuten*) of music in images appears as "Apollonian observation"—already, once again, a departure from and contradiction of an ostensibly "Dionysian" origin. One is left with "similes" *(Gleichnisse)* from which one interprets backwards, but not with the being or essence of origins.

Music is "interpreted [*interpretiert*] through the image of the will," just as the will is manifested through the aesthetic form of music. "Music itself," Nietzsche adds, "in its total sovereignty does not *need* image and concept, but merely *suffers* [*erträgt*] them alongside itself" (6; 1:43). But it not only suffers them but bears itself over into them—*sich überträgt*—as origination and source: from music to folk song and lyric and on to tragedy. The image of an origination and development of the arts from out of a spirit or origin in music is the contradictory appearance of images and concepts springing out from a locus of contradiction and nondetermination: neither music nor will but each only "as"—a simile for—the other. Music "compels to figurative speech [*zur Bilderrede nötigte*]," Nietzsche writes, and he adds that language can never "adequately exhaust" the world of music, as the latter "relates symbolically to the original contradiction and original pain the heart of the original-one and thus symbolizes a sphere that is beyond and before all appearances" (6; 1:43–44). Even as Nietzsche repeats and compounds "symbolically" a language of absolute origins, it is beyond and before all appearance and imagery, both transcendental and original: one does not know whether he is going or coming, except for the fact that it is still and already embedded in the appearance and reappearance of absolute imagery of contradiction. In relation to the "world of music," he concludes, "every phenomenal appearance is only a simile; therefore *language*, as the organ and symbol of phenomenal appearance, can never in any way reveal outwardly the deepest inside of music . . . its deepest meaning . . . cannot be brought one step nearer" (6; 1:44). The development of any concept or image from and for an origin, the origination of any image or concept of development, is neither more nor less than the springing out of a simile: the simile, metaphor, and image of and as *Ursprung*.

This original knot of origins—origin, music, and will, each appearing as the other, but only appearing as, similically—turns into "the origin of Greek tragedy" and its "standing out" *(entstehen)* from the tragic chorus, and so forth: the rehearsal and repetition of the metaphor of origination under the image of "development" *(Entwicklung)*, which Nietzsche later criticizes and rejects. Instead of pursuing this literary history, I would conclude this part, before turning to Lukács, with some remarks on some of Nietzsche's later versions of origination and their destiny.

Is it Nietzsche's destiny to be original? Like Hegel's "qualitativer Sprung," which, "a lightning bolt [*Blitz*], in one instant presents the image-structure [*Gebilde*] of the new world,"[8] Nietzsche never knew what hit him; his origin just leapt out at him: "I have in no case had the remotest sense of what was growing within me—all my abilities one day sprang forth [*hervorsprangen*] suddenly ripe, in their final perfection" (*Ecce Homo*, 2:1095–96). His Zarathustra had language spring out both toward and from him: "Here all of being's words and thesaurae spring open to me: here all being wants to become words, here all becoming wants to learn to speak from me" (*Also Sprach Zarathustra*, 3, "Die Heimkehr"; 3:432). To name being as it springs into language, to name its becoming language as what becoming always is and only needs to be seen and named as,[9] is Zarathustra's and Nietzsche's *Ursprung*, and also the motto to *Ecce Homo*—"werden, was man ist," become what you are. Being *(Sein)* becomes the becoming of language—the springing out of *Ursprünge* toward images, words, and metaphors—which it always, *ursprünglich*, is.

This is also Zarathustra's and Nietzsche's destiny: from Hegel's *Ursprung* as *Blitz* to the lightning bolts of *Ursprünge*. "There is . . . no art of speech before Zarathustra," Nietzsche writes in *Ecce Homo*, and in this original language, this language of origination, "lightning bolts [are] hurled ahead toward hitherto unguessed futures" (2:1135). Nietzsche's lightning bolts—"What I am today, *where* I am today—at a height where I no longer speak with words, but with lightning bolts" (2:1116)—point toward both a future and a past, as all *Ursprünge* do, and neither past nor future is yet named or seen before such naming of the "origins" that mark their breaking out and division. In the section of *Ecce Homo* called "Why I Am a Destiny," Nietzsche calls himself "a destiny—he breaks the history of mankind into two pieces. One lives *before* him, one lives *after* him. . . . The lightning bolt of truth struck" (2:1158). Lightning strikes, not once but repeatedly, in the form of origins that mark and remark all moments of the appearance of truth as the breaking of history (histories) into two pieces—before and after—and the manifestation of the *in between:* the *Ursprung* springing out and toward.

The destiny of origins, however, is to atrophy, through forgetfulness, into beginnings and sources. The authority of the bolt of truth in Nietzsche—or of thinking, in Heidegger—is not an origin of and for authority. Only forgetting, Nietzsche argued in the "Truth and Lie" essay, lets one believe in a truth as something substantial or fundamental or static; and this forgetting forgets above all the "truth" of an origin as the origination of truth. This origination may spring out, dance, "fall to" one (*Zufall* as *zufallen, accidere*),[10] or strike like lightning, but it does not stand still, nor does it lead to or stand on a ground or foundation. When it does, an origin becomes either a contradiction—as in the argument of *The Birth of Tragedy*—or an error, as Nietzsche argues in the passage on "Ursprung der Erkenntnis" in *The Gay Science* (110; 2:116–18). Nietzsche's origins would become their contradiction or error were they to become anything at all but what they "are"—the springings out of metaphor—and so it would be an error to understand and name them as anything other than the "original speaking against" and errancy of the *Ursprung*. The destiny of Nietzsche's *Ursprünge*, of course, is *to become,* and therefore not remain "as," these contradictions and errors: the becoming *(Werden)* not of what they are—origins, lightning bolts—but of sources, beginnings, histories.

Lukács's movement beyond Nietzsche would be everything the *Ursprung* is not: history and (as) the arrival at and departure from a foundation. But Nietzsche as one of Lukács's origins marks and remarks the appearance of Lukács's "truth" as the repeated breaking of his history into two pieces—before and after. What leaps out of this breach is the *in between:* the *Ursprung,* springing, leaping, out of its historical argument and toward a story. Models of "generic" development that we have analyzed in this study—Wissenschaft from the history of art, Flaubert's realism from Dante's figuralism—are concentrated in Lukács's *Theory of the Novel* as they were in Nietzsche's *Birth of Tragedy:* the generic "development" *(Entstehung,* or standing apart) of all histories from out of and away from their origins, of all origins as *Ursprünge,* first leaps. Nietzsche's "original" problem, which is that of the vibratory, reduplicating motion between a philosophic problem of origins and a literary history, becomes Lukács's repetition with a special twist or inversion: to depart from philosophy to a literary history (of the novel) in order to arrive at a philosophy—of the novel and then of life and reality. Lukács's narrative of and toward theory is not, as it "develops," developmental, but leaps *(springt)* across its own theoretical abysses, which are the *Abgründe* of *Ursprünge.* I do not believe a complete and coherent (systematic) reading of *The Theory of the Novel* exists or could exist, certainly not here. Nor that of Lukács's career after the book. It means very different things when critics as diverse as Paul de Man, Fredric Jameson, and J. M. Bernstein insist on the continuity of Lukács's work, for Marxist critics' developmental and alternately retrospective and prospective interpretations[11] are deeply at odds with de Man's equipoised critique.[12] Lukács himself tells a story—a literary history in its own right, for it is an autobiography—that allows him to break with a past as he recuperates it on the ground of a true story. Between the break and the ground are the story but also the leap and abyss of his truth.

In his critical retrospective preface of 1962, Lukács recounts *The Theory of the Novel*'s methodological location among the largely Kantian "*geisteswissenschaftlichen* tendencies" of Dilthey, Simmel, and Weber and says, "I found myself then in the process of transition from Kant to Hegel" (6; 12).[13] Then a story extends, and with it a breach within the story. He complains of "distortions" in the methods of the *geisteswissenschaftlichen* school and adds: "This naturally does not mean that for the author [*Verfasser*] of 'The Theory of the Novel' the way toward discovering interesting connections was in principle blocked. Here again I give only the most characteristic example: the analysis of the role of time in 'L'Éducation sentimentale'" (8; 14). A story of discoveries has within it a break between a past author and a present narrator (the *ich*). A page later the story is of developments from *out* of roots: "Even if rooted [*wurzelnd*] in the realm of the *Geisteswissenschaften*, this book contains—within the given limitations—certain traits that became significant in their later development. It has already been remarked that the author of 'The Theory of the Novel' had become a Hegelian" (9; 15). But the "development" is already *out* of Hegel, as well:

> The author of "The Theory of the Novel" . . . sought a historically founded [*fundierte*] universal dialectic of the genres, grounded [*begründete*] in the essence of aesthetic categories, in the essence of literary forms, that aspires to a more intimate connection between category and history than he found in Hegel himself; he sought to grasp intellectually a persistence within change, an inner transformation within the enduring validity of essence. His method nonetheless remains extremely abstract in many respects, especially in very important connections, cut off from concrete social-historical realities. (10–11; 16–17)

The "author" worked in the past, but the dialectic he sought still aspires, in the present (*anstrebt*, not *anstrebte*), to join category and history more closely than in Hegel, and the method of the book also still remains (*bleibt*), in the present. Who and where is this "author," separate from the present-tense narrator and his account of the book's aspirations? Lost in the past, and from the "I" who is Georg Lukács writing the preface in 1962. Until this recovery of a narrative trajectory toward a speaking, knowing "I": "It was only 15 years later that I succeeded [*gelang es mir*]—naturally already on Marxist soil [*auf marxistischem Boden*]—in finding a way to the solution." The "I" is now back in the past, but on a "way" *(Weg)* that leads to the present tense and position of the preface's author. This was when, countering what he calls "vulgar sociology" of the Stalinist period, Lukács was trying to "unearth [*auszugraben*] Marx's authentic aesthetics and develop it further [*weiterzubilden*]" and came upon "a real historical-systematic method" (11; 17).

There is one last paragraph of interest in this preface. Lukács says that "the aesthetic problematic of the present" "stems from out of the Hegelian heritage [*aus dem Hegelschen Erbe stammt*]." The previous paragraph had just broken, in its tenses, between a past of Hegel's achievement and the present "aspirations" of a dialectic. It will appear that, paradoxically, the continuity of what "stems" from Hegel's "legacy" is precisely that of a break. As Lukács summarizes his version of Hegel's "world of prose" (and it is not our concern to show how wrong this version is), he concludes:

> Thus art becomes problematic precisely because reality becomes unproblematic. The formally similar conception of "The Theory of the Novel" is in fact fully the opposite: the problematic of the form of the novel is here the mirror-image of a world that is out of joint. Thus here the "prose" of life is only one symptom among many others that reality from now on provides an unfavorable soil [*Boden*] for art; thus the central problem of the form of the novel is the artistic settling of accounts with the closed and total forms that emerge [*entsteigen*] from a totality of being rounded in itself [*in sich abgerundeten*]—and with any world of forms immanently complete in itself. And this not out of artistic, but out of historical-philosophical grounds [*geschichtsphilosophisch Gründen*]. (11; 17)

Marxist "soil" *(Boden)* allowed Lukács to know and tell that out of Hegel's legacy there "stems," not an adequate dialectic of category and history, but the condition of "unfavorable soil" in reality. Art cannot grow from bad soil, but good dialectics can from Marxist soil. What is the difference? Just as Lukács's *Theory of the Novel* sought, even then, a "historically founded universal dialectic of genres," "grounded [*begründete*] in the essence of literary forms," now the *ground* can be found for the difference between productive and unproductive soils, but not an aesthetic one: rather the real Marxist-dialectical "historical-philosophical grounds." Reality's soil and its historical-philosophical grounds— reality, history, and philosophy—are Marxist, which is what Lukács becomes, knows, and tells when he refinds his identity with the "author" of *The Theory of the Novel*. But this identity depends on a development *(Entwicklung, Werden)* from out of Hegel that is at once, paradoxically, a break between the past and the present, once-good soil and now-bad stuff, Hegel's dialectic and Marx's. Lukács's story spans a breach, or leaps over it.

The story we shall turn to in *The Theory of the Novel* is that of history from out of philosophy—like the preface's story of Marx from out of Hegel—and then the attempt of the literary history of the novel to (re)achieve its philosophic theory. This story that emerges from an origin (*Ursprung*) in "a totality of being rounded in itself" is of a break with and out of that origin. The origin, rounded (*abgerundet*) and total, breaks as the story breaks with it, leaps out and over a breach now gaping between origin and story. This is an abyss (*Abgrund*).[14] The story of a break with the rounded (*abgerundet*) yields the "abysmalized" (*abgegründet*). This original slippage in Lukács's signifiers faces, across the pages, the grounded (*begründete*) "essence of literary forms" that his *Theory of the Novel* at once sought in its pre-Marxist past and still produces in its textual present.

The present after the past was not always for Lukács over an abyss. In *History and Class Consciousness*, the present is the end of history and the presentation of its goal and truth, without being any less historical—any less than history—for this achievement. In his preface to the first edition, of 1923, Lukács says the contents are no more "than an *interpretation*, an exposition of Marx's doctrine *in Marx's sense* [*im Sinne von Marx*]" (51; xliii).[15] This much is sheer historicism, to understand the past as it understood itself. Lukács continues: "This aim and goal [*Zielsetzung*] is determined by the view that in Marx's doctrine and method the *correct method* for the knowledge of society and history has *finally* [*endlich*] been found. This method is historical [*historisch*] in its most inner essence." Lukács's own claim is doubly historical, eschatological, and circular in *its* inner essence. The goal (*Ziel*) that he aims at, that of a historicist understanding of Marx, is determined (*bestimmt*) by the view that this goal provides the true method for knowing history: the method of the goal anticipates the possibility of connecting present and past, Lukács and Marx, truth and history—aim and goal. The end—of historicism, of connections between present and past—has (*endlich*) been found before Lukács begins toward the goal. But this is no more than historicism, in which the possibility of knowing the past as it was is given already to and in the present's methods of submitting to the authority and truth of the past. Lukács continues, not only pointing out the obvious "self-application" of the method to and within his own essays but also claiming that such thoroughgoing historicism—in the past, understood in its sense, the final, thoroughly historical method for the correct understanding of history—is really present knowledge:

"According to this understanding of Marxist method its preeminent goal [*vornehmstes Ziel*] is *knowledge of the present*" (51–52; xliii). So the goal above, or before, the goal of and in the past (historicist Marxism, the final correct method, knowledge of history) is the goal of the present. It is not that (the goal of) history is one-sidedly before the present (Lukács's essays in *History and Class Consciousness*) but that (the goal of) the present is also before history and historicism. Lukács's trajectory is the seamless circular connectedness of past and present as the (Marxist) end—aim finally reached as goal—of history in history's (Marx's) historicist knowledge.

This connectedness of history within itself such that it includes present, past, and the knowledge of the one by the other, which Lukács and his celebrators promote as *totality*,[16] was not always there as objective knowledge or class consciousness, of course, but *becomes* history in becoming known as such. In the major section, "The Antinomies of Bourgeois Thought," of the volume's major essay, "Reification and the Consciousness of the Proletariat," Lukács writes that "classical philosophy"—i.e., up through Hegel—"worked out the new substance that for the first time [*zum erstenmal*] comes to view, and that now philosophically lies at the ground [*zugrunde liegende*] of the order and connectedness of things: *history* [*die Geschichte*]" (258; 143). What lies at the ground first comes up into view—a historical event—and in this "vertical" connectedness, as it were, "things" (everything, the totality of things) emerge as history, so that a past, one-time event *and* present knowledge, history *and* philosophy, are this connectedness as it is known as history. Here, where history and structure ("the order and connectedness of things") are identified, is also the "standpoint of the proletariat": "genesis and history . . . coincide or, put more precisely, are merely moments of the same process"—the structural history of genesis and history itself are equally processlike—and "determinants [*Bestimmungen*] of existence" must appear in "their succession, their coherence and their connection [*ihre Abfolge, ihr Zusammenhang und ihre Verknüpfung*] as moments of the historical process itself, as structuring [*struktive*] characteristics of the present" (282; 159). So structure and history structure and historicize the present.

This doubling and circling of history and structure, past and present, recall the joining of past "author" and present narrator in Lukács's preface to *The Theory of the Novel;* here, they join the text's first-person *plural* (collective, class-based) voice with the authority of *its* past: "the dialectical method as the method of history remained reserved for that class that was able to discover in itself from out of its life-ground [*von ihrem Lebensgrund aus*] the identical subject-object, the subject of action, the 'we' of genesis [*das 'Wir' der Genesis*]: the proletariat" (267; 148–49). Precisely as in *The Theory*'s preface, the joining of a first-person voice with a past that now joins a present is also the fusing of a fructive *soil* with a historical-philosophic *ground*—a "life-ground" (*Lebensgrund*). Now the present has and can tell its story; this story is history, having become the story. Lukács's reduplications of history—which rehearse the present study's entire exposition of the idealist Wissenschaft of history as the events of history (*Geschichte* as *das Geschehene*) becoming their knowing or *Wissen* in that Wissenschaft also called history (*Geschichte*)—are exact and succinct:

> History [*Die Geschichte*] appears no longer as an enigmatic happening of events [*ein rätselhaftes Geschehen*] *to which* men and things are subjected, or which must be explained by the intervention of transcendental powers or made meaningful by reference to values transcendent of history. . . . *history is precisely the history of* [*die Geschichte ist gerade die Geschichte der*] *the unbroken overthrow* [*ununterbrochenen Umwälzung*] *of the forms of objectivity that shape human existence.* . . . From this standpoint alone does history really become the history [*wird die Geschichte wirklich zur Geschichte*] of man. . . . History becomes the history of [*Die Geschichte wird zur Geschichte der*] the forms of objectivity that form [*bilden*] the environment and inner world of man, and that he tries to master [*bewältigen*] in thought, practice, art, etc. (321–22, 325; 185–86, 188)

In each of these formulations of "history becoming the history of," history (*Geschichte*) becomes a story or narrative (*Geschichte*) told—knowingly, as correct or true Wissenschaft—of that history and is thus the revealed, illuminated *ground* of history, which otherwise is a "dark allegory" (the technical meaning for that "enigmatic happening of events"), *Geschehen* without its *Geschichte*.

The story of history is of "mastery" and "overthrow," the rhetoric of class struggle and revolution, but more (and still) enigmatically, it is a narrative of "unbroken overthrow." The unbrokenness is the connectedness, the totality, provided by true history as total narrative; the overthrow or revolution (*Umwälzung*) is ultimately the overturning of events in and into their history; but a narrative of unbroken overthrow would be at once continuous and of a break with a past—continuously discontinuous. Would it flow or leap, discover or cover over? The question is, once again, that of Lukács's (and Marx's) relation to Hegel. The history of dialectics has to be a "step beyond" its history, and so, for the first time, its real history:

> The great step that Marxism, as the scholarly and scientific [*wissenschaftlicher*] standpoint of the proletariat, here makes beyond Hegel [*Der grosse*

Schritt . . . über Hegel hinaus], consists in its comprehending the determinations of reflection not as an 'eternal' stage in the grasping of reality as such but rather as the necessary existential and intellectual form of bourgeois society, of the reification of being and of thought, and thereby discovers the dialectic in history itself. Thus, the dialectic here is not imported into history and its story [*in die Geschichte hineingetragen*] or commented upon with the aid of history and its story [*an der Hand der Geschichte erläutert*] (as very often with Hegel) but rather is *read out* [*herausgelesen*] of history and its story itself as its necessary form of appearance at this determined stage of development, and made conscious as such. (308; 177)

Where the history from Hegel to Marx becomes Lukács's story of the "great step beyond" Hegel to Marx—where dialectics is genuinely in the story of history, so that it can be "read out" *(herausgelesen)* and not just "read in" *(hineingetragen)* or commented upon with its help—is both an unbroken narrative of a "developmental stage" *(Entwicklungstufe)* and a story of turning Hegel over, breaking with his dialectics, and stepping beyond. The story of the continuity is also the story of a break and breach in history; the stepping beyond itself is a leap over that breach.

The ambiguity *(Zweideutigkeit)* of Lukács's reduplicative and duplicitous "history of history" *(Geschichte der Geschichte)* as the "unbroken" story of a discontinuous history is the ambiguity of its origin in Hegel. Hegel is where the story starts and breaks. In the first two sentences of "The Antinomies of Bourgeois Thought," Lukács writes first that "modern critical philosophy steps out and stands apart from [*entstanden . . . aus*] the reified structure of consciousness." His English translator Rodney Livingstone captures much of Lukács's ambivalence in having translated this as "springs from," for the story would have it both ways: modern critical philosophy, including Hegel, arises from *(entsehen)* but would step beyond or apart from (the strong sense of the prefix *ent-*) its ground—the step to Marx, and into history as its knowing story. But for the story to begin and continue, it should not leap but grow, as if genetically, and so the next sentence reads: "As opposed to earlier philosophic positions, the specific problems of modern critical philosophy stem from [*stammen . . . aus*] this structure" (209; 110–11). The history does not originate with a leap from and over a ground but begins root-and-stem from its soil. History must begin already in its story, not in an origin.

Especially not if the story's origin is Hegel. With this we can return to *The Theory of the Novel*, where we shall restrict ourselves to three points: its origin, its leaps, its end. Perhaps the best-known thing about the text is its beginning with the image of the "closed culture" of the "age of the epic," which is Lukács's version of the Greece of the Homeric epic. But the first sentence is an allusion to Hegel, its origin: "Blessed are those times for which the starry sky is the landmap of paths that one may take and is to take, and when its paths are lit by the light of the stars" (21; 29). The allusion, by way of contrast and paradox, is to Hegel's preface to his *Phenomenology*. Here, stars are the map for the land, the heaven *(Himmel)* reflects the earth, to look up is to see down, and to be up is to cast light down. There, in the *Phenomenology*, Hegel begins by speaking of philosophy in a mistaken current view that asks for "feeling" and "edification" from it:

> Corresponding to this demand is the strenuous and almost zealous and frenzied effort to tear men out of their having become immersed in the sensuous, common and particular, and to direct their gaze up to the stars [*Sternen*]; as if, having altogether forgotten the divine, they, like the worm, were at the point of satisfying themselves with dust and water. Formerly they had a heaven [*Himmel*] adorned with a vast wealth of thoughts and images. For everything that is, the meaning lay in the thread of light through which it was joined to the heaven [*Von allem, was ist, lag die Bedeutung in dem Lichtfaden, durch den es an den Himmel geknüpft war*]; instead of lingering in *this* world, the gaze fled on this thread beyond it, up to the divine essence, up to—if one may put it so—a present on the far side [*jenseitigen Gegenwart*]. The eye of the spirit had to be directed by force toward the earthly and held fast to it; and it has taken a long time for that clarity which only the supra-worldly possessed to penetrate into the dullness and confusion in which the sense of things of this near side lay [*der Sinn des Diesseitigen*], and thus to make attention to the present as such—which was called *experience*—interesting and valid.— Now the opposite need appears to be at hand, sense [*der Sinn*] appears so fast rooted in the earthly that it needs just as much violence to raise it up.[17]

The allusion of Lukács to Hegel is obvious, the similarities striking, the differences compelling. Where Lukács begins with heaven and earth reflecting one another (down to his syntax: *Sterne* . . . *Wege* . . . *Wege* . . . *Sterne*), in the "blessed" past, Hegel begins with two distinct moments, present and past, and two opposed directions of movements. *Now*, it as if man has to direct his gaze to heaven, in opposition to earth; *once*, in the past *(Sonst)*, the light of heaven so illuminated the earth that one fled earth right up to heaven and had to be forced back down to earth; *now* (again), the gaze needs to be forced back up to heaven (again). The symmetries in each case are consistent, but reversed: in Lukács, up means (illuminates) down, in Hegel, up means not-down,

down means not-up (each illumination of one is a non-illumination of the other). So, too, the times and their "direction," as it were, are symmetrical and, we shall see, reversed: Hegel's age of access to the heavenly was, is no longer, but would be again ("now," when the gaze would be raised upward again), while Lukács's age of the epic was, is no longer, and . . . would *not* be again.

This last qualification hangs from another relation-and-reversal between the two passages, which is their respective positions vis-à-vis philosophy. Lukács's beginning is *before* philosophy, not only in the conventional sense that it starts with Homer, at the beginning of literary history and thus before Plato and the history of Greek and post-Greek philosophy, but also in an *absolute* past with respect to philosophy. His first page had continued, it may be recalled, with the Novalis quotation that "philosophy is actually homesickness," that philosophy is "always a symptom of the tear between inside and outside, a sign of the essential distinction between the I and the world [which were "never permanently foreign to one another" in this past]," none of which, including philosophy, existed "then," when the "landmap" was given with the stars: "For what," Lukács asks rhetorically, "is the task of true philosophy, if not to draw that archetypal landmap?" The map does not need to be drawn, because it is already given, at the beginning, *before* philosophy. Hegel, on the other hand, is *after* philosophy, in an absolute present with respect to it: his story of philosophy has it first having led men's gaze away from earth to the transcendental stars, then forcing that gaze back to the earth, as if to the empirical, only "now" to be called upon to "edify" man by redirecting the gaze back up (to what the previous paragraph sarcastically listed as the beautiful, the holy, the eternal, religion, and love). In Hegel's absolute present, after the story of philosophy that the *Phenomenology* is and on the threshold of the system of philosophy that the preface is and announces, philosophy is after its narrative history and before—in the face of—itself.

But Lukács is also not only before philosophy at the beginning of his story but after Hegel at the opening of his text. It is subtitled "a historical-philosophical essay" ("ein geschichtsphilosophischer Versuch"), and the allusion to Hegel signals that it is *after* him. At his beginning, Lukács is after—and according to—his origin: he springs and leaps out of it. His pre- or *Ur*-historical beginning at the beginning of Western literary history posits already "completion" and "rounded" totality:

> So all the soul's doing becomes meaningful and round in this duality: complete in meaning and complete for the senses [*vollendet in dem Sinn und vollendet für die Sinne*]; round, because the soul rests in itself during

its acting; round, because its action separates itself from it and, having become itself, finds its own center and draws a closed circle around itself. (21; 19)

This completion and totality at the beginning of history begins the story where it would end, in that it is, after Hegel, the exact opposite of Hegel in the placement of completion and totality.[18] But it remains retrospective, and post-Hegelian or "after" his model, in its singling out of the philosophical as the *determining*, as if history had revealed its philosophic content: philosophy is here "the form-determining and the content-giving of literature [*das Formbestimmende und das Inhaltgebende der Dichtung*]" (21; 29). And yet, once again, this Hegelian assumption does not mark a closing, resolving, or "completion" of its assumed correlative, for philosophy is "always a symptom of the tear . . . , a sign of essential difference . . . , of incongruence." It keeps signifying or pointing to the *Riss*. For Hegel, on his threshold *after* history and at its "qualitative leap" (*qualitativer Sprung*) of origin, philosophy's spirit is "the whole that, from out of its succession and extension, has returned into itself, the resultant [*gewordene*] *simple concept* of the whole." For Hegel, this philosophy is still history, but history of, after, and according to philosophy: "But the reality of this simple whole consists in this, that each of those shapes that have become [*gewordenen*] moments now once again develop and give themselves shape, but in their new element, in the meaning that has come about [*in dem gewordenen Sinne*]."[19]

Beginning his story before philosophy, but after his origin in Hegel, Lukács's literary history leaps into this breach, this *Riss*, between origin and beginning. As a story of history (*Geschichte der Geschichte*) it would tell of time, history, and their beginnings as if before this *Riss*, and before philosophy, and so cover or bridge over any breach between its philosophic origin and its narrative-historical beginning. As philosophy of history nonetheless (*ein geschichtsphilosophischer Versuch*), it is always already, from its "beginning" in and out of—standing out and apart from (*entstehend*)—its origin, the time of history in the face of that breach: the leap of history out of an origin, over a breach or gap (*Abgrund*), and not its growth out of a ground. The difference between Lukács's beginning to/and his narrative history and his origin in/after his philosophical "ground" is the difference within *Ursprung*: as origin and that which leaps or springs out of and away from itself.

There are several consequences to this original beginning and beginning *Ursprung*, or leap, in *The Theory of the Novel*, several shapes that it takes. One is that Lukács's literary history of the novel, which takes the epic as the "a priori home [*Heimat*] of [its] genre," with closure and completion as the characteristics of this "original principle [*Urprinzip*]," can then only tell "homelessness" as the story that springs from the origin: "the ultimate foundations [*Grundlagen*] of literary shaping [*Gestaltens*] became homeless [*heimatlos*]" (31; 40–41). This accounts, of course, for the dreariness of its themes—the pathos of loss, alienation, disillusionment, and so on—but also, more interestingly, for the shape of *The Theory* itself. It becomes, like the novel after its origin in the epic, the historical track or trait after *its* origin in philosophy, seeking the end of its story after the loss of an origin of closure and totality now forever denied it. De Man correctly compares and contrasts *The Theory* in this respect with its origin: "It is the Novel itself that tells us the history of its own development, very much as, in Hegel's *Phenomenology*, it is the Spirit who narrates its own voyage. With this crucial difference, however, that since Hegel's Spirit has reached a full understanding of its own being, it can claim unchallengeable authority, a point which Lukács's novelistic consciousness, by its own avowal, is never allowed to reach."[20] Chasing the end of its story (as the novel), the end of its history (as literary history of the novel), is *The Theory*'s shape of chasing time after an origin, for if the epic form "does not know the passage of time," for there there is "no qualitative difference between experiencing past and present" (113; 126), here, after the "qualitative leap," or *Ursprung*, the novel and *The Theory* know nothing else. This also explains why Lukács's book would have its second part, symmetrically the other of its first part's history after the origin, be a "typology of the form of the novel," as the attempt to close and bring time to a standstill after its origination into nothing but passage.[21]

Benjamin's essay "The Storyteller," and the present study's chapter on it, will explore the shape, extension, and end that may be given to Lukács's insight that the problem of the novel is the problem of time—in Lukács's writing of its history, in Benjamin's reading of its story. Here, I would remark that a different close reading of *The Theory* would show that at virtually every juncture in Lukács's argument and history where a narrative step, link, or transition must be made, a leap *(Sprung)* marks and remarks its origin. The *Sprung* marks and remarks the *Ursprung*, that which would spring from it, itself. Whether it is Lukács on the "qualitative differences" and "unbridgeable abysses" *(unüberbrückbare Abgründe)* that appear in his epic origin between immanence and transcendence, self and world (24–26; 32–34) or in his brief treatments of the caesurae that mark his triads, such as the lyric-novella and literary subjectivity, each between the epic and the novel (43, 45; 52, 53), the leap (the term *Sprung*) springs out of his text to mark the jump his history must originally and repeatedly make for there to be history and histories at all.[22] Dante, who in Lukács's literary history as well as in the authoritative one by today's leading Dantist is the very figure of the transition from epic to novel,[23] is also the very figure of the *Sprung* (29, 45, 88, see also 50–51, 59, 72; 37, 53, 102, see also 59–60, 68, 82–83). Time's origin would yield history but repeats as history's leaps; *natura non facit saltus*, but *historia saltare debit*. And since the epic originally stands for and on the ground of the empirical world—"For the epic, the world at any given moment is an ultimate principle; it is empirical in its decisive and all-determining transcendental ground [*Grund*] . . . it can never, given its form, overcome the breadth and depth, the roundedness [*Abrundung*] and sensuousness, the wealth and ordered nature of historically given life" (37; 46)—so Lukács's ultimate leap is not further into the novel and its history, but into "real history" as the epic's successor, and out of *The Theory* into Marxism—to the "ground" of a doubly remarked "history of history," which, we have seen in *History and Class Consciousness*, would repeat its epic *Ursprung* in and out of history after Hegel, continuously discontinuous.

But like the "abysmalizing" (*Abgründung*) we can glimpse in this rounded world (*Abrundung*), as we did in Lukács's retrospective preface and as Lukács suggests in his own occasional use of the term *Abgrund* (22, 26, 51; 30, 34, 60), the ultimate or ending leap toward solid ground less "bridges over" a gap than springs over and carries over its origin. Like Nietzsche's "Im Grund war die Kluft nicht überbrückt,"[24] Lukács's history carries over or metaphorizes (*überträgt*) its origin as the metaphor of history; the metaphor *history* is in carrying over its origin, the metaphor *origin* is in springing and carrying out its history. The only end to this duplicity of original *Widersprüche*—which is the doubling and redoubling of tropes, the tropes of origin and history—would be the false-bottomed (*gegründet, abgegründet*) ground of a hope that could become developmentally and historically (*werden* become *geworden*) a performance, an effective ethical-political performative: a *promise* of history contained, closed, totalized as memory, the redeemed past, knowledge and reality.

The end of Lukács's history of the novel in *The Theory of the Novel* promises such an end. Time, the name for "the greatest discrepancy between idea and reality" (107; 120), the very sign of homelessness and a breach between life and meaning (108; 122), would become the totality of duration (*durée*), "something existing in and for itself, a concrete and organic continuum" (112; 125).[25]

> Everything that happens [*alles was geschieht*] is meaningless, fragmentary, and mournful [*trauervoll*], but it is always irradiated by hope or by mem-

ory [*immer durchstrahlt von der Hoffnung oder von der Erinnerung*]. . . .
And in memory this steady struggle [of life] transforms itself into an interesting and incomprehensible path [*unbegreiflichen Weg*] that yet is
bound with untearable threads [*mit unzerreissbaren Fäden . . . gebunden*]
to the present, experienced instant. (112; 126)

This astonishing passage takes Lukács and his reader back to his origin
and forward to his future leap. "Everything that happens" (*alles was
geschieht*) is life and will become history (*Geschichte*), and even as it has
been novelistically lost in *The Theory*, homeless and without end in its
literary history of the novel, it now finds its end in its origin. In naming
Hegelian *Erinnerung*, the passage more precisely recalls its origin in epic
Greece and in Hegel's preface to the *Phenomenology:* the light coming
down, the path (*Weg*) so illuminated, the threads (*Fäden*) that are untearable (*unzerreissbar*) because healing (or coming before) any tear
(*Riss*), the origin's verticality of imagery now "transformed" into a temporal connectedness and coherence of a present with its past and thus of
a story with its origin, beginning, development, and history. This *Erinnerung*, which would redeem a past in making it a narrative path to a
present, we may now understand not only as Lukács's end to (the history and theory of) the novel but as his hope for (his future of) history
and historicism in a present and leading to a future:

> And this instant is so rich with the duration that advances upon it and
> leads beyond it . . . that this wealth shares itself with the past and the
> lost as well [*auch dem Vergangenen und Verlorenen mitteilt*] and even adorns
> [*ziert*] events past, which then went unremarked, with the value of expe-
> rience. And so, in a remarkable and melancholy paradox, the condition
> of failure is the moment of value [*ist . . . das Gescheitertsein das Moment
> des Werts*]; the thought and experience of what life denied, the source
> [*Quelle*] from which the fullness of life seems to flow. What is shaped is
> the thorough absence of any fulfillment of meaning, but the shaping ele-
> vates itself to the rich and rounded fullness of a real totality of life. (112–
> 13; 126)

As if the preceding passage could not have become any more remarkable, only to be outdone here, the Hegelian *Erinnerung* takes on its
proto-dialectical form of not just transformation but reversal and yet
preservation—of past into present, worthlessness into value, denial into
fulfillment. But this textual present of Lukács's reading of Flaubert's
Éducation sentimentale is not only the memory of a novel's narrative, nor
his recovery of a doubled origin—epic and Hegelian—for his novelistic
history, but the very promise of the thoroughgoing historicism (albeit
liberally mixed with Dilthey's *Erlebnis*) of his future Marxist *History*

and Class Consciousness. After this origin, nothing would be lost to historicism's presence of the past or to Marxism's totality of reality, history, and the value of values: true knowledge as the connection of present and past.

That was the future of that textual present. It is less interesting that Lukács acknowledged, with its technical tropological name, that this is *paradox* than that he acknowledged the "melancholy" light that already (or still) bathes that which was and still is "mournful." The memory that would irradiate a past and yield hope—the end of the novel, the end of historicism, the end of history—is the hope for a memory. Now, as Marxism becomes a memory of the hope for a present and a future, itself without hope or future, scarcely without a present—as it becomes history—the origin of its end is remarkable, perhaps melancholic, certainly interesting. A promise does not need to be fulfilled for history to be meaningful, especially when history is—as it is—that which leaps out of and carries over an origin. Lukács's and the twentieth century's Marxism has an origin less in Marx, perhaps, than in Hegel, Nietzsche, and the historicism that they found and unground—that they originate. To read the failure of a promise as a failure of history is still to believe that history can be grounded, or that it can end its story meaningfully. Lukács's dialectic, within *The Theory of the Novel* and between it and his Marxism, would be "historically founded" and also "grounded in the essence of literary forms." We shall have learned from his example, one of the most eloquent failures of our tradition, when we know that history should be read as the literary form and problem it is, while politics and its promises need, not history at all, but only a future for their original performance.

7

History as Rhetorical Enactment: Walter Benjamin's Theses "On the Concept of History"

The association of Walter Benjamin with the Frankfurt School, and with Marxism more generally, is a large part of the story of his reception to date, but it is probably ending. With it, the highly politicized reception of his last text, his theses "On the Concept of History" ("Über den Begriff der Geschichte"), may change as well. The importance of Benjamin's writings on history and the philosophy of history can scarcely be in question, and it will be the purpose of the remaining chapters of the present study to explore them in the context of the problem of allegory and history as it is bequeathed to the German literary-historical tradition after Hegel. What can be and is in question is whether the dimensions of Benjamin's writings on history—the theory of history and historiography and the practice of his own kind of literary history—can be subsumed within a Marxist or otherwise politically revolutionary problematic. Some (although by no means all) of Benjamin's later writings on history are laced with a Marxian vocabulary, and the combination of the theses being both a *last* text and a text marked by the martyrdom of Benjamin's suicide at the French-Spanish border in 1940, has made its reading in terms of political empowerment—desperate hopes or naive enthusiasms therefor—inevitable. Benjamin seems to have been the first to be skeptical about this potential reception. The text was not intended for publication, because, as he wrote in 1940, "it would open both the door and the gate to enthusiastic misunderstanding," but it acquired another status after his death.[1] For its 1942 mimeographing in Los Angeles by the Institute for Social Research, Theodor Adorno could write: "Benjamin's death makes the publication a duty. The text

183

has become a testament [*Vermächtnis*]. Its fragmentary form includes the charge [*Auftrag*] to keep faith with the truth of these thoughts through thinking" (GS, 1:1223–24). Published in Benjamin's own French version in 1947 and in German in 1950 and again in 1955, it began to receive increasing attention in the sixties and is now one of the most widely known and quoted parts of his canon. Much of the commentary on this small text has been thoroughly thematic, by which I mean that friends, scholars, critics, and polemicists largely undertake a paraphrase and rewriting of its themes in advance and in command of any further analytic reading of the text's enabling language, structures, or arguments.[2] Unsurprisingly, as we shall see, the thematics are repeatedly those of Benjamin's conjoining and/or confusing of a political-philosophical, specifically Marxist dimension in the theses with a theological, specifically messianic one, and if this is felt to be a problem (it understandably usually is), then the mode of "solution" has been to argue these "sides" almost symmetrically: either to save Benjamin for Marxism or to privilege Marx's philosophy of history and theory of political action over Benjamin's; either to save Benjamin from theology or to write him off as irretrievably mystified; in any case, to keep Benjamin between Marxism and messianic theology, between desperate calls for revolutionary political action and muddled fantasies of salvation.

The present chapter undertakes to read, beyond or beneath this polemical brushfire, the ways in which Benjamin's text necessarily emerges as a story, without altogether merging with it, without, that is, becoming a thematics without residue, *sans reste*. Thematics declare the truth of a text to be paraphrasable, but the terms that a truth of this text might take cannot be assumed in the first place. Rather, a close and critical reading, "brushing [the text] against the grain" of its thematics as Benjamin's theses would do to historiography—"die Geschichte gegen den Strich zu bürsten" (thesis 7)—can alone display and decide the conditions of possibility of such "truth(s)."

> *Briefly, the little work is clear and disentangling (despite all metaphoricity and Judaism) and one thinks with horror of how small the number is of those who are ready even to misunderstand something like this.*
>
> —Bertolt Brecht, August 1941[3]

The theses, in the nondefinitive version we have (cf. GS, 1:1252–59), scarcely present a linear unit. They open with a "false" beginning, like a rhetorical facade or trapdoor—a beginning that, as we shall see, is not even theirs and that marks a space of manipulation within it—and they follow through a series of numbered sections (sometimes clearly linked

to one another, sometimes not), only to "end" with a double ending—
two lettered sections, which may or may not have been intended for
exclusion but which, as they stand, invite some questions: Is a qualitative distinction to be indicated by the switch from numbers to letters?
If there are two lettered units, could there have been three (or four, or
more), or are the two to be considered alternatives, exclusive or otherwise?[4] Does this text end?

Editors have always thought so, and called it the "theses." Although
this "genre" or subgenre came, in Benjamin's hands, to conjoin with a
practice of theory apparently weighted toward *praxis* (as opposed to a
theory's conventional departure from a thesis or arrival at a concept), it
indissolubly retained characteristics of the question, the aphorism, the
postulate, the hypothesis, and the ironic tone (see Pierre Missac, M,
323–33, and Rolf Tiedemann, M, 111–12). Furthermore, it remains in
important respects in the shadows of two predominant models: Marx
and Luther. Marx's "Theses on Feuerbach"—like Benjamin's, having a
curious history, being jotted down in 1845, published by Engels in
1888, and given their definitive editing only in 1932—"end" with the
famous eleventh thesis: "The philosophers have only variously *interpreted* the world; it is a matter of *changing* it."[5] This appears to be in
direct response to the Hegelian position—which Marx reproduces as
the scholarly and scientific *(wissenschaftlich)* position as late as the third
edition of *Kapital* in 1883—that the thinking of philosophy is a *Nachdenken,* a reflection or meditation (i.e., thinking "according to") but
also a retrospection (i.e., thinking "after").[6] Of Luther's ninety-five
Wittenberg theses from 1517, while essentially directed against the
practice of selling indulgences for the sacrament of penance, many are
concerned with what can be done by the living (the present) for the dead
(the past), the answer to which is, very little indeed, as shall prove
ironic for Benjamin's theses and their apparent hopes from beyond the
grave. The Wittenberg theses also manifest Luther's *Schriftprinzip* of
the individual, unmediated interpretation of Scripture, *sui ipsius in-
terpres.*[7]

The point here is not as simple as Missac's claim that Luther and
Marx represent, respectively, "the inclination toward metaphysics and
the concern for the concrete" (M, 319). Rather, Benjamin's theses on
history locate themselves within a German tradition of "theses," themselves of the greatest historical import (the Reformation and Marxism)
and presenting antithetical but, as such, mutually determining positions. If Benjamin's theses partake of this tradition's gesture toward historical importance, they also may be understood as awkwardly strad-
dling the tradition's alternate models. Marx would shift thought and

writing from being an afterthought to having a predetermining and in-forming status; Luther would remove doctrinal thinking and writing (at least the Church's) from an obtrusive interpretive interference between the present individual and the past deed, life, or text. Where the one would move from interpreting the world or history to changing it, the other would move toward an ever more individual and pure interpreta-tion, even the interpretation of the text by itself, apparently without any secondary, mediating allegory. Marx would have thought and its writing be performative, with the efficacy of the text to be judged, not by its epistemological or constative value, but by its power to produce a change in the world. For Luther, the text (Scripture, *Schrift*) always already is performative, performing its own exegesis. Benjamin's theses may be situated between these two models of "theses": between a polit-ical rhetoric that would assume a performative dimension and a rhetoric of religious allegory that would perform its own exegesis, interpret-ing—and thereby dissolving and "defiguralizing"—its own figural rhetoric. Among Benjamin's most loaded terms in the theses are the performative ones: *Aufgabe* ("task") and *Anspruch* ("claim"). The ques-tion of reading the theses thus becomes one of their performance: what tasks and claims would the theses perform, and how?

The central image of the ninth thesis—Missac goes so far as to claim that the theses are grounded not in ideas but in two fundamental images (M, 325)—is that of the Angelus Novus. The image appears already in the 1920s in Benjamin's writing (when he also acquires Klee's painting of the same name), with the critic presented as "evangelic," as "bringing news," not, however, of *ana*strophe, a positive turn or turning around, but of *cata*strophe, a turning down, destruction or disaster. The image appears here in a subgenre or literary form that is as well a compact rhetorical structure: the emblem, a Renaissance and more especially a baroque structure of considerable popularity, especially after Andrea Alciati's *Emblematum libellus* of 1531 and its numerous subsequent edi-tions, and one that Benjamin knew and appreciated at least from the time of his studies for his book on the baroque, *Ursprung des deutschen Trauerspiels*.[8] Conventionally, an emblem includes a picture *(pictura)* fol-lowed by a title or motto *(inscriptio)*, which is followed in turn by a "caption" *(subscriptio);* sometimes, the motto is distinct from the title and substitutes for the "caption."

In Benjamin's thesis, a first glance might tell us that there is a picture ("There is a picture [*Bild*] by Klee . . . "), followed by its name or title (" . . . called 'Angelus Novus'")[9] and then by a description of it that would accord with the *subscriptio* slot in the structure reserved for the "caption" or motto. But this would be a misunderstanding of a deceptively contrived structure. Actually, one first encounters an inscription, lines from a poem by Gershom Scholem occasioned by the Klee picture. Then one is given a "picture," not the real picture by Klee (or its reproduction), which may or may not be known to us, but a verbal image that describes or "presents" it to us. And below or at the end of this "picture," dovetailing with it, the description turns into the subscription of an interpretation. This interpretation—as the *subscriptio* was to do in the baroque emblem—turns us back to the picture and inscription.

There can be discriminating disputes about the differences between Klee's painting and Benjamin's description of it, as well as about the significance of these differences.[10] But this seems to miss a basic and essential point: here there is no Klee painting but rather only a single Benjaminian structure: a verbal emblem inscribing its "visual" component or image. Moreover, the interpretation and its object are, paradoxically, mutually determining. The English translation by Harry Zohn is very misleading here. As Benjamin's text turns to the image's interpretation, it reads: "The angel of history must appear like this [*muss so aussehen*]," that is, like Benjamin's description of Klee's *Angelus Novus*, which he has just provided us. Zohn has: "This is how one pictures the angel of history." Rather than an active interpretation ("one pictures"), there is here a passive interpretation with an imperative construction ("must appear [to]"). The unfolding allegory of the angel of history "must" appear "this" way, for its description is enfolded in, and inscribed in the service of, the allegorical structure of the emblem. There is here neither an active nor a passive viewer—neither Benjamin nor anyone else—viewing but rather a *view* (an interpretation or an allegorization) of an image, both inscribed together in a single discursive, specifically rhetorical structure. The allegorical subscription "must" be as the inscribed *pictura* or *Bild* has it, just as the picture or image "must" be as it is allegorically inscribed, sandwiched between its equally interpretive *inscriptio* and *subscriptio*. The imperative force of the interpretation is not volitional or substantial, and the interpretation is neither accurate nor inaccurate, certainly neither "true" nor "false"—both the imperative and the interpretation are structural, even "artificial" in the sense that they are implicated and imbricated in the artifice of the emblem. "The angel of history must appear like this," that is, as it appears *and is* in the emblem.

That the allegorical interpretation is complex and ironic should go without saying. The past that the angel sees ("Where a chain of events appears before *us*, there *he* sees one single catastrophe, which ceaselessly piles ruins upon ruins and throws them at his feet") is *Trümmer*, ruins, fragments, pieces—the shards of a tradition. One theological alternative, that of the kabbalistic *tikkun*, making whole the broken vessel, is rejected: "He would like to linger, awaken the dead and join what has been smashed back together [*das Zerschlagnen zusammenfügen*]. But. . . ." The angel of history would redeem—"awaken," resurrect—the past but is instead propelled forward while nonetheless always looking back (here there is an allusion to Friedrich Schlegel's *Athenäum* fragment no. 80, "The historian is a backwards-turned prophet"): "But a storm is blowing from paradise and has got caught in his wings and is so strong that the angel can't close them anymore. This storm irresistibly drives him into the future to which he turns his back, while the pile of ruins before him grows toward heaven."

The image of the angel is likewise sandwiched between the "future" of allegorization before it and the "past" of inscription toward which it remains turned, like an emblem's picture, which, structurally, it is. This propulsion, which gets one nowhere or leaves one stuck in the same place, is ironically called "progress" ("That which we call progress, is *this* storm"), a concept already ironized in thesis 8 and to be given another ironic dimension in 11, when the "storm" *(Sturm)* that here propels the negative movement forward will be associated with the so-called positive forward movement of the "stream" *(Strom)* of technological development. We shall see how, as in this protostructure of the image and the emblem, an image for history must ironically "progress" into a narrative account even as it would also be arrested in a standstill and standoff between future and past. Our initial point here may be to observe that in this central thesis on a view of history, we are dealing with a verbal image inscribed within a rhetorical structure or form that, together, yield an ironic allegory. The allegory is that the image belongs meaningfully—as the condition of its possible meaning—to the structure of emblematizing allegoresis that informs and displays it, and the irony is that there is no getting out except by "progressing" into a story—a version of Benjamin's "history"—that it itself gives the lie to. The allegory is ironic in that it displays the paradox of a picture and its interpretation, an image and its allegory, both of which in the emblem are already rhetorically operative and determining vis-à-vis each other, and thus they neither "must" nor even can be otherwise, either as a literal art-historical description or as a variously "true" or "false," politically "correct" or "incorrect" interpretation. In the development of my reading of the theses, Tiedemann's assertion that "the Messiah, salvation, the angel and the Antichrist—they appear as images, analogies and similes in the theses, and not literally [*buchstäblich*]" (M, 95) will have to be stood on its head. The rhetoricity of Benjamin's theses, starting with that of the angel, is quite literally—materially, and textually citable—in the text.

Benjamin's critique of historicism focuses on several of its truth claims. Historicism holds that the truth of history is always there, available for us: "'The truth will not run away from us'—this saying, which comes from Gottfried Keller, indicates in historicism's image of history precisely the point at which it will be smashed through [*durchschlagen*] by historical materialism" (5). Historicism maintains that there is such a thing as "the 'eternal' image of the past" (16) and that this truth is Ranke's knowledge of "the way it really was" (6; in Benjamin's slight misquotation of Ranke, "wie es denn eigentlich gewesen ist"). The seventh thesis is his longest single critique of historicism.[11] Historicist truth as what once was is connected with historicist hermeneutics through a couple of key terms: Dilthey's *nacherleben* and Schleiermacher's *Einfühlung*. And Benjamin claims that this hermeneutics and the historical vision it serves suggest larger social-political developments. The Enlightenment's universal claims for mankind show themselves to be bourgeois class ideology in the nineteenth century, and universal history or Hegelian *Weltgeschichte* reduces to discrete nationalisms and nationalistic histories. Benjamin's identification of historicist narrative linking present to past as a "triumphal procession" relates this whole historical development, which includes historicism, back to the Renaissance and its literary form of the triumph, a specific narrative mode in complicity, as thesis 8 also suggests, with an arbitrary, violent, and even "barbaric" "norm" called "progress." References by Benjamin to other aspects of this progression—its "chain of events" (9) and "causality" (A)—further highlight the relationship he has drawn between the progressive norm and certain narrative presuppositions.[12]

This sketchy introduction of Benjamin's wide-ranging and powerful critique invites us to consider closely the historical thinking and writing that he opposes to historicism. In thesis 2, his argument is that just as the outlook of the present does not envy the future, but seeks happiness, fulfillment, or "redemption" (*Erlösung*) in present occasions and opportunities (which otherwise pass away), so a historical presentation (*Vorstellung*) ought not to look from the present toward the future but rather ought to redeem the past—its missed opportunities—in the present. As I shall be using the terms here, the former, rejected alternative is that of *prolepsis*, an anticipation of a future event or fulfillment in and from the point of the present, while the latter alternative, which is the one Benjamin advocates, is that of *metalepsis*, a retrospective assignation of a relationship between present and past. But while one can (for the sake of the present moment's argument) have prolepsis without metalepsis, one cannot have metalepsis without prolepsis. The movement connecting the present to the past—metalepsis strictly speaking—as, for example, in having the present be an effect of a past cause or an answer to a past claim or need, necessarily involves a correlative prolepsis—what I will call a metaleptic prolepsis—with which one moves from the past back to the present: the past anticipated its effect, response, or fulfillment in a present that was "future" for it but is present now. This two-way street is actually a single, unitary tropological structure: the metalepsis that gets one from the present to the related past presupposes a corresponding "return" prolepsis, and this prolepsis is predicated upon the metalepsis and as such is a "metaleptic prolepsis." This, I would suggest, is the inner workings or structure of what Benjamin, in thesis 2, calls the "secret agreement" (*geheime Verabredung*) between past and present.

The double negative of the prefixes of *Ver-ab-redung* corresponds to the negativity of Benjamin's circumlocution for the present: "the time to which the course [*Verlauf*] of our own existence has once assigned [*verwiesen*] us," where *verwiesen* also means "exiled." The same word is used for the present's understanding of the past and the latter's future-oriented understanding of the present: "The past carries with it a temporal index through which it is referred [*verwiesen*] to redemption." Referring to the present as a kind of exile, assigning it that meaning, is of one piece with the past signaling for redemption or fulfillment. The present understanding moves itself back into the past (metalepsis), and the past moves forward into the present (metaleptic prolepsis). The paradox, or negativity, of the structure is that the past would performatively "claim" the present, while this claim is predicated upon the metaleptic *turn* or trope that turns the past into—interprets or reads it as—a passive or already written sign ready to make the claim, "a secret index through which it is referred to redemption." The question which dimension of the structure has priority is as undecidable as the language of "reflection" and "image" that opens the thesis ("This reflection leads to this: that the image of happiness that we cherish . . . "). Is the image only a (product of a) reflection, or is it available "outside" or "before" it, so as to produce its reflection? The problem in thesis 1, of mirrors and the illusions they create (and to which I shall return), here casts its reflection on the question of historical perspectives. As thesis 3 explicitly states ("To be sure, only [*erst*] a redeemed mankind fully receives its past"), the present would already have to be (conceived of as) redeemed or fulfilled, the product of a metaleptic prolepsis, in order passively to "receive" (*zufallen*), or actively to conceive, the historical fullness of the past. And this would be to have, as the product of a metalepsis, the past as "citable"—"Which is to say: only to a redeemed mankind has its past become citable [*zitierbar*] in each of its moments"—as a sign or text "refer[ring] to redemption."

The fourth thesis extends the tropological structure of historical understanding as metalepsis and prolepsis to the Marxian problematic of infrastructure and superstructure: "The class struggle, which is always before the eyes of a historian schooled in Marx, is a struggle for the crude and material things without which there would be no fine and spiritual ones." Just as the pious and messianic epigraph to the thesis from Hegel can be translated into its vulgar version more contemporary to Benjamin (and surely alluded to by him here)—Brecht's "Erst kommt das Fressen, dann kommt die Moral" ("First comes grub, then morality")—so does Benjamin translate what had been reified as a one-way spatial hierarchy into its real temporal structure. Infrastructure may produce superstructure, but the latter has a retroactive, or metaleptic, critical effect on the former ("they work back into the depths of time"). The cultural past, now the "spoils" *(Beute)* of the ruling present, will continue to turn or trope against this rule and toward an alternate reception, that is, another future, as Benjamin compares the past to a flower turning toward the rising sun of a redeemed and redeeming present ("thus by dint of a secret kind of heliotropism, the past [*das Gewesene*] strives to turn toward *that* sun which is rising in the sky of history"). The "historical materialist," the redeemed historian, is enjoined to "understand this most inconspicuous of all transformations [*diese unscheinbarste von allen Veränderungen*]," this "secret kind of heliotropism." To understand this heliotropological structure is to see what is inconspicuous, namely, the *Schein* or play of rhetorical appearance in the "unscheinbarste von allen Veränderungen," the "secret" tropological structure—like the "secret agreement"—which links past and present in having each turn or trope toward ("transform") the other in metaleptic and proleptic operations.[13]

Thesis 5 tells of "grasping" the image of the past by and in the present and of there being no "true image" *(wahres Bild)* of history except as it is understood "as having been meant" ("als in ihm gemeint") for the particular present moment. The status of the "true image"—an image that recurs in thesis 7 as the "genuine historical image"—may already be suspect after the play of illusion, reflection, and image in the first two theses. There is the added paradox of this image being "fleeting" and "flashing" ("huscht vorbei," "aufblitzt") but also available to being grasped or, more literally, held fast *(festhalten)*. But the fundamental paradox here is twofold: that of the "true image" itself and of history as an image. A "true image" would not appear to be the historical thing itself;[14] it must then correspond to something in such a way as to be true. But such a correspondence theory of historical truth is the very historicism Benjamin criticizes. For "true historiography," then, as well as for false historicism, history is an image. The difference here would be that "true history" understands that its image is caught and coheres in a structure, as did the image of the Angelus Novus, the angel of history, in its allegorical emblem. The structure here for Benjamin, which constitutes a coherence theory of historical truth, is one of past and present, which are related to each other as intention is to understanding: the present moment knows itself as intended by a past image, and thus it grasps or comprehends and holds on to the past ("it is an irretrievable image of the past that threatens to disappear with each present moment [*jeder Gegenwart*] that does not recognize itself as intended in it [in the past, *als in ihm gemeint*]"). Understanding that would correspond to intention—this describes an ideal circuit of communication and brings with it, however implicitly, an idealist hermeneutics. Such idealist assumptions as are implied in thesis 5 are actually a continuation, a carrying over or rhetorical reinscription of the initial rhetorical inscription of the past as a sign or text offering meaning for the present, an inscription by and of metalepsis and prolepsis.

"To articulate the past historically"—for this is now the issue— means "to take possession of a memory [*Erinnerung*] as it flashes up in a moment of danger" (6). Paradoxically again, in this thesis the unexpected (*unversehens*) and fleeting moment combines with deliberate, intentional acts of mastery (*bemächtigen* and *festhalten*). As the Messiah is also the "overcomer" (*Überwinder*) of the Antichrist, the "true historian" asserts mastery over that which is handed over (*Überlieferung*, or tradition) and which would otherwise be slavishly in the hands of a conformist ruling ideology. History is transmitted or handed over in the triumphal procession (7) of historicism; it is to be overpowered and taken over by the historical materialist, so that this narrative of history might be overcome. The narrative *transmissio* or *Überlieferung* is to become, or give way to, the *translatio* or *Übertragung* of "true history," the overtroping of metaleptic historical interpretation. Historiography is to be overtrumped at its own game and become historiotropography.

> *You would be surely not the last, but perhaps the most* incomprehensible, *victim of the confusion between religion and politics, the working out of which in their genuine relation can be awaited from no one more clearly than from you.*

> —Gershom Scholem to Benjamin, 30 March 1931[15]

Benjamin's theses conflate "true" or "genuine" history with that of "historical materialism." My own discourse would do the same, albeit in a different and non-ideological way. The immediate objects of his polemical critique are the "idealism" of historicism and its adoption by Social Democracy, and he argues for the alternative of a revolutionary, materialist historiography. I would argue that the fundamental feature of what deserves to be called idealism here is the assumed correspondence between present knowledge (or "history" as it is done or written) and past event (or "history" as what happened), whether this is sanctioned by transcendental principles, epistemological rules, professional practices, political platforms, or plain old unconscious habits. Now historicism, with its correspondence theory of truth, is one form of such idealism. The apparent alternative to this is what I shall call, following Benjamin, the materialism of history and its writing: the rhetorical construction of structures within which past and present cohere so as to produce meaning, which then, empowered by this coherence, may be called "truth." In the materialism of the theses, the material is that of the *Bild*, or image, and the activity of the "historical materialist" is image-making. Thesis 12 speaks of the "oppressed class" as the "subject of historical knowledge," but Benjamin's French version reveals his theoretical point more clearly: there he has the "artisan of historical knowledge" (GS, 1:1264), that is, the maker or artificer. What he makes is an image of historical sense "wherein the past comes together with the present in a constellation" (GS, 1:1242). Benjamin's historiography as the construction of rhetorical structures that produce historical significance and understanding would be a part of Benjamin's broader materialist tropology, the projects of which are epistemological and metaphysical as well as historical.[16]

Benjamin's critique is almost always profounder than his local target. Thus, in thesis 13 his attack upon the Social Democrats' "concept of progress" is actually upon all the Enlightenment precepts that historicism and its political wing embody: those of universal, infinite, and irresistible progress. His critique becomes radical in the sense that it aims at what they all have in common, that is, at their root, or *radix*. And this is a common concept of time, such that historical progress (*Fortschritt*) is predicated upon temporal progression (*Fortgang*). His political critique becomes a critique of temporality, which is to be construed not as a preexistent time-line (or, in the analogy of thesis 15, borrowed from Baudelaire, as a clock that measures time indefinitely and thus emptily) but rather as a constructed structure that yields meaning (such as a calendar that allows the past to be recalled in each present moment).

The product of structures of temporality is history—as it is understood *and* as it is made. Thesis 14 opens: "History is the object of a construction whose place is formed [*bildet*] not by homogeneous and empty time but rather by time (ful)filled [*erfüllte*] by 'nowtime' [*Jetztzeit*]" (and not, as in Zohn's egregious mistranslation, "History is the subject of a structure whose site is not homogeneous, empty time, but time filled by the presence of the now"). History is the goal that would be arrived at, or produced, by a construction, the place of which is imag(in)ed or made (*bildet*) by a structure of temporality: the time of *Jetztzeit*. This time is filled or fulfilled (*erfüllte*) according to the structure of metalepsis and metaleptic prolepsis, which conceives of a present fulfilling or redeeming a past and, therefore, of a past "filling," intending or determining a present. The tropological structure of temporality yields an image (*Bild*) of the present as historically filled and filling: as a historical consciousness at once filled full by its temporal self-consciousness as a historical present and fulfilling a historical past through its present, rhetorically structured and structuring action of "making" history in its "doing," its being read and written. Gerhard Kaiser notes the "ambivalence" (M, 62) of this sentence in thesis 14 referring to both the happened and the interpreted history, but it is actually triply valent, referring to the *writing* of history as well. Benjamin's specific example in this thesis is of a "present" (the French Revolution) "citing" (*zitiern*) a "past" (Rome), a past that has already been understood, or read, as a text because the same structure inscribes, or writes, it as an "index referring to redemption" (2).

Elsewhere Benjamin wrote that the "historical index of images means . . . that they only become readable at a certain time. . . . This 'now' [*Jetzt*] is the 'now' of a certain 'knowability' [*Erkennbarkeit*]. . . . This is the occasion for a decisive turning away from the concept of 'timeless truth.' But truth is not—as Marxism claims—only a temporal function of knowing, but rather is bound to a kernel of time [*Zeitkern*] which is fixed at once in what is known and in the knower."[17] The "now" of reading and writing history at once determines the readability of historical images and is determined by them, as they must already be written. The "truth" of such history is neither timeless nor arbitrarily associated with the subjective temporality of a historical consciousness but rather is inscribed within the temporality of the tropological—metaleptic and proleptic—structure functioning in any given present, producing both past meaning and present understanding. History is made, Benjamin's thesis argues, in its being so written and read. Krista Greffrath, in her contribution to the *Materialien*, asserts that this "unity" of making and writing history is "no unity of differences, but rather unmediated equivalence, metaphorical identification," which can be saved from "political romanticism" only through reliance on a "party-line interpretation" (M, 220–21). But this is either the fear of Stalinism or its advocacy. Rather, the "ruling class" (14) always already has its historical "line" (or narrative) on the reading and writing of the historical past and present. The "dialectical" or "revolutionary" "leap" (*Sprung*) from out of the present to the past and back to a sublated (*aufgehoben*) present would at once reread, rewrite, and (re)make history. Kaiser understands this as "the representation of the possibility, but not the certainty, of salvation . . . instead of the model of prefiguration and fulfillment" (M, 52). But the representation and the model are indistinguishable. Benjamin's model or structure of prolepsis (prefiguration) and metalepsis (fulfillment) is precisely the condition of possibility for the rhetorical enactment of another historical understanding and present that would be the end of "history" as we have known it, as it has been written and read up until "now." The "leap," or overtroping, out of a predetermined history and into "true history" would be the springing of the springs of the ruling historical mechanism, those structures which determine historical locations and options. It would be the *Sprung* by which history is sprung from its narrative, leaving it behind like a broken spring.

Thesis 16 states that this "leap" takes place in "a present which is not a transition [*Übergang*] but in which time is answered for [*einsteht*] and comes to a standstill [*Stillstand*]." But one's suspicions should always be raised by a positive positioning that would be achieved by litotes (as it is here with "A historical materialist cannot do without [*nicht verzichten*] the notion of a present"), and we may recall that many of Benjamin's theses (5–7, 11, 12, and 17) argue by negative definition, by defining their positions against prevailing ones. As Irving Wohlfarth formulates the paradox here, it is "an affirmation of the transient which suspends the transitional."[18] The "leap" of thesis 14, like the "overcoming" and "handing over" of 6 and 7, is such a "transition" or translation. At such moments, time does not so much stand still as it is answered for or "guaranteed" (Zohn's version, "in which time stands still and has come to a stop," misses the *einstehen* and yields only a redundancy). One "time," the past, is answered for in another, the present; they are both guaranteed by a structure in which each is interrelated and codetermined. The "guarantee," then, is provided not by the authority of history but by the tropological structure of history, history as it stops and locates time by and within this structure. The structure provides the story of the author, of his authority. Whether by "quotation" or "reading," Benjamin here "aims to reconcile the alternative between using and interpreting the past,"[19] for exactly here, after the rhetoric of action in theses 14 and 15, he explicitly states that he is speaking of writing: "This notion defines precisely the present in which he is writing history for his own person [*für seine Person*]." This phrase, "for his own person" (missing in Zohn's "the present in which he himself is writing history"), is a reinscription of the structure wherein the past is determined by present writing and the present receives its authority as an author from this determination. "Knowledge at a historical instant, however, is always the knowledge of an instant," Benjamin wrote (GS, 1:1233); reversed, we have the knowledge of a historical instant, a past, being knowledge at an instant—present knowledge. The making of history is this rhetorical enactment or writing of both past and present, the writing of a text or script, "even if these texts masquerade in the guise of wars or revolutions."[20] And this writing is always already a reading. Benjamin wrote elsewhere: "The historical method is a philological one founded by the book of life. 'Read what was never written,' it says in Hofmannsthal. The reader to think of here is the true historian" (GS, 1:1238).[21] What was never written or enacted in the past and thus does not yet—before a present—constitute a text can be read in, and thus is inscribed by and in, the material structure of history: by and in its rhetorical text.

Such is the "constructive principle" of "materialist historiography" (17). In this thesis, which Benjamin singled out as containing the "hidden but decisive methodological connection" with his earlier work of the 1930s,[22] the historian is said to "recognize a sign," like the "index referring to redemption" of thesis 2, a sign constructed or written in by the tropological structure of metalepsis and prolepsis. As already in his *Trauerspiel* book, where Benjamin analyzed time not as the continuum of "one thing after another" (*Nacheinander*) but as a "spatial image" (*Raumbild*), time here is an imagistic space—like the "place" (*Ort*) of thesis 14—figuratively depicted as a "constellation" or "monad." Time is caught in the *Stillstand* of this rhetorical structure and written and read as *history*, as a specific past and present. As Gerhard Kaiser puts it, "'Now-time' and history distinguish themselves from mere present and mere past through the constellative relationship in which they become 'now-time' and history" (M, 68). Just as "leaping" out of the present was at once the overpowering and capturing of a past (6 and 14), so is the "arrest" of present thought in a "constellation" or "monad" at the same time the "blasting out" (*heraussprengen*) of a past: "The historical materialist . . . blasts a specific life out of the era, a specific work out of the lifework. The result of this method is that in the work the lifework is preserved [*aufbewahrt*] and negated and elevated [*aufgehoben*]; in the lifework, the era; and in the era, the entire course of history" (17).

The term *aufgehoben* would qualify this method as dialectical, what Benjamin elsewhere called "a dialectic in *Stillstand*." In Benjamin's elaboration there (GS, 1:1250), this entails understanding his method as founded upon a "law" or "schema," a schematization of the radical temporality of the tropological structure: radically temporal because at any given moment a "blasting out" from a false continuity is also a "standing still" of the dislocated piece of time thus isolated, and each such dislocation of a past is also a location of a present. The "blast," no less tropological than the "leap," both preserves and sublates *(hebt auf)*, manifesting the *Zweideutigkeit*, a fundamental ambiguity or paradox, of the rhetorical structure. The product of its operation in this thesis is the synecdochal structure of parts and wholes that preserve and sublate history in(to) a new rhetorical form, a continuity that is an overtly tropological construct rather than a naively narrative representation of an ostensible "flow" (or "stream") of time. When thesis A accents only the posthumous, metaleptic dimension of history and historiography—its making and writing—and gives this an active cast in speaking of the historian's "grasping" *(erfassen)*, it flattens the prefigurative and predetermining dimensions of a "history" that is also necessarily already there, grasping the historian in the selfsame structure: made and written, waiting to be (re)read and rewritten.

Benjamin's theses display a sustained rhetoric of violence: cutting through (5); seizing, overcoming, fanning the spark (6); breaking (7); blasting out (14, 17); exploding (15, 16); and the constellation receiving a shock (17). Many of these include the sense of the sudden, which combines with other imagery of the momentary (the "instant" that "flashes" in 5–7) and the unexpected (6). I would suggest that this rhetoric of violence and irruptive temporality, in addition to displaying one aspect of a desperate pathos in a dark moment, is one representational projection of the violence and the radical temporality of rhetoric; and that for the very reason of *this* danger of language, the rhetoric of Benjamin's text is rarely noticed in any manner other than celebratory remarks upon its revolutionary or anarchistic gestures. In the linguistic sense I am suggesting, the "moment of danger" that "flashes up" for the historian is the danger of radical suspension between the tropological and temporal structures that make history both an image and its other, a narrative: that constitute its rhetorical enactment in the temporality of both a reading of what has only just been written—which, qua reading, tends toward narrative—and a writing, or inscribed image, of what must already have been read for the image to respond or "answer." This danger of rhetoricity is destabilizing of all thematics, those of Benjamin's argument as well as of his interpreters and critics. Under this understanding, Benjamin's text would not provide what one of his editors, Hermann Schweppenhäuser, considers the blueprint for "forming the instruments that allow for the manufacture of a hardened construction out of an image rushing past" (M, 11). On the contrary, it is the hardened—material, textual—construct whose structure produces and is produced by the "rushing" or radically temporal rhetorical images in the act(s) of their being read and (re)written. It provides an understanding of history in which each "instant of humanity" is founded upon "the fundamental citability [*Zitierbarkeit*] of [the historical] object" (GS, 1:1233), that is, in which human being always already is and yet ever still remains to be written and read as a sign in a text. But as an image or a story?

It is one purpose of the remainder of the present study, in this chapter and the subsequent ones on Benjamin, to explore this question and try to supply an answer. In a version of his fragment "On the Mimetic Faculty" known as the "Doctrine of the Similar" ("Lehre vom Ähnlichen"), Benjamin writes of rhetorical understanding in terms remarkably similar to those he uses for historical understanding: "This perception of similarity is in each case bound to a flashing up [*Aufblitzen*]. It rushes by, and is perhaps to be won back, but cannot really be held fast like other perceptions. It offers itself to the eye as fleetingly and passingly as a constellation of stars. The perception of similarities thus appears bound to a moment of time" (GS, 2:206–7). This account of rhetorical understanding is also our account of Benjamin's understanding of history as rhetorical enactment.

The place and mode of such rhetorical enactment is portrayed through various terms for the act of memory. Irving Wohlfarth usefully associates Benjamin's use of *Eingedenken* and *Gedächtnis*, based on his "Storyteller" essay, and he distinguishes Benjamin's *Gedächtnis* from *Erinnerung* along the lines of a passage from his essay "On Some Motifs in Baudelaire,"[23] but as we shall have further occasion to see in the following chapters, Benjamin's employment of terms for acts of memory is not clearly and consistently distinct. So here, for example, he explicitly speaks of the "true historian" seizing possession of an *Erinnerung* in thesis 6. In theses 15 and B, the memorial term is *Eingedenken*, which may be translated, not as "remembrance" (as Zohn and Wohlfarth choose to), but as "mindfulness." What this translation would mean to capture is the "innering" or interiorizing of the "past" by the mind, which *Eingedenken* has in common with *Erinnerung*. When we recall that this past is an image (*Bild*), its "innering" becomes associated with *Ein-bild-ungskraft*, or imagination; the origin of this term in medieval mysticism apparently involved *in-bilden* as the making of the image of

Christ within one's soul, and thus, like Benjamin's *Eingedenken*, it is a "birth [from *nascere*] of the image (with)in." This "innering" of the past is further coupled with the notion of a present "in which time is answered for [*ein-steht*]" by the historian writing history "for himself" (16). And the "historically conceived [*historisch Begriffenen*]" has time in its "inside" or "interior" (*Innern*) in thesis 17.

Interiorization, or "innering," is, then, the mode and place of Benjamin's rhetorical enactment of a past in a present and a present through a past. But as I argued above, this "inside" or "in" is not the autonomous mind or consciousness of some historical subject simply off writing history "for himself" but is rather constituted *within* the same tropological structure as is history, within the "fit" of metalepsis and prolepsis to one another. Benjamin wrote that "history in the strict sense is thus an image out of involuntary mindfulness [*unwillkürliches Eingedenken*],[24] an image that suddenly deposits or sets itself into [*sich einstellt*] the subject of history in an instant of danger" (GS, 1:1243). The historical image both comes out of and deposits itself into the subject's "inside" in an instant of rhetoricity that gives him his in-stance, or stance in history. The subject is with-in the structure that produces a present moment or stance in-between metalepsis and metaleptic prolepsis. From this tenuous tropological and temporal situation, not yet a position but always already positing, the image of an "I" in a rhetorical structure will constitute a narrative of historical meaning and understanding. In brief, it will tell a story.

Benjamin explicitly attacks the notion of history writing as storytelling when he condemns "the whore of 'Once upon a time' in the bordello of historicism" (16), but this renders his own storytelling only more ironic. In thesis 15, for example, he writes of an incident that supposedly occurred in Paris during the July revolution of 1830 and then quotes an "eyewitness," namely, Hugo (from *Choses vues*). But the "image" Hugo provides must be either historicism's "the way it really was" (which it may or may not be) or a story (which it certainly is). There is no "incident" outside of its narrative, nor any "eyewitness" account unmediated by the tropes of such a narrative. It is the rhetoric of another such narrative that, we shall see in conclusion, tells the story of Benjamin's theses "On the Concept of History."

All that remains to be said—and, in a sense, all that has been said—about the mechanism or structure of Benjamin's theses is contained in their first section. Thesis 1 tells a story: it begins, "As is well-known [*Bekanntlich soll es*]," but an earlier version has the more loquacious, "As is well-known, the legend has circulated for a long time [*Es lief bekanntlich eine zeitlang die Legende . . . um*]," and the French says simply, "On raconte qu'il aurait existé" (GS, 1:1247, 1260). The story or legend it tells is of an "automatic" chessplayer invented by one Wolfgang von Kempelen, but as with Hugo's verse, it recounts this historical "event" through some direct mediation: that of Edgar Allan Poe's story "Maelzel's Chess-Player," translated in Baudelaire's *Nouvelles histoires extraordinaires* and read by Benjamin in the Baudelaire translation.[25] Poe himself worked through some half a dozen prior texts to argue that the "true history" of the "machine" is that it is a fake—it was all done with mirrors—for it had a man inside. Benjamin does Poe one better by using the "story" to introduce another story, about a machine called "historical materialism."

Hermann Schweppenhäuser, Helmut Pfotenhauer, and Rolf Tiedemann are all on to something when they characterize the relationship between the paraphrase of the Poe story and the use to which Benjamin puts it as one between "sign" and "meaning" or between "image" and "interpretation" (M, 15, 28, 96ff.). The structure, in fact, recalls that of the "Angelus Novus," an image embedded in a rhetorical structure—an allegorical emblem—that generates a story about history; here, a story has been rendered into an image and will regenerate a story: a parable, or allegory. The "apparatus" of the chess-playing machine has a hunchback inside "pulling the strings," but in the analogy to historical materialism that Benjamin draws, the relationship is explicitly reversed: the "puppet . . . can take theology [i.e., the hunchback], which today, as we know, is small and ugly, into its service [*die Puppe, die man 'historischen Materialismus' nennt . . . die Theologie in ihren Dienst nimmt, die heute bekanntlich klein und hässlich ist*]." The extent to which this reversal causes problems for admirably informed readers of Benjamin is remarkable: Jürgen Habermas in an otherwise persuasive essay ends by missing the clear distinction and would reverse what Benjamin already has reversed;[26] Gerhard Kaiser would "let the image speak for itself" and thus would undo Benjamin's reversal (M, 44–45); and the one "vulgar Marxist" in the discussion, Heinz-Dieter Kittsteiner, reads the passage accurately but then would have historical materialism somehow "sublate" the "mystical" into the "rational" (M, 30). The thematics of this confusion—the reasons for it and the errors it leads to—are of considerable interest, but that is another story. Here, my point is that the thesis displays a chiasmic reversal (B':A'::A:B) in the form of a "philosophic" analogy ("To this apparatus one can imagine a counterpart [*Gegenstück*] in philosophy"). The rhetorical "apparatus" is in control of, or masters, the philosophic topic or thesis just as the automaton masters the hunchback. Tiedemann points out that both puppet and hunchback are brought together into the single apparatus of the automatic chess-player, but he then would have Benjamin in charge of, or "choosing," such rhetorical manipulation (M, 97–98). I would point out rather that what Tiedemann says of the first thesis—that two parts (puppet and hunchback, rhetoric and philosophy) are brought together within a single apparatus or construction—is true of the whole text of the theses: the material apparatus of a complex rhetorical construction, in charge even of the ostensible distinctions among its "imagistic" and "philo-sophic" parts. Thus, in the figure of the first thesis, the apparatus makes a "countermove" (*Gegenzuge*) to the move of another player who is outside the apparatus—"an automaton that was constructed in such a way that it could reply to each move by a chessplayer with a counter-move"—but the positing, or "move," of the figure itself, the image's tropological apparatus or rhetorical structure, can only be met by a re-active "counterpart" (*Gegenstück*) on the part of the "philosophical" analogy. In this thesis, philosophical or thematic argument is "in the service" of, or having its strings pulled by, the rhetorical structure. Ben-jamin does not "choose" here but opens his theses with a "counter-move" to that move already made "outside" his own text—by the text by Poe, the translation by Baudelaire, the carrying over and handing down of and by tropes and traditions in the already constituted field of intertextuality.

> *There have been many attempts at solving the mystery of the Automaton. The most general opinion in relation to it, an opinion not too unfrequently adopted by men who should have known better, was, as we have before said, that no immediate human agency was employed—in other words, that the machine was purely a machine and nothing else.*
>
> —Poe

To have implied that Benjamin did not act as "any immediate human agency" vis-à-vis the rhetorical structure of his text (with the stress on "immediate") is not to say that his theses are a "pure machine." Rhetor-ical structures and texts can be quite impure, especially in the relations of their stories to their images. The reception of redemption is quite explicitly associated by Benjamin with the accidental (*Zufall*) in theses 3 and 4. Or in thesis 15, in Hugo's anecdote, clocks are said to have been fired upon "independently and simultaneously." To this image, Benjamin adds that Hugo "may have owed his divination"—which in-terpretation is less Hugo's than Benjamin's, his story of revolutionary violence bringing time to a standstill—"to the rhyme." The rhyme of "tour" and "jour," this acoustic image or play of the signifiers in Hugo's verse, generates the evidence—less "eyewitness" *(Augenzeuge)* than "earwitness"—for the story. And Benjamin himself fails to note the crucial but equally arbitrary double entendre of *tour* as both the clock tower and the *turn*, the troping over of the present in the moment of revolution.

These sorts of "accidents" *(Zufälle)* will always fall out of any understanding of rhetorical structures available through a Marxist thematics, and they fall to the analytic task of a tropological poetics of historiography. Tiedemann would have Benjamin's rhetoricity inscribed by rules:

> The emphasis with which Benjamin's thought as a whole uses metaphorical language itself already forbids one from being satisfied with the mere dissolution of his metaphors, similes, and analogies. If Benjamin is playing a game there, then there must be rules to the game; if this is more than arbitrariness . . . then one can suppose that there are objective-historical grounds for these rules. (M, 95)

But the sense of rhetorical structures and their operation may finally be as lacking in "objective-historical" foundation as it is beyond a formalist understanding of rules or language games. It may be, in a borrowing of Benjamin's borrowing from Proust, involuntarily *(unwillkürlich)* tropological and tropologically involuntary. Thus, in thesis B, the "alternate ending" to the theses, when Benjamin shifts from political history to eschatology, from metalepsis to a tentative, subjunctive prolepsis ("For every second was the little gate through which the Messiah might enter"), and from statement to parable, this rhetorical shift may be understood as the theses' final shift to allegory. This allegory represents the *shift* of allegory itself, wherein every temporal event—"every second" of all of history—forever signifies, points to, or shifts to another, by way of the figure of the Messiah. But what, after all, is a Messiah? An allegory of allegory, a sign standing in the absence of its meaning, "that signifies precisely the non-being of what it presents" (GS, 1:406). The Messiah is also an image for a story-to-come.

In another version, Benjamin added one last sentence to this "last ending" to the theses: "The hinge [*Angel*] in which [the little gate] swings is *Eingedenken*" (GS, 1:1252). The eschatological "hinge" is *Eingedenken*, that attentive mindfulness of history whose tropological structure of metalepsis and prolepsis provides the folds, angles, and pivots where a story—even the Messiah—might enter and lodge or displace itself. But what are we to make of the relationship between this *Angel* and Benjamin's *Engel*, or "angel"? Nothing, perhaps, except that it appears accidental: an arbitrary or involuntary (*unwillkürlich*) association of graphemes, be it by the slip of a writer's pen or the slip of a reader's eye, a written image that can be the site and cite of Benjamin's coming story. We are still reading it.

8

Benjamin, Baudelaire, and the Allegory of History

In Benjamin's theses, his last testament on history and historiography, historical meaning reveals itself in and as an image. The historical image is the mode of existence of the truth of history, but this truth is not a representational one vis-à-vis an "eternal" past (the position of historicism, which Benjamin attacks) but a productive one vis-à-vis the agent and present moment by which the image is constituted. Within the formulations of what he calls his "historical materialist" theory of historiography and historical action, he constructs a theory of reading and rewriting the past, not in the manner of a historicist reconstruction of what actually was (or might have been) the case, but treating the past as its pointing toward, calling out for, intending, and provoking its rewriting by the present and for the sake of both the past, which might otherwise slip away, and the present, which might otherwise become like the past, "unredeemed." Historical meaning, according to this formulation, would mean that the past means *otherwise* than it did in the past, and this is part of Benjamin's genuinely *dialectical* construction; for as Hegel said in the "Preface" to his *Phenomenology*, "meaning experiences that it means otherwise than it intended."[1]

In the previous chapter, an analysis of the theses exposed their position as a kind of *literary* historiography and specifically as a rhetorical or allegorical theory of history, where tropes and allegory are the means of the *production* of historical meaning (in the movement from events to images), so that with Benjamin historiography can be said to transform itself into "historiotropography." But is there a perspective within which Benjamin's theory of the construction of the historical image evaluates itself? Is there a historical register—or some other kind— upon which Benjamin's argument locates the historical image and its truth-value? Already in the last chapter, we could notice the pull of stories upon the historical images: Benjamin's own stories of salvation, as partial or qualified as they are, and the stories of his interpreters, which would make the theses into the occasions for narratives about a lost past or a hoped-for future. The theses' own historical register would seem to be, obviously enough, the immediate pressure of the power of European fascism, and specifically the Hitler-Stalin pact; but as obvious as this seems to his retrospective reader, this location of his argument occurs for the most part only sotto voce and does not itself become an explicit object of critical or metahistorical reflection in his text. His studies of Baudelaire in the context of nineteenth-century Paris, on the other hand, would seem to be the more promising place to pursue a more searching answer to our question of the perspectives, historical or otherwise, within which Benjamin situates his discussion of historical meaning as a tropological and allegorical image. And what if the historical images and their incorporations within narratives and arguments are themselves absolute, ahistorical, resistant of all rehistoricizing? If so, then Benjamin's critique of historicism in the name of a more radical historical truth would reveal itself as radical beyond any rehistoricizing political front or orientation, going to the root of our ascriptions of meaning to time.

The value of posing the question this way—the historicizable or non-historicizable character of what Benjamin considers historical meaning—is not only that it reintroduces some balance into recent Anglo-American "reconstructions" of Benjamin's thoughts on history.[2] It also may allow Benjamin's instance to cast some light upon the similarly structured contemporary (and not only contemporary) debate on literary theory and literary history, which alternately fears the subsumption of literature's historicity into literary theory and effects or wishes a re-historicization of theory. When it is additionally seen that Benjamin's work here focuses upon the figure of Charles Baudelaire, an interest in the relations between literature and history only receives a finer point, for Baudelaire has long stood (for Marcel Raymond as for Hugo Friedrich, for Edmund Wilson as for Monroe K. Spears) at a historical watershed in literary history's constructions of its narratives of the differences and the connections between premodern and modern poetry.[3] The exemplary value of Benjamin's late work on Baudelaire may be that it casts a *mise en scène* for all these dramas of history and theory: the attempt at a sophisticated historical understanding of great literature and the theoretical lesson to be drawn from its results.

> *Benjamin is here. He's working on an essay about Baudelaire. . . .*
> *It's all mysticism within a posture against mysticism. It's in such a form that*

the materialist construction of history is being implemented! It's all rather frightening.

—Bertolt Brecht, 25 July 1938[4]

From Benjamin's project for what he called a "total history" (*Gesamtgeschichte*) of Paris in the nineteenth century, an unfinished work known as the *Passagen-Werk*, there issued his renewed work on Baudelaire, some three hundred pages of chapters, drafts, notes, and exposés that are today collectively called *Charles Baudelaire, Ein Lyriker im Zeitalter des Hochkapitalismus*, and have been edited separately from the work on Baudelaire that remained within the *Passagen* project. (I say "renewed work" on Baudelaire because Benjamin had, of course, published a translation of Baudelaire's *Tableaux parisiens* in 1923.) When Benjamin began to refocus his attention on Baudelaire in 1937, he had in mind a single essay, but by the time he had finished "Das Paris des Second Empire bei Baudelaire" in 1938, he had a three-part study— "Die Boheme," "Der Flaneur," "Die Moderne"—and this he now saw as, altogether, only the second part of what was to be a book in three parts. His letters from this period speak of the historical character of his study in a twofold sense: his analysis and evaluation of Baudelaire are to be historical rather than formalist or biographical, and they are supposed to enable Benjamin to move from reading literature to writing history.[5] Of his projected book, the first part was to be called "Baudelaire als Allegoriker": "[It] will demonstrate the authoritative significance of allegory in the *Fleurs du mal*. It presents the construction of the allegorical perspective in Baudelaire."[6] The claim is furthermore for an explicitly dialectical treatment of allegory in Baudelaire. For if the planned first part was to pose the "question" or "problem," the third, provisionally titled "Das Neue und Immergleiche," later "Die Ware als poetischer Gegenstand," would present what Benjamin called the "synthesis" or "social solution,"[7] while the second part, the part actually written, "provides the data necessary for this solution [and] is, generally speaking, that of the antithesis."[8]

This projected movement sketched in Benjamin's letters to Horkheimer is from a question of literary form and structure to its "social solution" in the commodity understood as both a social factum and, in itself, a formal structure for the representation of value. But the project went unfulfilled, in its being left both incomplete and initially unwelcomed. Horkheimer and Adorno rejected the second part, "Das Paris des Second Empire," when it was sent to the *Zeitschrift für Sozialforschung* for publication. Adorno's critical response has become famous in Marxist literary-theoretical circles; I quote here only in part:

The motifs are collected but not pursued. . . . Panorama and "trace" ["*Spur*"], *flaneur* and arcade, the modern and the ever-the-same [*immer Gleiches*], *without* theoretical interpretation . . . this dialectic thus falls apart around one point: mediation. There is a governing tendency throughout to relate Baudelaire's pragmatic content immediately to neighboring aspects of the social history of his time, and indeed to aspects of an economic sort whenever possible. . . . I consider it methodologically infelicitous [*methodisch unglücklich*] to use striking individual aspects of the superstructure in a so-called "materialist" manner, in that one sets them unmediately or even causally in relation to corresponding aspects of the infrastructure. The materialist determination of cultural characteristics is possible only by way of mediation through the total process [*Gesamtprozess*]. . . . The "mediation" that I miss, and that I find covered up by materialist-historiographic conjuring [*materialistisch-historiographische Beschwörung*], is really nothing other than precisely the theory that your work neglects. The neglecting of theory affects a kind of empiricism . . . thus one could say that the work resides at the crossroads of magic and positivism. This spot is bewitched [*verhext*]. Only theory can break the spell: your own, ruthless, thoroughly speculative theory.[9]

This is the accusation against vulgar Marxism. Adorno criticizes the lack of *theoretical* interpretation, noting instead a merely circumstantial collation of Marxist-historicist "facts" in unmediated "correspondence" with Baudelaire's texts, a reference to social-historical overview without interpretive engagement of a theoretical (instead of merely a historical) "Gesamtprozess"; in short, empirical or positivistic facts without dialectical or critical theory.

Benjamin's dignified response notes Adorno's exaggeration and misrepresentation and reminds him that "the philosophical foundations of the book are not capable of being surveyed from the perspective of the second part [i.e., "Das Paris des Second Empire"]."

The construction demands that the second part of the book be constituted essentially out of philological material. Here it is a matter . . . of a methodological precaution. . . . the philological interpretation of the author is to be sublated by dialectical materialists in a Hegelian manner [*auf hegelsche Art aufzuheben*].[10]

In this remarkable response to Adorno's accusation that Benjamin lacked dialectical mediation or speculative theory and was telling stories instead—"wo Historie und Magie oszillieren," Adorno had written—Benjamin replies by telling him a story: a story of the theory to be supplied when he finishes telling his story of Baudelaire.[11] Adorno's principled position remained that this was not "theory," that history and literature had not yet been integrated in a legitimately theoretical way.

The "solution" was never written. The essay "On Some Motifs in Baudelaire" ("Über einige Motive bei Baudelaire") was written instead.[12] Only after almost a dozen pages does this essay actually take up the Baudelaire of the earlier study, and then in a greatly self-limited form. Sections on the crowd are preserved and even improved. A striking interpretation of the poem "A une passante" is presented in a new form, and there is a dense section (no. 10) on the topic of Baudelaire's *correspondances*. But otherwise everything from "Das Paris des Second Empire" drops out, including the theory of the commodity, that long-promised dialectical "social solution" to the problem of Baudelaire's allegory. What also drops out is a discrete half-page buried in the middle of "Die Moderne" of "Das Paris des Second Empire": an interpretation of one of Baudelaire's greatest poems, "Le Cygne." If we now turn to his elliptical remarks on "Le Cygne," together with some of his notes on allegory in Baudelaire, a more adequate understanding may emerge of why the problem of allegory, together with "Le Cygne" itself, resisted its *historical* "social solution" in an interpretive model of the commodity.

Benjamin spoke of the "antinomy of appearance and significance [*Schein und Bedeutung*] [as] fundamental for the development of the problem of *allegory* as well as that of phantasmagoria" (1174).[13] Such an antinomy might appear to suggest a dissolution of appearance in a signifying movement toward significance; in Benjamin's paragraph on "Le Cygne," for example, Paris is described as being in "constant movement" but also "*erstarrt*," ossified: "It becomes brittle like glass, but also like glass, [it becomes] transparent—that is, with respect to its significance [*auf ihre Bedeutung hin*]" (SE, 585–86). But rather than designating a static opposition between two sides, or a simple overcoming of one by the other, "antinomy" here actually indicates for Benjamin a persistent and unresolved interaction between the two. On the one hand, he wrote that "the allegorical mode of perception [*Anschauungsweise*] is always built upon a devalued world of appearances" (1151). Here, in "Le Cygne," the city and its associations are said by Benjamin to be destroyed, devalued—fragile, decayed: "Paris's status is fragile: it is surrounded with emblems [*Sinnbildern*] of fragility. Creaturely ones: the negress and the swan; and historical ones: Andromaque, 'Hector's widow, and wife of Helenus.' Mourning for what was and hopelessness toward what is coming [*Trauer über das was war und Hoffnungslosigkeit in das Kommende*] is the trait common to the emblems" (SE, 586). But this assertion of Baudelaire's allegorical negation of the world of appearances does not imply a movement from the negative appearances and emblems to their dissolution and resolution in some positive allegorical significance in the manner of some Platonizing kinds of allegory. (It will remain to the last chapter of this study to examine more fully Benjamin's argument about "negative" emblems and their "dissolution" in allegorical significance.) Rather, in Benjamin's suggestions about "Le Cygne," modern and ancient images are said to be formally and thematically related in the poem: "This decrepitude [*Hinfälligkeit*] is that in which the modern and the ancient are finally and most intimately related" (SE, 585). And so the meaning or idea behind this explicitly allegorical poem is apparently one of the suspension and interpenetration of contraries. Ancient and modern are blended (Benjamin's term is *Durchdringung*, "permeation" [SE, 585]), both as allegorical appearance *(Schein) and as* its significance *(Bedeutung)*, which means that appearance and meaning are themselves also blended.

What we have, then, is an "antinomy" of appearance and meaning but also a "playing together" *(Ineinanderspielen)* of them, an "extinguishing" *(Auslöschung)* of appearance in meaning but also their "blending." Such are the nuances of Benjamin's model of allegory in Baudelaire. With specific respect to his remarks on "Le Cygne," one sees that if imagery and meaning, like ancient and modern, have "decay" in common, then there is something in common between his structural understanding of Baudelaire's allegory and his thematic understanding of "Le Cygne." "Hopelessness toward what is coming" is shared by ancient and modern in "Le Cygne" because each will decay; this is a thematic understanding attributed to the poem, specifically a temporal one. The *meaning* of decay or coming to an end—represented in the poem in such lines as "Le vieux Paris n'est plus" and "Paris change!"—brings with it, for Benjamin, a structural imperative: the allegorical image. "What one knows that one will soon no longer have before one—this is what becomes an image," he wrote (SE, 590).[14] The meaning of decay or ending is allegorically preserved in an image of decay or ending. But qua image—and here is a paradox—the temporal process is apparently arrested, and the meaning is *of* this arrest or *Stillstand:* temporality is of decay, it means decay, and yet as temporality it halts *in* decay. Rather than having a continuous temporal movement or trajectory between ancient and modern, beginning and end, one has in the allegorical image time—ancient or modern, each past or passing—frozen in advance as always already passing, "images . . . from out of the ocean of the 'past before the past' [*Vorvergangenheit*]" (1148). Thus, in Benjamin's paradox, Baudelaire's allegorical poems represent temporality as decay, permanently and in advance—the modern as the ancient—but thereby preserve it anew, as if original and enduring. A circularity is implied here: the modern decays as the ancient does; the meaning of decay is

the occasion for its imagery; the imagery as such fulfills the meaning—
something has become an image, no longer alive—but also contradicts
it, preserving the negative temporality as a *Vorvergangenheit* that could
then be followed by ancient and modern, each in decay. The circularity,
however, is arrested. To follow the circle is not to arrive at a "future,"
even a negative or repeating one: "Baudelaire is no pessimist. He is not
one, because for him there is a taboo upon the future" (ZP, 657). The
allegorical, one recalls, was "built upon a devalued world of appearances"; it is "a destruction of the organic and the animate" (ZP, 669,
670). Instead of an organic *circle*, with past decaying into future and
future into past, there is a semi-*circularity* frozen in the flight of its arc:
"the power of ossification [is] a kind of mimesis of death that appears a
hundred times in Baudelaire's poetry" (SE, 587). In allegory, life is *represented*, but precisely as an allegorical mimesis or *Bild*, as the representation of death: "Whatever is struck by the allegorical intention is sev-
ered from the contexts of life: it is at once destroyed and conserved
[*zerschlagen und konserviert zugleich*]. Allegory holds fast to ruins [*Trüm-
mern*]. It offers the image of ossified unrest [*das Bild der erstarrten Un-
ruhe*]" (ZP, 666). Ossified unrest; "life that signifies death" (ZP, 667);
the modern signifying—devalued, already decayed—the ancient; the
image conserving life's meaning as that which is already dead precisely
by destroying it as life and "conserving" it as an image: Benjamin's Bau-
delairean allegory.

Now the commodity structure was, in Benjamin's design for his project, supposed to indicate a social *and historical* "solution" to Baudelaire's allegorical perspective. To his note that "the allegorical mode of
perception is always built upon a devalued world of appearances," he
immediately added: "The specific devaluation of the thingly world
[*Entwertung der Dingwelt*] that lies in the commodity is the foundation
of Baudelaire's allegorical intention" (1151). Allegory is built upon a
devalued world of appearances, and the devalued thingly world of the
commodity is supposed to be the specific foundation of Baudelaire's allegory. But implicitly, in Benjamin's move from the *appearance* to the
thing-as-commodity, the devalued world would reassume value as the
material, thingly, concrete "foundation" for the allegorical perspective.
This would indeed appear to be Benjamin's intention in his initial
claims for the commodity as the dialectical "social solution" to the
problem of Baudelaire's allegory. Thus, as a *historical* argument about
allegory, and as a *methodological* step in his "dialectical" construction of
such a historical argument, Benjamin could write: "The commodity has
stepped into the place of the allegorical *form* of perception [*Die Ware ist
an die Stelle der allegorischen Anschauungsform getreten*]" (ZP, 686; my

emphasis): a formal—indeed, Kantian—category has been supplanted by, or replaced and substituted for, a material-historical one. This would be Benjamin's "materialist" fulfillment of the literary problem of allegory.

Or has the commodity thereby become allegorical? This question of a material "foundation" or substitution for the allegorically dominated and devalued "world of appearances" comes to the fore in another of Benjamin's late writings in "Zentralpark": "The devaluation of the thingly world in allegory is surpassed [*überboten*] within the thingly world itself through the commodity" (ZP, 660). What happens within allegory—the devaluation of the thingly world to its being a mere "world of appearances"—is exceeded or surpassed (*überboten*) within the thingly world itself by the commodity. Our understanding of this assertion depends, in effect, upon our translation of *überboten*. For on the one hand, allegory is "surpassed" by the structure and effect of the commodity itself *within* the material world, but on the other hand, "surpassed" does not mean "bypassed," let alone "canceled," "overcome," or *aufgehoben*, and thus it is not so much that allegory is outbid or overtrumped by the commodity as that the commodity itself (re)introduces the allegorical structure "within the thingly or material world itself." The commodity does not end, overcome, or dialectically resolve allegory: it repeats it. Two further notes from "Zentralpark," side by side, may elaborate this. First, "with the new modes of production leading to imitations, appearance precipitated into the commodities [*schlägt sich der Schein in den Waren nieder*]." New modes of production, themselves imitating, imitatable, and imitated, lead to the precipitation of allegorical semblances into the structures of the commodities themselves. Appearance and the "world of appearances" are not overcome; rather, commodities become the new—or continued—allegories. Then, in the second note, immediately appended to the preceding one, "There is for people as they are today only one radical novelty, and it is always the same: death" (ZP, 668). The claim of "radical novelty" for modern man in fact precipitates into the ever-the-same; the only new thing or experience is the same as it always was: death, the "one" thing that can only be experienced as new, and is always experienced as such. That these two notes link the new with the ever-the-same, just as they link the commodity with allegory, is no accident; one recalls that the planned "part" of the Baudelaire book on "die Ware als poetischer Gegenstand" was also originally entitled "Das Neue und das Immerwiedergleiche."

What, then, of the commodity form as a social-economic fact that might pose as a dialectical historical "solution" to the allegorical perspective? How could it transform the structural characterization of allegory—appearance and significance reciprocally representing decay and death—if it is itself a repetition of allegory and, as newness, also means the ever-the-same: allegory and death? Another note from "Zentralpark" reads: "The dialectic of commodity-production: the novelty [*Neuheit*] of the product receives (as a stimulus to demand) a formerly unknown significance [*eine bisher unbekannte Bedeutung*]; the ever-the-same [*das Immerwiedergleiche*] appears strikingly in mass production for the first time" (ZP, 680). The novelty of a product, as a stimulus to demand, receives a new significance, namely, as new—a significance of the commodity as appearance, independent of its original- or use-value as thing. But the "new" significance—the "formerly unknown"—is, in what Benjamin calls the "dialectic of commodity-production," the ever-the-sameness of commodities as commodities, as products for demand rather than use, as appearances with a significance that now appears as allegorical: like the meaning of death behind the modern, the ever-the-same is behind the new. The "newness," the "previously unheard of," the "for the first time"—all markers of historical occurrence in Benjamin's exact formulation—reveal their meaning in this note as allegorical: the ever-the-same. Thus, Benjamin's "dialectic" not only turns, as the commodity does, into allegory; the whole note as referential to a historical event—for it intends itself as such—undercuts its own claim for (historical) novelty by displaying its structure and significance as (allegorical) repetition of the same.

The commodity, then, would appear to have scarce chance of "resolving" Benjamin's problem of Baudelaire's allegorical perspective, since as a phenomenon literally signifying a material social-historical event, it is also made, in Benjamin's hands, to reveal its structure and significance as allegory. We are now perhaps closer to understanding why both the problem of allegory and the structure of the commodity drop out of the Baudelaire study in its last stage. But our conclusion cannot simply be that Baudelaire's allegory receives no historical resolution for Benjamin, because Benjamin knew, in some sense, that his proposed historical answer—the commodity—bore within it the sameness and the re-placement, the reappearance, of his problem: the appearance and significance of allegory. A reading of "Le Cygne" may show what actually becomes of the devalued, thingly world of appearances within Baudelaire's allegory and Benjamin's history. An allegory of history lies within their respective stories of allegory.

Comme tout ce que vous faites, monsieur, votre Cygne est une idée. Commes toutes les idées vraies, il a des profondeurs. Ce cygne dans la poussière a sous lui plus d'abîmes que le cygne des eaux sans fond du lac de Gaube. Ces abîmes, on les entrevoit dans vos vers.

—Hugo to Baudelaire, upon receiving "Le Cygne," 18 December 1859[15]

In a seminal study from 1960, Hans Robert Jauss argued that "Le Cygne"'s representations submit to a process of "derealization" *(Entrealisierung)* and that exterior referents or objects are ultimately absent as a consequence of the "alienating" character and operations of the poem's allegorical and mythic imagery (Andromaque, the swan). Instead of the allegorical representation of a prior, or better, a *timeless* truth within or through reality—the Platonic tradition of allegory—the allegorical imagery is here in a negative or discordant relation to its significance, inverting allegorical truth into a self-referential sense of lost significance and, together with this, inverting worldly representation into the representation of its absence.[16] More recently, Wolfgang Fietkau has scrupulously pursued the complications of the poem regarding both its own language and the language of its sources (Racine, Ovid, Virgil) in order to tease out layer after layer of realistic reference and rhetorical ambivalence, avowal, and reservation; his goal is finally, through the accumulation of massive evidence from contemporary political and cultural documents, and with an eye for what he calls the "univocality of the ambiguity" *(Eindeutigkeit der Zweideutigkeit)* of the poem, an interpretation of "Le Cygne" as a political allegory about the bourgeois republic and Louis Bonaparte (Andromaque and Pyrrhus, respectively), the failed revolution of 1848 and the coming of the Commune in 1871.[17] These two studies of "Le Cygne" are among the best of those few that have attempted to learn from Benjamin's work on Baudelaire since it was left among the scattered notes of the *Passagen* project:[18] Jauss follows Benjamin in his accent upon the tension between, on the one hand, the allegorical image and its significance and, on the other hand, the "devalued world of appearances" of Baudelaire's allegory; Fietkau, with an explicitness that approaches devotion, recalls his master in his skillful use of Benjamin's translations as interpretive tools, his attention to Benjamin's notions of the commodity and the whore (apropos of Andromaque), and his self-avowed indebtedness to Benjamin's studies for the "theoretical armature" or model for his own social-historical interpretation of literature. Yet despite what one could call Fietkau's philology of excess, neither interpretation pursues the Benjaminian reading of "Le Cygne" sketched in "Das Paris des Second Empire bei Baudelaire" to the point of being able to account for its having dropped out of the last stage of the Baudelaire studies.

Benjamin's several pages on Baudelaire's "Le Cygne" are thus a compelling if elliptical legacy. Perhaps despite, but also because of, the poem's manifest centrality to the interpreter's overall understanding of the poet, the task of a detailed reading of the poem in question falls away before the appearance that the poem "reads itself" in accordance with a Benjaminian view. Indeed, "Le Cygne" appears to correspond with uncanny accuracy to Benjamin's most fundamental theses concerning Baudelaire and his allegory. The poem's refrainlike announcement, "je pense à . . . ," dominating the poem from beginning to end, signals memory of the ancient (Troy, Epirus), the mythological (the swan), the proto-historical (the comparison to Ovid's first man), and, of course, the near-contemporary Paris that is passing away, becoming "Le vieux Paris" in the face of its modernization.[19] If memory is in fact indifferently called forth toward the more recent as well as the most ancient, the contemporary real as well as the mythological, the sense of the "blending" *(Durchdringung)* of the modern and the ancient with which Benjamin introduced his brief discussion of "Le Cygne" (SE, 585) is already implicated in the poem's first strophe.

> *Andromaque, je pense à vous! Ce petit fleuve,*
> *Pauvre et triste miroir où jadis resplendit*
> *L'immense majesté de vos douleurs de veuve,*
> *Ce Simoïs menteur qui par vos pleurs grandit*

The figure from antiquity of whom the poetic persona thinks is herself already a newer or later version of herself, in Epirus (a "new" Troy) instead of her original Troy, beside "Ce Simoïs menteur" instead of the real one (not to mention her being perhaps Racine's Andromaque as much as or more than Virgil's, or the way in which she recalls as well her stepmother Hecuba in Ovid's *Metamorphoses* 13, saving her son Hector's ashes as she is dragged away from his tomb): the persona calls to mind an image of antiquity that is itself, in turn, an image of an earlier antiquity, an image engaged in image-making. Thus, the skillful transition from the first to the second strophe,

> *A fécondé soudain ma mémoire fertile,*
> *Comme je traversais le nouveau Carrousel.*
> *Le vieux Paris n'est plus (la forme d'une ville*
> *Change plus vite, hélas! que le coeur d'un mortel);*

from Andromaque (back) to the new ("le nouveau Carrousel"), reduplicates the structural movement of the first, as a Benjaminian understanding of Baudelaire would now expand from the image of antiquity as itself both old and new, original and image, to include in this doubled image one standing for "the modern" as well, as if the modern came out of that ancient *Vorgergangenheit*. The "new" Paris recalls the old one that is passing away ("Le vieux Paris n'est plus"), and it semantically recalls or provokes the image of the ancient in the first strophe. But as the poem is read sequentially, it is the first strophe's doubled image of antiquity that precedes, leads to, and already implies the doubled image *(nouveau-vieux)* of modernity in the second one. Each strophe is the image *(Bild)* of the other's significance *(Bedeutung)*, each at once the original or "old" and the new, the replacement, the "menteur."

This in-mixing *(Ineinanderspielen)* of image and significance, old and new, ancient and modern, in the first two strophes, which prevents their strict separation along the lines of "mere image" and "true" allegorical meaning or reference, continues in the second strophe's last two lines. At first glance, the image of Paris changing (from "vieux" to "nouveau") and of time decaying ("Le vieux . . . n'est plus") would seem to signify an opposing allegorical meaning: Paris and time may pass, but the feelings of a mortal heart do not (in accordance with the lines' parallel oppositions of *forme* as exterior and *coeur* as interior, *ville* as inorganic and *mortel* as human). Upon closer examination, however, even these parenthetical lines exchange image and significance amongst themselves and with the preceding ones as well. The "coeur," after all, changes as well, if not as rapidly as a city, and thus the apparent constancy of one's memories as opposed to the exterior images itself changes into the very movement of change between old and new, new and old. To the extent that the lines also recall Andromaque, still acting out her sufferings as Hector's widow while the "form" of her city (Troy) has changed from original to copy or image, the apparent *meaning* of the phrase for the "modern" or present moment is that there is a constant, remembering persona amidst the material and temporal change and novelty (and loss). But with reference back to the first strophe, the meaning of these lines then reappears as an *image* for the very image and significance of antiquity—its change and thus its loss manifest themselves in the reduplication of images—so that the modern appears as the ancient, the meaning as the image, and vice versa. It is neither exaggeration nor parody to say, together with Benjamin, that in these eight lines, each "new element" *(Neues)* appears as such *and* reappears as "the ever-the-same" *(das Immerwiedergleiche)*.

If I have lingered this long over the first two strophes, it has been in the effort to present a part of the poem under the focus of a "Benjaminian" lens with enough persuasive power to allow me to forgo a similar reconstruction of its remaining strophes. The material for such a reconstruction would not be lacking. The third and fourth strophes,

Je ne vois qu'en esprit tout ce camp de baraques,
Ces tas de chapiteaux ébauchés et de fûts,
Les herbes, les gros blocs verdis par l'eau des flaques,
Et, brillant aux carreaux, le bric-à-brac confus.

Là s'étalait jadis une ménagerie;
Là je vis, un matin, à l'heure où sous les cieux
Froids et clairs le Travail s'éveille, où la voirie
Pousse un sombre ouragan dans l'air silencieux,

correspond, in the details of the technical meanings of certain words
("camp de baraques," "voirie"), to Benjamin's stress on the importance
of what he called the "Haussmannisierung" of Paris for an understanding of Baudelaire, while at the same time the strophes allow a sense of
antiquity to shine through the images of the modern, in the manner in
which Benjamin thought Haussmann's modernization of Paris to represent a memorial to the dead.[20] Of the first strophe of the second part of
the poem,

Paris change! mais rien dans ma mélancolie
N'a bougé! palais neufs, échafaudages, blocs,
Vieux faubourgs, tout pour moi devient allégorie,
Et mes chers souvenirs sont plus lourds que des rocs.

Benjamin wrote in a note that it "has the movement of a cradle rocking
back and forth between modern and ancient" (1142). He might have
added that with the subtle shift from the second strophe's "Change plus
vite . . . que . . . " to this strophe's "change! mais rien . . . N'a
bougé!," the first part's allegory of modern and ancient now appears
under the Benjaminian hat of melancholy ("During the Passion of the
melancholic, allegories are the stations of the cross" [ZP, 663]). In the
second part's first strophe, the more there is the new ("change!"), the
more there is the ever-the-same of melancholy: as Benjamin wrote,
"mourning for what was and hopelessness toward what is coming." The
termini technici of Benjamin's theory are gathered here as they rarely are
in a single Baudelaire poem, so that the lines might serve as a motto for
Benjamin's studies: "neufs . . . Vieux . . . tout pour moi devient allégorie." And the "souvenirs" heavier than the "rocs," while obviously
reflecting the persistence of memory in the poem and the immediate
claim of unbudging melancholy, as opposed to the stone forms of the
city that are all-too-light or easily changed, these memories are also,
through the hyperbolic comparison, made material, reified, like Benjamin's *Erinnerung* or *Andenken* deposited into a devalued thingly world.

As the second part of the poem concludes, the persistence of memory ("Je pense" repeated three times: "Je pense à mon grand cygne, avec ses gestes fous," "Je pense à la négresse, amaigrie et phthisique," "Je pense aux matelots oubliés dans une île") is repeatedly linked to an even greater persistence of the image. Once it has been said that "Aussi devant ce Louvre *une* image m'opprime" (my emphasis), as if actualizing in its oppression the "weight" of the preceding "souvenirs," all the images recur: first "ce Louvre" (as opposed to the older, unchanged one), then the swan, then Andromaque, then a new one—the Negress—finally an image of the allegorico-melancholic image itself, "quiconque a perdu ce qui ne se retrouve / Jamais, jamais!"[21] As Benjamin said: "What one knows that one will soon no longer have before one—this is what becomes an image." In other words, an image of time: the poem's temporality displayed in its unfolding of images of time as change, as unfulfillment ("un désir sans trêve"), as emptiness ("un tombeau vide"), as loss ("les cocotiers absents"), ultimately as decay and death.

It is as if, after an anecdote of memory in the poem's first part, the "souvenirs" of the second part have set off, with the appearance of one image, a series of imagistic memories that can know no anecdotal or narrative end: time, under the allegorical structure of ancient and modern, new and ever-the-same, will know no historical, ex post facto narrative construction, but rather only the iterative or repetitive "Je pense à," with each thought being of the unchanging loss brought about by changing time. The persona's "I" stands, not *after,* but forever before or in the face of this temporality; and as a result it has no stance or character other than that of the image itself. Each allegorical "mask" here—Paris, swan, Andromaque, Negress, "whomever" ("quiconque"); the modern, the natural, the mythological, the ancient, the exotic, the human—each is at home in Baudelaire's temporality, and each mask that the melancholic gazes at is the death mask of time.

But with this, I would not want a reading of "Le Cygne" to have its last word, if only because the last strophe has yet to be glanced at. The present reading of "Le Cygne" has been entirely thematic to this point in its attempts to lay bare the Benjaminian theme of allegory in a central Baudelaire poem. But if now, in an attempt to understand the poem's "last word," we look more closely, images of a different sort may emerge—no less allegorical, perhaps, but in a different relation to their significance. And we may take a guiding hint from Hannah Arendt, who, responding to Adorno in Benjamin's posthumous defense, praised Benjamin's understanding of the Marxian superstructure-substructure (i.e., infrastructure) relationship as "in a precise sense, a metaphorical one." She went on to say that he understood "the theory of the superstructure as the final doctrine of metaphorical thinking . . . he directly related the superstructure to the so-called 'material' substructure, which to him meant the totality of sensually experienced data."[22] Our task, in other words, is to pursue to a limit the "metaphorics" that arise from and return to the "material . . . of sensually experienced data" and to raise there the question of a *material* dimension of Baudelaire's text and of allegory on the far side of Benjamin's "materialist" social-historical model as well as Arendt's "material"-sensualist (or phenomenal) model of a metaphoric or imagistic substructure to Benjamin's own allegoresis.

One may note the oppositions of *vieux-nouveau* and *plein-vide* implicit in the line "Un vieux Souvenir sonne à plein souffle du cor":

> *Ainsi dans la forêt où mon esprit s'exile*
> *Un vieux Souvenir sonne à plein souffle du cor!*
> *Je pense aux matelots oubliés dans une île,*
> *Aux captifs, aux vaincus! . . . à bien d'autres encor!*

In the line, we hear the poem's preceding lines echoed in the words "vieux," "Souvenir," "plein." Rendered thematic, the horn's call to the hunt would be for a kind of semiotic pursuit of the poem's allegorical significance, which hitherto has repeatedly reverted from new to old, old to new, in an iterative series of allegorical memories within a structure of melancholy: "Je pense à . . . Je pense à . . . Je pense à. . . ." Such pursuit would be *à l'infini*—"à bien d'autres encor!" the *cor*-rhyme implies—and there would be no "last word" to Baudelaire's allegory but that of an unhappy consciousness, infinitely reflecting itself in the echo. But along with the strictly verbal repetitions in this line, another path of signification unfolds. This path leads back to the "souvenir" of the anecdote of the poem's first part: "Là je vis, un matin . . . Un cygne." The swan is also, as "mythe étrange et fatal," a *"vieux* Souvenir," the oldest—the mythical—element in the poem, such as Andromaque, already imitating Troy, could never be. The only "son" ("Un vieux Souvenir sonne . . . ") or expression in the poem has indeed been the swan's "Eau, quand donc pleuvras tu?" And the sounds of this line echo those of the line of the swan far more dominantly than they anticipate their echo in the end-rhyme: *"sonne* à *plein* souffle du *cor"* / "le *coeur plein* de *son* beau lac natal," where the sounds in question reflect one another across the length of the poem in a kind of palindrome.

Phenomenally, then, as Arendt's "sensually experienced data" in relation to possible significance, the line sounds like the swan. Specifically, it sounds as a Latinism: "plein souffle du cor" may *refer* to the hunting horn, but it *signifies* as well a full horn or *cornucopia*. The tension between "cor"—sounding like "corps," with its associations of substantial presence—and the "souffle" of air or breath corresponds in its implicit irony to that between the *cornucopia* as the presence of a harvest and the "vieux Souvenir" as the sound, through horn and air, of absence.

If the line of the "vieux Souvenir" sounds like the swan *and* like a cornucopia, this is because the swan was invoked with the same ironic fullness: "le coeur plein de son beau lac natal." Perhaps like a horn ("coeur plein de son"), perhaps like a cornucopia itself (full of its natural ambience), but certainly full of sound: "plein de *son* b*eau* lac" as full of the sound of water. The phenomenal signifier *eau* signifies within another sign *(beau)* the very significance that is being ironically represented; there is no water *except* as the sound of water in the absence of its meaning as referent or representation. What the swan finally "says" or sounds, of course, is: "Eau" ("Eau, quand donc pleuvras-tu?").

Jonathan Culler has insightfully observed that when the swan "speaks," it apostrophizes water, and as the only utterance in the poem that might stand in a mimetic relation to the persona's own apostrophe ("Andromaque, je pense à vous!"), it in fact apostrophizes apostrophe: to want to say "Eau," as *vouloir-dire* or intention, is to say "o!" phonetically or phenomenally.[23] But this bird "plein de [l']'eau' [the sound 'ô']" is located, representationally, in the absence of water: "Pres d'un ruisseau sans eau," as ironically as the cornucopia invoked by a "plein souffle du cor" full of air. "Un ruisseau sans eau" is "ruisseau" "sans eau": *ruisseau,* not even a full sound of "ruisseau," but a strange half-absence, a sign that cancels the substantiality of what it appears to announce even as it phenomenally announces it.[24]

These associations of sound and meaning are sustained at the level of what appears—or sounds. The reading of "Le Cygne" along the lines of Benjamin's understanding of Baudelaire's allegory unfolded relations of image and significance such that old and new, ancient and modern, and image and significance themselves were explained in a structure of allegorical repetition trapped within melancholic memory: change as the ever-the-same, temporality as decay, meaning as the face of death. A thematic reading of the last strophe suggested "more of the same": "à bien d'autres encor," *ad infinitum*. It was at this point that attention was called to another dimension of the image in Benjamin's model of allegory and in Baudelaire's poem: the image as sound-image, signifying within and across the words as semantically signifying images. It now remains to inquire into "material significance" *au pied de la lettre* and in its relation to allegory and history.

The ruse of a "ruisseau sans eau" is not only that there is no water and therefore no "ruisseau," which is why the swan must apostrophize "eau" rather than represent it. More largely, the poem's problematic of representations or images of presence turning into meanings of absence—its problematic of allegory—is implied as well. From the poem's perspective, representation, including allegorical representation, is a ruse, ironic and cruelly so. The first such representation is the poem's opening apostrophe to Andromaque. Fietkau and others have explored the ambiguities and reversals of this representation: is "Ce petit fleuve" a representational image drawn from the Place du Carrousel that invokes the memory—and apostrophe—of Andromaque beside her "Simoïs menteur," or is it the "Simoïs menteur" itself, a representation within the memory of and apostrophe to Andromaque, that is then compared to a representation—"un ruisseau sans eau"—in the Place du Carrousel?[25] And as allegorical representation—modern for ancient and/or ancient for modern—is it not also an image for the lost original of literary history, the "original" literary-historical Simoïs of Troy? In any case, or in all cases, it is "menteur," *falsa* (Virgil's *falsi Simoentis ad undam*), a ruse or fiction. It represents allegorical representation (i.e., the absence of what is represented) but still does so *within* the thematics of the loss of an original.

The primary loss represented here is not that of a river but that of a man, a husband, Hector. Andromaque is identified in each part as "veuve," and what is she doing beside this stream but mourning a loss through death? "Ce Simoïs menteur," lying as a representation of a river, does not (mis)represent a river so much as it does—obliquely, metonymically—an absent body, or an unfilled tomb. For Andromaque, fallen from the arms of her husband when he fell in battle, has fallen "Auprès d'un tombeau vide en extase courbée." The sounds of this line are called to one's attention by the repetition of *tombée / tombeau* and the rhyme of *tombée / courbée;* and given the first strophe's image of Andromaque filling the little stream with her tears, one might also hear the watery sounds of a "ruisseau sans eau" "*Au*pres d'un tom*beau.*" Hearing such sounds, one is reminded that they signify—allegorically—the absence of their meaning: ruisseau *sans eau*. What, then, of the *tombeau?*

"Auprès d'un tombeau vide en extase courbée": Andromaque, near or next to an empty tomb, lowered, weakened, bent or curbed in ecstasy. What falls most immediately out of one's comprehension of this line is the phrase "en extase." It falls out of Benjamin's translation of the line altogether: "Die übern leeren Sarkophag gelitten."[26] The most recent Pléiade edition of Baudelaire's works usefully cites as a parallel his *Fusées*, section 3, where, with a reference to the same passage from Ovid as figures in "Le Cygne" (*Metamorphoses* 1, vv. 84–85), the word *extase* is used for sexual orgasm: "Et le visage humain, qu'Ovide croyait façonné pour refléter les astres, le voilà qui ne parle plus qu'une expression de férocité folle, ou qui se détend dans une espèce de mort. Car, certes, je croirais faire un sacrilège en appliquant le mot: extase à cette sorte de décomposition."[27]

What is more to the point here than sexual orgasm is death. The line in "Le Cygne" represents a thematics of death, and in *Fusées*, even as Baudelaire speaks of sex and ecstasy, he is also speaking of death ("une espèce de mort," "cette sorte de décomposition"). Or of a *kind* of death, a *sort* of decomposition. For death is supposed to be the loss or departure of *anima, âme*, or soul from the body as the latter decays through time to the point of "decomposition," a decomposing of the unity or the *correspondance* of *corps* and *esprit*. This "decomposition" is precisely the meaning of ecstasy, and of the line in which the word appears: *ek-stasis*, the soul outside of the body, Andromaque alive, as memory and mourning, next to and bent over the sign of the absent body.

But here there is a reversal: not the lost soul or spirit of life but the lost body. Fietkau suggests that the *tombeau vide* "is not the exile's reproduction, but the original left empty before the walls of Troy,"[28] and with this insight our reading of the line can begin to conclude. In the "original" of literary history—Homer—before Virgil's and Racine's Epirus, or Baudelaire's "Simoïs menteur" (or Ovid's Hecuba salvaging Hector's ashes), the body is missing from the grave. The lost original, as corporeal *factum*, makes each grave or memorial image a sign of the lost referent. It means, as image, that there is only an image of loss, a *tombeau vide* or an empty crypt, *en extase* or de-composed from a meaning that it cannot contain but can only represent as missing. Thus, the "tombeau vide" and the "ruisseau sans eau" are each a *menteur*, or ruse, empty as literal or referential signs but figurally or allegorically representing this emptiness as their meaning: the loss of meaning, of intended meaning, as its allegorical meaning. What is the case for the grave and the stream—that they cannot represent their meaning other than as its absence—is likewise so for the swan and Andromaque: the swan, "le coeur plein de son beau lac natal," when its heart or center in fact represents only the absence of fullness and water in the expression of "Eau/O," a nonrepresentational apostrophe or a sign invoking an absent meaning; Andromaque, "embodying" loss in her irrecoverable distance or disembodiment, as a sign of mourning, from the object or meaning of her loss. This means that she is herself *en extase*, decomposed from, or only a figure of, her meaning, for to be repeatedly—from Virgil to Baudelaire—representing loss "next to" a *tombeau vide* is to be a *tombeau vide* herself, as each is a sign of lost meaning. Andromaque is less life preserved and preserving as memory, "next to" the image of material loss, the tomb of the missing body, than she is herself an image of loss or death signifying, through repetition or reiteration, the allegorical image "next to" her: a figure of a figure. And this is exactly what the line in question means. *Auprès d'un tombeau vide* is not corporeal contiguity with a lost corpus (including not the literary-historical corpus of *tradition*, the "handing down" of the sign of Andromaque). It is not a full sign for a meaning of emptiness but a figural image of a figural image: *auprès de* as also meaning *en comparaison de;* Andromaque brought into comparison with the figure of the empty tomb, sign of the lost original it nonetheless re-presents: the allegorical sign. As the swan also means: "Le cygne": *le signe.*[29]

In each of these homophonies, the poem brings together a phenomenal-"materialist" dimension with a tropological-material one, the very material of tropes. *Auprès de* as contiguity or metonymy ("next to") means spatiality, proximity, co-presence, all of which are phenomenally or "materially" representational; *auprès de* as comparison or simile ("in comparison with") means analogy, which is tropological rather than phenomenal. These two senses and dimensions of *auprès de* are themselves "next to" each other, contiguously or phenomenally, *and* "in comparison with" each other, tropologically: they are one mark divided in itself into phenomenality and an other, tropological material, as, in Benjamin's model of the allegorical sign, appearance *(Schein)* divides from significance *(Bedeutung)*, the literal from the allegorical. So, too, with the *signe* of the *cygne*. *Le cygne* is representational, and as a visual, imagistic sign (the swan) expresses an oral one (its apostrophe to water), the representationality remains within the phenomenal dimension. *Le signe* is an aural pun, and its signification (the rhetorical sign of the sign) is tropological: *le cygne* sounds, phenomenally, like *le signe*, but *le signe* means *le signe* along no such phenomenal register. *Le cygne* and *le signe* are phenomenally (aurally) identical but mean a difference the *signe* of which is not phenomenal alone. Rather, each sign *(cygne/signe)* is the phenomenalization of the other's tropological material, as the swan expresses, aurally, the verbal sign ("le cygne" sounds as "le signe," as its "Eau" sounded as "O"), and the signs for sound (*c, y, g, n, e*) construct the imagistic swan, which is the sounds' deconstruction (they mean not the fullness or presence of the representation but its emptiness or absence). The tropology is other than its phenomenalization, just as in

Benjamin's allegorical sign, there is *Durchdringung* or *Ineinanderspielen*, and still the "speaking otherwise" of allegory. The sign *cygne/signe* is the sign of its difference.

One could pursue this analysis one step further and say that *le cygne* and *le signe* are *auprès de* one another, both "next to" and "in comparison with" one another in the single sign; as proximity or contiguity, this would be a phenomenalization of the "difference within," and as analogy, this would be its tropography: the sign as phenomenal (*cygne*) in comparison with its nonphenomenal meaning as sign (*signe*). This difference could then be phenomenally signified and compared again in turn, and so on, "à bien d'autres encor!" Similarly, the two senses of *auprès de* are the *cygne/signe* of one another, one the phenomenalization of the verbal, one the verbalization of the phenomenal, and each the *sign within* the other, the other within the sign. Furthermore, the two senses of *auprès de* and the doublet *cygne/signe* are themselves next to, in comparison with, the phenomenal image for, and the sign of the others. In each of these pairings, multiplications, and divisions within, there is not one phenomenal ("sensually based") foundation for the trope, as if its "materialist" substructure, but the *linguistic positing* of the possible phenomenalization of the difference between the phenomenal and the tropological. Language—*le c/signe* in its/their near-indivisibility—posits marks of difference and iterability, and these are the minimal constituents of materiality as they are the minimal constituents of the sign and of history.

What is at stake here is the possible relation of allegory to history. Allegory, in the "full" sense of "tout pour moi devient allégorie" that may be read in Baudelaire's "Le Cygne"—not just new and old or Paris and Troy but the verbal signs themselves "becoming allegory," becoming otherwise to and within (next to and in comparison with) themselves—depends *materially* upon signs that signify rather than upon historical minds (literary, materialist, or otherwise) that remember or are melancholic. This leads to the allegorical stake of Benjamin's and Baudelaire's histories. If, in the example of "Le Cygne," Western literary history—from its "origin" in Homer—is represented as the repeated, reiterated allegorical re-presentation of a lost original, then there is never any standpoint from which the history can be told or written as meaning the literal recovery of lost life-events. The sign of the *tombeau vide* in "Le Cygne" is the *c/signe* as the *tombeau vide*, its material dimension "auprès de" and "en exstase" from (the absence of) life, history, even the corpse, the bones, the mere "signs" of the (missing) body. Of such material, there can only be another fictive representation, "Simoïs menteur," or allegorical narrative in which the allegorical representation

223

stands for, *auprès de*, the lost original and tells, as its literal narrative or history, a "false," fictive story of its maintenance across history. Such allegorical signs of/as empty tombs install not a "vieux Souvenir" as an interiorization of meaning (*Erinnerung*), as history told to the point of its being known (i.e., as narrative), but rather the empty tombs of historical signs as the site and cite (the "s/cite") of memorization, reiteration, and a radical thought of history. Benjamin's *Gedächtnis* or *Andenken*, Baudelaire's "Je pense à," and Hegel's *Denken* are signs of holding on to loss in and as language that figurally means—and repeatedly, ceaselessly reminds of—the loss of its meaning, even as historians and their narrative history would represent literally or "historically" the forgetting of this loss in an amnesia that calls itself a recovery.

These thoughts from Baudelaire are not far from Benjamin. The more he meditated upon the historical in Baudelaire, the more he remained with the allegorical. His most advanced notes on Baudelaire's allegory center on the commodity, and what he had first conceived as the social-historical "solution" to the problem came to be characterized as a problem of the body, the dead body: the corpse or *Leiche*. Like "decomposition" in the *extase* of Baudelaire's "Le Cygne," this is less a case of evolution—"progress"—than one of *de*volution: the "historical" event of the commodity having become the un- or transhistorical one of the sign of death, the nineteenth century devolving—nonnarratively but reiterably—into the seventeenth century and beyond. One of the last notes of "Zentralpark" reads:

> In the nineteenth century melancholy displays a different character than it did in the seventeenth. The key [*Schlüsselfigur*] to the earlier allegory is the corpse. The key to the later allegory is "mindfulness" [*Andenken*]. "Mindfulness" is the schema for the metamorphosis of the commodity into an object for the collector. The "correspondences" are, accordingly, the endlessly multiple resonances [*Anklänge*] of each act of mindfulness upon the other. "J'ai plus de souvenirs que si j'avais mille ans." (ZP, 689)

Is this a history of allegory or an allegory of history? Benjamin's language of "key figure" and "schema" points to the latter. Benjamin could spend several years collecting notes on baroque corpses, several more collecting them on the bourgeois commodity. In neither case did he write a history of allegory beyond such a figural "schema." Allegory is that which resists historiography even as it provokes history as its own representation, as the ongoing narrative toward recovered meaning, *and* the unremembering (*unerinnernde*) memory (*Andenken* or *Gedächtnis*) of loss—and this is the allegory, as well as the irony, of history.[30]

Where Hölderlin could write in "Mnemosyne" of the goddess of memory and the mother of the muses, "Lang ist / Die Zeit, es ereignet sich aber / Das Wahre" (loosely translatable as "the waiting time is long, but what is true does happen"), Benjamin writes, recalling Hölderlin momentarily, "What happens is the 'ever-the-same' [*Es ereignet sich 'immer dasselbe'*]." He then adds immediately: "*Spleen* is nothing but the quintessence of historical experience" (1151). *Andenken,* or "mindfulness"—a deteriorated mode of memory in Benjamin's vocabulary, neither *Gedächtnis* nor *Eingendenken*—would wish to turn the allegorical signs (corpses, commodities) into historical meanings but collects them instead, writing lists of notes ("bien d'autres encor!") instead of narratives. "'Mindfulness' [*Andenken*] is the secularized relic. . . . The relic comes from the corpse, 'mindfulness' from experience that has died away" (ZP, 681). It remains for a later chapter, in its treatment of Benjamin's *Ursprung des deutschen Trauerspiels,* to uncover something of the investment and betrayal behind the historian's melancholic mask of allegory. In the meantime, any historian can say, with Baudelaire's second "Spleen" poem and with Benjamin as well, "J'ai plus de souvenirs que si j'avais mille ans"—but no experience except as that which has died away. Behind the hyperbolic line lies a modest truth. The corpses are the historical texts, the relics their language, as signs of missing bodies of meaning. *Andenken* is our secularized—historical—mode of repetition, as readers reading. What remains buried but also missing in this allegory of reading is history: "For spleen," Benjamin wrote, "what is buried is the 'transcendental subject' of historical consciousness" (ZP, 661). He might have added: buried in an empty tomb.

9

Death and Authority: Benjamin's "The Storyteller"

"**D**ie Zeit ist vorbei, in der es auf Zeit nicht ankam" ("The time is past in which time did not matter"). This sentence, quoted from Paul Valéry, appears in Walter Benjamin's essay "Der Erzähler" ("The Storyteller").[1] It sounds better in Benjamin's German translation than in the French original ("Le temps est passé où le temps ne comptait pas"), because Benjamin's version exposes the deep paradox the thought contains. Valéry is writing of the passing of patient, time-consuming handicrafts (miniatures, ivory carvings, stone polishing, lacquers); his point is that that time is past when one was not concerned about time. Benjamin recasts this as, literally, "the time is [gone] past in which it did not come down to time." Not only is that time past—come and gone—but at that time, time did not even enter (into consideration). The paradox is that a time can pass in which time itself did not seem to pass and that with this passing, not only a time (an epoch) is past, but time itself is at stake, passing away, a matter of concern: *Es kommt darauf an*. Time counts because it ends, is ending.

Benjamin wrote "The Storyteller" in 1936, having been in his Paris exile since 1933 and unmistakably aware that for Jews, Germans, and European intelligence alike, it was a matter of time. The date, however, while slightly earlier than the theses "On the Concept of History" and the unfinished book on Baudelaire, leaves this essay unisolated with respect to his other projects; by the evidence of early notes for some of the parts of the essay, its thoughts date back to the late 1920s, and in the late 1930s he writes of its continued centrality to the projects he was then engaged in—the Baudelaire book and the *Passagen-Werk* (GS, 2:1279). Indeed, "The Storyteller" is Benjamin's major statement on narrative and history, the better-known theses notwithstanding, and one of the most brilliantly crafted essays by this or any other writer. In the series of late works by Benjamin on history and literary history, its

226

dominant position emerges as one moves backward from the very last writings, and its shadow also stretches behind it back upon the other major work that will still have to concern any serious consideration of Benjamin on history: his book, *Origin of the German Trauerspiel*. In the theses "On the Concept of History," history was seen to emerge as an image, a rhetorical image at all times about to explode from one narrative and enter into another called an allegory of reading. In the Baudelaire project, the object of historical study was seen to emerge as a trope for death, the compulsive, repetitive character of which seemed to threaten all historical study lest it become truly *literary* history in attending to the transformation of signs into tropes. In "The Storyteller," Benjamin combines the rhetorical image, the theme and trope of death, and an exemplary instance of literary history to bring history to an edge of allegories of history.

Time was, when time did not matter. But times pass—that time, too. Benjamin's object of study and cause for concern is storytelling (GS, 2:1276–77). But it is telling that in studying storytelling, he keeps it a *present*, not-yet-past or "historical" concern, even as his claim is that it is passing away. Specifically, his claim, as he put it already in a fragment from 1928–29, is that "the art of telling stories is coming to an end [*zu Ende geht*]" (GS, 2:1281); his achievement is to tell *this* story—that stories are coming to an end—in such a way that storytelling becomes historical and becomes present to us at one and the same time. For something to become present in passing away—to live in its death, as it were—is, for Benjamin, history. But it only happens if history is *made* present.

The most direct way to begin to approach this series of paradoxes, which is at once Benjamin's theory of history and his writing of literary history, is via the language and imagery of his essay's introductory account. "The storyteller," Benjamin writes, "—however familiarly the name resounds for us—is by no means altogether present [*gegenwärtig*] to us in his living efficacy. He is already something remote from us, and becoming ever more remote [*und weiter noch sich Entfernendes*]" (GS, 2:438). However familiar the name "storyteller" is to us, and thus apparently alive to consciousness or at least to recent memory, he is not himself effectively or actually (*wirksam*) present and, in fact, is withdrawing from us, becoming ever more distant or remote. But this nonpresence, Benjamin's precision indicates, is not yet an absence; rather, it is a distancing, a withdrawing, a *present* participial *absenting*. This nearness that presents a distancing recalls a Karl Kraus aphorism that Benjamin quotes elsewhere: "The more closely you look at a word, the more distantly [*ferner*] it looks back."[2] So, too, the image Benjamin uses here to "represent" Nikolai Leskov: "To represent a Leskov as storyteller is not to bring him nearer to us, but rather much more to increase our distance from him." This becomes precisely Benjamin's *historical* claim: that at a present moment (*his* present moment, 1936, or the 1920s and 1930s more broadly), "the art of storytelling is coming to an end [*zu Ende geht*]," and that the experience of this end*ing* can be a daily, present one. The "distancing [*Entfernung*]" which Leskov, for example, gains for the reader, causes the "large, simple features that make up the storyteller to stand out in him," and—Benjamin introduces the image of seeing a face or animal appear in a rock from a certain distance—"this distance and perspective are prescribed to us by an experience that we have almost daily. It says to us that the art of storytelling is coming to an end" (GS, 2:438, 439).

The shifts in Benjamin's perspectives are perhaps momentarily confusing but ultimately not at all contradictory. They establish a pattern in which images, visually present and as if immediate, yield stories about temporal distancing or passing away, which stories are then told as *present histories*, histories presented to the present. Benjamin begins by shifting from an event in time to an image in space (the storyteller's withdrawing, a face in a rock). He also then shifts from this image—of the storyteller in Leskov's "features"—to the narrative of its disappearance, of storytelling's coming to an end. And he also shifts from one present perspective to another. What is *not* present is the efficacy of the storyteller: he is withdrawing. What *is* present is this experience: of the withdrawal, of the art of storytelling coming to an end. What is going away from us in the first claim, is, curiously, coming toward us—presenting itself to us—in the second: we see the end coming toward us, as it were. Benjamin seeks to see storytelling from the end, from the point of ending, to be more precise—for it is a present experience, not a static spot—and yet the present, he implies, has not yet *grasped* this ending as such, for the name "storyteller" can be said still to sound familiar, not yet archaic or "historical."

Benjamin will in the course of the essay adduce many *historical* reasons or causes for the decline and ending of storytelling, and his first reason is a massive one: storytelling comes to an end, "it is as if the capacity to exchange experience has been taken from us," and "one cause of this phenomenon lies ready at hand: experience has fallen [*gefallen*] in value" (GS, 2:439). This reasoning is of a piece with his Marxist analysis, conveyed here and elsewhere (as, for example, in "Zentralpark" and elsewhere in the Baudelaire project), that the exchange values of commodity culture in fact inhibit the exchange of experience.[3] But here the image of a *fall* may be seen to function in direct relation to the story of an ending. For Benjamin immediately adds the fear: "And it looks as if it [experience] will keep falling into bottomlessness" (GS, 2:439). To say, then, that storytelling is coming to an end and that we are, daily, experiencing this ending is, rhetorically, the check—the stop, the handhold—for an image of the falling away of experience toward an abyss of bottomlessness. Benjamin hyperbolically raises the stakes of this fall in value: "Every glance in the paper shows that it [experience] has reached a new low, that not only the image of the external world but the image of the moral world as well has overnight undergone changes that one never held to be possible." This anxiety is of daily (and nightly) changes, to the point of experiencing what one would have thought impossible to experience, namely, the infinite, endless falling away of experience. This massive reason for the decline of storytelling—the tumbling loss of experience—itself has a cause: the event of World War I is named as the time when "a process began . . . that since then has not come to a stop [*nicht zum Stillstand gekommen ist*]" (GS, 2:439). What threatens not to stop—what Benjamin then calls our becoming "poorer in communicable experience"—but only to keep falling is given a *Stillstand*, a standstill, by being "seen" and told from the perspective of its historical ending. "The art of storytelling is coming to an end."

Stories may be, in Benjamin's view, the most valuable, the most necessary things: the condition of possibility for experience, for a healthy humanity, for a human history. For him, there is no such thing as the pejorative "mere story," while a *sheer* story would be as pure a find, or as purely made a thing, as one could desire. It is the task of an interpretation of this essay not merely to retell his story about storytelling's coming to an end but also, more painstakingly, to arrange its parts, to connect its points, so that its imagistic structure, its "figure-construction" or *constellation* of the storyteller with respect to history, may emerge, not so much like a face in a rock as like a figure in points of light spread across the essay's pages. Here, in the essay's first section, the image of storytelling's ending is one of this image becoming present against the background of the recent and still present endlessness of experience's loss. One thing will not come to an end; something else is coming to an end. The section ends with an image of World War I's battlefields: a generation "stood under the open sky in a landscape in which nothing remained unchanged but the clouds, and beneath them, in a forcefield of destructive torrents and explosions, the tiny, fragile human body" (GS, 2:439). This is an image of apocalypse, of all things changed, the world turned upside down, before the last change—the disappearance of man. The image is apocalyptic of experience and experience's communication precisely because it will not end: man is still there witnessing, the changes still occurring; it ends experience and communication because *it*, the changing, will not end. To match this apocalyptic image is the function of an eschatological story: telling the story of the last thing, the end of storytelling.

An image in space, the apocalyptic battlefields under the empty sky, being met with a story in time—this structure of exchange or shift becomes, in Benjamin's hands, part of what constitutes stories, and of what stories do. They transfer—transmit, carry over—between space and time, distance and proximity, the long ago and the right now. What stories are and do—their image—and what can be told of them—the story of their ending—are increasingly conjoined in the next several sections of "The Storyteller," in the sense that one will twist into the other. So, for example, to give "the figure of the storyteller its full corporeality," Benjamin says one must "present [*vergegenwärtigt*]" to oneself two groups of "many nameless storytellers": the ones who come from afar and the ones who stay at home and know its stories and traditions (GS, 2:440). The storytellers in the one group overcome spatial distance by their travels; the others overcome temporal distance by knowing and preserving the past of the home. Together, they constitute the "full" image of the storyteller. But what is being *told* of the storyteller, correspondingly, is that he is entering into temporal distance—passing—via terms of spatial distancing (*Entfernendes, Abstand, Entfernung*). Storytelling combines the past with distance in a present time and place; the storyteller is becoming past, and becoming ever more distant, in and from the present.

So, too, if one asks what else storytelling does, and what its departure or passing signals, one finds a similar correspondence in Benjamin's report. The very capacity to "present [*vergegenwärtigen*]" the two groups of storytellers "in their archaic representatives" (the sedentary farmer and the merchant seaman [GS, 2:440]) is, as Benjamin's precise language indicates, to link the past and the present into a continuity; it is this continuity that is being threatened by the same present (*Gegenwart*) in which the figure of the storyteller is passing away or becoming historical. It turns out that for Benjamin, this continuity instanced in storytelling extends even into the future. One of Benjamin's central categories for storytelling is its *utility*: "every true story . . . carries, openly or secretly, its usefulness [*Nutzen*] along with itself. This usefulness might consist in one case in a moral, in another in a practical instruction, in yet another in a proverb or a maxim for living—in every case, the storyteller is a man who has counsel for the listener." This specific utility of giving counsel is, Benjamin avows, future-oriented: "Counsel is less the answer to a question than a proposal concerning the continuation of a (just now unfolding) narrative" (GS, 2:442). It is this image of a narrative—from afar, from the past—"just now unfolding," that is, in a present of telling and listening, and leading to "counsel" about its continuation, that is precisely the image of a temporal continuity from past across present to future. At the very moment (or spot) in his essay where he sketches such an image of temporal continuity, Benjamin then correspondingly tells the story of its rupture or breakage. He immediately adds the sentence, "In order to seek it [counsel], one had to be able to tell it [the story] in the first place." The continuity toward a future—counsel about how to continue—paradoxically hinges on a story's ending, in the sense that it could be told up to its conclusion at the present point: ending so that it might continue, as it were. And this sentence, with this point, is the swivel point in Benjamin's argument, for now he (re)tells the story of storytelling up to the point of its ending: "Counsel, woven into the material of lived life, is wisdom. The art of storytelling is reaching its end, because the epic side of truth—wisdom—is dying out. But this is a process that comes from afar." Benjamin's language—the "coming from afar," for example—signals his storytelling; telling the story up to the point of threatening its very constitutive nature of continuity then at once breaks with storytelling, consigning it toward a past, and preserves it in a still-present "reaching its end," and "dying out." So storytelling continues to maintain itself, however mortally, toward an immediate if short-lived future: the present ending.

To present something as losing its future-orientation focuses upon this present as a terminal point, and no mere moment of transition.[4] Paradoxically, such presentation takes the form of *presenting* a state of affairs—the state of storytelling—*as history for "us"* (the "we" of Benjamin's contemporaneity). The weight of the term "history," in this usage special to Benjamin, needs to be clarified. Historicist "history" has been known, at least since Collingwood and Gadamer, to have as its hermeneutics a theory of question-and-answer: either the past represents its answer to a question or problem posed to it at its time, and the present historian has to rediscover this question; or the past poses a question to the present, which then has to discover its own answer.[5] Benjamin decisively broke with this historicism, as seen in his critique in the theses "On the Concept of History" or here in this essay with his dismissal that the "counsel [that stories give] is [not] an answer to a question." To present a state of affairs as history for us means, for Benjamin, to grasp it for the present as achieving meaning, being fulfilled or ending in and at a present moment and place: for example, assuming tellable form for us as a story whose ending we experience (see or "hear"). But Benjamin's story about storytelling's coming to an end takes the form not so much of a story told in order to be retold (to be "continued") as of—as his essay is about to unfold—a written literary history, specifically the historical meaning of the trajectory from storytelling to the reading of novels. The story of storytelling's *becoming history*—ending, passing away—is presented, in and for the present, as the history that emerges from reading the novel: the presentation of history via that narrative form alive for us on the far side or flipside *(Kehrseite)* of the end of storytelling. It is as history that a present ending presents itself. Ironically, then, if storytelling traditionally (in the past) implies a proposal about a story's continuation—in this case, counsel as to how storytelling is to continue—and, for this, it also requires that the story be told up to that point, then here the story that storytelling is coming to an end (that it does not continue) requires that it be told up to that point *as history:* as becoming history, and specifically as yielding the historical presentation of the novel.

Benjamin's views on the novel here, as his early notes already announce, are a self-avowed theory of the novel and of epic-narrative forms (GS, 2:1276–77). Indeed, as he well knew, they are also his reading and rewriting of Lukács's *Theory of the Novel.* That the novel rises out of the decline of storytelling and all the continuity of mouth-to-ear transmission that it presents, is, for example, a counter-image to Lukács's novel descending from the precipitous rupture with the totalized epic forms of a certain image of Hellenism; so, too, is the novel's bookish form a counter-image to storytelling's oral tradition, and both these features are in conspicuous contrast to Lukács's treatment, which nowhere mentions these media differentially specific to the respective narrative forms.[6] But Benjamin's argument about the appearance of the novel—and the appearance of the novel in his argument—occurs in relation to a central feature of his theory of storytelling. This is its handling of death. Several other features of storytelling for Benjamin need to be drawn out of his essay before this dramatic interlocking of story, death, and novel may be unfolded. These features may be designated as the *authority* of storytelling—one version of this authority, at least—and a further aspect of its relation to time, which is *accumulation.*

Both authority and accumulation, as features of storytelling, draw upon and reinstantiate Benjamin's central claim that storytelling constitutes a temporal continuity. "The intelligence that comes from afar," which is Benjamin's summary version of what stories bring—"be it the spatial [distance] of foreign lands or the temporal [kind] of a handing down"—has *eo ipso* an authority *(Autorität)* that is independent, Benjamin adds, of whether its validity can be controlled or verified (GS,

2:444). This is not the authority of an authoritative author or proper name; Benjamin has already insisted upon the namelessness of the storyteller, or, rather, the multiple tellers of stories. Benjamin instead means the authority that comes with sheer increase or accrual, as if deploying the etymological force of *auctoritas/auctor* deriving from *augere*, "to increase." An image for this may be like a snowball, which the farther it rolls, the more it increases; or in an image Benjamin will shortly introduce, like a pearl, which over time increases its layers, its size and value—its "authority"—as well. With specific respect to time, this sense of authority by virtue of having come from afar is the same as that of the "aura" and "authenticity" that Benjamin attributed to one-of-a-kind original works of art in his well-known essay "The Work of Art in the Age of Its Technical Reproducibility": "It is on the unique existence [of the work of art] and nowhere else that the history to which the work has been subjected in the course of its existence is accomplished. . . . The authenticity of something is the sum of everything in it capable of being passed on from its origin forward, from its material duration up to its historical testimony . . . [this] is the authority of something." [7]

The *authority* of such things—originals, original stories—is not only that they have accreted time to themselves but that this accumulated time also resists a dissolution lest it be as a momentous release. They *preserve* time up to a present presentation of this accumulated time. In a contrast Benjamin pessimistically deploys, unlike everyday news or information, they do not instantly explain themselves away: "[It is] now no longer intelligence that comes from afar, but information that provides a handle for the nearest thing, which one prefers to hear" (GS, 2:444). Stories, on the other hand, come without—are "held free of"—explanation, in order to be preserved for interpretation; in this manner, as Benjamin says of the exemplary story of Psammenitus told in Herodotus and retold by Montaigne, "it preserves its force gathered within it and is capable of unfolding even after a long time. . . . It resembles seeds of wheat, which have lain closed, airtight, for thousands of years in the bowels of the pyramids, and have preserved their seed-force up to the present day" (GS, 2:446).

This last image, of a "seed" of time preserving its force up to a present moment of release, retains the structure of paradoxical turning that was embodied in the essay's first image of storytelling's drawing away from, but also coming to an end in, the present. That is, the imagery is of stories coming from and drawing back away into a distance but being seen as such—as such vehicles for the "authority" of time—precisely at a *present* moment of release-cum-extinction. A seed stops being a seed, a story ends, at the moments of their release—like Hegel's "qualitative leap."[8] A similar turn from the distant past and from preserved time to a present moment and perspective occurs with the feature of *accumulation*. It was in referring to activities of the accumulation of time that Benjamin drew upon Valéry, who first introduced natural examples of such activities—pearls, vintage wines—before turning to human examples. Valéry called them "the precious product of a long chain of causes each like the other"; Benjamin immediately added: "But the accumulation [*Anhäufung*] of such causes would have its temporal limit only at perfection" (GS, 2:448). Valéry's "long chain of causes each like the other" may be understood temporally as the succession of like moments, each linked one to the other in a chain, the individual links of which do not distinguish themselves. Benjamin's "temporal limit" of "perfection" is a fullness of time, indeed, an eternity; the first sentence of the next section of this essay quotes Valéry's conclusion, to the effect that "It is almost as if the disappearance of the thought of eternity coincided with the growing aversion to sustained effort" (GS, 2:449).

Now, accumulation of moments into a chain leading to and ending at eternity is Benjamin's version of a history that would counter historicism's. Whereas historicism as he analyzed and criticized it in his theses "On the Concept of History" has a chain of moments in which each one is attributed significance in its ostensible uniqueness and distinction, but the chain itself has no direction or telos but merely passes through "homogeneous and empty time," Benjamin's image of history is the opposite: a chain of like moments, but leading to and ending in their release in eternity. In the theses, the pessimistically colored image was of the Angelus Novus, facing the past as a "Trümmer*haufen*," a *heap* of ruins growing up to heaven;[9] here, it is the "Anhäufung," the heaping up or accumulation of like causes, like moments. Historicism in Benjamin's caustic phrasing is a bordello where the historian dissipates (*ausgeben*) himself with the whore of "once upon a time," precisely a false "'eternal' image of the past" because it was located in the past;[10] here, in "The Storyteller," accumulated moments retain their temporal charge or force, for the story "does not expend [*verausgabt*] itself. It preserves its force gathered within it and is capable of unfolding even after a long time." Historicism does not *yield* eternity or any end to time precisely because it privileges—claims to "eternize"—a distinct moment in the past. Stories, and the access to a *made* history they provide, may end in eternity when they end or break with the continuity of time that they themselves constitute: when they *become* history.[11]

"Die Zeit ist vorbei, in der es auf Zeit nicht ankam." When time passes, and it is no longer a time when it did not come down to time, is this eternity? Not at all. But it is a perspective of eternity, which is to say a perspective upon the discontinuous, the present, and the timely, focused upon—seized, grasped, or brought to a standstill—as such. The "fall" into the merely historical or (the same thing for Benjamin) into the historicist, which is the narrative version of what his essay first introduced as an infinite, bottomless falling away of experience, is itself made historical—made present and timely. The theses "On the Concept of History" attacked and opposed this fall. "The Storyteller" essay, rather more like the essay on "The Work of Art in the Age of Its Technical Reproducibility," wants to turn falling and ending—loss—into rise and gain. In the language of that slightly earlier essay,

> Two processes [of the reproducibility of art-objects for mass distribution and for repeated actualization] lead to a powerful shattering of the traditional—a shattering of tradition that is the flipside of the present crisis and renewal of humanity [*die die Kehrseite der gegenwärtigen Krise und Erneuerung der Menschheit ist*]. . . . Its social significance, even in its most positive form, and precisely in this, is unthinkable without this, its destructive, its cathartic side: the liquidation of the value of tradition in the cultural inheritance.[12]

"Shattering," like the "explosion" in the theses, is the violent, terminal ending of a heretofore continuous and apparently seamless chain of handings-down. In "The Storyteller," Benjamin calls this coming-to-an-end, or death. His perspective is from the end point—an ending—sighting upon and bringing into focus and presentation at once a vanishing and its obverse, an appearance. With broad historical sweep, he speaks of "secular historical forces of production that very gradually withdrew storytelling from out of the realm of living discourse and at the same time make discernible a new beauty in what is disappearing [*eine neue Schönheit in dem Entschwindenden fühlbar macht*]" (GS, 2:442). The history of the story's ending, leaving time—dying—can yield the historical presentation of the novel.

An apparently continuous passing of the cultural baton from story to novel, from disappearance to appearance, is precisely what Benjamin's argument does *not* mean. If death means birth, then death altogether loses its meaning in such a casual organicism. Benjamin's conceptual difficulty here was already apparent in that sentence quoted above, to the effect that "The art of storytelling is reaching its end, because the epic side of truth—wisdom—is dying out." What is the argumentative force of "because"? Does the death of wisdom *cause* storytelling to end? Or is it rather—since wisdom is, as Benjamin describes it, an *effect* of storytelling's giving of counsel—that storytelling is ending "because," tautologically, storytelling's effect is dying out? Benjamin is trying to *tell* an end, a death; this cannot be done as an argument, but rather only as a story that would *present history*—make history present in its release or issue. This is where Benjamin's "history of the novel" and what has already been described as his eschatological perspective conjoin. Two sentences from this essay can introduce evidence of history's entwinement with death and eschatology.

"The earliest sign of a process at whose end the decline of storytelling stands is the rise of the novel at the beginning of modern times" (GS, 2:442). The connection between end and beginning, decline and rise, is not organic but semiotic-interpretive: a sign is read. A beginning, like the beginning of an arc, already, at its initial rise, signals its decline: alpha means omega; both are parts of the same "process." But when decline has *its* end in ending, in death, this end of storytelling will mean—signify—a particular life and afterlife (no longer a birth or rise) for the novel: its (re)presentation of a death undergone or submitted to by storytelling. Another way of putting this is to say that when storytelling becomes history, it signifies the novel's *historical* meaning—its "afterview," seen from the point of view of the end point—the meaning the novel now holds and releases for the history preceding it (and presently passing away). "The thought of eternity has always had its strongest source [*Quelle*] in death," Benjamin wrote immediately after quoting Valéry on the disappearance of this thought (GS, 2:449). The *source* for thinking eternity is death, like the presentation of an event's ultimate meaning occurring or being released in its ending. A last thing (death) is a first (source), and this "first" thing is of the thought of the last thing after the last: of eternity. When Benjamin adds that "if this thought [of eternity] disappears, then we conclude that the face of death must have changed [*muss das Gesicht des Todes ein anderes geworden sein*]," the eschatological perspective, which can claim to view death itself ("and there shall be no more death . . . for the former things are passed away" [Revelations 21:4]), reinvokes the thought of eternity, which was just said to be disappearing, but also—precisely because it is a question of death and eternity—reintroduces terms and structures of allegory into Benjamin's discourse and story.

With his return to an image—the face of death (like the features of the storyteller), rather than, say, the *story* of wisdom's dying out—there will be, on the one hand, the reappearance of his practice of generating stories out of images and, on the other, the turn or troping toward the specific rhetorical structure of allegory. And this latter feature for at least two reasons: because Benjamin's exact phrasing indicates already an allegorical dimension of death's face "becoming other [*anders werden*]," *allos-agoureuein* meaning "to speak otherwise"; and because the face of death is itself, for Benjamin, a privileged sign of allegory as a limit to narrative form.[13] The concluding sentence to this paragraph in Benjamin—"It turns out that this change [*Veränderung*] is identical with the one that diminished the communicability of experience to the same degree that the art of storytelling came to an end" (GS, 2:449)—underscores that the introductory and heretofore predominant concerns of his essay, such as the loss of communicable experience and the end of storytelling, will overlap precisely with what is here being announced as the eschatological view and allegorical meaning of the image of death.[14]

Images of death and their allegorical meaning become the hinges upon which Benjamin's historical argument about storytelling's end and reading the ends of novels hangs and turns. This imagery should be unpacked carefully, for it is not some gratuitous filler or lining to an otherwise autonomous argument but rather the very material and mechanism of the argument's delivery, above all in the deviations or swerves among the images themselves. It may be recalled that Benjamin's images of storytelling's powerful continuity have included an unbroken chain, an accumulation of layers, and a still-fructive seed. On the other hand, images of historical dangers to this continuity have been couched in the language of falling, distancing, and ending. To the extent that such dangers of ending are located by him—and with considerable plausibility—in modern or recent times, it would appear that "the death of storytelling" is a specifically historical image, attributable to historical causes, at a particular historical juncture. So, for example, Benjamin privileged the boredom of certain kinds of labor and the capacity for listening that such boredom favors as conditions for sustaining the continuity of storytelling.

> To tell stories is always the art of retelling them, and this art is lost when the stories are no longer retained. It is lost because one no longer weaves and spins, during which one listens to the stories. . . . Where the rhythm of work has taken hold of the listener, he listens to the stories there in such a way that the talent for telling them comes to him by itself. (GS, 2:446–47)

However true or untrue this claim might be, it is a social-historical image of the conditions that might sustain the continuity of storytelling: the conditions of handwork, specifically of weaving. But Benjamin tellingly does not next introduce a further social-historical image of, say, small-scale weaving being replaced by a mass textile industry. Rather, his image unfolds a mythological dimension, and this means that it becomes absorbed as allegory. His paragraph continues: "Thus the net is provided in which the talent to tell stories is cradled. And thus it is unraveling today at every end, after having been tied together for thousands of years within the surroundings of the most ancient forms of craftsmanship" (GS, 2:447). Weaving as a condition for storytelling becomes—in Benjamin's hands, it weaves—the image of a net that contains storytelling and the condition for its continuity. But how does the net (or web, *Netz*) begin to unravel? The image of the weaving first includes spinning but not measuring or cutting. That is, the mythological image of the three fates constituting life, its span, and its end is at first scarcely adumbrated. But then it is picked up like a loose thread, in precisely the threads of that net that have become loosened. A *cut* has been introduced, the cut of meaning that cuts into and across the image: weaving becomes unraveled, and the social-historical becomes the fateful.[15] "All ends" are becoming unraveled; in Benjamin's expansively allegorical language, an end to storytelling includes multiple ends within the net such an image casts.

What this image certainly includes is the implication that for Benjamin, death—implied in the thread cut by Atropos after having been spun by Clotho—comes only at the end of the "historical" argument about storytelling interwoven with the handwork of weaving. The thread that is spun is also measured and cut—this is an allegorical image and meaning for life becoming death. Benjamin likewise has death's image located in the argument about storytelling's ending together with the thought of eternity. When he claims that "the face of death must have changed" for conditions of the communicability of experience or the thought of eternity to have changed radically as well, he once again combines a social-historical image with an allegorical one. His historical claim about changes in death's face regards its masking and its disappearance: "In the course of the nineteenth century, bourgeois society . . . made it possible for people to withdraw from the sight of the dying." If Benjamin claims that formerly death was *everywhere* ("Formerly, not a house, scarcely a room in which someone had not already died"), he also asserts that death was *always:* he immediately adds parenthetically, "The Middle Ages also felt spatially that which makes the inscription on a sundial on Ibiza significant as a temporal feeling [*Zeitgefühl*]: *Ultima multis*" (GS, 2:449). The image of the face of death, Benjamin suggests, is like the face of a sundial across which a shadow continuously passes: every instant is the last one for many; the face of death is at all times many faces, potentially *all* faces. Benjamin's social-historical argument about the expulsion of death from the public sphere and finally from the private (domestic) sphere as well may be what it may—true or false—but his imagery here, at first glance, signifies the same allegorical meaning that he represents by such other imagery as the chain of storytelling and listening and retelling, or the layers of patient handwork. In each set of images, a continuous and ongoing passage of time and/or labor conserves itself in the constant signification—and hence, *preservation*—of its meaning. The "chain" or "accumulation" ("piling up," *Anhäufung*) of like causes had, in Benjamin's words, "its temporal threshold only at perfection." So, too, the chain of storytellings had its temporal limit at a potential for eternity—an eternity of storytelling—just as its spatial "coverage" of near and far overlapped with the temporal coverage of the long-ago of the story, the right-now of its counsel, and the next-time of its retelling. Here, with the sundial on Ibiza, death is at all times and (because) at all places: in every room, on every spot on the dial that life's shadow touches. This would be an allegory of continuity, expansion, plenitude, albeit of death.

But if it were seen that storytelling unraveled or was cut by its own fate within the very imagery of its continuous weaving, how might "the face of death" change its allegorical significance across the imagery of its continually repeated presence? In the conjunction of two further images of death's repetitions—images that continue to bring together the circular and the keeping of time—the essay indicates a swerve, a deviation that yields a different story. The end of the essay's next section likens the regularity of death in *Naturgeschichte* to that in a certain clock: "In it death appears with the same regular repetition as the reaper does in the processions that take place around the cathedral clock at noon" (GS, 2:451). And the end of the following section further elaborates this image: "[The storyteller's] gaze does not stray from that numbered dial in front of which walks the procession of creatures, in which death variously [*je nachdem*] has its place as the leader or as the last wretched straggler" (GS, 2:452). The image in each case is of a mechanical clock with an automated circulating wheel of figures representing death and its effects: the reaping of the creaturely world. That the procession is regular and circular is of a piece with the essay's previous imagery for the storyteller, where to go away meant coming back with intelligence from afar, or where to finish hearing a story meant rebeginning it in the next telling. But these two images of the cathedral clock swerve significantly from that of the sundial, and so, too, does their allegorical meaning of the "face of death." The imagery is of a post-medieval, *mechanical* clock,[16] and in it death is actually *figured* rather than globally signified as in the inscription "Ultima multis."

A feature of the mechanical clock as well as of the procession of automata around it is that the time piece—the hands on the clock face, the figures of the procession—moves forward *haltingly*, whereas the shadow on the sundial moves *continuously*, albeit gradually. In other words, the continuity of the earlier "face of death" across a clock face gives way to the discontinuity—the starting and stopping—of the pausing and advancing clock hand or the similarly jerking figures of the mechanical procession. In Benjamin's "modern" image, time comes repeatedly to a *Stillstand:* it stands still, marks time, and figures death.[17]

The allegorical image of death "itself," in the figure of the reaper, similarly enacts the halting and radically altering transition from life to death. In this respect it seems right that Benjamin's customarily fine and exact phrasing should have the figure of death appear *je nachdem* as first or last. *Je nachdem* means "according to [the conditions]," in this case, the conditions of observation that note the figure's movement. Its meaning qua allegorical figure is accordingly not only that its procession is circularly repeating—death is never gone for long—but that death itself changes its position from cause to consequence, from beginning to end. Looked at from one perspective, the face of death starts the procession of time. But after the mechanical succession of starts and stops, pauses and clicks, an altered perspective sees it following behind, the consequence and end of its beginning and also the leveled, "humanized," or creaturely companion of its victims: at once the sign of death as the reaper and its meaning—after the clicks—in just another human form.

Death with a human face—such is the changing "face of death" in Benjamin's allegorical treatment, and if he has already said that its changes no longer yield access to eternity (for which it is no longer the "strongest source"), this is because in his allegory, the face of human death yields history instead. It has been argued that for Benjamin, history is the standing still of time in a present moment that releases its allegorical meaning. In his literary history of narrative forms, this standstill is occurring as the figure of time's continuity in the form of storytelling comes to a halt in the form of death—as one used to stop the clock's pendulum at the moment of death—and indeed, the end of storytelling is here being told around altered images of the face of death. The halting and altering of an allegorical procession of deaths introduces the specifically literary history in Benjamin's essay—the succession of storytelling by the form of the novel—and a specifically *literary* allegory of Benjamin's history emerges from his attention to the figures of death in the telling of stories and the reading of novels. That is, literature in its narrative forms—stories, novels, and, it will be seen, histories—takes shape for Benjamin along the line that connects one experience of a face of death (the dying man) to another, strictly literary figuration of this experience: reading the end of a novel as a figure for death, including one's own. Between beginning a story and ending a novel is Benjamin's reading of the literal passing of time, and his allegory of reading one's living in this loss: a reduced presence at a deferred closing time.

At the center of his theory of storytelling Benjamin tells how stories begin with an ending, which claim is also applicable to his theory of historiography. "It is not only man's knowledge or wisdom but above all his lived life—and this is the stuff out of which stories [*Geschichten*] are made—that first takes on transmissible form at the moment of death" (GS, 2:449). "Transmissible form" (Benjamin's *tradierbare Form* signals the broad claim for *tradition* or "handing down" in general that is being made here) requires a terminal point with its introduction of a past tense ("*lived* life"), and if this is in some sense self-evident for the biography of a lived life, it is no less obvious that Benjamin means to include histories within the reach of his claim about stories, hence his use of *Geschichten* where he might otherwise, contextually, have been expected to use *Erzählungen*.[18] But his argument here is not the formal one that a series must be closed before it can be recounted, or that a temporal sequence can be narrated only retrospectively; rather, Benjamin pins this claim to an ostensible experience of the face of death:

> Just as a sequence of images sets itself in motion inside a man as his life runs out—consisting of the views of his own person in which, without being aware of it, he has encountered himself—so the unforgettable suddenly arises in his expressions and looks, and communicates to everything that concerned him the authority that, in dying, even the poorest peddler possesses for the living gathered around him. (GS, 2:449–50)

Several features of this remarkable sentence may be noted and scrutinized. The preceding claim for a lived or past life draws its support by back-pedaling to a moment of being present at a passing away from life to death, just as the accompanying claim for transmissibility draws from the imagery of actual bystanders co-present at the moment of death and ostensibly having something "unforgettable" and "authoritative" imparted to them. This "authority" is communicated (*mitteilen* is Benjamin's term) first to one's own life-experience—by the "unforgettable"[19]—but then immediately shared by the surrounding witnesses; but this circuit is already implied by the face of the dying one, on whose "expressions and looks" the unforgettable visibly appears. An allegory—of ephemeral life assuming timelessness or unforgettability at the moment of its dying away—appears in the altering face of the dying man. And the allegory is in fact (like all allegories) a doubled thing about a doubled object. Benjamin would have it two ways about two things here. The ways are that both timelessness and ongoing time can emerge at once: the "unforgettable" appears with death in order to survive it, but the ongoing temporality of storytelling is about to be simultaneously initiated. The doubled object of Benjamin's allegory here is the real "lived life" and death of a man (which emerges into a story) and, emblematically, the life and "death" of storytelling being told here, in his essay, as *its* story or narrative: emerging as history at the historical moment that it is coming to an end or dying away. And so, to the extent that this allegory includes among its objects history, its meaning will come to be about the dying out of a length of narrative time and about living in this loss, this death, this diminishing spot of closing time.

But most interesting in this passage is the deceptively familiar claim about a series of images appearing to a person at the moment of death. Benjamin does not seem to worry over the logical paradox that informs this belief, less a Cretan's paradox than a version of Zeno's, less that dead men tell no lies than that they tell no stories, while the *nearly* dead who survive to tell, perhaps, of a series of images appearing to them can hardly be counted reliable sources for what really happens with the *really* dying. But a paradox nonetheless comes to inhabit Benjamin's use of this topos: the paradox of an inside being used as an analogy for an outside. "Just as" *(So wie)* a man encounters himself *inwardly* in a narrativelike series of autobiographical images (self-discovery, self-knowledge), "so" one communicates at the moment of dying not only with one's own past ("everything that concerned him") but with everyone around or outside him. How should one account for interiority becoming exterior, surface appearance as well as communication, and why should this matter?

The stakes in Benjamin's analogy are those of founding storytelling on an image—of the face of death—that is actually not that of hearing a story but that of an experience far more interior, private, and silent in kind. For Benjamin's very next sentence, which also concludes this section of the essay, is, "At the origin of the story told [*Am Ursprung des Erzählten*] stands this authority." And the opening of the following section reads: "Death is the sanction of all that the storyteller can report. He has borrowed his authority from death" (GS, 2:450). At this core of Benjamin's theory, after the unfolding of his history of storytelling's coming to an end in *its* death (the essay's first ten sections), one finds its *origin* enfolded in a corresponding moment of death. And this death is at once a real one (any real death of any historical person, including the poorest) and an allegorical one: an origin for the authority and the possible authorship of a literary form. A form comes to an end, a death, and that story, that literary history, comes to tell at just this juncture of its origin, its historical condition of possibility, in death.

These large and masterful strokes whereby Benjamin's literary history leads to and complements his literary theory of the form of storytelling should not while dazzling us also blind us to the paradoxical analogy on which they turn. A second image of sharing death, as it were, recalls this first one, and since it does so when discussing not the story but the novel, it raises explicitly issues of exteriority and interiority, public and private, that otherwise lie only implicitly in the skillful if deceptive analogy that Benjamin employed in his first use of the image. The fourteenth section begins by recalling the transmission of unforgettability by even the poorest soul that ended the tenth: "'No one,' Pascal says, 'dies so poor that he does not leave something behind.' Surely it is so with memories as well—only that these do not always find an heir. The novelist takes custody of this estate, and seldom without deep melancholy" (GS, 2:454). In this claim, the poor still always have something to hand down, but the changed circumstances—so Benjamin's social-historical argument about the hiding away of death by bourgeois society—mean that there may not really be anyone gathered around to receive the inheritance. And if storytelling, in Benjamin's view, could immediately turn death into origin, and loss (of life) into gain (of authority), the novelist rather more bleakly handles memories that may be going nowhere. But there is a deeper reason for the deep melancholy attributed to the novelist, and it begins to emerge as Benjamin, continuing this section, pays homage to Lukács's *Theory of the Novel*.

A long string of quotations from Lukács's text concludes to the effect that the overcoming of that "power of time" that separates meaning and life and constitutes the form of the novel can occur only when past life becomes compressed in memory by a character's "divinatory-intuitive grasping of the unattained and therefore inexpressible meaning of life" (GS, 2:455). Lukács speaks of what happens to a literary character inside a novel (Frédéric Moreau of *L'Éducation sentimentale* is the privileged example), and his strained formulation of a "grasping of the unattained and therefore inexpressible" indicates the thoroughgoing fictionality of the "experience," as well as, strictly speaking, the unarticulated nature of what is being attributed to the character. But when Benjamin picks up his own prose again, he is suddenly outside the novel but also "grasping" back in: "The 'meaning of life' is indeed the center around which the novel moves. But the quest for it is nothing other than the initial expression of perplexity with which its reader sees himself deposited in precisely this written life" (GS, 2:455). Here, it is not the character "remembering" inside the narrative given him in the novel (like Frédéric and Deslauriers at the end of Flaubert's *L'Éducation sentimentale*) but an uneasily explicit version of Benjamin's earlier image of the real man dying with his narrative (biographical) meaningfulness while surrounded by real witnesses to whom such a narrative and its authority are supposedly communicated. Here, however, the life that may or may not achieve meaning is the fictional one of the novel, while the struggle, "perplexity," and directionality are all on the part of the readers outside, "looking" in and "seeing" themselves in a "written life."

That a reader might "see himself deposited in this written life" means that he might see life as a series of images assuming narrative (and narratable) form at the instant of death, except that here, in a crucial swerve, the images must already have *assumed* narrative form, and the instant of death must not be occurring but rather already have *occurred*. In other words, the tenses must be changed—the co-present moment become a past one—for the life is said to be already *written*. The reader of a novel does not share, by witnessing, a co-present moment of life becoming narrative as it (life) dies, but enters into a time-lag wherein one "sees" life in an afterview, inscribed as past and over, as if it were only what it always already was. Reading one's being deposited in a written life, unlike seeing a story emerge from an "unforgettably" transformed face, is seeing oneself in and as history: the living having passed into being written, seen already from the end point of a reading.

The definitive, that is, noncontinued and therefore terminally historical nature of such a reading "experience"—reading one's deposit into a written life—is accentuated by Benjamin in his contrast of the novel with the story. A story originated in and was sanctioned by an "end"— a death—that initiated an ongoing continuity, but "the novel achieves an end that is more proper to it, in a stricter sense, than to any story. Actually there is no story for which the question of how it continued would not be legitimate." Not only legitimate but, one is inclined to add, necessary to and constitutive of storytelling, according to Benjamin's own theory. "The novel, on the other hand," he continues, "cannot hope to take the smallest step beyond that limit at which it invites the reader to a divinatory representation of the meaning of life by writing a 'Finis' beneath the pages of the text" (GS, 2:455). Novels come to definitive ends, and *this* experience—material, textual—is "transmitted" to the reader as a communication, an "invitation" to "anticipate [*ahnen*] a representation" of the possible meaning of a life at the moment it definitively ends. To observe or partake of this moment in reading is to be present at a past, at once to read the written and to be in the face of history. And in this the novel, like history for Benjamin, is eschatological, for it presents the afterview: a view upon the last thing after which there is no more "next"; the last thing after the last or, in Benjamin's words, "no hope to take the smallest step beyond the limit."

The limit here is no longer the pathos-laden or existential image of a real person's death but its transformed face: the end of a character's fiction and the end of a novel's pages. Meaning—and with it memory, transmissibility, authority, the origin for a story, sanction—either will or will not emerge at this juncture, which is also the threshold between life and *lived* life, or history. The reader's position at a novel's end, with its concomitant injunction that one "anticipate" one's meaning, one's having lived up to the point of being fully written ("seeing oneself deposited in this written life"), is momentarily suspended when Benjamin returns, in the next section, to the social and existential dimensions of the novel reader's solitude in contrast to the story listener's keeping "company" with the storyteller.[20] But as Benjamin's rhetoric heightens the sense of the reader's solitude, he introduces imagery that increasingly focuses on a reader's orientation and movement toward the end of his reading material: the more solitary he is, the more the reader "devours" (*verschlingen*) the novel's material (*Stoff*). "Indeed, he annihilates, he devours the material as fire does logs in a fireplace. The tension that runs through a novel is very much like the draft that stimulates the flame in the fireplace and animates its play" (GS, 2:456). As Benjamin contrasts the companionship and communicability of the situation of storytelling with that of novel reading, his language for the latter centers on its consuming, combusting characteristics but also on its precise location of the "flame" in this event. The flame is the reader's, or a figure for the reader himself. And this is noteworthy because where the dying man was said to exhibit an illuminating appearance that transmitted authority for storytelling to those gathered around him ("so geht mit einem Mal in seinen Mienen und Blicken das Unvergessliche auf . . . ," where the verb *aufgehen* indicates a sudden illumination, like the turning on of a light), with novel reading it is the *reader* who catches fire and throws off light, as it were. More precisely still, where the dying man lit up and died, the reader is an *animated* or "enlivened" flame.[21] Across this more or less constant imagery of light, the dying man who became an illumination and an origin has given way to the fictional written life in novel form, which in burning animates its reader.

What is at stake in this imagery is the passing of light and life, both their transmittal and their passing away. One claim, for storytelling, was that death and the life-narrative that constitutes itself at its moment might communicate an illumination, through however many media-tions (illumination-authority-sanction/origin-storytelling), across its threshold. A counterclaim, about novel reading, is now that at an abso-lute terminal point of a life-narrative—the end of the novel—an illumi-nation nonetheless still blazes up, but as if at the cost of "seeing" oneself in a text's written life and *not* crossing its threshold so much as catching fire along the narrative line and up to its very limit. The stakes are that what can serve as an origin in one case is a terminus (a *terminus ad quem*) in the other and that a "real" source for metaphoric light in the first case is replaced by thoroughly artificial (fictional) light and heat in the sec-ond. But Benjamin raises the stakes higher still.

He first continues his imagery with apparent irony: "It is a dry mate-rial on which the burning interest of the reader feeds." The irony that such dry, novelistic feed may yield such a burning interest rests upon the truth of the literal level of the image—that dry tinder flares up all the quicker and brighter. But the force of "dry," as in dead or inanimate, is immediately drawn out.

> "A man who dies at thirty-five," Moritz Heimann once said, "is at every point in his life a man who dies at thirty-five." Nothing is more dubious than this sentence—but only because it has the tense wrong. The truth that is intended here reads: a man who died at thirty-five will appear *to remembrance* [*dem Eingedenken*] at every point of his life as a man who dies at thirty-five. In other words: the sentence, which is meaningless for real life, is indisputable for remembered life. One cannot represent the es-sence of a character in a novel any better than this sentence does. It says that the "meaning" of his life is only released at his death. But now the reader of the novel really seeks people from whom he reads off the "mean-ing of life." And so he must, one way or another, know in advance that he shares [*miterlebt*] their death. If need be, the figurative one: the end of the novel. But better yet, the literal one. (456)

The introduction of the past—past time, the past tense, the passing of life into death—has introduced *meaning*. Benjamin's words are exact-ing: where there was a "meaningless" sentence "for real life," there is an "indisputable" "truth" for remembered life. The remembered here is not, however, necessarily of a real life, let alone of that real moment of death isolated in the scene about the "origin" of storytelling. Rather, Benjamin is drawing his sense of meaningfulness and truth from narra-tive form: the earlier "series of images" ostensibly flashing up an instant before extinction is now the form of remembered life *tout court*, and this, as his next two sentences indicate, is modeled on the *novelistic char*-

acter (Romanfigur).[22] This does not mean that the claim is any less universal, only that the vector, as it were, points from fiction to allegorical truth rather than from life to storytelling. The "death" (in quotes because fictional) of the character, exactly like the death of the real man in the earlier image, "unlocks" meaning. Now when the reader turns to people, he notably "sees" them in and through a *textual* model: not as with Benjamin's example of the dying man, who yields the authority and origin of storytelling, but rather like that phrasing of a reader, who "sees himself deposited in this written life," with the allegorical truth that such a figure "signifies precisely the nonbeing of what it presents."[23] For here Benjamin uses the German verb *ablesen* to describe the novel reader's turn toward people: he would not so much "gather" or "collect" (this would be *auflesen*) but more precisely, he would *read off* the "meaning of life" from people *as textual characters.* His "knowing in advance" that he shares their experience of death is not drawn from a lived experience of surrounding a death bed—banished from Benjamin's portrait of bourgeois society—but from the practice of reading up to but not beyond "that limit at which [the novel] invites the reader to a divinatory representation of the meaning of life by writing a 'Finis.'" If Benjamin can still nostalgically "prefer" the actual, literal death experience of a character, he signals its dispensability by granting priority to the "if need be" case of the figurative experience of "death" in a novel's ending precisely by mentioning it first.

Fictional characters in the novel give the reader to understand that death—a definite end—awaits them and, therefore, him. He is "reading off" his life and meaning from theirs. Even as Benjamin underscores the communicability or mediation achieved between the novel's fiction and the real reading of the real, material ending of the text, he is bringing us—*his* readers—toward an astonishing end and *décalage.* As reading a novel is likened throughout this essay to the realization or becoming of history—time definitively, terminally past, releasing its meaning at a present moment as "its reader sees himself deposited in this written life"—the very moment of experiencing such a history in and *as* a present ("den Lebenssinn ahnend sich zu vergegenwärtigen") remains marked by a thoroughgoing fictionality:

> The novel, therefore, is significant not because it represents—didactically, as it were—a stranger's fate for us but rather because this stranger's fate, due to the flame by which it is consumed, gives us a warmth that we never gain from our own. What draws the reader to the novel is the hope of warming his shivering life around a death of which he reads. (GS, 2:456–57)

The sharing of "truth" and "meaning" becomes less the shining forth of light—illumination or enlightenment—than the shedding of warmth. And the "flame" of reading that consumes the "stranger's fate" gives off a warmth that one can never experience in reality. Benjamin's rigorous and astringent "never"—"die wir aus unserem eigenen [Schicksal] nie gewinnen"—may give the lie to his earlier historical image of a meaningful, illuminating drawing of experience from another's death; that is, he may hereby declare that to have been a serviceable fiction. Or his "we" here may be strictly contemporary, in which case that earlier "historical" image and experience is now a dead, cold history for us. In any case, the *we now* never get warm from death.[24] The death is "figurative" (the novel ends) or literal (the character dies) but in either case fictional, and the warmth metaphoric. The moment of ending the novel may be materially real; the moment of ending reading in meaning is, as was first said, "anticipatory," while here it is *virtual*. Virtual because it does not so much *remember a fictional life and meaning* as it *hopes to remember a real one*.

The figurative gap both between fiction and life and between history and life remains inscribed in this *almost present* moment of reading meaning. To read the novel's end and remember its (through its character's) meaning is real with respect to the fictional life and gives an almost present warmth—*almost* present because it remains enclosed within the covers of the book, closed within the time that runs out at "The End," and not beyond. But the reader outside the book—across its threshold—is still shivering, the warmth is still metaphoric, and the gap or pause between a figurative death "shared" and a meaning almost realized is no less powerful for being conceptual. The conceptual difference between realizing (remembering) life as history when it is dead and over, and waiting for the arrival of meaning at an asymptotically unachieved crossing of an end is the *décalage*—the halt in the narrative, the gap in the argument—within Benjamin's essay. The story yields the novel, so his literary history tells us. The novel yields history, so his narrative actually tells its allegorical reading. And the latter two narrative forms yield a "meaning of life" that is always true and never ours.

The conceptual gap in Benjamin's account of novel reading and its enactment of meaning may be compared with the halt or pause identified in his imagery of the modern "face of death" as the mechanical clock marked the onward march of death. In neither case is an end not reached; on the contrary, the end is as ineluctably there as ever, and the temporal force of chronology—one minute after another—is not in question here. Rather, the forms and material of its marking are, along with the significance that can be produced. In the case of the mechanical clock, the pause between one moment of life and the next marked by the allegorical figure of death was found to emblematize that the appearance of allegory is a certain separation from the mere passage of time, not the *Ultima multis* of any and all instants of the shadow of time upon the sundial, where there is always the sun on either side, but the specificity of death's face appearing, momentarily halted, as if detached from a "real" (living) chronology or temporality that is otherwise (felt as/to be) continuous. Benjamin introduced his differing versions of the "face of death" in clock faces as he was arguing for the changed situations of the social-historical experience of death and the consequent changes in narrative transmittal of such experience. As if, in his somewhat hyperbolic formulation, every moment and every room had once been the scene of a dying away, so, with equal constancy, every collective witnessing of such death scenes yielded testimony for telling stories of life's assumption of narrative form and communicable meaningfulness. The coloration of Benjamin's account is nostalgic and strangely positive: what might otherwise be thought to indicate a transcendental region ("the unforgettable") is here "leveled" into the existential claim of a witnessing and the literary-historical constitution of storytelling and, ultimately, a tradition of narrative that extends and sustains the very features deriving from such a moment: authority, an origin, sanction, communication, and transmission.

Within the context of Benjamin's practice of literary history in his essay, the moment when he is about to account for the social-historical causes for the coming to an end of storytelling is the moment when his history sounds most like storytelling and his version of the story promises most to survive itself in literary history. That is, Benjamin's literary history sounds like storytelling because, as if having been witness to the latter's death in the present, he has the sanction and authority immediately to tell its story—to pick up a thread that is becoming untied and continue to weave a seamless narrative. And so storytelling as well gains access not only to a kind of unforgettability but also to a kind of "historical eternity": the eternity of the historical record, of the all-remembered, the all-recalled after death.[25] No sentence so powerfully represents the survival of the end of storytelling in the narrative form of literary history as the one that converts death into birth, loss into afterlife: "The earliest symptom of a process whose end is the decline of storytelling is the rise of the novel at the beginning of modern times." This seems to confirm his claim that "there is no story for which the question as to how it continued would not be legitimate"—including the story of storytelling. And so that imagery attributed to the story—

the weave, the net, the chain, the tradition, the handing down—spreads continuously across the length of Benjamin's literary history. Storytelling comes to an end, and this means—yields as allegory—that it is more continuous or inwoven than ever in the narrative of literary history. But such an account, faithful to a series of features of Benjamin's imagery and argumentation, and testifying to the persuasive power of his historical account, stops short of the significance of the changed face of death and the changed features of reading an end in the experience of the narrative form of the novel.

If there was nostalgia and pathos (the two are never far apart) in Benjamin's account of the death scene that was also the continuous birth scene of storytelling, there is every temptation to feel an equivalent existential *frisson* around his account of the "shivering" novel reader trying to warm his life around the dying flame of the novelistic character's narrative. But the "experience" here, as the life of a character becomes his history, and as a present of reading becomes its passing into the past at the finish line of "Finis," is that of a pause in the face of an end rather than a crossing of the threshold in a continuous passage. The "experience" is less existential than paradoxical, less meaningful even at the level of loss than meaningless in its dimension of unattainability. Zeno's paradox, in this case of a reader ever warming his figurative hands around the dying flame signaled at an end that he can reach but not cross, is a representation of a conceptual halt or check on the near side of all "real" chronology that runs on nonetheless.

Loss—if this is still an appropriate (appropriately cleansed or disinfected) term—is not, then, of *time's* continuity through narrative forms but of its remembering in either a collective or a continuous form. Benjamin's insistence on the solitude *(Einsamkeit)* of the novel reader matches his attention to the *punctual* or *solitary* character of remembering in the modern narrative forms of the novel and literary history: they remember or keep mindful of *(eindenken)* the *one* (the *ein[e]*) rather than "re-membering" the many into the continuous.[26] An irony of his allegory of literary history, therefore, is that even as he can weave the death of storytelling into the ongoing story of narrative forms, his "life" of novel reading is a repeated punctuality rather than an ongoing continuity: an almost-present-ending at a figurative death, end*lessly* kept in mind *(eingedacht)* in an unresolved, unremembered, untransmitted non-authority of death's meaningfulness. "Unforgettability" is here neither the immanence of the transcendental nor the transmission of the existentially meaningful within the collective but the haunting unforgettability of a ghost. Reading the novel is not the birth of some new and yet still continuous or traditional form of knowledge, communication, and wisdom but the stillbirth of a "still reading": still reading death, around a faint but fixed flame of attention at the end of a page.[27]

This "end" (dead end) of literary history in Benjamin's "Storyteller" is also the punctual, allegorical point at which his theory of history leaves one at present. History for Benjamin is a coming to an end, and this still-ending in the face of death is a reading of history that has not yet concluded, even as time keeps running out. That time passes does not mean that any reading of the past time can get beyond the terminal line that marks a threshold (not a passage) between a literal mark left by death and an allegorical or figurative dimension of that mark's meaningfulness. Or rather, "getting beyond" that line is, for Benjamin, nonnarrative: it does not assume the form of a remembering that can be passed on and thus re-membered with other moments, by other readers reading. It is instead a shift of axes, which may be designated as the paradigmatic option. The closing sections of Benjamin's essay return, somewhat abruptly but with an unmistakable conviction and sense of need (time is running out), to Nikolai Leskov as the figure of the storyteller. And if the reader of his essay had been halted, shivering, at the figure of an uncrossable line and a dying but still burning figurative life, he is here invited into depths and up to heights.

The horizontal or syntagmatic axis of Benjamin's literary history—from storytelling to novel reading, but no further—is here tipped endwise into the vertical or paradigmatic one of a hierarchy of creatures and gradations of knowledge. One can hear the sense of release from a bind that the very next section's language of liberated vertical movement conveys:

> All great storytellers have in common the lightness with which they move up and down the rungs of their experience as on a ladder. A ladder reaching down into the earth's center and losing itself in the clouds is the image of a collective experience for which even the deepest shock of each individual's experience, namely death, represents no impediment and limit. (GS, 2:457)

The "shock" of death, which yielded that halt or pause in Benjamin's image of reading at the end of the novel, would here, in this image, be recuperated as if with that much greater force, including the force to expand an individual experience into its collective reception. ("'And they lived happily every after,' says the fairy tale," says the next sentence, in which the German phrase even more directly captures Benjamin's bypassing of death: "Und wenn sie nicht gestorben sind, so leben sie heute noch.")

Benjamin returns in these closing sections to his claims that storytelling provides good counsel *(guter Rat)* and that at its most efficacious it leaves behind happiness *(Gluck)*. Happiness at *its* height has man liberated from a mythic, entrapping nature but still participating in nature, precisely because he is able to move to its heights: "'Escaped as in a fairy tale' are the creations that lead the procession of the Leskovian creatures: the righteous ones. . . . The righteous man is the advocate for the creaturely and at the same time its highest embodiment. . . . With this Leskov sees the height of the creaturely attained and at the same time presumably a bridge between this world and the other" (GS, 2:459–60).[28] That the figure from storytelling could be both creaturely and a bridge, ladder, or peak reaching from that realm to the heavenly is a clear sign of this verticality's allegorical structure: it is at once the sign of the material level and means the overcoming of the level of that sign. But if here the allegory is of a saving, triumphant procession (the symmetrical counterpart to death leading or following the procession of men), Benjamin's vertical axis can recall a *fallen* nature as well, like that *Naturgeschichte* in which death regularly appears.[29] In fact, below *Naturgeschichte* with its rhythm of deaths is a "bottom" of nature *beneath* life and death. "The hierarchy of the creaturely world, which has its apex in the righteous man, reaches by many gradations down into the abyss of the inanimate [*Unbelebten*]" (GS, 2:460). For Benjamin, the righteous man gives voice to all of this nature, including its inanimate abyss, and is himself quintessentially given voice by Leskov the storyteller. In this he figures precisely an allegorical *conversion* (Benjamin's terms are *umgewandelt* and *Umschlag*)[30] of "depravity into saintliness," of low into high, but also of syntagmatic into paradigmatic, of historical narrative into allegory, even if this means descending back to the depths of that vertical dimension: "a natural prophecy of petrified, inanimate nature concerning the historical world in which he himself lives" (GS, 2:463).[31]

This is identifiable as allegory for Benjamin because the representation of such meaning occurs not only across all rungs of a hierarchy but across all time as well and even out of time. The inanimate can mean ("prophesy") the historical, and the historical world "in which [the storyteller] himself lives" can become in his allegorical hands the sign of the fateful end of this history. To the storyteller "it is granted . . . to reach back to a whole lifetime." This image still recalls the historian's— and the authoritative narrator's—"horizontal" grasp back across expired time. But it just as suddenly tips or tilts into the "vertical" image of surviving one's own death: "His gift is the ability to narrate his life; his distinction, to be able to narrate his *entire* life" (GS, 2:464). Not only to "read" it—to have that "series of images" not only appear but be read and understood to the end—but to live beyond the reading in order to tell it: to pass on one's *own* legacy, to write one's own history. The survival of death would also be the resurrection of that cold, inanimate nature in a warm afterlife: "The storyteller—he is the man who could let the wick of his life be consumed completely by the gentle flame of his story" (GS, 2:464–65). Not a shivering reading but an autocombustion of material—human life, historical events—into the language of their meaning. At a moment of death, the wick consumed completely, its authority would turn into the total authorship of a story of life. The storyteller also, finally, goes up in smoke at the self-consuming end of Benjamin's story of the same name. If history is, for Benjamin, to live in time's death, then the history of the storyteller is to live in his self-mortification: the essay's symmetrical counterpart to its opening apocalyptic image of "the tiny, fragile human body" beneath destructive forces, where here the disappearance of the "last man"—the storyteller—would complete such a foreboding of the disappearance of man.

This is Benjamin's eschatological piety, his appeal to "the storyteller join[ing] the ranks of the teachers and sages" (GS, 2:464). "The storyteller," his essay concludes, "is the figure in which the righteous man encounters himself" (GS, 2:465). That it is also allegory is also signaled by his passing remarks that at the very historical present of his closing section, storytelling lies in waste and in ruins.[32] His greatest claims for storytelling occur just short of its historical ending, and just after its historical end; his allegory of history is exactly that a highest meaning is claimed to emerge from out of this gap between an ending and an end. Call this the *absence* of history, or its ruins upon which his allegory is erected. Benjamin's paradigmatic-allegorical option is available at all times but operative at no historical time, not unlike any philosophic allegory of history over or beyond history—such as a philosophy of epic-narrative forms over or beyond literary history, or a metahistory over and beyond historiography. But such an image of remembering all (Benjamin remembering all that Leskov stands for) is held in tension with a historical moment when the unforgettable does not emerge but crumbles or dies away. In plain historical terms, this is *every* moment, every time that closes upon itself. In the literary-historical terms that Benjamin's essay has defined, his recalling of *all* that the story stands for—a metahistorical recall of verbal narrative since its prehistory, "the voice of the nameless storyteller who existed before all written textuality [*vor allem Schrifttum*]" (GS, 2:462)—occurs at a limit at which Benjamin's reader is invited to read narrative death, both the end of storytelling and the figure of death at the end of every novel: closing time. It remains for a reading of Benjamin's *Ursprung des deutschen Trauerspiels* to demonstrate that an allegory above history is still precisely an allegory *of* history: reading its absence, contemplating the face of death, and seeing an "origin" not of meaning except as of mourning.

10

End and Origin: Benjamin's *Ursprung des deutschen Trauerspiels*

One can also fall *into heights, just as into depths.*
—Hölderlin

"Origin is the goal," Benjamin quoted Karl Kraus as saying.[1] For Benjamin as well, the origin is the goal: the goal of historical studies and thus the end it would reach. A limit and perhaps also a terminal point, an end to history, where history ends. But what originates at such an end-in-origin? The structure of historical representation—of that mode of signification and discourse we call "history," as something scholars and intellectuals "do"—stands forth and displays itself, under Benjamin's treatment, as the allegory it is: the allegory of history. Allegory is the origin of history.

When Benjamin writes his *Ursprung des deutschen Trauerspiels* in 1924–25, it is his second book-length study (after his 1919 dissertation on the concept of *Kunstkritik* in German romanticism) but his first sustained work on representations of history and the philosophy of history.[2] As we have seen, it was not to be his last such effort, but it may remain his most stunning contribution to the problem, and within his own body of work the most decisive. And thus it is given a place of privilege in this study—the end spot for the original contribution of the *Ursprung*—after the preceding chapters on Benjamin's texts on history and literary history. For in those texts' arguments for history as a rhetorical image of a messianic breakthrough of time (the theses "On the Concept of History"), as an allegorical re-presentation of death (the Baudelaire project), and as a narrative problem of reading a near-meaning at a nearly ending moment ("The Storyteller"), the fragmentary, sometimes elliptical, and often obscure sets of Benjamin's thoughts on history and its structures are but extensions and probes sent out from the virtual core, which is his *Ursprung des deutschen Trauerspiels*. Reading Benjamin backwards, as it were, against the grain of the *oeuvre*'s chronology of composition, as well as against a certain tendency to celebrate his last-written works as his ultimate statements, we may finally reach a beginning at and from which to read Benjamin.

To read the *Ursprung des deutschen Trauerspiels* in the context of the present study is to come as close as we shall finally be able to understanding the linkage of allegory and history. And to do this will mean to have to unpack those two terms across the book's treatment of its principal topic—the baroque *Trauerspiel*—and within its matrix of other key terms, above all, the term and concept "origin."[3] The sequential treatment the book provides is itself one of powerful antitheses and remarkable reversals, while the set of terms generated by its "Epistemo-Critical Prologue" displays a kind of plastic topography in which one or more terms will envelop or be layered upon others, only to have their relations reformulated a step or two later. An initial series of expository declarations, however apophantic they may appear, and however provisional they must remain, can lead to a more refined reading of the actual deployment of the argument in this, Benjamin's densest and most luminous work.[4]

In letters that contain some of the earliest notes for the *Ursprung*, Benjamin referred to "the deduction of the form of the *Trauerspiel* from out of the theory of allegory" and to what was to be the work's first chapter: "On History in the Mirror of the *Trauerspiel*" (873, 875).[5] This would suggest a hierarchical ordering, with a theory of allegory having priority for a deduction of the object of study, which is the *Trauerspiel*, which in its turn is the mirror giving access to a certain image of history; and while neither phrase from these notes survives in the final version of the book, the generative power of a theory of allegory to produce an understanding of history is certainly retained as the work's central accomplishment. But the "Epistemo-Critical Prologue," which presents the book's methodological apparatus (together with its polemical bravado, which can be ignored for our purposes), has nothing to say explicitly about allegory but a great deal to say about philosophy and its approaches to criticism and history. That Benjamin should be able to assert summarily that "philosophical history [is] the *Wissenschaft* of 'origin'" (227) obliges us to understand these terms in advance of an inquiry into allegory. His philosophical approach to history, also called "philosophical criticism [*Kritik*]" by him, is specifically distinguished from the disciplinary practice of literary history as he and his academic contemporaries understood it;[6] but to the extent that Benjamin arrives, via a treatment of the problem of history in the understanding of works of literature, at an allegorical—that is, literary-rhetorical—rendering of history, his *Ursprung* is indeed an instance of *literary* history in the structural sense that the present study has been seeking to display.

Philosophy, Benjamin holds, is "the representation of truth," and the truth is "made present in the dance of represented ideas" as "something representing itself" (207–09). Unabashedly Platonist, Benjamin maintains that the representation of such ideas as self-representing is the task of philosophy; and if its general project will also include "the salvation [*Rettung*] of phenomena by means of ideas" (214), so the more specific task of philosophy in the face of the beautiful—the task of *Kunstphilosophie*, or "philosophical criticism"—will be to move from the forms of art, phenomenal as they are, to the representations of their ideas. This movement from things and their phenomenal appearance to their "salvation" in ideas is itself a mediated one, first by way of concepts (*Begriffe*). Concepts, Benjamin holds, break phenomena into their "elements," and it is only as such that phenomena enter, "saved," into ideas.[7]

But what are these ideas, apart from something self-representing and a still-vague "salvation of phenomena"? Here is where a second step of mediation between phenomena and ideas enters. For the phenomena, although dissolved or broken down by their conceptual grasp (*Begriff*, "concept," from *begreifen*, "to conceive," "to grasp together") into "elements," are retained (or "saved") as the concrete, "thingly [*dingliche*]" stuff of which the ideas are constructed and via which they represent themselves:

> As the salvation of phenomena by means of ideas accomplishes itself, so does the representation of ideas in the medium of the empirical. For not in themselves do ideas represent themselves, but solely and exclusively in an ordering of concrete elements in the concept. And indeed they do this as their [the elements'] configuration. (214)

Benjamin immediately adds that the phenomena are not "incorporated" (*einverleibt*) or "contained" (*enthalten*) in ideas, which are rather the phenomena's "objective virtual arrangement," "their objective interpretation." A striking and, for Benjamin, typical analogical image renders this point clearly. "The idea belongs to a fundamentally different realm than that which it grasps [*das von ihr Erfasste*]. . . . The ideas relate to things as constellations ["starry images," *Sternbilder*] to the stars" (214). As stars, the things are what they are—minerals and gases, one presumes—but as constellations, they are or have become representations. Benjamin adds that "the ideas are eternal constellations [*Konstellationen*]"—this qualification will interest us shortly—and continues: "and as the elements are grasped [*erfasst*] as points in such constellations, the phenomena are at once divided and saved." Breaking apart and then saving as well, in the mode and service of representation: this allows Benjamin to conclude that philosophy's task vis-à-vis things is a double one that is in fact two faces of a single project, "the salvation of phenomena and the representation of ideas" (215).

Now this vocabulary—vertical, hierarchical, theological, or at least thoroughly Platonic and idealist (Benjamin quotes the Platonic byword *ta phainomena sozein*)—begins to take on a special interest as it opens onto a temporally constituted field. Although the language of ordering, arrangement, and constellation is admittedly spatial, it also already implies an activity (it was also called an "interpretation"), and the temporality evident in such activity as "salvation" (all these terms are substantive participles) will become more focused as Benjamin explains both the character of the material entering into the idea qua representation and the significance of the representation itself. As the choice of the term "elements" already suggests, the material is partial, individuated, and Benjamin has also said that phenomena are "divided" into such "punctual" elements; but while these elements are then also said to be "singular and extreme," it is precisely their coherence *and their survival in the mode of this coherence* that is accomplished in the representation: "The idea is described as the shaping of the coherence [*Gestaltung des Zusammenhanges*] within which the singular and extreme stands alongside its counterpart . . . ideas come to life only where extremes are gathered around them" (215). Similarly, as Benjamin asserted from the start that "unity" (*Einheit*) is an immediately presupposed determination of truth,[8] he goes on to identify *totality* as a contribution the representations of ideas make to their constitutive particulars: "There is no analogy between the relationship of the individual [phenomenon] to the idea and its relationship to the concept: in the latter it falls under the concept and remains what it was—individuality; in the former it stands in the idea and becomes what it was not—totality. This is its Platonic 'salvation'" (227). It is in between these claims for the shaping of the singular into its coherence and the saving of the individual in the idea's totality that the specifically temporal and, indeed, historical character of the "saving of phenomena" is worked out in Benjamin's argument. It will also emerge later in our analysis—but the phrase "becomes what it was not" already suggests it—that the structure of this operation is allegory itself.

Benjamin appears to believe that both truth's "form" and the ideas are coequally fundamental, given or immanent in the very status of truth's existence and ontologically qualified as "being" (*Sein*). Thus, "for the truth, [method] is self-representation and therefore immanent in it as form. This form derives not from a coherence within consciousness—as in the methodology of knowledge [*Erkenntnis*]—but from a being" (209; cf. 210). Philosophy has to "remain true to the law of its form as the representation of truth" (208). The truth in turn, it may be recalled, is present in the "dance" of represented ideas. And so philosophical criticism will have to serve the self-representation of truth in the ideas. Now Benjamin boldly declares that "in the sense that it has for an art-philosophical [*kunstphilosophischen*] treatment, the *Trauerspiel* is an idea" (218). How is this idea to be represented? Much later in the text of the *Ursprung*, in a paragraph that will concern us again, Benjamin puts it with rare clarity and conciseness as follows: "It is the object of philosophical criticism to demonstrate that the function of the art form is precisely this: to make historical factual-contents [*Sachgehalte*], such as lie at the basis of every important work, into philosophical truth-contents [*Wahrheitsgehalten*]" (358).[9] And so the temporally transformative operation of the ideas as the "interpretation" of phenomena, and of philosophical criticism as the representation of ideas, may be developed in the instance of the *Trauerspiel*, which is at once a series of historically existent and determined art works *and* precisely one such "idea." This will be done when Benjamin further qualifies his project in this book as "philosophical history," as "the *Wissenschaft* of 'origin' [*Ursprung*]," and, in a draft exposé for the work that corresponds precisely to this passage in the "Epistemo-Critical Prologue," adds: "Accordingly the 'origin' [*'Ursprung'*] of the German *Trauerspiel* is its idea developed in its concrete fullness [*seine in konkreter Fülle entwickelte Idee*]" (227 and 951).

The "origin" of an idea is not its beginning but rather its "concrete fullness." What might this mean more specifically? Benjamin has summarized a transformation of "historical factual-contents" into "philosophical truth-contents." A dense paragraph in the prologue brings out the temporal transformation enacted upon the historical material, which is—or rather, in their plural historical instances, *are*—the *Trauerspiel*, in order to get at its "origin." Benjamin insists that "origin" is a "thoroughly historical category" and yet that it "has nothing in common with rise or development [*Entstehung*]." Working then with the root sense of the word, immediately intuitable to any speaker of German, he says: "In the 'origin' [*Ursprung*] it is not any process of becoming [*Werden*] of that which has sprung forth [*Entsprungenen*] that is meant, but rather that which springs out of becoming and passing away [*dem Werden und Vergehen Entspringendes*]" (226).[10] This decisive sentence signals that "origin," an "original springing out," is precisely that which does not *begin* a process but *ends* one—springs out of it, leaves it forever. The process it leaves and ends is that of temporal development, both the coming into being of something and its passing away.

Now let us take Benjamin at his word when he insisted that "origin" is a thoroughly historical category and assume that he knows what he is talking about. Earlier in this same paragraph he remarked on the general skepticism that has followed upon "the impossibility of a deductive unfolding of art forms" and favorably quoted Croce on "that genetic and concrete classification which in any case is not 'classification' but rather is to be called history" (225). So when Benjamin sketches his idea of "origin," he is not denying history but affirming it—in its meaning and its "concrete fullness." But such meaning is on the far side, or outside, of the sheer passage of historical time: history as it happens is not history as it means; the latter is only possible with history as it happened. History as "origin" is never "just the facts, ma'am": "The 'original' [*Ursprüngliche*] never makes itself available to be discerned in the sheer, manifest existence of the factual, and its rhythm stands open only to a doubled insight [*Doppeleinsicht*]" (226). This "doubled insight"—which will interest us again both for the feature of its doubleness and for its sense of the optical—turns out to requalify the "springing out of becoming and passing away" that is "origin." For it is not only that history has to *have happened* for there to be "origin"; it is also that there has to be "origin" for history to have really happened. That is, "origin" not only comes after but ends, fills, or fulfills. The next sentences in Benjamin's paragraph read:

> It [the rhythm of the "original"] needs to be recognized as restoration, as reestablishment on the one hand but, precisely because of this, as the incomplete, the unfinished [*Unvollendetes*] on the other. In every instance of the "origin" the shape is determined [*bestimmt sich*] in which an idea again and again confronts and engages [*sich auseinandersetzt*] the historical world, until it lies complete [*vollendet*] in the totality of its history. (226)

The two-sided or double-handed proposition of the first sentence here unfolds precisely into the second, in a motion between the incomplete and the complete that also simultaneously holds the two together and coexistent. If "origin" *re*stores, *re*establishes, and thus *re*turns to something past, by this very action it determines that past as not yet "finished" or "complete" or altogether over. And yet it *also* thereby does the finishing or completing just marked as "not yet": the historical world, not yet complete by virtue of its sheer facticity, becomes complete in its totality as the idea. When an idea is completely represented in its history, its history is likewise complete in its totality, and the relation of idea to history is the springing out of "origin."

And "origin," Benjamin repeats, "does not stand out from the factual findings; rather, it concerns their pre- and post-history [*Vor- und Nachgeschichte*]" (226). This "pre- and post-history" must not be thought of simply as an extended historical time surrounding some particular historical event or events.[11] Rather, the "pre- and post-" here ought to be thought rigorously as that which might precede and follow after historical events themselves, as their ideational (idealike) "origin." The idea is there before and after, as imprint and trace. Or as its unique instantiation in the course of history and its *return* ("restoration, reestablishment") to finish it off. As Benjamin's next sentences put it, first referring to "the dialectic that is inherent in 'origin,'" "it [the dialectic] shows singularity and repetition to be conditioned by one another in all essentials" (226).[12] The single and the repeated, in their codetermination, are history and idea, brought together as "origin." Events happen and events mean; when you have one and then the other, you have "pre- and post-history," history become "original." Thus in his following paragraph Benjamin can write, at first puzzlingly, that "that which is grasped in the idea of the 'origin' has history only still as a content, no longer as a happening [*ein Geschehn*] that could have occurred to it" (227). On the one hand, this means no more—and no less—than that history is over, finished, and can no longer happen *as it did,* now that it is grasped as a content for something else, which is exactly the "origin" now lying manifest. But on the other hand, the term "content" *(Gehalt)* recalls the contrast *Sachgehalt/Wahrheitsgehalt,* as "content" here has turned—"dialectically," in a doubled insight or perspective—from factual material of what happened into truth-content in and of the representation of the idea. History is now "inside" the "shape" of "origin," given form rather than just giving itself extension as it runs—occurs, passes—on and on: "Only now is history known inwardly, and to be sure no longer in a boundless sense, but rather in that sense relating to essential being [*in dem aufs wesenhafte Sein bezogene Sinne*], which allows it [history] to be designated as that being's pre- and post-history" (227). So, indeed, "pre- and post-history" have limits—contours and shape—*that* are recognizable as the image of "origin."

Benjamin concludes this line of thought with some further sentences that at once introduce a new term (one that will reappear crucially in the body of the book) and repeat some earlier ones. First: "The pre- and post-history of such essences [*Wesen*] is, as a sign of their salvation [*Rettung*] or gathering [*Einsammlung*] into the preserve of the world of ideas, not pure history but rather natural history." What Benjamin appears to want to evoke here with the term "natural history" *(Natur-geschichte)*—and this can only be a provisional account, to be supplemented as the term's use is expanded later—is the nonhuman, that is, noneventful character just suggested ("no longer as a happening that could have occurred"), but as well a spatial and static sense of history as fixed, almost geologically so. For in the following sentences to which our attention is to be called, the inhuman, the fixed or completed, and the static come to the fore:

> The life of works and forms, which only under this protection unfolds itself clearly and undisturbed by the human, is a natural life. If this saved or salvaged being [*gerettete Sein*] is established in the idea, then the presence of the non-actual or improper [*uneigentlichen*]—that is, natural-historical—pre- and post-history is virtual. It is no longer pragmatically real, but rather, as natural history, it is to be read off from the completed status, brought to rest—from the essence [*am vollendeten und zur Ruhe gekommenen Status, der Wesenheit, abzulesen*]. (227–28)[13]

No more a history in which events could still befall it, this "natural history" is "undisturbed by human being" and its *pragmata* or actions and may be so because it is completed and "brought to rest." It is, in other words, over and brought to its end—what Benjamin calls "origin"—but it is not dead but rather living, living a "natural life" within the full expanse of its pre-history and post-history. The apparently innocent (because colloquial) reference to "reading off" such completion and totality, such fullness, of history may already suggest that history as what happened has been transformed into or at least recharacterized as a text, perhaps even a script. But it certainly indicates that, to recall the earlier phrase of Benjamin's about the individual fact, it has become what it was not: not history unfolding across time but history unfolded and limited *within* its time, "established" in the idea as "origin." Benjamin reuses the verb *feststellen*, "to establish" or, literally, "to place in a fixed manner," and reemphasizes the overcoming of a still-dynamic temporality as he concludes this line of thought by recalling "the tendency of all philosophical conceptual formation . . . to establish [*feststellen*] the becoming of phenomena in their being," and then adding: "For the concept of being in philosophical *Wissenschaft* is not satisfied by the phenomenon, but rather only by consuming its history" (228). *Aufzeh-rung*, "consumption"—as with Hegel's end to his *Phenomenology*, so here, the allegory behind a consuming of history will need to be unpacked.

In the immediate context of Benjamin's methodological apparatus, "consumption" is displayed in terms of time's wear: death, ruination, and what might follow. A letter's version of Benjamin's early thoughts on the *Ursprung* first coins a phrase that was to become famous and then links this with the claim for "establishing" life beyond its living temporality: "Criticism is the mortification of works. Not an intensification of consciousness in them (romantic!), but knowledge's taking up residence [*Ansiedlung des Wissens*] within them . . . the task of the interpretation of art works is: to gather creaturely life within the idea. To fix or establish [*Festzustellen*]" (889).[14] Mortification, or "making dead," is evidently how knowledge takes up residence in works, fixing them and their natural, creaturely life in the idea (like the above phrase's "establish the becoming of phenomena in their being"). When this passage shows up later in the final version of the *Ursprung*, it is in a context where the payoff of death and ruination could not be more explicit. This is the context of Benjamin's argument about historical factual-content being transformed into philosophical truth-content, in a sentence we have already had occasion to glance at. The passage begins with a re-written version of the sentence in question: "Criticism is the mortification of works. . . . Mortification of the works: thus not—romantically—an awakening of consciousness in the living ones, but knowledge's taking up residence within them, the ones that have died off [*in ihnen, den abgestorbenen*]." Here, the taking up of residence by knowledge is not just via the works' "mortification" but *in* their very dead forms. There then follows, several sentences later, the claim about factual-content and truth-content, now in its full context of deathly transformation:

> It is the object of philosophical criticism to demonstrate that the function of the art form is precisely this: to make historical factual-contents, such as lie at the basis of every important work, into philosophical truth-contents. This remodeling [*Umbildung*] of the factual-contents into truth-content makes the decay of efficacy [*Verfall der Wirkung*] . . . into the ground for a rebirth, in which all ephemeral beauty fully falls away [*vollends dahinfällt*] and the work maintains itself as a ruin. In the allegorical construction of the baroque *Trauerspiel*, such ruined forms of the saved artwork [*trümmerhafte Formen des geretteten Kunstwerks*] have always stood out clearly. (357–58)

The transformation, or remodeling—literally, the "re-imaging"—of historical contents into philosophical truth here names and displays its paradoxes as the structure of allegory itself. The "making dead" of works is the establishment of a residence for the life of knowledge, collecting creaturely or natural life in such knowledge. The "fall" in the German *Verfall*, or in the Latin *cadere* of its English translation as "decay," is the "re-imaged" sign for "the ground for a rebirth"; the "falling away" of the "ephemeral," the merely transient, yields a "fullness" of falling such that the work no longer falls but stands or maintains itself—"as a ruin." And thus this ruination is saving or salvaging: saving the phenomena is what philosophical criticism does when it sees time's passage or falling away (its "ephemeral" quality) as its transformation into its truthful meaning.

Allegory displays the ruined forms of the saved, the saved in the form of the ruined. To speak of "re-imaging" here is exact to Benjamin's language, but it needs to be understood as the radically paradoxical "re-imaging" of something into its other, and thus as *alle-gorical*. The passage of historical time, in this model, becomes what it was not yet "fully"—its *past*, its falling away, its death—and what it is not—its *overcoming*, or "rebirth," as its meaning or truth. Benjamin believed that in this treatment of history within the artwork, philosophical criticism was itself reduplicative of the art form of the *Trauerspiel* itself. Just as "historical factual-contents" are the basis of the work, "historical life . . . is [the *Trauerspiel*'s] content, its true object" (242–43). And if such historical content may, in Benjamin's general model, be transformed into its philosophic truth, the *Trauerspiel* itself may transform its content of history into "the representation of history as a *Trauerspiel*" (321). This latter formulation means that history's allegorical treatment would yield, as its allegorical "re-imaging," its meaning as the display of its very allegorical structure.

History ruined and reborn, reborn as and in ruins, *is* allegory in that the "other" of history, its falling away, becomes its meaning. Benjamin claims that during the baroque, "one believed one could grasp the *Trauerspiel* with one's own hands in the course of history itself; one needed no more than to find the words" (243). This implies that another dimension of the claimed allegorical structure of history is the insight into history as discourse, as the becoming of a language of signs. "Whatever this time grasps, its Midas-hand transforms into a signifier [*ein Bedeutendes*]. Transformation of all kinds was its element; and its schema was allegory" (403). As we turn to the body of Benjamin's argument about the allegory of history in the baroque *Trauerspiel*, it is this dimension of history's becoming language that must be examined such that its constitutive aspects of reading and becoming read may appear. The allegory of history in the *Trauerspiel* not only entails a reading of allegory but yields an allegory of reading.

From very nearly the beginning of his presentation of the baroque *Trauerspiel*, Benjamin poses the extreme and often counterintuitive versions of history and time that inform this art form and its world vision. Not surprisingly, these versions are in the face of a fall and its consequences, but the consequences themselves may surprise in their own versions and ramifications of falling. Benjamin does not present a familiar Fall with its eventually happy, redemptive end. Rather,

> In the theological-juridical mode of thought that is so characteristic of the [seventeenth] century, there speaks the delaying, deferring exaggeration or overstraining [*verzögernde Überspannung*] of transcendence that lies at the basis of all the provocative worldly accents [*Diesseitsakzenten*] of the baroque. For, antithetic to the historical ideal of restoration, the idea of catastrophe stands before it. (246)

The "turning down" (*kata-strophe*) that stands before the baroque does not promise a restoration of another world but instead remains tied to "this side" (*Diesseits*) and in fact exaggerates the antithesis between a here and a beyond (an *über*, a *trans*). Even the catastrophe will not occur—befall—and get itself over with; the deferral defers, the "excess tension" (*Überspannung*) exaggerates itself. Sartre's "change is not conceivable except as catastrophe" would even be too hopeful a view for this situation. If catastrophe were to occur, it might not "turn down" so much as just fall, or plummet, some more; thus, "the religious man of the baroque holds so tightly to the world because he feels himself driven along with it toward a cataract" (246). Because the falling would be without an ending, there is no desire that the fall occur, that anything fall away:

> There is no baroque eschatology; and for that very reason there is a mechanism that piles up and exalts all that is earthly before it is handed over to its end. The hereafter [*Jenseits*] is emptied of all that contains even the slightest breath of the world, and the baroque acquires from it a plenitude of things that had customarily escaped any [artistic] shaping and, at its highpoint, brings them in a drastic shape into the light of day, in order to clear an ultimate [*letzten*] heaven and put it, like a vacuum, in a position to annihilate the world one day [*dereins*] with catastrophic violence. (246)[15]

This remarkable image strains history and its end to an "annihilistic" conclusion. Rather than encourage or propel the historical world toward a redemptive end, the baroque—in Benjamin's portrait—piles up (*häuft*) the earthly, as if in a grotesque parody of a scholar's tower toward heaven. It will be handed over to an end nonetheless, but not before the near side and the far side (*Diesseits, Jenseits*) are emptied of one another and left thoroughly antithetical. The image appears to tend toward such a radical opposition of an end freed of the world and a world freed of the end, an apparently anti-eschatological or immanent historicism opposed to an empty transcendence. But this appearance—*Schein*—is, in Benjamin's treatment, a forestructure of divine nihilism: a violent turning down that renders the world nil. The vacuum of the empty heaven would come to evacuate the world, leave it null and void, when a last (*letzt*) meets a first (*dereinst*) in a deferred but not for that reason canceled eschatological moment.

Benjamin's portrait of the *Trauerspiel* thus announces a structure of last things despite itself: an absence of its doctrine, qua eschatology, nonetheless poses an antithesis between the presence of the world and the absence of its end and meaning, which antithesis will strain or oppose its paired terms toward a catastrophic conclusion. But in the meantime the very deferral of the end appears to turn time, not into a catastrophic (and potentially redemptive) closure, but into another other—a spatial nonpassage. Benjamin's language is, once again and not for the last time, of a fall, a strange fall-back in the face of a falling away: "a consequence of the loss ["falling-out," *Ausfall*] of all eschatology is the attempt to find comfort for the renunciation of a state of grace in a falling back [*Rückfall*] upon a sheer state of creation" (259–60). Time seems not to progress toward a promise but to revert to a stasis:

> Here, as in other spheres of baroque life, what is decisive is the transposition [*Umsetzung*] of originally temporal data into a spatial inauthenticity [*Uneigentlichkeit*] and simultaneity. . . . Where the Middle Ages present for our view the decrepitude [*Hinfälligkeit*] of world events and the transience of the creature as stations on the way to salvation, the German *Trauerspiel* altogether buries itself [*vergräbt sich*] in the disconsolateness of the earthly condition. If it knows a redemption, this is more in the depth of this destiny itself than in the fulfillment of a divine plan of salvation. (260)

If the creaturely state appears not as a state of grace before a Fall, nor as a postlapsarian moment promised redemption, then the temporal register that it indicates appears arrested and thus distorted. The temporal is transposed into its other, the spatial, but the spatial is inauthentic (*uneigentlich*) and figurative (also *uneigentlich*) because *it* really is *its* other (the temporal), only figuratively so. Temporality "is" spatial simultaneity, which means that it has the structure of a sign that not only *is not* what it indicates or means but *means* the opposite of or opposition to its signifier. A "fall" of historical events and a transience of the creaturely, however, do not yet mean *their* reversal as and into salvation (so Benjamin would portray medieval Passion plots); rather, the fall seem-

266

ingly cannot go far enough, as it buries itself ever more deeply in the earthly, as if in the merely spatial. And yet a redemption is nonetheless still held out, if, however paradoxically, in a fall of time into the depths of the spatial, rather than in time's "fulfillment." It will await the very end of Benjamin's argument on allegory and *Trauerspiel* to explicate the tensions here implied between buried depths and the heights of salvation.

A reduction of the temporal to an apparently spatial "state" yields, in the *Trauerspiel*, what Benjamin calls "the sequence of dramatic actions unfold[ing] [*rollt sich . . . ab*] as in the days of creation, when it was not history that occurred [*da nicht Geschichte sich ereignete*]" (270). This formulation might suggest a hypostasis of a prelapsarian state of grace, but it is rather that history is reduced to or inverted back into its pre-beginning and that drama "unfolds," but as if without narrative (also *Geschichte*). Benjamin's continuation of his argument draws out such paradoxes: "It is not eternity but the restoration of paradisal timelessness that opposes the disconsolate course of world-chronicle" (271). This much is indeed reversion out of history and back to timelessness, and yet it is clearly nonredemptive, yielding not eternity but a *space before* time's unfolding in(to) a narrative. And in fact it is not so much *out* of history as putting history *back into* a space, for Benjamin's next sentence reads: "History takes up residence in the setting." Still narrative—and hence, as a condition of possibility, potentially dramatic—the *Trauerspiel* is also spatial, enclosing history such that its story cannot unroll or unfold out of its space. (Benjamin, quoting the scholar of the baroque Herbert Cysarz—and anticipating his own, later work on Paris in the nineteenth century—also calls this "panoramatic," a "collection of all that is memorable.") Thus, "the temporal movement is captured and analyzed in a spatial image [*Raumbild*]" (271). History reverts to timelessness qua setting but still unfolds qua dramatic narrative; the "paradisal timelessness" is not in fact without time, but would display temporality without its historical unfolding beyond its confines.

What Benjamin later in his *Ursprung* calls the baroque's "rendering present [*Vergegenwärtigung*] of time in space . . . its transformation into the strictly present" (370), is here captured conceptually in his language of the image, the *Bild:* the *Raumbild* that encloses and absorbs time's unfolding, which—otherwise—would be history. Thematically this is the court, and dramaturgically it is the setting of the play, the *Trauerspiel*, but structurally it is the spatial and visual (*Raum-bild*) that can represent a temporality that might unfold without its going anywhere "else," such as time not becoming history nor the story of its departure from an origin. It is, in other words, an image like a calendar or a clock.[16] It is also a visual image of the invisible, an image of its other. *Sternbilder*, or constellations, for Benjamin, it may be recalled, belong to a fundamentally different realm than that which they grasp; they divide phenomena into the punctual, the singular, and the extreme before "saving" them in the image or idea. Here, the *Raumbild* divides temporality from its historical unfolding or "rolling out" and guards it in a spatial presence or present. That this should befall time introduces into Benjamin's argument *both* the other face of a time that does not lead to temporal redemption *and* the structure of a discourse that would itself be counterprogressive.

History as "counterprogressive" would mean, in Benjamin's understanding, that human history does not progress beyond its creaturely beginnings, but remains mired in the state of createdness and its immediate fallen consequences. What he calls "the natural-historical transformation of history in the baroque drama" (299) is best understood in terms of a counterpart to progress that is not stasis but rather *fate*. "Fate," Benjamin writes, "is meaningful only as a natural-historical category in the spirit of the restoration-theology of the Counter Reformation. It is the elemental force of nature in historical occurrence [*im historischen Geschehen*], which itself is not entirely nature, since the state of creation still reflects the light of grace" (308). In this complex image, fate is natural-historical, but precisely mixed—natural and historical, not entirely natural—because the fallen state of creation is still bathed in the light of grace from above. But the human history that issues from this state does not leave it behind; this is not like Milton's end to *Paradise Lost*,

> *Some natural tears they dropp'd, but wip'd them soon;*
> *The World was all before them, where to choose*
> *Thir place of rest, and Providence thir guide:*

$$(12.\ 645\text{--}47)$$

where a natural inheritance is "wiped" away and providential or salvation history is about to begin. Rather, as Benjamin's argument immediately continues, "[the light of grace] is mirrored in the swamp of Adamic guilt": the descent from heaven of an origin to human history is still reflected in the course that is consequent, but is reflected foully. Grace falls into creation and is reflected in that fall; and so the human history that would follow falls as well. This "elemental force of nature" is called fate, and Benjamin clarifies the natural-fatality of this natural-history as follows:

> The genuine notion of fate should have its decisive motive sought in an eternal sense of such [natural] determination. . . . It does not lie in factual inevitability. The core of the notion of fate is much more the conviction that guilt—which in this context is always creaturely guilt (in Christian terms: original sin), not moral fault by an agent—releases, through however fleeting a manifestation, causality as the instrument of irresistibly unfolding [*unaufhaltsam sich entrollenden*] fatalities. Fate is the entelechy of occurrence in the field of guilt. (308)

An *original* sin, in this view, yields not an escape from its consequences in a final eternity or timelessness but a fateful eternality or timelessness of its consequences, a determination more powerful that sheer factual inevitability (Benjamin has in mind here the causal determinism of natural laws). Causality is here not a natural law but a natural fate, an instrument in the service of that which unfolds or "unrolls" (*entrollt*). But what thus unrolls does not lead beyond its very condition; it remains entombed, enclosed, encaptured, or otherwise merged in its "original" setting. The entelechy—the realization of the potential, of the cause that gives form—is of events that are fated to remain as they are, in their "field of guilt."

If guilt is the condition of natural (created), fallen man, as a consequence of an original Fall, the fallen nonetheless keeps falling, and this is its fate. Fate and, with it, history do not unfold out of or beyond this condition, but they do appear to aim at an end. "Fate leads to death [*rollt dem Tode zu*]. It is not punishment but expiation, an expression of the subjection or fallenness [*Verfallenheit*] of guilty life before the law of the natural" (310). Death appeases, or gives a kind of peace to, fate by signaling that the fallen condition submits to this, its very naturalness: death as the law of nature. On the one hand, fate is that which "unhaltably rolls on," but on the other, it "rolls or leads to" death. Death is the fated (irresistible) entelechy of fate and thus the end—goal and closure—of occurrence in the baroque natural-historical version of man's condition.

Benjamin's language of falling, which has permeated his discussion of the *Trauerspiel* thus far, may be traced a step further in order to have it lead to his portrait of the human subject in the face of such a deathly world-view. This step is the one in which the world itself falls into sheer *things*. "Even the life of apparently dead things wins power over human life once the latter has sunk [*versunken*] into the company of the merely creaturely. The effectiveness of the thing in the sphere of guilt is a harbinger [*Vorbote*] of death" (311). For man sunken or fallen among nature, things themselves—inanimate or, in Benjamin's oxymoron, having only "the life of dead things"—presignal or prefigure death.

Dramaturgically, this accounts, in Benjamin's claim, for the preponderant role the thing plays as a stage property (*Requisit*) in the *Trauerspiel*. It foreshadows death and means this very foreshadowing, that is, that creaturely life goes nowhere, but unrolls to its death. "The meaning of the stage property," Benjamin says, is "accident [*Zufall*] as the breaking down of action or occurrence [*Geschehen*] into thinglike fragmented elements" (312). In the immediate context, Benjamin's *Geschehen* clearly refers to dramatic action, as he sketches the arrest of fluid action in the foregrounded stage presence of discontinuous things. But in the larger context of the first half of his *Ursprung*, Benjamin's choice and linkage of terms is precise: as occurrence merges with or otherwise does not escape the confines of the sheer creaturely world—as human history becomes "natural history"—the consequence of falling is that things themselves fall apart (become *abgestückt*) and that "befalling to" ("accidence," *Zufall*) is the extreme form of occurrence under the law of fate. Accidentality, or that which befalls, is in this sense not the opposite of fatality but rather its mode of appearance. Fate befalls man; his history becomes thinglike; the life of dead things foreshadows the death that fate leads to. This is the fate of an original fall.

The unimaginable bleakness of such a world-view has, in fact, not only the local habitation of the baroque *Trauerspiel* but the name (and image) of melancholy. When Benjamin summarizes the view of the *Trauerspiel* with references to Lutheranism and Shakespeare's *Hamlet*, he describes "the dark belief in the subjection to fate, in its befalling one [*Schicksalsverfallenheit*]," and continues: "All value was removed from human actions. Something new arose: an empty world" (317). Benjamin calls this "existence as . . . a field of ruins of unfinished, inauthentic actions" (318). In the face of fate, death, and an empty or half-empty world, at best filled with deathlike things and ruined actions, the names of "mourning" and "melancholy" designate both a position, or posture, and a reaction. It is here that an action upon or reaction to the world-view so bleakly portrayed will also be about to appear. "Mourning [*Trauer*] is the disposition in which feeling reanimates the emptied world as a mask, in order to have an enigmatic pleasure in its sight." The term *reanimation*, or revival (*neubeleben*), describing a reaction to deathly emptiness, already suggests a reversal of fortunes, and "enigmatic pleasure" (*rätselhaftes Genügen*) similarly surprises by its incongruity in the face of the deathly images that have just preceded it. "The theory of mourning . . . is only to be unfolded in the description of that world which opens up under the gaze of the melancholy man" (318).[17] Mourning and melancholy will respond in a doubled sense to the mournful world already attributed to the *Trauerspiel*. They are at once its subjective re-presentation and a reversing response, as powerful a reversal as, say, the opposition of "reanimation" to death.

Before turning to several passages in which Benjamin depicts the reversing response of the *Melancholiker*, it will be consistent with his argument first to spell out further the form of the world that presents itself to his gaze. Each of Benjamin's key terms describing history and its fall reappears in this characterization of the *Trauerspiel*, but with the two signal additions that the world represented in the *Trauerspiel* is *allegory* and *script:*

> When, with the *Trauerspiel*, history merges [*hineinwandert*] into the stage setting, it does so as script [*Schrift*]. On the face of nature "history" stands written in the characters of transience [*Zeichenschrift der Vergängnis*]. The allegorical physiognomy of nature-history [*Natur-Geschichte*] that is put on stage by the *Trauerspiel* is present in reality [*ist wirklich gegenwärtig*] as ruin. In the ruin history has sensually [*sinnlich*] moved into the stage setting. And, shaped in this way, history does not display itself as the process of an eternal life, but much more as the proceeding of irresistible decay [*unaufhaltsamen Verfalls*]. Allegory thereby declares itself on the far side of beauty. Allegories are in the realm of thoughts what ruins are in the realm of things. (353–54)

The spatial enclosing and freezing of history in the stage setting reaches here an end point in its containment and fixing as script, as sheer written signs *(Zeichenschrift)*, as if they spelled "history." History, which does not progress beyond the creaturely condition of *Natur-Geschichte*, is thus embodied in nature, which signifies "history." But the embodiment paradoxically is cast in the "characters of transience": the fixed meaning is, at least literally (as letters), of passing away. And so the visual, physical embodiment is not just nature but the ruin. Nature in all its massive reality *is* transience, *is* ruination, and Benjamin calls this the "real," "present" counterpart to its allegorical representation on stage in the *Trauerspiel*. The sensuous or sensorially *(sinnlich)* real version of history is nature's decline into the ruin in *its* real, sense-based natural world. Once again, this is not history's progressing beyond itself to eternity, nor its preserving a pristine timelessness, but its ceaseless falling or decay. Such sensuous decay is, intuitively, "on the far side of beauty," and as allegory it is the meaningful version ("in the realm of thoughts") of the concrete, thingly version of decay seen as ruination.[18]

History falls and is captured in creaturely nature-history. Together, they are inscribed with temporality in its sense as sheer transience; the physical or sensuous embodiment of this inscription is the ruin. Such a "regression" in nature—a fall opposite to a progression—appears to offer no redemption:

> Nature remained the great teacher for the writers of this period. But to them she appeared not in bud and bloom but rather in the overripeness and decay [*Verfall*] of her creations. Nature appeared to them as eternal transience [*ewige Vergängnis*], and in this alone did the saturnine gaze of those generations recognize history. . . . In decay [*Verfall*], and in it alone, does historical occurrence [*das historische Geschehen*] shrivel up and merge into the stage setting. The essence of these decaying things [*verfallenden Dinge*] is the extreme opposite of the concept of transfigured nature. . . . The nature in which the image of the course of history imprints itself is the fallen one [*die gefallene*]. . . . [Things] carry on the authorization of their allegorical signifying [*Bedeutens*] the seal [*Siegelbild*] of the all-too-earthly. Never do they transfigure themselves from within. (355–56)

The oxymoron "eternal transience" retrieves Benjamin's argument about not timelessness but an eternity of history lying in the face of the creaturely condition. Here, it is nature—the "sensuous" appearance of decay or falling—that means history. Historical occurrence itself, the very *act* of time, becomes decay or falls. And this image of history appears to be at the polar extreme from a salvation history's image of transfiguration (*Verklärung*). And yet the activity of transfiguration, however little it may be empowered "from within" the fallen, all-too-earthly things themselves, nevertheless continues to hover about them, "outside," as it were. In those things is imprinted (*eindrücken*) the course of history, but its meaning is—allegorically—elsewhere and otherwise: not where it is read, in script or sealing image (*Siegelbild*), but in *its* other of a read*ing*.

The response to history in fallen nature, and to their representation in allegory, will be (a) reading. When history falls, in Benjamin's analysis, it falls into allegorical images, and all of these images—the fragment, Yorick's skull for Hamlet, mere nature, ruins—constitute script as if so many letters or characters: "The image in the field of allegorical intuition is a fragment, a rune" (352), and here the fragment (*Bruchstück*) alliterates with the letter (*Buchstabe*), and the angled letter or rune (*Rune*) sounds and looks like the fallen ruin (*Ruine*). Where reading meets the written, there is temporality meeting the spatial, significance about to appear at or about the signifiers: extremes are about to touch. As the oxymoron just glanced at might have hinted, "eternal transience" is not out of place in such an encounter of nature as script and history as its meaning; elsewhere, Benjamin describes allegory as being "most enduringly in residence there where transience and eternity [*Vergänglichkeit und Ewigkeit*] encountered each other most closely" (397).

The antinomic relation of transience and eternity, or of history as time and nature as space, may collapse together in *Natur-Geschichte* as in allegory, but if we are to understand this "collapse," if such it be, the extremes that inform allegory must be pursued one step further. Allegory itself forms one pole in a set of extremes recalled to our attention in recent years by Paul de Man, who himself retrieved much of his insight from Benjamin's *Ursprung*.[19] This pair of extremes is, of course, symbol and allegory:

> Within the decisive category of time . . . the relationship between symbol and allegory may be incisively and formally established. While in the symbol decline [*Untergang*] is transfigured and the transfigured face of nature is fleetingly revealed in the light of redemption, in allegory there lies before the eyes of the observer the *facies hippocratica* of history as an ossified primordial landscape [*erstarrte Urlandschaft*]. History, in all that it from the beginning has of the untimely, the sorrowful, the failed, is expressed in a face—no, in a death's head. . . . This is the core of the allegorical view, of the baroque, secular [*weltlich*] exposition of history as the Passion story [*Leidensgeschichte*] of the world; it is significant [*bedeutend*] only in the stations of its decay [*Verfalls*]. The more the significance, the more the subjection or falling (un)to death [*Soviel Bedeutung, soviel Todverfallenheit*], since death engraves most deeply the jagged line of demarcation between *physis* and significance. But if nature is always subject or fallen (un)to death [*todverfallen*], it is also always allegorical. Significance and death are as temporalized and produced [*gezeitigt*] in historical unfolding as they are, as seeds, tightly wound in upon one another [*enge ineinandergreifen*] in the creature's graceless state of sin. (342–43)

While all the terms associated with a Christian theology of salvation—*Verklärung*, transfiguration, revelation, redemption—appear aligned with the symbol, allegory appears to its observer (we shall have occasion to return to the explicitness of this image of allegory "coming into view") as the physiognomic pre-image or foreshadowing (the *facies hippocratica*) of history as a petrified desert. But at this instant when allegory represents history in its iterative negativity—the *un*timely, the sorrowful, the failed or missed (*Verfehltes*)—and in the very image of the death's head or the skull, ossified mankind (re)turned to ruin, world history in its sorrow (*Leidvolles*) is represented as passionate (*Leidensgeschichte*). The turn from fall to resurrection is already implied here, if not yet at all unfolded in its implications, and it is not unimportant, but crucial, to note that Benjamin's prose communicates this reversal in two employments of the figure of chiasmus. First, "The *world*ly exposition of *history* as the Passion *story* (history, *Geschichte*) of the *world*," wherein the secular or worldly is (re)claimed by the very other with which it is contrasted. But this is admittedly still under the (allegorical) sign of a fall; the stations are not yet of the cross, but only of sorrowful decay, and the relation appears parallel, not reversed: "the more the significance, the more the subjection or fallenness to death." But this is precisely where the second chiasmus appears: "The more the *significance*, the more the subjection or fallenness to *death*, since *death* engraves most deeply the jagged line of demarcation between physis and *significance*."

The point of reversal, the fulcrum for allegorical leverage here, is where death divides *physis* from *significance:* where death divides from itself, divides its literal letters from its significance, between "death" and "death" in the middle of the chiasmus, "death, since death." This divide is called by Benjamin the engraving of the line of demarcation, and the term "engraving" *(eingräben)* is itself doubled or allegorical, for it recalls the portrayal of history fallen, encaptured, sunken, and indeed *entombed (vergräbt)* that filled much of the first part of the *Ursprung* and is as well, here in the discussion of allegory, the very *terminus technicus* for writing, for inscribing a mark of difference. Just as in Keats's famous line from the opening of *The Fall of Hyperion*, "When this warm scribe my hand is in the grave" (l. 18),[20] Benjamin's word writes itself into the grave of writing, and retrieves death for writing, in the middle of the chiasmus itself. Death as physical, natural death divides from itself, in allegorical writing, to become the mark, line, script or demarcation of death, engraved or inscribed no longer as itself but as the significance of the sign. *The point of death is the point of writing.* The "historical unfolding" of the reversal enfolded in the chiasmus is what, in Benjamin's last line here, summarizes the trajectory of the *Ursprung*'s entire argument to this point: from the original loss of grace, the original sin, the first fall, to the unwinding of what is coimplicated (*ineinandergegriffen*) in the two "seed" words "death" and "significance."

It turns out that the turn or reversal from death into its significance and the allegiances and betrayals that, in Benjamin's argument, come with this are adumbrated in his brief analysis of the *Melancholiker*. The meaning to which the melancholic has access begins at the depths of a fall: "All the wisdom of the melancholic is slave to the nether world [*der Tiefe hörig*]; it is won from immersion or sunkenness [*Versenkung*] in the life of creaturely things, and nothing of the sound of revelation [*Offenbarung*] reaches it" (330). To this familiar contrast between the creaturely things and a spiritual salvation is added one between enclosure in depths and an impossible opening up *(Offenbarung)* from above. But the claim of "wisdom" for this position already suggests an ambivalent evaluation. What does the melancholic know? According to Benjamin, the melancholic turns from men to things (and this would explain, within certain *Trauerspiele*, the courtier's turn from the ruler to the sheer things of his rule—crown, royal purple, scepter) and displays loyalty only toward the latter: "Melancholy betrays the world for the sake of knowledge. But its enduring immersion or sunkenness [*Versunkenheit*] takes up the dead things into its contemplation, in order to save [*retten*] them" (334). From *this* depth of immersion in the thingly, a rising or taking up (*nimmt . . . auf*) appears in the melancholic's contemplative knowledge and promises salvation. Here, this reversal of depth toward heights, of the dead toward the saved, is called "dialectical" by Benjamin: disloyalty to man, loyalty to things, and, in their inverting reflection, a redeeming aspect of such a disloyal displacement of loyalties. For loyalty, Benjamin says, "is the rhythm of emanatingly descending levels of intention in which the ascending ones of neo-Platonic theosophy reflect themselves correlatively transformed [*beziehungsvoll verwandelt sich abspiegeln*]" (334). Descent can mean—via the means of melancholic knowledge—its inverting, transforming reflection into ascent, like death into salvation, or disloyalty into loyalty.

The specific language of mirror reflections turning and thus transforming opposites into one another is repeated and further enhanced in Benjamin's last paragraph on the melancholic. This is his portrait of Hamlet. Respecting the "style and language" of the *Trauerspiel*, he credits "the bold twist [*Wendung*] with which Renaissance speculations caught sight, in the features of the tearful observer/contemplator [Dürer's "medieval" *Melancholia*—as Benjamin somewhat anachronistically considers it], of the reflection of a distant light, shining back from out of the ground of sunkenness [*Versenkung*]" (334). This passage dazzles by its reversals. The conceptual point is to situate the baroque in both its medieval and its post-Renaissance aspects; but the "Renaissance" aspect reflects ("speculates"), and twists in reflecting, the "medieval," Düreresque one: what is thus "caught sight of" (*gewahrten*) out of sunken and dark depths is the reflection of light. Not only is darkness "reflected"—inverted—into light but the entire focus has been reversed: from Dürer's melancholic persona looking at once away and as if inwards to the viewer now looking above and behind, catching a reflection back upward. The human figure who is said to correspond to this "dichotomy [*Zwiespalt*] of neo-antique and medieval lighting" in the carefully composed Benjaminian image is Hamlet. "His life, as the exemplary, pre-imaged [*vorbildlich*] object provided to his mourning, points, before its extinction, to the Christian providence [*Vorsehung*], in whose bosom his mournful images are transfigured [*verkehren*] into blessed existence" (335). As an example or pre-image *(Vorbild)* for mourning, Hamlet's life declines toward death, but then it reverses its indication and prefigures or fore-sees providence; thus the image of mourning is itself inverted and transfigured into its other of blessedness. "Only in a life of this princely kind," Benjamin continues, "is melancholy redeemed *[löst sich ein]* by confronting itself" (335). The self-confrontation of the image, we have seen, is its specular reversal, from an image before one's mourning—a *Vorbild*—to a fore-image of providence *(Vorsehung):* from death to redemption *(Erlösung).*

Although Benjamin claims the singularity of the figure of Hamlet in the context of the *Trauerspiel* ("Shakespeare alone was capable of striking Christian sparks from the baroque rigidity of the melancholic, as un-Stoic as it was un-Christian, as pseudo-antique as it was pseudo-pietistic" [335]), his own construction of the figure of Hamlet is itself not singular but part of a double structure: a pre-image or prefiguration of *its* reflection at the end of Benjamin's *Ursprung.* For as Benjamin protesteth perhaps too much the utter uniqueness of Hamlet ("in this drama [lies] the unique play of the overcoming [of Saturn's line and the marks of *acedia*] in the spirit of Christianity"; "Only in this prince does melancholic sunkenness *[Versenkung]* arrive at Christianity" [335]), his own construction—we have been quoting from the very last paragraph of the first half of the *Ursprung*—anticipates its symmetrical counterpart at the other end of the other half. To return, then, to Benjamin's discussion of allegory, history, and *Trauerspiel* is to follow the precise language and imagery of reversal and "salvation."

"Criticism as mortification of works" would have seemed to tend unilinearly toward a site of death; as Benjamin's thought had continued, "not an awakening of consciousness in the living, but knowledge's taking up residence within them, the dead ones." But he continued with a claim we have already glanced at, namely, "that the function of the art form is precisely this: to make historical factual-contents, such as lie at the basis of every important work, into philosophical truth-contents." This innocent "to make" is in fact not unilinear but transformative and reversing. History in its transience becomes philosophy in its truth. The structure, as Benjamin's next sentences, together with our commentary to this point, make clear, is one of *allegorical* descent and reversal into otherness. "This transformation *[Umbildung]* of factual-contents into truth-content makes decay of efficacy *[Verfall der Wirkung]* . . . into the ground for a rebirth *[Grund einer Neugeburt]*, in which all ephemeral beauty fully falls away *[vollends dahinfällt]* and the work maintains itself as ruin" (358). The transformation, or literally, the re-imaging *(Umbildung)*, that the sentence describes is one of reversing historical signs into images of their other or opposed, allegorical meanings: so *Sachgehalte* become *Wahrheitsgehalt*, but falling *(Verfall)* also suddenly becomes a standing on a "ground," and the death associated with the decay of history and beauty becomes a rebirth that would "maintain" itself on their far side. "Fully falling away" itself reverses as if to stand upright, with head up *(behaupten,* "to maintain," is built around *Haupt,* "head": to show oneself the master—chief, head—of something). When beauty falls away and the ruin appears, this means the very reversal of ruination into rebirth. Benjamin concludes this paragraph by acknowledging his allegorical operation and linking it to the theme and project of salvation: "In the allegorical construction [*Aufbau*] of the baroque *Trauerspiel* such ruined [*trümmerhafte*] forms of the saved [*geretteten*] work of art have always stood out clearly" (358).[21] The allegorical builds up *(aufbauen)* from what is falling or in decay, but it also builds up by building *down* to the form of the ruined: it constructs by deconstruction, as it were. But not only does this reverse up and down, it also reverses an intuitive sense of before and after, for the "ruined form," which customarily would be thought to appear after an earlier moment of an unruined condition, here stands out "from always" *(von jeher).* The final paradox of reversal in this allegorical construction is that of "the ruined form of the saved." From transient historical effect *(Wirkung)* and ephemeral beauty to truth *and/in/on* ruination, there is not a continuity of falling but a flipping, reversing fall into heights. What is beginning to emerge out of such figures as chiasmus, paradox, and allegory?

The reversal implied in "the ruined form of the saved" pursues the arc of reversal seen in the figure of the melancholic—from death to redemption—but also retrieves the theme and operation of saving or salvaging from the "Epistemo-Critical Prologue." Indeed, Benjamin draws out saving *(Rettung)* as the principal function of allegory, just as "saving the phenomena" was the principal operation on the part of the philosophic critic. "The insight into the transience of things [*ins Vergängliche der Dinge*], and the concern to save them in eternity [*sie ins Ewige zu retten*], is one of the strongest motifs in the allegorical" (397). On his next page, Benjamin likens the operation of allegorical "saving" to the apparently more familiar and mundane one of reading:

> To be named . . . remains, perhaps, always a presentiment of mourning. But how much more so not to be named, but only to be read, to be read uncertainly by the allegorist and to have become highly significant only through him. The more nature and antiquity were felt as guilt-laden, the more obligatory was their allegorical interpretation as their only still-foreseeable saving [*Rettung*]. (398)

277

The merely natural, or, better, the *fallen* natural, gets elevated to a *high* significance *(hochbedeutend)* in allegorical reading. Such reading is not only the now-familiar reversal of low to high, or of transience into eternity—but is, as Hegel doubted, the familiar for that reason the known?—but of writing ("the demarcation line between nature and significance") into the read.

The transformation or re-imaging performed by allegorical reading cannot maintain an accord or unilinear correspondence between sign and meaning, even at the extremes of "transience" and "eternity," or "fall" and "heights." Rather, it will put the sign and its relation to its significance at stake, to the point where their very relation might, as itself a sign, signify their discord. As Benjamin's next sentence on the page in question puts it, "For in the midst of the knowing degradation of the object, the melancholic intention keeps faith [*bewahrt . . . die Treue*] with its being as a thing [*seinen Dingsein*] in an incomparable way" (398). Now this appears to indicate a fixation upon the thing itself (in this context, the thing as signifier), despite its degradation, or, rather, in its very mode of fallenness: a melancholic refusal to give it up (or over) to death, on the far side of the "demarcation line" between *physis* and death. A refusal to read the line of *Schrift* engraved by death. But how could this be its "saving" *(Rettung)*, let alone the kind of dialectical "saving of phenomena" Benjamin has already sketched? Allegorical reading—allegory as allegory of reading—will needs be a refusal of the refusal to read, that is, a refusal of the refusal to give up the sign of and by death. But in such a case, could allegorical reading be faithful, or "keep the faith"? Several pages later, Benjamin writes that "the mute creature is capable of hoping for salvation through the signified [*Rettung durchs Bedeutete*]" (401). "Keeping faith" with a thing in its being and saving it through its significance are in the signifying relation that signifies their discord. Allegory is this relation of alterity, and allegorical reading is the passage across the line demarcating the signifier from the signified.

Benjamin's analysis of allegory in the baroque *Trauerspiel* has led to this threshold of *crossing the line:* of reading a line between nature and significance—a line "engraved" by death and a line that is writing—and of confronting the "extremes" of the thingly, the creaturely, the fallen, on the one hand and, on the other, its "saving" in an allegorical reversal of the script into its higher meaning. The moment of crossing or turning over the line *as reading* would appear to allow—indeed, to necessitate—that Benjamin have it both ways: to retain the thing as mere signifier, "hoping for salvation through the signified," and to have its elevation and salvation in that reversal of the low into the high, the transient into the eternal. Will Benjamin's analysis ultimately underwrite such an understanding of the doubled structure of allegory as one that allows both ways and levels?

There are at least two sentences in Benjamin's *Ursprung* that, in their pithy and puzzling character, exemplify this problem of doubled "ways" and levels of meaning in a possible reversibility of statement. The first occurs in the context of Benjamin's critical discussion of theories of Greek tragedy, where (under the influence of his friend Christian Florens Rang's views) he is seeking to account for what he calls a "dual significance" or "dual power" of tragic death and then of tragic suffering. If suffering, as in Aeschylus's *Oresteia* or Sophocles's *Oedipus*, substitutes for sacrificial death, as "the subjection or fallenness to death [*Todverfallenseins*] is replaced by a 'fit' [*Anfall*] that both atones to gods and announces a new order," then—here is the first sentence—"Death thereby becomes salvation [*Rettung*]: death-crisis [*Todeskrisis*]" (286). The sentence represents a transformation of death, via suffering, into salvation—a fallenness *(Verfallensein)* to death gives way to a new falling upon *(Anfall)*—and this transformation is in fact a reversal indicated quite technically by the term "crisis": the turning point of a decision. In this sketch of Attic tragedy, death at a moment of crisis becomes the crisis of a moment of death, the turning or reversing of death into salvation, the decision that death *means* salvation. Death dies as death and yet is saved in the claim that it means salvation.

The second sentence of this kind occurs directly in Benjamin's discussion of allegory and poses the question of a *perspective* upon reversibility of meaning; and, once again, it specifically concerns the meaning of death. The sentence and its theme are introduced by a reprise of Benjamin's now-familiar argument about the decay or fall of nature as the precondition of allegory and its reversals:

> If then in death the spirit becomes free in the manner of spirits, it is also only then that the body attains its highest right. For this is self-evident: the allegorization of *physis* can be energetically pursued only on the corpse. And the characters of the *Trauerspiel* die because it is only thus, as corpses, that they enter into the allegorical homeland. Not for the sake of immortality do they die, but for the sake of the corpse. (391–92)

An initial paradox here is that the fall and decay of the body into the corpse is preliminary to its coming into its "highest right." The structure here appears to be one of antithesis, as body becomes most like sheer *physis* or dead matter, while spirit becomes most "spiritlike" *(auf Geisterweise)*, but the lowest will join with or enter into the highest, even as this "allegorical homeland" is explicitly (consistent with Benjamin's argument throughout) said to be not an antithesis to death but its very pursuit: "for the sake of the corpse." The sentence in question then follows: "Produktion der Leiche ist, vom Tode her betrachtet, das Leben" ("Observed from the point of view of death, the production of the corpse is life") (392).

One aspect of the meaning of this sentence is the very reversal it performs: we see not a vanishing point of life called death but *from* the vanishing point back upon a temporal fullness of life, seen as such for the first, and last, time. This understanding of the sentence, which seems true to one dimension of its meaning, would correspond exactly to the claim in Benjamin's "Storyteller" for the meaningful "last glance" of the dying man in the face of his future, now-authorized storytellers.[22] But a second aspect of the sentence conveys a different sense. The perspective of death is not immortality but the passing away *of* the body, yielding only its meaning as life; the corpse *produces* life as its "other" leftover precisely when there is no (living) body left over. As Benjamin's argument immediately continues, "Not only in the loss of limbs, not only in the changes of the aging body, but in all the processes of elimination and purification does the corpselike fall away from the body piece by piece" (392). "Observed from the point of view of death" means, not a static or permanent perspective, but the very dying away of death. At the end of a process of decay or falling (*Verfall*), the occasion—death—itself "falls away." Death means, allegorically, life.

The fall of life into death, like that of time into "natural-history," "produces" the falling away of death and the meaning of life: the "salvation" of the fallen. The line of script engraved by death between nature and significance will, when the script is read into meaning, allow nature to "fall away" and its allegorical other, the spiritual meaning of the bodily letter, to emerge across the line, at and as its far side. But is this account accurate with respect to the instance of reading? Does one read *away* the letter in allegorical reading, as if erasing it? Does the corpse—the letter, the script—"engraved" by death upon the creaturely condition and its history, give way to its other of meaning so thoroughly, without "leftover" or obstruction?

The reversal of perspectives implied in Benjamin's sentence on "the production of the corpse" being life may be the point at which these questions can be clarified. The discussion heretofore may have suggested that a reversibility of perspective entails only first one view, then another: first a view of death from the point of view of life, then of life from the perspective of death—or first of script as the dividing line between nature and its meaning, then of meaning as the far side, the other or crossing of that line—with the further suggestion that the "first this, then this" are not discontinuous but temporally connected by a figure of reversibility as one of narrative sequence. But the notion of reversibility, like its tropological embodiment in and as chiasmus, entails not merely first one view and then an other—even *the* other of the first—but one view *turning into* the other, reversing a temporal position of "now" into another: still "now" but not sequentially advanced or otherwise elsewhere but rather *reiterated*. When antitheses reverse, they turn into one another, "now" and "now." Benjamin has a thesaurus of closely related terms that represent just this attempted reversibility, and they are impacted in the most crucial of his passages on allegory. All his terms of fall and of transfiguration would appear to reach the end of their trajectory in this language and imagery of reversibility. And if the theory of allegory is also the structure of the understanding of the meaning of history as "origin," as an original springing out of time, then the relation of such "origin" to allegorical reversal will have to be clarified as well.

The passage in question, long and complex, comes scarcely three pages from the end of the work:

As those who stumble turn over and over in falling [*im Fallen sich überschlagen*], so would the allegorical intention fall [*fiele*] from emblem to emblem [*von Sinnbild zu Sinnbild*] down into the dizziness of its bottomless depths,[23] were it not that, precisely in the most extreme of these depths, it had so to jump round or reverse [*umspringen*] that all its darkness, haughtiness, and distance from God appears as nothing but self-delusion. Yet it is to misunderstand the allegorical altogether if one severs the store of images [*Bilderschatz*] in which this turn-around [*Umschwung*] into the sanctity of salvation [*in das Heil der Rettung*] accomplishes itself from that gloomy one that means death and hell. For precisely in visions of the intoxication of annihilation, in which everything earthly collapses into a field of ruins [*zum Trümmerfeld zusammenstürzt*], there is revealed [*enthüllt*] less the ideal of allegorical contemplative sunkenness [*Versenkung*] than its limit. The disconsolate confusion of Golgotha [*Schädelstätte*], such as can be read out of a thousand engravings and descriptions of the period as the schema of allegorical figures, is not just the emblem [*Sinnbild*] of the desolation of all human existence. In it transitoriness [*Vergänglichkeit*] is not so much signified, allegorically represented, as— itself signifying—put forth as allegory. As the allegory of resurrection. Ultimately the allegorical observation jumps round or reverses [*springt . . . um*] in the death signs of the baroque—thus for the first time in the returning, redeeming [*erlösend*] part of its wide arc. . . . In God's world the allegorist awakens. "Yea, / when the highest comes to harvest the graveyard, / then will I, a death's head, be an angel's face" [Lohenstein]. This cracks the code of the most fragmented, the most died-away, the most scattered. With this, admittedly, allegory loses everything that most properly belongs to it: the secret, privileged knowledge, the arbitrary mastery in the realm of dead things, the supposed endlessness of the void of hope. All this vanishes with this *one* turn-around [*Umschwung*], in which the allegorical contemplative sunkenness [*Versenkung*] has to clear away the last phantasmagoria of the objective and, left entirely on its own, rediscovers itself, no longer playfully in the earthly world of things, but seriously beneath heaven. This indeed is the essence of melancholic contemplative sunkenness [*Versenkung*], that its ultimate objects, in which it believes it can most fully secure the abject [*des Verworfnen*] for itself, invert [*umschlagen*] into allegories, that the allegories fulfill and deny the nothingness in which they are represented [*das Nichts, in dem sie sich darstellen, erfüllen und verleugnen*], just as the intention, in the end, does not remain faithful in gazing upon bones, but faithlessly springs over [*überspringt*] to resurrection. (405–6)

Benjamin's argument here about the ultimate reversals by and, indeed, *of* allegory unfolds across his seven staged uses of the related terms for this very image: *überschlagen, umspringen, Umschwung, umspringen* again, *Umschwung* again, *umschlagen,* and *überspringen.* Across the argument's constant narrative of a fall and a sunkenness, which language recapitulates that of the *Ursprung*'s entire presentation of the *Trauerspiel* and its versions of history and melancholy, the falling as well as each of the moments of its arc submit to allegorical reversals, up to the limit of allegory's reversal of itself. What might this, Benjamin's penultimate piece of argumentation in the *Ursprung,* mean?

A freefall of tumbling turning (*überschlagen*) reverses (*umspringen*) at its very bottom but just in time; thus a fall and all the bleak imagery associated with it turn or invert into a sheer delusion of falling. But this *volte-face* or about-turn (*Umschwung*) is not *from* the imagery of falling but *in* it, "undissociated," as Eliot might have put it. The imagery and its incorporation into allegorical emblems are the same for the fall and its turn-around into "salvation" (*Rettung*). What is indicated here is the possible error of literal reading—of reading, say, a fall to mean a fall: an image (*Bild*) to mean what the image shows. This, in allegory, is delusion, for instead, the allegorical image or emblem (*Sinnbild*) means the image (*Bild*) *plus* its reversing sense (*Sinn*). All the falling *means* its reversal, but precisely because the falling signifies (is the signifier for) its reversal, the latter meaning of "salvation" cannot be dissociated from the imagery. The principle of reversal that operates between sign and allegorical meaning is, Benjamin tells us, at the limit of annihilation. That is, the images in their negativity of death, hell, and ruination "reveal" not their self-evident meaning—an-nihilation, or radical negation

(Vernichtung)—but the limit of such allegorical falling and sinking *(Versenkung)* at the very edge of annihilation. This is not an undialectical doing away with the negative—its "simple" annihilation, as it were—but rather a claim that the negative *is*, literally, itself and means, allegorically, its other, and the reversal from the one to the other is *at the limit* of the imagery's preserved negative literal meaning: it negates *and* preserves itself. The allegorical emblem *(Sinnbild)* for "the desolation of human existence" at once presents this in an image and means something more. What Golgotha signifies literally is negativity, death, mortality, transitoriness *(Vergänglichkeit)* as the very condition of history and temporality; but under the conditions of its status as an allegorical representation *(allegorisch dargestellt)*, these meanings are themselves signifiers in the service of a further, other signification. "Itself signifying, put forth as allegory," death means resurrection.

Were this an instance of traditional Christian allegoresis, it would be tired and uninteresting, but in Benjamin's hands the argument comes to mean otherwise. The problem, as it emerges, has less to do with the allegorical meaning of, here, resurrection than with the allegorical signifier—the image, the emblem—of death. In terms of his argument about history, it has less to do with an end (an overcoming) of history in its redemption than with an end to history in its "origin" as a sign—the allegorical sign. For Benjamin's argument has insisted that the image and its allegorical meaning cannot be dissociated: that not to misunderstand allegory is to understand the imagery "in which this turn-around into the sanctity of salvation" *is* the imagery of death and hell. As the paragraph continues here, the allegorical observation or gaze "jumps round or reverses" in the "signs of death." What is dramatized here is the instance and instants of reading, and the dramatization is itself imagistic. For the reversal of seeing death and having it mean "redemption" is conceptual and implies, perhaps, an image of mirror reversal, of a turn into an opposite. But if one "sees" (in the mind's eye) an image of reversal that means the inversion of literal into allegorical meaning, one also *reads* literally another image: a "jumping round" that, in its arc, is a reversal not of meanings attached to a sign but of the views upon sign and meaning. At one instant on the arc, one views *(betrachtet)* the sign that means death, and at another instant on the same arc, one views the allegorical meaning, which is redemption. The sign curves or tropes into its meaning.

Is one seeing ("viewing"), or reading, or seeing reading? In Benjamin's allegorical construction, seeing (viewing, *betrachten*) is seeing otherwise, reading is seeing signs read as (other) meanings. Yet just as the "arc" inscribed here is the same, only turning, so is the image seen/read

the same. "Awakening in God's world," the allegorist must be the same
one gazing, for otherwise there is no "awakening," no arc that connects
one condition with its reversal or other, and similarly, the "I" that
speaks in the Lohenstein quote as "a death's head" is still that deathly
sign even as it comes to mean "an angel's face." When Benjamin nonetheless continues that "allegory loses everything that most properly belongs to it," even this loss may be understood as a remaining true or
faithful to itself qua allegory. For what "most properly belongs" to allegory is the improper, the figurality or otherness of meaning to sign, and
so "loss" may mean "gain." "With *one* turn-around," allegorical falling
and sinking (*Versenkung*) sinks beyond objective things—even the most
fragmented, died-away, and scattered among them—and, left only with
falling, inverts this into a rise: "no longer playfully in the earthly world
of things, but seriously beneath heaven." Falling into heights.

But here it is no longer the allegorical gaze (*Betrachtung*) or attitude
of contemplative immersion or sunkenness that inverts, but the objects
themselves. The "ultimate objects," which might yield the abject itself,
invert (*umschlagen*) into allegories, which allegories—doubled and thus
true to their structures—fulfill the "nothingness" of the fallen world in
which they are represented *and* deny this, their selves. Benjamin's argument about the inversion of allegories in this last sentence seems to
say, however, something more exact and more astonishing. When objects become—by the *Umschlagen*—allegories, then allegories "represent" themselves in nothingness; thus, the "last objects" become nothing, are annihilated, and to that extent the allegories "fulfill" or fill to
the fullness of nothingness the last, abject things, in which they pose
themselves. Benjamin's sentence takes the form of a chiasmus, with the
"inversion" precisely at the point of chiasmatic reversal: literally (preserving the German syntax), the *last things* " . . . into *allegories* invert,
that they [*the allegories*] the nothingness [= the *last things*], in which
they represent themselves, fulfill." Both the structure and the repetition
of the verb *darstellen* recall the paragraph's earlier formulation, which
now, retrospectively, reveals itself as a chiasmus as well: transitoriness
was "not so much . . . *allegorically represented* (or posed there, *dargestellt*) as—itself signifying—*put forth* (or proffered there, *dargeboten*) as
allegory." This first chiasmus now clarifies itself as the posing and erasing of the transitoriness: "allegorically represented," but to the extent
that it is also "proffered as allegory," it is the negation of transitoriness
in the allegorical meaning of resurrection. In the latter chiasmus, the
very fulfilling of nothingness by and in allegories is also its denial, for it
is not—any longer—empty or void, but full. One word means two
things—to fulfill nothingness, to make it fully itself, and to unmake it,

to make it not void but full—and so two words mean one thing: to fulfill and to deny. To *read* one word, one sign, in allegory is to read two meanings and to see two signs that contract into one another.

This is allegorical *Darstellung*, in which to pose is to dis-pose or to take away. So, too, Benjamin's "allegorical intention" cannot remain intent on one object: in gazing at bones, it turns faithless and does not remain true to them but springs across or transcends faithlessly to resurrection. Dead bones stand with a spring in their legs, but with a double faithlessness ("nicht treu . . . treulos"). This last of the seven terms and images for allegorical reversal is, amidst its faithlessness, the truest. For instead of inverting or turning around one thing into another meaning, here there is just a leap over *(Sprung über)* from faithless denial to faithless fulfillment.[24] *Treulos* modifies the springing away from gazing upon bones and *means*—allegorically, otherwise—the arrival at resurrection, which is the denial of the former, literal (grammatical) sense: the very leap is untrue. To be "true" to its meaning, it must be untrue to its sign, and so the sign cannot remain true to itself *or* to its meaning. Allegory is the denial of the sign.

The stakes and leftovers are time, history, and bones. In allegory, the signified cannot be at one with the signifier. If the sign is the stuff of history, "transitoriness" and "the desolation of all human existence," then its meaning—in allegory—cannot be its own, but must be its other: history is not the fulfillment of its meaning *(Sinnerfüllung)* but its becoming fulfilled in its nothingness, and thereby denied. Allegory forces itself upon Benjamin's "original" construction of history for the reason that what he, through the lens of the baroque *Trauerspiel*, considers the "phenomenal"—eventful, temporal—character of historical occurrence cannot be allowed to fall continuously into transitoriness and ruination, unless this very condition becomes the occasion (the sign) of its reversing "salvation" into its meaning. History, for Benjamin as for Hegel and for all historicism, cannot be allowed to be a story without meaning or, what is the same thing, a story whose only meaning is the literal loss, or fall, of presence in time's passing into past. And so the *Ursprung*'s allegorical construction is neither more nor less than a fundamental restatement of the modern Western historical paradigm: that history *(Geschichte)* as what happens *(das Geschehene)* might mean—across, over, and despite its temporal passage and passing away—history as narrative discourse *(Geschichte)*, that is, a story of meaning and understanding. But Benjamin's allegory of history displays the spring or leap from the former to the latter as "untrue," faithless. The negativity that attaches even to a leap away from fallen ruins and over into their salvation remains, but in what form of remainder? And what is the mark of the gap between a narrative of history and its understanding as an allegory of reading?

History's allegorical treatment yields *its meaning* as the display of its allegorical structure, which Benjamin has qualified as "fulfillment and denial" of its literal signs and which the present analysis has already characterized as the signifying relation that signifies the discord within the terms of the relation. That the meaning of history is the denial of the historical sign means that this alterity constitutive of history is always a threshold of the readability—or unreadability—of allegory. For how to read its signs when they mean their "faithless" undoing? Crossing the line of demarcation, the image of the narrative script of history, is not merely to reverse nor to hang on to a swinging, pendulumlike arc (suspended in oscillation) that might carry one over from, say, fall to rise, and do so in the very act of falling. Reading history as allegory is, in Benjamin's model, to encounter *Ursprung*—"that which springs out of becoming and passing away"—as a faithless springing over of the line of script, signed of and by death, which literally or as letters is the deathly falling and entombing of events into their literal narrative chronology ("this happens," *Geschehen*, writing itself as "this happened," *Geschichte*). On one side of the line is death, on the other a faithlessness to it. The line itself would be continuous, an image of narrative as of the historical "time-line," as in Benjamin's ceaselessly sustained language and imagery of falling and sinking, the very type of narrative continuity that he could admire in "The Storyteller" and oppose, in his "Theses," to a far less believable "line" of progress or development. Discontinuity, on the other hand, would be the price but also the means of its escape in a "springing over." To read "over" or across this line—is this to spring over reading its signs?

If allegory divides the sign, and doubles reading, leaving the signifier "significant only through the allegorist" and his reading (cf. 398)—which at once deny its letter and fulfill it as this negating spirit—then the possible "coherence and survival" of the phenomenal that Benjamin's *Ursprung* promised must be requestioned at this, the locus of the allegorical sign as the very sign of historical time. Contrasting symbol and allegory, Benjamin wrote that "the mystical *Nu* becomes the contemporary, actual 'now' [*das aktuelle 'Jetzt'*]; the symbol becomes distorted into the allegorical" (358).[25] In allegory the time is always "now" distorted and displaced from another "now" now "then," never to be rejoined, never "then *and* now." Its punctual timing is, in an image Benjamin sustains through his last text on history, the flashing, *blitzartig* momentlike-ness of reading. In an apparent aside, Benjamin had remarked that "fundamentally, then, the *Trauerspiel*, cultivated in the realm of the allegorical, is according to its form a kind of reading-drama [*Lesedrama*]. . . . the situations changed infrequently, but when they did, then in a flash [*blitzartig*], like the look of the print-type when one turns the page" (361).

Such an image of seeing the allegorical *Trauerspiel* as an emblem, a *Sinnbild* or sensuous image, of reading represents the "now" and "now" of flashing print and pages in their very punctuality, singularity, and extremity, to reinvoke Benjamin's characterization of phenomena as they enter into the "original" idea. The "rhythm" of the "origin," which may now be understood as the discontinuous punctuality of allegorical reading—"now" sign, "now" meaning—was said to yield only to a *Doppeleinsicht* (cf. 226). The "doubled insight" into allegory as fulfilling and denying connects sign and meaning in the very manner of disconnection or discord, as the (new, doubled) sign of allegory. But the language of sight and insight is pursued one step further in Benjamin's argument. Immediately after the long paragraph that falls from "turning over" to "springing over," Benjamin continues:

> "With weeping we strewed the seed in the fallow rows / and went away mournfully [*und giengen traurig aus*]" [von Birken]. Allegory goes away empty-handed. Sheer evil, which it cherished as enduring profundity, exists only in it, is allegory pure and simple, signifies something other than it [evil] is [*bedeutet etwas anderes als es ist*]. And indeed, it signifies precisely the non-being of what it presents [*bedeutet es genau das Nichtsein dessen, was es vorstellt*]. (406)

The very faithlessness "in view of the bones" (*im Anblick der Gebeine*) with which the preceding paragraph concluded is allegory's "springing over" of its own shadow, its denial of the body of evil that casts its signifying shadow or self-presentation: allegory means the other of what it is, and it means "precisely the non-being of that which it presents," that is, evil. So even faithfulness to things despite their degradation[26] can mean faithlessness toward them when, in allegory, they mean their self-cancellation or denial in fulfillment. "Now" there, "now" not (or not being), is the double rhythm of such allegorical overcoming or "springing over" of the fallen, ruined, hellish, evil line or narrative inscribed by history. But where is "there" when the "now" is predicated on non-being (*Nichtsein*)? Reading non-being would be the "double-insight" that in reading history as allegory, one is arriving "now," at the juncture of every historical sign, at its "saving" meaning only at the cost of a canceling—blinding—that empowers such insight, namely, the blinding to the cancellation of the history as sign(s). History the passing/

passed/past is the *Ursprung*, the springing over of its being, "now" its shadow or non-being, into history the saved.

Allegory as the denial of the sign, or the non-being of what it presents, is not, however, an easy leave-taking from the things of history. The allegorical knowledge that Benjamin would attribute to the melancholic—that "the knowledge of evil has no object," that "the allegorical, as abstraction, as a capacity of the spirit of language itself [*als ein Vermögen des Sprachgeistes selbst*], is at home in the fall into sin" (407)—may lighten, for some, the *claims* of history but does not relieve or otherwise sublate the burden of its material *stuff*. For allegories mean not only the non-being of their means of representation but blindness to this insight:

> [Allegories] are not real, and they have that for which they stand [*das, als was sie dastehn*] only in the subjective view of melancholy; they are this view, which is annihilated [*vernichten*] by its own products, as they signify only its blindness. (406)

This is the place, not to reargue a hackneyed debate over "subjective" versus "objective" or positive constructions of history, but rather to draw on Benjamin's argument about the necessarily subjective character of allegorical—and all linguistic—construction. (For where but in delusive cratalytic or onomatopoetic conventions, or in the otherworldly realism of Saul Kripke's "rigid designators," could one believe in an "objectivity" of the signified's relation to the signifier?) When allegories of history mean the denial and overcoming of their signs—history—in a saving "now" of historical meaning—also history—that springs out of the passing "then," the allegorical view in turn ("now," "now") is negated by the non-being of the representations, which now mean only the blindness to the insight into historical nothingness.

Blindness is the truth of, the faith (*Treue*) to, the insight of a faithless leap out of historical falling and to a saving meaning. The two moments, or points, of the "original spring" or "origin" (*Ursprung*) of historical meaning are as irremediably separate as Benjamin had held the baroque's "emblematic representation of [nature's] meaning . . . to remain, as allegorical, irremediably separate from its historical realization" (347).[27] History's meaning is separate from history's signs—"now," and "now"—and this separation is the "annihilation," the radical negation (*Vernichtung*), of the former's standing, for *they*, the latter, only fall. The consequence of such a structure, for Benjamin, is that history can never become "stations on the way to salvation," but remains a non-narrative reading of disjunction. The images and flashing instants of a messianic explosion out of narrative lies (lines) of progressivism; the reconfigurations of allegorical structures of death in the sixteenth and nineteenth centuries, without a story line between; the narratives of storytelling and novel reading leading to a liminal non-meaning or reading of meaninglessness: these "irremediable separations" of historical reading from the stuff—the signs—of history are Benjamin's allegories of history as allegories of reading, which reading undoes the narrative of allegorical salvation, be this messianic, Marxist, literary-historical, or otherwise. That we scarcely have a clue how to read non-narratively only underscores the constitutive disjunctions that inhabit allegories of reading and their unreadability.[28]

Undoing salvation leaves allegory at a loss. In the final paragraph of his *Ursprung*, contrasting "the intervention of God in the work of art" in Calderón's baroque dramas with "the deficient development of the intrigue" in German *Trauerspiele*, Benjamin remarks that what is missing in the latter is "allegorical totality . . . thanks to which, in the image of the apotheosis, one of the images of the series stands out as different in kind and gives mourning at one and the same time its cue for entry and exit [*der Trauer Einsatz und Ausgang zugleich wiest*]" (409). But once mourning has laid down its stake *(Einsatz)*, it takes its leave neither readily nor without cost. Allegory, Benjamin had begun his conclusion by saying, "exits empty" ("Leer aus geht die Allegorie"), echoing von Birken's line of mournful exit ("und giengen traurig aus"). But mourning, as in Freud's understanding of melancholy, will not give up the sign of the lost object—the signs of historical time—without the cost of faithlessness and untruth *(Untreue)*, and the sign of this giving up or refusal of the refusal to give up is the *Ursprung* with which allegory springs away from history's signs and, "faithlessly," over to history's meaning. The leap or spring that at once constitutes and undoes the connection of signs and meanings, narratives and readings, and history *(Geschichte--das Geschehene)* and history *(Geschichte-Erzählung)*, also separates bones from resurrection. For it is not the bones that rise again; when the allegorist "faithlessly springs over to resurrection," he ultimately "does not remain true or faithful [*treu*] in view of the bones." But the place of the bones is, in Benjamin's allegory as in Hegel's, the place of Calvary: Golgotha, the *Schädelstätte*, or "place of the skull" (405). If the bones are "buried," they are no less entombed and engraven in writing. Called "the nothing in which they [allegories . . . of history] represent themselves," the bones are the inscription from which historical meaning can "originate" or spring only as the otherwise mournful historical "view" springs over and away from their faithful reading. History is always the unread.

Or else it is its spirit as the undead, hauntingly *revenant*, "auf Geisterweise." A rising up, or *Auferstehung,* that "originates" in the fulfilling *and* denying of the law of the fall would be different, irremediably so, from the bones that—unconsumable remains—lie behind as leftovers, the remainders and reminders of allegoresis as its unreadable script. As the inscription of a reminder, the otherness of history to itself comes back to haunt that forgetting letting-go by which historical meaning would be on the far side of death, its very sign. To see anything at all, history must be blinded to the otherness of the chalky line upon which it hangs, so as not to fall. But in allowing sight of this much, history, like Hölderlin's Oedipus, may have one eye too many.

Afterword

History and Literature
in the University

H istory is always crossing the literary—the allegorical—
line that relates and divides events and their possible discursive knowledge. The only difference would seem to be
whether history thinks it is being faithful or faithless,
truthful or untrue, to itself. A *literary* history, as I have
sought to understand it in this book, would know that the only mode of
its truth is its denial of its historical material in its knowing fulfillment
as history. The question remains whether this would make any institutional difference.

As far as I know, nobody has ever founded a university literature curriculum *against* history. The preponderance of historically defined
teaching and research in the modern university's study of literature
leaves history today a horizon beyond which we can scarcely think. Literary studies in the university are still the heir to the historicism after
Hegel.

In the name of what literary theory tries to do—to inquire and argue
toward principled views of its object, and their consequences for true
knowledge, as well as knowledge of their true consequences—we ought
to be teaching and discussing the *conflicts* of theories in the institutions
of literary study; in this I agree with Gerald Graff. But the curricula,
the classrooms, and the scholarly journals' pages would soon enough
repose themselves on familiar historicist cushions and headrests, believing these to be foundations, for I assume that the majority of university
professors of literature will quite understandably prefer a sense of certainty that may be false to an uncertainty that may be true. And so I do
not see any present institutional alternative to literature's university
teaching and scholarship (*Wissenschaft*) massively construed and delimited by historicism as I have tried to analyze it in this book.

History in the university, even when it is housed in its social sciences
divisions and not in the humanities, cannot do without places and ac-

tions linked to past times: historical events or series of events, the minimal constituents of its object. And so a "return to narrative" or a counterturn to quantitative analysis, any ostensibly new invention of its objects of study or any conservative defense of its periods and privileged actors, would still leave the institution of historical knowledge and its discourses in the face of the events (history as what happened) doubled as their descriptions and accounts (history as what is known, thought, understood), which is the minimal point of departure of the allegorical structure I have laid out here. With specific respect to the current novel mode of historical studies of literature—the new historicism—it will, by its own success and its own historical tenets, not be new for long, and then it will reveal itself as what it was all along: historicism, only with jazzier materials, licentious crossdressing, and lurid tales of crime and punishment, and the like, than its nineteenth-century Teutonic predecessors, with their dull diplomacy and familiar court politics. Historicism or historical study of any kind, to the extent that it names and tells, renames and retells—to the extent that it *writes*—literature as a series of past events, remains within the allegories of history after Hegel.

Is it conceivable to think of university scholarly study (*Wissenschaft*) of literature "after history"? It seems to me that some university studies—physics, for example, as far as I can tell—have been able to construe their "objects" as theoretically understandable independent of their status as historically determinable events or things. The scientific comprehension of its "matter," then, is on the far side of the historical mode of existence of any such matters. An analogy much more humble and closer to home may be drawn from studies of language. The historical study of languages—the nineteenth-century *Wissenschaft* of philology, and its heritage—may be viewed either as having led to the development of nondiachronic linguistic and rhetorical studies or as having been rudely replaced by them (Saussure scholarship, for example, can understand him in both respects, as a development from and an overcoming of diachronic philology). But in either case, the linguistic object is once again available to nonhistorical constructions and analyses, without needing to overlook any of the evidence of historical linguistics. Wilhelm von Humboldt already knew that the historical understanding of language—or of other human events—was not only not incompatible with but reasonably founded upon and oriented toward a true *idea* of language's structures and operations. As anyone knows from having learned earlier forms of language, knowing *what they meant* both assumes and aims toward knowing *how they mean*.

If it is thinkable that the material of literature's production and reading—language—may be constructed and analyzed in the manner of a fundamental matter, then surely it is conceivable that the attempt will be made (and will have been made) to understand literature, after all its history, as the set of its structures of and operations upon its material and upon mind, together with their consequences. This is, of course, nothing less than the fundamental project of literary theory undertaken in Hegel's *Aesthetics*. In the recent university, Northrop Frye and Paul de Man stand as the remarkable instances of efforts to understand literature after history. From *The Anatomy of Criticism* to *The Great Code* and from *Blindness and Insight* to *Allegories of Reading*, patterns of literature and literary meaning emerge from its history without being relocatable within or on the terms of historicism. I think especially that after the remaining historicist defenses of the threshold of "literary modernity" are breached in the last two essays of the first edition of *Blindness and Insight*, the second part of *Allegories of Reading* and the ruthless readings of Shelley and Baudelaire collected in *The Rhetoric of Romanticism* present examples of what a poetics of literature and a theory of reading could be on the far side of literary history. I have no illusions about the resistances such theory will continue to provoke in a modern university that has thoroughly institutionalized historical *Wissenschaft*, but one should be grateful that the university is sufficiently capacious to support its own critical heresy. The possible continued interaction of literary studies with other nonhistorical *Wissenschaften* will depend on this license for counterparadigmatic inquiry.

But none of these achievements, by Frye or de Man or anyone else that I am aware of, are theory after narrative. If allegories of history leave us, at their most advanced articulations in Hegel and Benjamin, with non-narrative readings of history's disjunction and disarticulation, then we nevertheless still do not know what it would mean to read non-narratively after such constructions and deconstructions of history. Reading literature after history would seem to be to read everything that is there, in its history, and the nothing that, then, is. No longer history, no longer a story, but the unknown no-thing of literature's being known otherwise. And *this* would be literature, allegory, and reading after Hegel.

Notes

Chapter 1
HISTORY ENTERS THE UNIVERSITY

1. Josef Engel, "Die deutschen Universitäten und die Geschichtswissenschaft," *Historische Zeitschrift* 189 (1959), 223–378; the quoted paragraphs are from pp. 356–58, my translation. Throughout this study I have treated *Wissenschaft* as if it were an English word, for it is misleadingly translated for Anglo-American audiences as "science" and only awkwardly translated as "scientific study and scholarship." Its adjectival form, *wissenschaftlich*, I have translated as "scholarly and scientific," and the substantialized form of this adjective, *Wissenschaftlichkeit*, as "scholarly and scientific character."

2. Ernst Troeltsch, "Die Krisis des Historismus," *Die Neue Rundschau* 33 (1922), 572–90. Martin Heidegger may echo Troeltsch when he writes in *Sein und Zeit* (1927), 12th ed. (Tübingen: Max Niemeyer, 1972), sec. 3, p. 9: "The actual 'movement' of the Wissenschaften plays itself out in the more or less radical and self-transparent revision of fundamental concepts. The level of a Wissenschaft determines itself by the extent to which it is capable of a crisis in its fundamental concepts. In such immanent crises of the Wissenschaften, the relationship of the positively investigative questioning to the matter asked about itself begins to totter. All around today in the various disciplines, tendencies have awakened to reestablish research on new foundations."

3. Among literally hundreds of studies on this topic, three classic titles would be Karl Mannheim, "Historismus," *Archiv für Sozialwissenschaft und Sozialpolitik* 52 (1924), 1–60; Friedrich Meinecke, *Die Entstehung des Historismus* (1936), ed. Carl Hinrichs (Munich: R. Oldenbourg, 1959), in English as *Historism: The Rise of a New Historical Outlook*, trans. J. E. Anderson and H. D. Schmidt (London: Routledge & Kegan Paul, 1972); and Georg G. Iggers, *The German Conception of History: The National Tradition of Historical Thought from Herder to the Present* (Middletown, Conn.: Wesleyan U.P., 1968). Among many competing definitions of "historicism," I reproduce four brief ones here: "[the outlook] whereby the truth, meaning or value of anything is to be found in history" (Dwight E. Lee and Robert N. Beck, "The Meaning of 'Historicism,'" *American Historical Review* 59 [1953–54], 577); "to represent all phenomena of human life as essentially history and therefore as temporally conditioned and changeable" (Reinhard Wittram, *Das Interesse an der Geschichte* [Göttingen:

Vandenhoeck & Ruprecht, 1958], p. 58); "the tendency to interpret the whole of reality, including what . . . had been conceived as absolute and unchanging human values, in historical, that is to say relative, terms" (Hayden White, Introduction to *From History to Sociology: The Transition in German Historical Thinking*, by Carlo Antoni [Detroit: Wayne State U.P., 1959], p. xvii); and "a rule of historical inquiry that the significance of past actions must in the first instance be understood in terms of their agents' own beliefs about human nature, not in terms of our possibly very different ones; we must at least understand their own action-descriptions before we venture our own redescriptions" (Louis O. Mink, "Narrative Form as a Cognitive Instrument" [1978], in *Historical Understanding*, ed. Brian Fay, Eugene Golob, and Richard Vann [Ithaca: Cornell U.P., 1987], p. 194). Some literary students have recently given the term "historicism" a wide sense that tends to lose discriminating precision; so Marjorie Levinson, in her introduction to *Rethinking Historicism: Critical Readings in Romantic History* (Oxford: Blackwell, 1989), p. 2, would have "received historicist premises" be the injunction "to reveal the past, the object, either as it is/was in itself, or as it is intended in the sympathetic consciousness of the present." But other scholars associated with the so-called new historicism make it clear that this movement in literary and cultural studies has little to do with historicism conventionally conceived (see the list of "key assumptions" in H. Aram Veeser's Introduction, p. xi, and Stephen Greenblatt's "Towards a Poetics of Culture," pp. 1–14, in *The New Historicism*, ed. H. Aram Veeser [New York: Routledge, 1989]).

4. I have addressed some aspects of this in "Historical Realities" and "Short Response to E. D. Hirsch, Jr.," in *Criticism in the University*, TriQuarterly Series on Criticism and Culture, no. 1, ed. Gerald Graff and Reginald Gibbons (Evanston: Northwestern U.P., 1985), pp. 224–28 and 231–32, as well as in "Histories of the University: Kant and Humboldt," *MLN* 102, no. 3 (1987), 437–60.

5. With respect to Hegel, Henry Sussman has caught something of this double sense of his heritage in his *The Hegelian Aftermath: Readings in Hegel, Kierkegaard, Freud, Proust, and James* (Baltimore: Johns Hopkins U.P., 1982). Sussman, however, does not treat literary historians as such, nor does he discuss the same Hegel texts as I, or their place in the rise of the German Wissenschafts-university.

6. In this section I rely extensively upon the Engel monograph cited in n. 1; Emil Clemens Scherer, *Geschichte und Kirchengeschichte an der deutschen Universität: Ihre Anfänge im Zeitalter des Humanismus und ihre Ausbildung zu selbstständigen Disziplinen* (Freiburg: W. G. Korn, 1927); and Friedrich Paulsen, *Die deutschen Universitäten und das Universitätsstudium* (Berlin: A. Asher, 1902). I have also profited from the more general discussions contained in Charles E. McClelland, *State, Society, and University in Germany, 1700–1914* (Cambridge: Cambridge U.P., 1980), and Fritz Ringer, *The Decline of the German Mandarins: The German Academic Community, 1890–1933* (Cambridge, Mass.: Harvard U.P., 1969), and from the detailed studies by R. Steven Turner: "The Growth of Professorial Research in Prussia, 1818 to 1848—Causes and Context," *Histor-*

ical Studies in the Physical Sciences 3 (1971), 137–82; "University Reformers and Professional Scholarship in Germany, 1760–1806," in *The University in Society,* ed. Lawrence Stone (Princeton: Princeton U.P., 1974), 2:495–531; "Prussian Universities and the Concept of Research," *Internationales Archiv für Sozialgeschichte der deutschen Literatur* 5 (1980), 68–93; "The *Bildungsbürgertum* and the Learned Professions in Prussia, 1770–1830: The Origins of a Class," *Histoire sociale* 13, no. 25 (1980), 105–35; and "Historicism, *Kritik,* and the Prussian Professoriate, 1790 to 1840," in *Philologie und Hermeneutik im 19. Jahrhundert II,* ed. Mayotte Bollack and Heinz Wismann (Göttingen: Vandenhoeck & Ruprecht, 1983), pp. 450–78.

7. Herbert Butterfield, *Man on His Past: The Study of the History of Historical Scholarship* (Cambridge: Cambridge U.P., 1955), p. 15.

8. Engel, "Die deutschen Universitäten und die Geschichtswissenschaft," p. 238.

9. Eugenio Garin, *Italian Humanism,* trans. Peter Munz (New York: Harper & Row, 1965), p. 183.

10. Quoted in Scherer, *Geschichte und Kirchengeschichte,* p. 22. On the "exemplar theory of history," see George H. Nadel, "Philosophy of History before Historicism," *History and Theory* 3 (1964), 291–315, where he quotes as exemplary for this whole tradition the opening statements of Polybius's *Histories,* that history teaches "that the soundest education and training for a life of active politics is the study of history, and the surest and indeed the only method of learning how to bear the vicissitudes of fortune is to recall the calamities of others" (295). For an example of this view from the Anglo-Saxon tradition, see Thomas Hearne, *Ductor Historicus: or, A Short System of Universal History, and An Introduction of the Study of it,* 2d ed., 2 vols. (London, 1705), 1:113, where he calls "history" "a Science of infinite Benefit to Mankind" and then adds parenthetically, by way of explanation, "for 'tis by the Light it gives the Understanding, that Princes and Generals are enabled to avoid and hinder those evil Consequences that would hurt us all, and to direct the performance of such Actions as tend to our Protection and Defense" (quoted in Leo Braudy, *Narrative Form in History and Fiction: Hume, Fielding, and Gibbon* [Princeton: Princeton U.P., 1970], p. 8).

11. See Engel, "Die deutschen Universitäten und die Geschichtswissenschaft," p. 245.

12. Hans Blumenberg, *Die Legitimität der Neuzeit,* 2d ed. (Frankfurt am Main: Suhrkamp, 1976).

13. Nadel, "Philosophy of History before Historicism," p. 312.

14. Engel, "Die deutschen Universitäten und die Geschichtswissenschaft," p. 255.

15. Butterfield, *Man on His Past,* pp. 45–46. On Petrarch, see Theodor E. Mommsen, "Petrarch's Conception of the 'Dark Ages,'" *Speculum* 17 (April 1942), 226–42.

16. See, e.g., the pages on Samuel Pufendorf, scholar of natural and state law, in Peter Hanns Reill, *The German Enlightenment and the Rise of Historicism* (Berkeley and Los Angeles: U. of California P., 1975), pp. 15–22.

17. Engel, "Die deutschen Universitäten und die Geschichtswissenschaft," pp. 268–69.

18. For a classic statement of this view, see Stephen Toulmin, *Human Understanding* (Princeton: Princeton U.P., 1972), p. 84: "The rationality of a science is embodied not in the theoretical systems current in it at particular times, but in its procedures for discovery and conceptual change through time."

19. Engel, "Die deutschen Universitäten . . .," p. 273.

20. Butterfield, *Man on His Past*, pp. 5–10, 44–54.

21. Ibid., p. 37. For the promotional aspect of history at Göttingen, see Johan Claproth, *Der gegenwärtige Zustand der Göttingischen Universität in zweenen Briefen an einem vornehmen Herrn im Reiche* (Göttingen, 1748), p. 77 (quoted in Reill, *The German Enlightenment and the Rise of Historicism*, p. 38): "One finds that history is in excellent hands here. The historian is no longer considered a walking reference work from whom one hears about battles and sieges or learns the dates of great persons' births and deaths. Instead, it is accepted that the historian must teach us about the world. He must uncover the hidden causes of an event and show us the future that already resides in the past."

22. This double-edged aspect should be borne in mind when one confronts a sweeping generalization such as Helen P. Liebel's in her review of Reill in *History and Theory* 16, no. 2 (1977), p. 209, that "by 1700 and throughout the first part of the eighteenth century, history became an indispensable part of the German university curriculum." Even if this were true of universities other than Göttingen, the unaddressed question remains: which curriculum?

23. Fritz K. Ringer, "The German Academic Community," in *The Organization of Knowledge in Modern America, 1860–1920,* ed. Alexandria Oleson and John Voss (Baltimore: Johns Hopkins U.P., 1979), pp. 415–16.

24. Paulsen, *Die deutschen Universitäten und das Universitätsstudium*, p. 35.

25. Northrop Frye, *The Great Code: The Bible and Literature* (New York: Harcourt, Brace, Jovanovich, 1982), pp. 12–13.

26. Richard Rorty, "The Historiography of Philosophy: Four Genres," in *Philosophy in History,* ed. Richard Rorty, J. B. Schneewind and Quentin Skinner (Cambridge: Cambridge U.P., 1984), p. 11. Such a sense of "clear stories of progress to tell" thoroughly colors Wilhelm Dilthey's account of the rise of science (Wissenschaft), which might have been adduced next to Butterfield's version of the rise of historiography (see n. 7 above) for its similar naive progressivism but is more appropriately quoted here since, with the reference to Bacon, it alludes to a specific step taken with "modern" science: "The progress of the sciences goes on throughout all of history. This progress is steady, unbroken, unstopping, for it depends on the fact that concepts are transferable without loss [*restlos übertragbar*] from person to person and from age to age. In the whole domain of the understanding of life's expressions [*Lebensäusserungen*], it is here alone that such a transferability takes place. Thus, there is here a universal regularity in the succession of changes within humanity. And it assumes a striking place within the context of the signification of the changes; for according to a different law-governed relationship that Bacon first established, the knowledge of causal connectedness according to laws enabled the prediction of future

events [*Zukünftiges vorauszusagen*], and, through employment of the lawfulness of causal connections, the bringing-forth of intended effects through knowledge" (Dilthey, "Geschichtliche Entwicklung," addendum to *Der Aufbau der geschichtlichen Welt in den Geisteswissenschaften, Gesammelte Schriften*, ed. Bernhard Groethuysen [1926], 5th ed., vol. 7 [Göttingen: Vandenhoeck & Ruprecht, 1968], p. 346).

27. Heidegger, *Sein und Zeit*, sec. 3, p. 9 (see n. 2 above).

28. Jacques Derrida, "The Principle of Reason: The University in the Eyes of Its Pupils," trans. C. Porter and E. P. Morris, *Diacritics* 13, no. 3 (1983), 7.

29. Ibid., p. 8.

30. Ibid., p. 9.

31. Ibid., p. 8. Derrida has also written on Kant's *Streit* in "Mochlos ou le conflit des facultés," *Philosophies* 2 (1984), 21–53. See also my "Histories of the University."

32. *Der Streit der Fakultäten*, in Immanuel Kant, *Schriften zur Anthropologie, Geschichtsphilosophie, Politik und Pädagogik 1*, in *Werke*, ed. Wilhelm Weischedel (Frankfurt am Main: Suhrkamp, 1968), 11:280, 281.

33. Ibid., pp. 282, 299–300.

34. Ibid., pp. 285, 289, 290.

35. Ibid., p. 290.

36. Ibid., pp. 290, 291.

37. Ibid., p. 296.

38. On this general matter, see Derrida, "The Principle of Reason," pp. 9–10, and "Mochlos," passim.

39. See my "Histories of the University," pp. 453–56; and Yirmiahu Yovel, *Kant and the Philosophy of History* (Princeton: Princeton U.P., 1980), pp. 224–70, for extended discussions of this.

40. Kant, *Der Streit der Fakultäten*, p. 297.

41. Engel, "Die deutschen Universitäten und die Geschichtswissenschaft," p. 280.

42. See Reill, *The German Enlightenment and the Rise of Historicism*, pp. 34–45; and Butterfield, *Man on His Past*, pp. 46–49.

43. August Ludwig von Schlözer, *Weltgeschichte nach ihren Haupt-Theilen*, 3d ed. (Göttingen, 1785), p. 8, and *Vorstellung seiner Universal-Historie*, 2d ed. (Göttingen, 1775), p. 244 (both quoted in Butterfield, *Man on His Past*, p. 49).

44. Schlözer, *Vorstellung*, p. 45 (quoted in Reill, *The German Enlightenment and the Rise of Historicism*, p. 37).

45. Ibid., p. 46 (quoted in Reill, *The German Enlightenment and the Rise of Historicism*, p. 229).

46. Johann Christoph Gatterer, *Allgemeine Historische Bibliothek von Mitgliedern des Königlichen Instituts der Historischen Wissenschaften zu Göttingen* (Halle, 1767), 1:80–81, 85–86 (quoted in Reill, *The German Enlightenment and the Rise of Historicism*, pp. 42 and 230, my translation).

47. Ibid., pp. 77–78 (quoted in Reill, *The German Enlightenment and the Rise of Historicism*, pp. 116–17, my translation).

48. Mink, "Narrative Form as a Cognitive Instrument," pp. 188–92.

49. Kant, *Der Streit der Fakultäten*, p. 45; Mink, "Narrative Form as a Cognitive Instrument," p. 190.

50. Mink, "Narrative Form as a Cognitive Instrument," p. 136.

51. "Was heisst und zu welchem Ende studiert man Universalgeschichte?" in *Schillers Werke*, vol. 4, *Schriften*, ed. Hans Mayer and Golo Mann (Frankfurt am Main: Insel, 1966), p. 421, in English as "The Nature and Value of Universal History," in *History and Theory* 11 (1972), 321–34 (although here as elsewhere I provide my own translation from the German). For the remainder of the discussion of this work, page references to the Mayer-Mann edition will be given in the body of the text. Schiller had studied a little theology and law, and a little more medicine, and was an autodidact in history and philosophy. He had also published, in the fall of 1788, the first part of his *History of the Decline of the Netherlands*. Mann notes (p. 905) that Schiller was called to Jena to be a professor of history but was eventually appointed *Extraordinarius* (associate professor) of philosophy, since the chair for history was occupied.

52. *Vorlesungen über die Methode des akademischen Studiums*, in F. W. J. von Schelling, *Werke: Auswahl in drei Bänden*, vol. 2, *Schriften zur Identitätsphilosophie*, ed. Otto Weiss (Leipzig: Fritz Eckardt, 1907), pp. 542–44, in English as *On University Studies*, trans. E. S. Morgan, ed. Norbert Guterman (Athens: Ohio U.P., 1966). For the remainder of the discussion of this work, page references to the Weiss edition will be given in the body of the text. (The German text is also reprinted in *Die Idee der deutschen Universität: Die fünf Grundschriften*, ed. Ernst Anrich [Darmstadt: Wissenschaftliche Buchgesellschaft, 1956], pp. 1–123.) Schelling was appointed professor of philosophy at Jena in 1798, at the age of twenty-three, and edited the *Kritisches Journal der Philosophie* with Hegel in 1802 and 1803.

53. Schelling, *Philosophie der Kunst* (Darmstadt: Wissenschaftliche Buchgesellschaft, 1976), sec. 45, p. 96. The *Philosophie der Kunst*, first published posthumously in 1859, represents lectures Schelling gave at Jena in 1802–3 and again in 1804–5.

54. Ibid.

55. The first three hundred–odd pages of the first volume of Max Lenz's four-volume *Geschichte der königlichen Friedrich-Wilhelms-Universität zu Berlin* (Halle: Buchhandlung des Waisenhauses, 1910–18) narrate and document these developments. See also his "Freiheit und Macht im Lichte der Entwicklung der Universität Berlin," in Lenz, *Kleine historische Schriften, II: Von Luther zu Bismarck* (Munich and Berlin: R. Oldenbourg, 1922), pp. 258–74. A still-serviceable presentation of the Prussian reform movement is found in Friedrich Meinecke, *Das Zeitalter der deutschen Erhebung, 1795–1815* (1906), 7th ed. (Göttingen: Vandenhoeck & Ruprecht, 1963), in English as *The Age of German Liberation, 1795–1815*, trans. Peter Paret (Berkeley and Los Angeles: U. of California P., 1977), albeit with only two sentences (p. 92) on the University of Berlin.

56. Lenz, *Geschichte*, 1:37, 67; René König, *Vom Wesen der deutschen Universität* (1935; reprint, Darmstadt: Wissenschaftliche Buchgesellschaft, 1970), pp. 49–53.

57. Lenz, *Geschichte*, 1:160; see 1:88 and 108 for some of Wolf's thoughts on the university.

58. Schleiermacher, *Gelegentliche Gedanken über Universitäten in deutschem Sinn*, in *Fichte, Schleiermacher, Steffens über das Wesen der Universität*, ed. Eduard Spranger (Leipzig: Dürr, 1910); the quotes here and in the remainder of my paragraph are from sec. 2, pp. 125–28 (also in Anrich, *Die Idee der deutschen Universität*). On Schleiermacher's Berlin plan see Lenz, *Geschichte*, 1:124–30.

59. For example: "Thus through philosophy the view must already be opened into the two great areas of nature and history, and the most universal [*das Allgemeinste*] in both must be no less common to all [*allen gemein*]" (sec. 3, p. 140).

60. "Histories of the University."

61. In Spranger, *Fichte, Schleiermacher, Steffens über das Wesen der Universität* (also in Anrich, *Die Idee der deutschen Universität*); cited in the body of the text by section number.

62. See Lenz, *Geschichte*, 1:114–22, and "Fichtes Erlanger Professur," in Lenz, *Kleine Historische Schriften, II*, pp. 245–57.

63. Schleiermacher's more famous phrasing, "das Lernen des Lernens" ("the learning of learning," in *Gelegentliche Gedanken*, sec. 2, p. 127), echoes Fichte's here ("die Kunst des Erlernens überhaupt gelernt . . . wird"); although Fichte's text was first published in 1817, Schleiermacher might have known it directly or indirectly, through Humboldt, when he composed his own.

64. Engel, "Die deutschen Universitäten und die Geschichtswissenschaft," p. 288.

65. In sec. 25, Fichte divides—in a manner that recalls a similar division in Schelling—*Geschichte* into "history" and "nature," clearly indicating that both are areas of a posteriori knowledge: "All of history [*Geschichte*] divides itself into the history of fleeting appearance [*fliessenden Erscheinung*] and that of the enduring [*dauernden*]. The first is that which is particularly called history [*Geschichte*], or *Historie*, with its auxiliary Wissenschaften; the second is natural history [*Naturgeschichte*], which has its theoretical part in the doctrine of nature [*Naturlehre*]."

66. Lenz, *Geschichte*, 1:118.

67. Ranke names Fichte and confronts him with the charge of using concepts a priori to deduce history in at least two manuscripts from the 1830s (his own early years at the University of Berlin): "Geschichte und Philosophie," in the *Vorwort* to Leopold von Ranke, *Weltgeschichte*, Teil 9, Abt. 2, ed. Alfred Dove (Leipzig: Duncker & Humblot, 1888), pp. vii–xi; and—citing Fichte's 1804–5 lectures at Berlin, "Die Grundzüge des gegenwärtigen Zeitalters"—"Idee der Universalhistorie," first edited in Eberhard Kessel, "Rankes Idee der Universalhistorie," *Historische Zeitschrift* 178 (1954), 292–93. See as well, however, Ranke's use of Fichte's term in this formulation: "Were philosophy what it is supposed to be, and were historical study [*Historie*] perfectly clear and complete, they would both fully harmonize [*übereinstimmen*]. The historical Wissenschaft would permeate [*durchdringen*] its element with philosophic spirit" (ibid.,

p. 302). But when the otherwise distinguished historian Arnaldo Momigliano writes of Ranke's "reject[ing] the Hegelian a priori method of philosophy of history" ("A Hundred Years after Ranke," in *Studies in Historiography* [London: Weidenfeld & Nicolson, 1966], p. 105), he is simply not being a very good historian. Not only does Hegel never speak of concepts (or any "method") a priori with respect to the philosophy of history; it is also by no means clear that Ranke rejects Hegel at all. On this latter point, see my n. 12 in chap. 3, below, "Historical Anthropophagy."

68. Engel, "Die deutschen Universitäten und die Geschichtswissenschaft," p. 302.

69. Ibid., p. 294.

70. On Bopp, see Michel Foucault, *Les Mots et les choses: une archéologie des sciences humaines* (Paris: Gallimard, 1966), pp. 292–307, especially this remarkable passage, in which the advance claimed for Bopp corresponds to one between chronology (chronicle) and history, between finding historical facts as they are and rewriting them so that they read as if already so written: "Il a fallu traiter le sanskrit, le grec, le latin, l'allemand dans une simultanéité systématique; on a dû, en rupture de toute chronologie, les installer dans un temps fraternel, pour que leurs structures deviennent transparentes et qu'une histoire des langues s'y laisse lire. Ici comme ailleurs, les mises en série chronologiques ont dû être effacées, leurs éléments redistribués, et une histoire nouvelle s'est alors constituée qui n'énonce pas seulement le mode de succession des êtres et leur enchaînement dans le temps, mais les modalités de leur formation. L'empiricité—il s'agit aussi bien des individus naturels que des mots par quoi on peut les nommer—est désormais traversée par l'Histoire et dans toute l'épaisseur de son être. L'ordre du temps commence" (306).

71. Lenz, *Geschichte*, 2:136, 137.

72. Engel, "Die deutschen Universitäten und die Geschichtswissenschaft," p. 303.

73. There is an extended discussion of Ranke in the aftermath of Hegel in Hayden White, *Metahistory: The Historical Imagination in Nineteenth-Century Europe* (Baltimore: Johns Hopkins U.P., 1973), pp. 163–90, although White repeats the received idea of Ranke's "rejection" of "the a priori philosophizing of Hegel" (164; see n. 67 above). See also the briefer discussion of Droysen after Hegel, pp. 267–73.

74. *Historische Zeitschrift* 76 (1896), 2, quoted in Engel, "Die deutschen Universitäten und die Geschichtswissenschaft," p. 347.

Chapter 2

HISTORY AND HEGEL

1. See, e.g., the foregrounding of Hegel in the second volume of Max Lenz's authoritative history of the University of Berlin, *Geschichte der königlichen Friedrich-Wilhilms-Universität zu Berlin*, 4 vols. (Halle: Buchhandlung des Waisenhauses, 1910–18), 2:33–137. See also the many biographical and anecdotal

sketches in Ernst Simon, *Ranke und Hegel,* suppl. 15 of *Historische Zeitschrift* (Munich: R. Oldenbourg, 1928), pp. 16-120.

2. See, most recently, Jacques Derrida, "L'Age de Hegel," in GREPH (Groupe de recherches sur l'enseignement philosophique), *Qui a peur de la philosophie?* (Paris: Flammarion, 1977), pp. 73-107, esp. 105-6.

3. Alexandre Kojève, *Introduction à la lecture de Hegel* (Paris: Gallimard, 1947), p. 438.

4. On the step from the *Phenomenology* to the *Logic,* see the last chapter, "Phénoménologie et Logique: le savoir absolu," of Jean Hyppolite's classic *Genèse et structure de la "Phénoménologie de l'esprit" de Hegel* (Paris: Aubier Montaigne, 1946), pp. 553-83, as well as his essay "On the *Logic* of Hegel" (1955), in *Studies on Marx and Hegel,* ed. and trans. John O'Neill (New York: Harper & Row, 1973), pp. 169-84. For a more problematic version of history in the *Logic,* and the *Logic* in history, see Alfred Schmidt, *Geschichte und Struktur: Fragen einer marxistischen Historik* (Munich: C. Hanser, 1971).

5. G. W. F. Hegel, *Wissenschaft der Logik,* pt. 2, "Die subjektive Logik, oder Die Lehre vom Begriff," in *Werke,* ed. Eva Moldenhauer and Karl Markus Michel, 20 vols. (Frankfurt am Main: Suhrkamp, 1969-71), 6:260. Cf. from the introduction to the *Vorlesungen über die Philosophie der Geschichte,* in *Werke,* 12:103: "Indem somit der Geist einerseits die Realität, das Bestehen dessen, was er ist, aufhebt, gewinnt er zugleich das Wesen, den Gedanken, das Allgemeine dessen, was *er nur war.*"

6. Louis O. Mink, "History and Fiction as Modes of Comprehension" (1970), in *Historical Understanding,* ed. Brian Fay, Eugene Golob, and Richard Vann (Ithaca: Cornell U.P., 1987), p. 47. This "level," or "dimension," of the facts is what Wesley Morris calls "the mass of historical-experiential data," which he, like Mink, does not consider properly historical until it "is molded into the first principle of a meaningful continuity" (*Toward a New Historicism* [Princeton: Princeton U.P., 1972], p. 9).

7. Mink, "History and Fiction," 55, 46.

8. Mink, "Narrative as a Cognitive Instrument," typescript, pp. 2 and 3 (a shorter draft version of "Narrative Form as a Cognitive Instrument" (1978), which appears in *Historical Understanding,* pp. 182-203).

9. Richard Rorty, "The Historiography of Philosophy: Four Genres," in *Philosophy in History,* ed. Richard Rorty, J. B. Shneewind, and Quentin Skinner (Cambridge: Cambridge U.P., 1984), p. 26.

10. See C. G. Hempel, "The Function of General Laws in History," *Journal of Philosophy* 39 (1942), 35-48; and Karl Popper, *The Logic of Scientific Discovery* (New York: Basic Books, 1959).

11. Friedrich Schlegel, *Kritische Schriften,* ed. Wolfdietrich Rasch (Munich: C. Hanser, 1970), p. 34. We shall see this fragment alluded to by Walter Benjamin in his ninth thesis "On the Concept of History," the topic of chap. 7, below.

12. Mink, "History and Fiction," pp. 55-56.

13. See Stanley Fish, *Is There a Text in This Class? The Authority of Interpretive Communities* (Cambridge, Mass.: Harvard U.P., 1980), p. 14 and passim.

14. Paul de Man, "Sign and Symbol in Hegel's *Aesthetics,*" *Critical Inquiry* 8 (Summer 1982), 770.

15. Mink, "History and Fiction," p. 56.

Chapter 3
HISTORICAL ANTHROPOPHAGY AND ITS PASSING

Epigraph: Friedrich Engels to Conrad Schmidt, 1 November 1891, in *Karl Marx, Friedrich Engels: Werke,* ed. Inst. für Marxismus-Leninismus beim ZK d. SED, vol. 38 (Berlin: Dietz, 1968), p. 203: "Ohne Hegel geht's natürlich nicht, und der Mann will auch Zeit haben, bis er verdaut ist."

1. This reprise of the ending of the *Phänomenologie* begins at 3:589 and continues to its end on p. 591. The full last paragraph and a part of the penultimate one are reproduced, in German and in my modification of A. V. Miller's translation (*Hegel's "Phenomenology of Spirit"* [Oxford: Oxford U.P., 1977], pp. 492–93), as an appendix to this chapter.

2. See Jean Hyppolite, *Genèse et Structure de la "Phénoménologie de l'Esprit" de Hegel* (Paris: Aubier Montaigne, 1946), p. 582.

3. *Vorlesungen über die Philosophie der Geschichte, Werke,* 12:129, in English in *The Philosophy of History,* trans. J. Sibree (New York: Dover, 1956), p. 99; henceforth cited in the text by first the German page number(s), then the English. I have modified the English translation for accuracy where necessary.

4. On the fetish and its resistance to the dialectic in this part of the *Philosophy of History,* see Jacques Derrida, *GLAS* (Paris: Galilée, 1974), pp. 232–34.

5. Asia, on the other hand, is historical, comprehensible—and digestible. Although I say nothing about Hegel's historiography of Asia as a *beginning* in the *Philosophy of History* or in the *Aesthetics* in either this or the next chapter, it is worth quoting here Paul Valéry on "the Orient"—replete with his thoroughly and comprehensively Hegelian terminology—from his "Puissance de choix de l'Europe" (1938), in *Oeuvres,* ed. Jean Hytier, 2 vols. (Paris: Gallimard, 1960), 2:1556: "Au point de vue de la culture, je ne crois pas que nous ayons beaucoup à craindre *actuellement* de l'influence orientale. Elle ne nous est pas inconnue. Nous lui devons tous les commencements de nos arts et de nos connaissances. Nous pourrions bien accueillir ce qui nous viendrait de l'Orient, si quelque chose de neuf pouvait en venir,—dont je doute. Ce doute est précisément notre garantie et notre arme européene. D'ailleurs, la question, en ces matières, n'est que de *digérer.* Mais ce fut là précisément la grande affaire de la spécialité même de l'esprit européen à travers les âges. Notre rôle est de maintenir cette puissance de choix, de compréhension universelle et de transformation en substance nôtre, qui nous a faits ce que nous sommes. Les Grecs et les Romains nous ont montré comment l'on opère avec les monstres de l'Asie, comme on les traite par l'analyse, quels sucs l'on en retire" (Valéry's emphasis).

6. The relevant part of the *Enzyklopädie der philosophischen Wissenschaften im Grundrisse* (1830), *Zweiter Teil: Die Naturphilosophie, Mit den mündlichen Zu-*

sätzen, in *Werke*, vol. 9, appears on pp. 430–93, in English in *Hegel's Philosophy of Nature*, trans. A. V. Miller (Oxford: Clarendon, 1970), pp. 350–406; henceforth cited in the text by first the German page number(s), then the English. The most sustained reading of these passages that I am aware of is in Werner Hamacher, "Pleroma—zu Genesis und Struktur einer dialektischen Hermeneutik bei Hegel," his introduction to G. W. F. Hegel, *"Der Geist des Christentums": Schriften 1796–1800* (Berlin: Ullstein, 1978), pp. 263–90.

7. *Werke*, 9:344–45.

8. For a stunning assimilation of the problem of digestion in Hegel to that of reading, see Hamacher, "Pleroma," pp. 291–333.

9. Roman Jakobson, "Linguistics and Poetics," in *Style in Language*, ed. Thomas Sebeok (Cambridge, Mass.: MIT Press, 1960), p. 358.

10. In addition to the Hamacher section cited in n. 8 above, Quentin Lauer, *A Reading of Hegel's "Phenomenology of Spirit"* (New York: Fordham U.P., 1976), p. 268, and Donald P. Verene, *Hegel's Recollection: A Study of Images in the "Phenomenology of Spirit"* (Albany: SUNY Press, 1985), p. 7, each speak of the sublation of the stages of progress into *Erinnerung* as a linguistic move from a first to a second reading or a first to a second language.

11. "This book tries to comprehend in their unity all these and the other related histories of the Latin and Germanic nations. To history has been given the function of judging the past, of instructing fellow men for the profit of future years. The present attempt does not aspire to such lofty undertakings. It merely wants to show how things actually happened [*wie es eigentlich gewesen*]" (Leopold von Ranke, foreword to the first edition of *Geschichten der romanischen und germanischen Völker von 1494–1514* [1824], 3d ed. [Leipzig: Duncker & Humblot, 1885] [= *Sämtliche Werke*, 23], p. vii). For another remarkable approximation of the writing of history to something very much like Ranke's "wie es eigentlich gewesen," see Georg Büchner to his parents, 28 July 1835, in *Sämtliche Werke und Briefe*, ed. Werner R. Lehmann, 2 vols. (Hamburg: Christian Wegner, 1971), 2:443: "[Der dramatische Dichter] ist in meinen Augen nichts, als ein Geschichtsschreiber, steht aber *über* Letzterem dadurch, dass er uns die Geschichte zum zweiten Mal erschafft. . . . Seine höchste Aufgabe ist, der Geschichte, wie sie sich wirklich begeben, so nahe als möglich zu kommen."

12. The relation of Ranke to Hegel, to which professional historians have been repeatedly hostile, and professional philosophers mostly indifferent, remains a topic for historiographic inquiry. The most extended work on the subject is Ernst Simon's 1923 dissertation, published as suppl. 15 of the *Historische Zeitschrift* (Munich: R. Oldenbourg, 1928), which was written before Ranke's fragments on universal history and historical method from the 1830s were available; he does not draw the parallel I have just drawn between Ranke's "wie es eigentlich gewesen" and Hegel's "wie sie an ihnen selbst sind." For some remarks by Ranke that suggest his not-incompatible relation to Hegel's philosophy of history, see the edition of his fragments in Eberhard Kessel, "Rankes Idee der Universalhistorie," *Historische Zeitschrift* 178 (1954), 269–308: "History understood [*verstandene Geschichte*] is, in my opinion, the true philosophy

of history" ("Über Universalhistorie," p. 285); "Were philosophy that which it is supposed to be, and were historical study [*Historie*] so perfectly clear and complete, they would both fully harmonize [*übereinstimmen*]" ("Idee der Universalhistorie," p. 302); "History is not an opposite to, but a fulfillment of philosophy" ("Schluss einer Einleitung zur Vorlesung über neueste Geschichte," p. 304). In his "Einleitung zu einer Vorlesung über Universalhistorie," pp. 304–8, probably from 1833, Ranke recounts Hegel's lectures on the philosophy of history with considerable respect and accuracy of paraphrase; since Hegel's lectures were first published in 1837 but were given every two years from 1822 to 1830, and as Ranke was at the University of Berlin as an *Extraordinarius* from 1825 to 1827, it seems probable that Ranke either heard Hegel's lectures or had access to notes from them. See also my n. 67 to chap. 1, above.

13. Verene, *Hegel's Recollection*, p. 6, remarks that "what seemed to be the face, the living presence of mind or spirit suddenly becomes the *calvaria*—the skull lacking the lower jaw and facial portion. Here once again the image shows us what it is not: the concept as the element of the divine in the image has not attained its proper life." Verene (pp. 88–91) is also, to my knowledge, the only one who has connected the *Phenomenology*'s critique of phrenology, *Schädellehre* (3:244–62), with the privileged position of the *Schädelstätte* at its end: "Phenomenology is the 'recollection and the Calvary of absolute spirit.' The true sense of the skull is found only in phenomenology, not in phrenology. . . . The skull in phrenology, as Hegel says, is a *caput mortuum*. It is dead—dead, inert mind. Phenomenology is a logos of eros, of the life of mind, the self-movement of spirit toward the life of absolute knowing. Phrenology sounds like phenomenology. Phrenology is the inverted world, the upside-down version of phenomenology" (p. 89).

14. B. Kliban, *Never Eat Anything Bigger Than Your Head and Other Drawings* (New York: Workman, 1976), unpaginated.

15. *Werke*, 3:262. On this conjunction, see Hamacher, "Pleroma," and Verene, *Hegel's Recollection*.

16. I refer here to Cathy Caruth's studies of a historical unconscious in Freud's writings on human history, such as *Civilization and Its Discontents* (in her *Empirical Truths and Critical Fictions* [Baltimore: Johns Hopkins U.P., 1991]) and *Moses and Monotheism* (forthcoming).

17. *Werke*, 3:259–61.

18. In a draft version of a fragment titled "Romane lesen," Walter Benjamin writes: "The most ancient theory of nutrition is thus important for a knowledge of novel-reading, for it takes its departure from eating: it says that we nourish ourselves through the incorporation of the spirits of the eaten things [*durch Einverleibung der Geister der gegessenen Dinge*]. Now we admittedly don't nourish ourselves that way, but we do eat for the sake of such an incorporation. We also read for the sake of such an incorporation" (*Gesammelte Schriften*, ed. Rolf Tiedemann and Hermann Schweppenhäuser, 7 vols. [Frankfurt am Main: Suhrkamp, 1972–89], 4:1013). The relation of reading novels to doing history will be explored in chap. 9, below, on Benjamin's essay "The Storyteller," for which this fragment constitutes part of the context.

Chapter 4
MOURNFUL ANTHROPOMORPHISM AND ITS PASSING

Epigraph: Patrick Süskind, *Perfume: The Story of a Murderer,* trans. John E. Woods (New York: Alfred A Knopf, 1986), p. 35.

1. On *Aufhebung* as "relief" *(relève)* and on Hegel's dialectic as the "relieving" of oppositionality, see Jacques Derrida, "De l'économie restreinte à l'économie générale: un hegelianisme sans réserve,"in *L'Écriture et la différence* (Paris: Seuil, 1967), pp. 369–407; *Positions* (Paris: Minuit, 1972), pp. 55–61 and passim; and *GLAS* (Paris: Galilée, 1974).

2. Hayden White gives a lively account of the *Lectures on the Philosophy of History,* in the context of Hegel's remarks on historiographic prose in his *Aesthetics,* in *Metahistory: The Historical Imagination in Nineteenth-Century Europe* (Baltimore: Johns Hopkins U.P., 1973), pp. 81–131. Although this is not the place for an extended consideration of White's important work, it seems appropriate to distinguish his project from mine. White's interest in the tropes and "modes" or genres of history, drawing upon Vico, Jakobson, Burke, and Frye, is ultimately in a typology of generative models for historical narrative. He is, in his words, "forced to postulate a deep level of consciousness on which a historical thinker chooses conceptual strategies by which to explain or represent his data," which—called "acts of prefiguration" by White and "characterizable by the linguistic modes in which they are cast"—conform to "the four tropes of poetic language: Metaphor, Metonymy, Synecdoche, and Irony" (p. x). Whatever the inherent difficulty of this fundamental list of tropes (on this, see my contribution "Figure, Scheme, Trope," in the *Princeton Encyclopedia of Poetry and Poetics,* 3d ed., ed. T. V. F. Brogan et al. [Princeton: Princeton U.P., forthcoming]), my critical interest here is in the narrative of White's own argument wherein the past is a mass of documents or data, then "prefiguratively," at some conscious or unconscious level, a mental perception is constituted, which then yields the conceptual representation and explanation of data that is the historian's actual historical narrative and argument (pp. 30, 31). Here, White tells a generative story about data before tropes, and tropes before historiography—to the point of using an ambiguous phrase such as "the possible modes of historiography are . . . in reality *formalizations* of poetic insights that analytically precede them" (p. xii)—which recasts the properly "metahistorical" analytic problem of *before and after* in structures of narrative understanding into their precise unfolding in historians' narratives, including White's own. In other words, White's approach tells as a generative narrative or history what is in fact the reverse of his analytic procedure, which is—like all historians'—to come *after* their data and then to claim that "prefigurative" models (in White's case, *Ur*-tropes) necessarily "precede" the explanations they will give to these data, even as a phrase like "analytically precede" suggests in its ambiguity that the historian's analysis epistemologically precedes the generative or developmental claims that his narrative will then make for the ways in which data become their stories. As White's language of "deep structure" and "consciousness" suggests, his model also seems to need a universal psychology of historiography and its

poetics, whereas in this study my interest in the tropological and linguistic-material bases of allegories of history is rather in discursive conditions of possibility and structural consequences that have uniquely to do with letters. So, too, White's remarks on tropes in Hegel (pp. 86, 87) are different from my present attempt to read Hegel's tropes.

3. On the import of these late lectures, see Paul de Man, "Hegel on the Sublime," in *Displacement: Derrida and After*, ed. Mark Krupnick (Bloomington: Indiana U.P., 1983), pp. 149ff. See also Hegel's statement from the *Wissenschaft der Logik*, in *Werke*, ed. Eva Moldenhauer and Karl Markus Michel, 20 vols. (Frankfurt am Main: Suhrkamp, 1969–71), 6:260, quoted in chap. 2, above.

4. G. W. F. Hegel, *Vorlesungen über die Philosophie der Geschichte*, in *Werke*, 12:28: "Aber die göttliche Weisheit, d.i. die Vernunft, ist eine und dieselbe im Grossen wie in Kleinen, und wir müssen Gott nicht für zu schwach halten, seine Weisheit aufs Grosse anzuwenden. Unsere Erkenntnis geht darauf, die Einsicht zu gewinnen, dass das von der ewigen Weisheit Bezweckte wie auf dem Boden der Natur so auf dem Boden des in der Welt wirklichen und tätigen Geistes herausgekommen ist. Unsere Betrachtung ist insofern eine Theodizee, eine Rechtfertigung Gottes"; and p. 540: "Dass die Weltgeschichte dieser Entwicklungsgang und das wirkliche Werden des Geistes ist, unter dem wechselnden Schauspiele ihrer Geschichten—dies ist die wahrhafte *Theodizee*, die Rechtfertigung Gottes in der Geschichte." Further quotations from these lectures will be identified in the body of the text by volume and page number(s).

5. Hegel is here playing on the relation of reason (*Vernunft*) and perception (*Vernehmen*) and also recalling an earlier passage in the introduction: "Der einzige Gedanke, den die Philosophie mitbringt, ist aber der einfache Gedanke der *Vernunft*, dass die Vernunft die Welt beherrsche, dass es also auch in der Weltgeschichte vernünftig zugegangen sei" (12:20).

6. Cf. also Hegel's movement between "das Bestehen dessen, was er [der Geist] ist" and "das Allgemeine dessen, was *er nur war*" (12:103), quoted in full above in chap. 2, n. 5.

7. de Man, "Hegel on the Sublime," p. 142.

8. G. W. F. Hegel, *Vorlesungen über die Ästhetik*, in *Werke*, 13:21; henceforth cited in the text by volume and page numbers.

9. For a reading of a similar passage-of-appearance in Hegel—this between Wissenschaft and the appearance of Wissenschaft—see my "The Indifferent Reader: The Performance of Hegel's Introduction to the *Phenomenology*," *Diacritics* 11, no. 2 (Summer 1981), 68–82.

10. See, e.g., René Wellek, *A History of Modern Criticism: 1750–1950*, vol. 2, *The Romantic Age* (New Haven: Yale U.P., 1955), pp. 319–22; Willi Oelmüller, "Hegels Satz vom Ende der Kunst und das Problem der Philosophie der Kunst nach Hegel," *Philosophisches Jahrbuch* 73 (1965), 75–94; and Hans Robert Jauss, *Literaturgeschichte als Provokation* (Frankfurt am Main: Suhrkamp, 1973), pp. 112–14. Even so astute a philosopher as Dieter Henrich can treat Hegel's position as historicizing, although Henrich apparently does so in order to turn then to a more interesting reflection on the contemporaneity of Hegel's aesthetics (see Henrich, "Kunst und Kunstphilosophie der Gegenwart [Über-

legungen mit Rücksicht auf Hegel]," in *Immanente Ästhetik, Ästhetische Reflexion: Lyrik als Paradigma der Moderne—Poetik und Hermeneutik II*, ed. Wolfgang Iser [Munich: W. Fink, 1966], p. 15). See also the suggestive essay by Odo Marquard, "Kunst als Kompensation ihres Endes," in *Ästhetische Erfahrung*, ed. Willi Oelmüller (Paderborn: Schöningh, 1981), pp. 159–68.

11. See the immediately following sentence: "Thereby it [art] has lost [*verloren*] for us genuine truth and liveliness as well, and is rather more misplaced in our *presentation* [*Vorstellung*] than maintaining its earlier necessity in reality and occupying its higher place" (13:25).

12. See Paul de Man, *The Resistance to Theory* (Minneapolis: U. of Minnesota P., 1986), pp. 25–26, 55–57, 70, and 113; and, from a different perspective, Peter Szondi, *Einführung in die literarische Hermeneutik*, ed. Jean Bollack and Helen Stierlin (Frankfurt am Main: Suhrkamp, 1975), pp. 24–25.

13. The contrast is apparent, for the previous paragraph has explicitly introduced Hegel's own voice: "Es ist über diesen Punkt hier nur in der Kürze zu sagen, dass, welche Vorstellungen man sonst von Philosophie und vom Philosophieren haben möge, ich das Philosophieren durchaus als von Wissenschaftlichkeit untrennbar erachte" (13:26). Hegel here alludes to his statement in the preface to the *Phänomenologie des Geistes*, in *Werke*, 3:14: "Die wahre Gestalt, in welcher die Wahrheit existiert, kann allein das wissenschaftliche System derselben sein."

14. For one among several statements of classical art's exalted position see *Werke*, 13:111: "Die klassische Kunstform nämlich hat das Höchste erreicht, was die Versinnlichung der Kunst zu leisten vermag, und wenn an ihr etwas mangelhaft ist, so ist es nur die Kunst selber und die Beschränkheit der Kunstsphäre."

15. The very first such sketch may be found on the eleventh page of the *Aesthetics:* "Nur ein gewisser Kreis und Stufe der Wahrheit ist fähig, im Elemente des Kunstwerks dargestellt zu werden; es muss noch in ihrer eigenen Bestimmung liegen, zu dem Sinnlichen herauszugehen und in demselben sich adäquat sein zu können, um echter Inhalt für die Kunst zu sein, wie dies z.B. bei den griechischen Göttern der Fall ist" (13:23).

16. I owe to T. M. Knox's translation the rendering of *herausmachen* as "to proceed out into" in addition to my "to constitute itself into" (see Hegel, *Aesthetics: Lectures on Fine Art*, trans. T. M. Knox, 2 vols. [Oxford: Clarendon, 1975], 1:78).

17. On, for example, the examples of *this, here, now, I*, and *writing* in the sense-certainty chapter of the *Phenomenology*, see Andrzej Warminski, *Readings in Interpretation: Hölderlin, Hegel, Heidegger* (Minneapolis: U. of Minnesota P., 1987), pp. 163–79; and de Man, *Resistance to Theory*, pp. 41–43.

18. On Kant's "Einheit des Mannigfaltigen" in apperception (*Anschauung*), see Kant, *Kritik der reinen Vernunft*, in *Werke*, ed. Wilhelm Weischedel (Frankfurt am Main: Suhrkamp, 1974), 3:135 (= B130–31). For another Kantian formulation by Hegel in this section, see Hegel, *Werke*, 14:81: "Die allgemeinste und zugleich vollendeteste Vorstellung von ihrer Natur gibt uns ihre konzentrierte Individualität, insofern dieselbe aus der *Mannigfaltigkeit* von Bei-

wesenheiten, einzelnen Handlungen und Begebenheiten in den einen Brenn-
punkt ihrer einfachen *Einheit* mit sich zusammengefasst ist" (my emphasis).

19. The possible allusion is to Schlegel's famous *Athenäum* fragment no. 116,
with its depiction of romantic *Poesie* "zwischen dem Dargestellten und dem
Darstellenden, frei von allem realen und idealen Interesse, auf den Flügeln der
poetischen Reflexion in der Mitte schweben" (see Schlegel, *Kritische Schriften,*
ed. Wolfdietrich Rasch [Munich: C. Hanser, 1970], p. 39).

20. Knox, in his translation of the *Aesthetics,* 1:482, renders *hindurchergiesst*
as "permeates" and so blunts the distinction I am drawing.

21. On the place of the sublime in Hegel's *Aesthetics,* see de Man, "Hegel and
the Sublime," and especially the apparently puzzling claim, p. 144: "The sublime for Hegel is the absolutely beautiful."

22. The classic study of Hegel's dialectical appreciation of words remains
Jean-Luc Nancy, *La Remarque spéculative* (Paris: Galilée, 1973).

23. Paul de Man, *Allegories of Reading: Figural Language in Rousseau,
Nietzsche, Rilke, and Proust* (New Haven: Yale U.P., 1979), p. 300 and n. 21.

24. See Hegel, *Phänomenologie des Geistes,* in *Werke,* 3:82–95, and n. 17
above.

25. In here conjoining the punctuation of the text of the *Aesthetics* with the
authority of the proper name Hegel, I am only forcing an issue that has been
latent throughout this chapter, namely, that of the authority of the text of the
Aesthetics, given that the lectures were edited posthumously by his student
Heinrich Gustav Hotho from Hegel's notes reaching back to 1818 (but principally from 1823 to 1829), together with several transcriptions of students' notes,
and then lightly re-edited once again by Moldenhauer and Michel for the present version in the *Werke.* See *Werke,* 15:575–78, for the editors' account of the
textual status of the lectures. I am reading the text as we have it, with its own
authority; perhaps wherever I write *Hegel,* the reader should read "Hegel."

26. Hegel continues here to say that "art makes each of its constructs [*Gebilde*] into a thousand-eyed Argus, so that the inner soul and spirituality might
be seen at all points." In his commentary on the *Aesthetics,* "Hegels Lehre von
der Dichtung," in *Poetik und Geschichtsphilosophie,* ed. Senta Metz and Hans-
Hagen Hildebrandt, 2 vols. (Frankfurt am Main: Suhrkamp, 1974), 1:360,
426–27, Peter Szondi brilliantly associates this passage, as well as another that
we shall presently look at (14:131–32), with Rilke's poem "Archaischer Torso
Apollos."

27. See 13:61 and also, in the part of the *Encyclopaedia of Philosophical Wissenschaften* on "Assimilation," which we treated in the preceding chapter, *Werke,*
9:465–68.

28. I skip over the fact that the topic of satisfaction is introduced with a
reference to Napoleon:

> Satisfaction is the feeling of correspondence between our particular subjec-
> tivity and the condition of our determined state, be this given to us or
> brought about by us. Napoleon, for example, never more thoroughly ex-
> pressed his satisfaction than when he had succeeded at something with

which the whole world showed itself dissatisfied. For satisfaction is only the approval of my own being, acting, and doing, and the extreme of such approval can be recognized in that Philistine feeling that every accomplished man must bring with him. But this feeling and its expression are not the expression of the plastic eternal gods. (14:85–86)

As difficult as this passage is to understand, it is tempting to speculate on this section's improbable reassembling of Goethe, Napoleon, and Hegel in a Berlin lately regained by the Prussians, more than two decades after Hegel had finished his *Phenomenology* to the sounds of the "world spirit" Napoleon's victory at the battle of Jena, after which Napoleon wanted nothing so much as to meet Goethe, the author of *Werther.*

29. With respect to the divergence of meaning from the sign with which it is also juxtaposed, this characterizes allegory for Hegel as well as for us, and earlier in the *Aesthetics* (13:512) he had remarked on the cool "frostiness" (*Frostigkeit*) of allegory.

30. Knox's translation, "We read in their faces . . . ," *Aesthetics,* 1:485, seems wrong.

31. On this dimension of Hegel's thought, see Paul de Man, "Sign and Symbol in Hegel's *Aesthetics*," *Critical Inquiry* 8 (Summer 1982), 761–75.

Chapter 5
AUERBACH'S *MIMESIS*

1. Standard studies of nineteenth-century historicism available in English are Friedrich Meinecke, *Historism: The Rise of a New Historical Outlook* (1936), trans. J. E. Anderson and H. D. Schmidt (London: Routledge & Kegan Paul, 1972); James Westfall Thompson, *History of Historical Writing,* vol. 2, *The Eighteenth and Nineteenth Centuries* (New York: Macmillan, 1942); G. P. Gooch, *History and Historians in the Nineteenth Century* (Boston: Beacon Press, 1959); and Georg G. Iggers, *The German Conception of History: The National Tradition of Historical Thought from Herder to the Present* (Middletown, Conn.: Wesleyan U.P., 1968). See also Meinecke's late reconsideration, "Ranke and Burckhardt," in *German History: Some New German Views,* ed. Hans Kohn (London: George Allen & Unwin, 1954), pp. 141–56; and Arnaldo Momigliano, "A Hundred Years after Ranke," in *Studies in Historiography* (London: Weidenfeld & Nicolson, 1966), pp. 105–11. Similar studies of nineteenth-century literary history include the latter part of Ulrich von Wilamowitz-Moellendorff, *History of Classical Scholarship* (1921), trans. Alan Harris (Baltimore: Johns Hopkins U.P., 1982), pp. 105–78; and René Wellek, *A History of Modern Criticism: 1750–1950,* vol. 3, *The Later Nineteenth Century* (New Haven: Yale U.P., 1965). More recent and more interesting studies sometimes extend over historicist, historical-philosophical, and literary-historical achievements of the nineteenth century. Although they do not always accord with the methods and aims of the present study, I refer the reader to Michel Foucault, *Les Mots et les choses: une*

archéologie des sciences humaines (Paris: Gallimard, 1966), pt. 2, esp. pp. 229–33, 292–307, 339–46, and 378–85; Jacques Derrida, *De la grammatologie* (Paris: Minuit, 1967), pt. 1 (pp. 9–142); idem, "Cogito et histoire de la folie," in *L'Écriture et la différence* (Paris: Seuil, 1967), pp. 51–97; idem, "Les Fins de l'homme," in *Marges de la philosophie* (Paris: Minuit, 1972), pp. 129–64; Siegfried Kracauer, *History: The Last Things before the Last* (New York: Oxford U.P., 1969); Odo Marquard, *Schwierigkeiten mit der Geschichtsphilosophie* (Frankfurt am Main: Suhrkamp, 1973); Hayden White, *Metahistory: The Historical Imagination in Nineteenth-Century Europe* (Baltimore: Johns Hopkins U.P., 1973); Hans Robert Jauss, "Geschichte der Kunst und Historie," *Literaturgeschichte als Provokation* (Frankfurt am Main: Suhrkamp, 1973), pp. 208–51; Hannelore Schlaffer and Heinz Schlaffer, *Studien zum ästhetischen Historismus* (Frankfurt am Main: Suhrkamp, 1975); Wolf Lepenies, *Das Ende der Naturgeschichte: Wandel kultureller Selbstverständlichkeiten in den Wissenschaften des 18. und 19. Jahrhunderts* (Frankfurt am Main: Suhrkamp, 1978); Reinhart Koselleck, *Vergangene Zukunft: Zur Semantik geschichtlicher Zeiten* (Frankfurt am Main: Suhrkamp, 1979); Gerald Graff, *Professing Literature: An Institutional History* (Chicago: U. of Chicago P., 1987), esp. pp. 55–80; Peter Hohendahl, *Building a National Literature: The Case of Germany, 1830–1870*, trans. Renate Franciscono (Ithaca: Cornell U.P., 1989); and Lionel Gossman, *Between History and Literature* (Cambridge, Mass.: Harvard U.P., 1990).

2. Frederick Crews, "Criticism without Constraint," *Commentary* 73, no. 1 (1982), 69.

3. Frank Lentricchia, *After the New Criticism* (Chicago: U. of Chicago P., 1980).

4. Paul de Man, *Allegories of Reading: Figural Language in Rousseau, Nietzsche, Rilke, and Proust* (New Haven: Yale U.P., 1979), p. ix. De Man remarked about the significance of his and similar work for his "generation" in his brief introduction to the special issue he edited of *Studies in Romanticism* 18, no. 4 (1979), 495–99.

5. For de Man's most extended statements on the responses to literary theory, see *The Resistance to Theory* (Minneapolis: U. of Minnesota P., 1986), pp. 3–26. For the quote from Derrida, see *Mémoires for Paul de Man*, trans. Cecile Lindsay, Jonathan Culler, and Eduardo Cadava (New York: Columbia U.P., 1986), p. 42, n. 5.

6. For the canonizing treatment, see Charles Breslin, "Philosophy or Philology: Auerbach and Aesthetic Historicism," *Journal of the History of Ideas* 22 (1961), 369–81. Something closer to a close reading is David Carroll, "Mimesis Reconsidered: Literature, History, Ideology," *Diacritics* 5, no. 2 (1975), 5–12. Two considerations of *Mimesis* in the context of the philosophy of history are Friedrich Gogarten, "Das abendländische Geschichtsdenken: Bemerkungen zu dem Buch von Erich Auerbach 'Mimesis,'" *Zeitschrift für Theologie und Kirche* 51 (1954), 270–360, and Helmut Kuhn, "Literaturgeschichte als Geschichtsphilosophie," *Philosophische Rundschau* 11 (1973), 222–48; see also the pages on Auerbach in Karl Morrison, *The Mimetic Tradition of Reform in the West* (Prince-

ton: Princeton U.P., 1982), pp. 407–14. See Paul Bové, *Intellectuals in Power: A Genealogy of Critical Humanism* (New York: Columbia U.P., 1986), pp. 97–110, for a survey, however incomplete, of some of the reviews *Mimesis* received in America. The single extended consideration of Auerbach's *oeuvre* is by a German Romance scholar, Klaus Gronau, *Literarische Form und gesellschaftliche Entwicklung: Erich Auerbachs Beitrag zur Theorie und Methodologie der Literaturgeschichte* (Königstein: Anton Hain, 1979).

7. For Auerbach on the centrality of levels of style for his argument, see the epilogue to his *Mimesis: Dargestellte Wirklichkeit in der abendländischen Literatur* (Bern: Francke, 1946), in English as *Mimesis: The Representation of Reality in Western Literature*, trans. Willard R. Trask (Princeton: Princeton U.P., 1953), pp. 554, 555, henceforth cited in the body of the text by page number(s) only; and his "Epilegomena zu *Mimesis*," *Romanische Forschungen* 65 (1953), 5–10.

8. In this matter, Auerbach's method (his own differentiations notwithstanding) is essentially the same as that of Leo Spitzer, who, in "Linguistics and Literary History," likewise claimed to demonstrate the methodological continuity that obtains between the analysis of a particular word or stylistic feature of an author and the study of the author's psychology, his place among his people and their time, and ultimately, his place in the life of his language (see *Linguistics and Literary History: Essays in Stylistics* [Princeton: Princeton U.P., 1948], pp. 10ff.). This is part of what Morrison (*The Mimetic Tradition*, p. 413) considers the "mimesis" shared by Spitzer and Auerbach. For Auerbach's major statement on philology, see "Philologie und Weltliteratur" (1952), *Gesammelte Aufsätze zur romanischen Philologie* (Bern: Francke, 1967), in English as "Philology and Weltliteratur," trans. Maire Said and Edward Said, *Centennial Review* 13, no. 1 (1969), 1–17. On the continuing topicality of philology, see the special issue of *Comparative Literature Studies* 27, no. 1 (1990), publishing the proceedings of the 1988 Harvard symposium, "What Is Philology?"

9. Some sense of this may be gathered from the contrasting pairs of works by masters in the historicist tradition: Friedrich Meinecke's magisterial *Die Entstehung des Historismus* (1936), *Werke*, vol. 3, ed. Carl Hinrichs (Munich: R. Oldenbourg, 1959), followed after the war by *Die deutsche Katastrophe: Betrachtungen und Erinnerungen* (Zurich: Aero-Verlag, 1946); Ernst Troeltsch's "Die Krisis des Historismus," *Die Neue Rundschau* 33 (1922), 572–90, and *Der Historismus und seine Probleme* (Tübingen: J. C. B. Mohr, 1922), followed scarcely two years later by the hopeful *Der Historismus und seine Überwindung* (Berlin: R. Heise, 1924); and E. R. Curtius's short work *Deutscher Geist in Gefahr* (Stuttgart: Deutsche Verlagsanstalt, 1932), followed by the long march toward *European Literature and the Latin Middle Ages* (1948), trans. Willard R. Trask (New York: Pantheon, 1953).

10. For two critical assessments of German historiography by historians teaching in Germany, see Walther Hofer, "Toward a Revision of the German Concept of History" (1948), in *German History: Some New German Views*, ed. Hans Kohn (London: George Allen & Unwin, 1954), pp. 187–205; and Hans-Ulrich Wehler, "Historiography in Germany Today" (1979), in *Observations on*

"The Spiritual Situation of the Age," ed. Jürgen Habermas, trans. Andrew Buchwalter (Cambridge: MIT Press, 1984), pp. 221–55.

11. "Epilegomena zu *Mimesis*," p. 15. Cf. also his earlier remark in "Vico und Herder" (1932), *Gesammelte Aufsätze*, p. 223: "The modern conception of history as an immanent intelligible whole . . . arrives at its perfect philosophic expression in Hegel's work, and the foundations of its praxis with the scholars of the romantic period; the faculty which I represent—Romance philology—is one of the smaller branches of the tree of romantic historicism."

12. For an earlier treatment of Auerbach's studies of Vico and some of their relations to his understanding of *figura* and literary history, see my "Vico, Auerbach and Literary History," *Philological Quarterly* 60, no. 2 (1981), 239–55.

13. Erich Auerbach, "Figura" (1938), *Gesammelte Aufsätze*, in English in Auerbach, *Scenes from the Drama of European Literature*, trans. Ralph Manheim (New York: Meridian, 1959), pp. 11–76; henceforth cited as F.

14. The technical term for the fulfilling is *implere*, but the language of revealing, realizing, consummating, and so on, also appears.

15. For a stylistic anticipation of this argument, see the Christian typological and, indeed, figural language in Fritz Schalk's brief summary of the argument of *Mimesis* in his introduction to Auerbach's *Gesammelte Aufsätze*, p. 15: "If the classical literature which distinguished styles first appeared only as *a station on the way* to a figural literature which blended styles, then representation now leads from the Middle Ages to modern times as if to a *peak*, so that earlier art forms work almost like *shadows* that are *outshined* [*überglänzt*] by modernity" (my emphasis).

16. Erich Auerbach, *Dante als Dichter der irdischen Welt* (Berlin: W. de Gruyter, 1929), in English as *Dante, Poet of the Secular World*, trans. Ralph Manheim (Chicago: U. of Chicago P., 1961). In his "Figura" essay, Auerbach remarked that the interpretive theory of this early book—"which is already to be found in Hegel"—is actually figural (F, 71).

17. On the survival of the figural pattern in Auerbach, see my "Vico, Auerbach and Literary History."

18. I owe to a discussion with Richard Macksey the consideration that the very last chapter of *Mimesis*, on Virginia Woolf and Proust, is the terminal point where history yields not figural realism but autobiography and that it is this chapter and this genre that provide an ultimate model for Auerbach's historiography. It would require considerable additional work to integrate this insight into the present argument about Auerbach's figural narrative.

Chapter 6
NIETZSCHE'S *URSPRÜNGE*, LUKÁCS'S LEAPS

1. All Nietzsche texts are cited from *Werke in drei Bänden*, ed. Karl Schlechta (Munich: C. Hanser, 1966). Passages are first cited by the book and section numbers Nietzsche gave them (for *The Birth of Tragedy* and *The Gay Science*

there are only section numbers); then by the volume and page numbers in the Schlechta edition.

2. G. W. F. Hegel, preface to the *Phänomenologie des Geistes*, in *Werke*, ed. Eva Moldenhauer and Karl Markus Michel, 20 vols. (Frankfurt: Suhrkamp, 1969–71), 3:18, 19.

3. For an exception to the claimed uninteresting character of the second of the *Untimely Meditations*, see the exceptionally interesting treatment of this essay in Paul de Man, "Literary History and Literary Modernity," *Blindness and Insight: Essays in the Rhetoric of Contemporary Criticism* (New York: Oxford U.P., 1971), pp. 142–65, where much of the interest may be attributable to de Man's own argument and to the Baudelaire text with which he pairs Nietzsche. For some commentary on de Man's essay, see my "Lessons of Remembering and Forgetting," in *Reading de Man Reading*, ed. Lindsay Waters and Wlad Godzich (Minneapolis: U. of Minnesota P., 1989), pp. 254–55.

4. More extended analysis of the essay may be found in de Man, *Allegories of Reading: Figural Language in Rousseau, Nietzsche, Rilke, and Proust* (New Haven: Yale U.P., 1979), pp. 110–16, and *The Rhetoric of Romanticism* (New York: Columbia U.P., 1984), pp. 239–43.

5. On this motif of excess, see the following sentence from *The Birth of Tragedy*: "The excess [*Übermass*, 'over-measure'] uncovers itself as truth" (4; 1:34).

6. On *Entwicklung* as an important term and concept in Hegel's philosophy of history—and one I have not previously dwelt on in this study—see *Vorlesungen über die Philosophie der Geschichte*, in *Werke*, 12:24, 75–77, 86–88.

7. Just as this part of this chapter cannot be an extended reading of all of *The Birth of Tragedy*, so it cannot take meticulous account of the many powerful readings the text has recently received, among them Philippe Lacoue-Labarthe, "Le Détour," *Poétique* 5 (1971), 53–76; Paul de Man, "Genesis and Genealogy (Nietzsche)," in *Allegories of Reading*, pp. 79–102; and Andrzej Warminski, *Readings in Interpretation: Hölderlin, Hegel, Heidegger* (Minneapolis: U. of Minnesota P., 1987), pp. xxxv–lxi. De Man's reading of *The Birth of Tragedy*'s argument, his most extensive analysis of a single Nietzsche text, is not incompatible, I believe, with the claims I advance here about the nondevelopmental character of the text's moves from *Ursprünge* to a beginning.

8. See n. 2 above.

9. "What is originality?" Nietzsche asks. "To see something that carries no name as yet, that cannot yet be named or mentioned [*genannt*], although it's open to all eyes. The way men usually are, it takes a name to make something visible for them.—Those with originality have for the most part also been the name-givers." (*Fröhliche Wissenschaft*, 261; II, 158) To see something that has no name as yet, and to name it as such—as something that jumps out at us, that leaps or springs out as an *Ursprung*—is both originality, according to this aphorism from *The Gay Science*, and the very procedure of origination, according to the "Truth and Lie" essay or *The Birth of Tragedy*.

10. "Original.—Not that one is the first to see something new," Nietzsche writes, "but that one sees the old, the well-known, what has been seen and overlooked by everyone, as new—this distinguishes the really original minds.

The first discoverer is ordinarily that wholly familiar and spiritless fantast [or visionary: *Phantast*]—accident, *der Zufall*" ("Vermischte Meinungen und Sprüche," no. 200, in *Menschliches, Allzumenschliches*, Band 2; 1:814). The very old—the "original," the *vorzeitlich*—as new, as (re)originating, is what distinguishes *Ursprung* and the original thinker of origins: it is what falls to him.

11. Fredric Jameson, *Marxism and Form: Twentieth-Century Dialectical Theories of Literature* (Princeton: Princeton U.P., 1971), criticizes the nondevelopmental understanding of Lukács when he says that "Lukács's life work fails to be understood from the inside, as a set of solutions and problems developing out of one another according to their own inner logic and momentum" (p. 161) and asks rhetorically, "What if the earlier works proved to be fully comprehensible only in the light of the later ones?" (p. 163). J. M. Bernstein, *The Philosophy of the Novel: Lukács, Marxism, and the Dialectics of Form* (Brighton: Harvester Press, 1984), p. viii, boldly declares that his study—the most extensive of *The Theory of the Novel* that I am aware of in any language—tries "to read his pre-Marxist theory of the novel from the perspective of his Marxist social theory." Bernstein's retrospective approach, developmental like Jameson's, arrives at a prospective meaning drawn from his key text, Lukács's *History and Class Consciousness:* "The theory of Marxism is a theory of political narrative; the truth of Marxist theory is a political and narrative truth; its writing addresses us as possible members of a future collective subjectivity; our self-recognition in the story we hear, our grasping of our past and future in terms of the story told is an act of political identification by which we begin to become who we might be" (pp. 266–67). This prospective interpretation accords, I believe, with Jameson's later rereading of Lukács in his *The Political Unconscious: Narrative as a Socially Symbolic Act* (Ithaca: Cornell U.P., 1981), pp. 50–55 and 63, and with his more general remarks on Marxism, history, and narrative, pp. 100–102 and 281–99.

12. de Man, *Blindness and Insight*, p. 52: "Whatever one may think of Lukács, he is certainly an important enough mind to be studied as a whole, and the critical interpretation of his thought has not been helped by the oversimplified division that has been established. The weaknesses of the later work are already present from the beginning, and some of the early strength remains operative throughout."

13. Georg Lukács, *Die Theorie des Romans: Ein geschichtsphilosophischer Versuch über die Formen der grossen Epik*, published in 1916 and, in book form, in 1920 (Neuwied and Berlin: Luchterhand, 1971), in English as *The Theory of the Novel: A Historico-philosophical Essay on the Forms of Great Epic Literature*, trans. Anna Bostock (Cambridge, Mass.: MIT Press, 1971). Although I have translated all quotations here myself, for ease of reference I cite in the body of the text the MIT pagination after a semicolon that follows the pagination of the Luchterhand paperback edition.

14. In his *Die Zerstörung der Vernunft* (Neuwied: Luchterhand, 1962), p. 219, Lukács scorned Schopenhauer and then "leading German intellectuals," including Adorno by name, for residing at the "Grand Hotel Abgrund" (cited in his preface to *Die Theorie*, p. 16; Eng., p. 22).

15. Georg Lukács, *Geschichte und Klassenbewusstsein: Studien über marxistische Dialektik* (1923) (Darmstadt and Neuwied: Luchterhand, 1970), in English as *History and Class Consciousness: Studies in Marxist Dialectics*, trans. Rodney Livingstone (Cambridge, Mass.: MIT Press, 1971). As above, I have translated all quotations here myself, but for ease of reference I cite in the body of the text the MIT pagination after a semicolon that follows the pagination of the Luchterhand paperback edition.

16. For a classic statement from early in *History and Class Consciousness* of totality as the totality of reality as history, and of history as thought, see "What is Orthodox Marxism?": "Only in this context, which joins together the individual facts of social life, as moments of the historical development, into a *totality*, is a knowledge of the facts as knowledge of *reality* possible. This knowledge . . . progresses from [simple determinants] to the knowledge of the concrete totality as the reproduction of reality in thought. . . . Marx's dictum, 'the relations of production of every society form a whole,' is precisely the methodological point of departure and key for the *historical* [*historischen*] knowledge of social relations" (69 and 71; 8, 9).

17. Hegel, preface to *Phänomenologie*, 3:16, 17, in English as *Hegel's "Phenomenology of Spirit,"* trans. A. V. Miller (Oxford: Oxford U.P., 1977), p. 5 (translation slightly modified).

18. See Hegel, *Vorlesungen über die Philosophie der Geschichte*, on historical development and on perfection: "*So ist der Geist in ihm selbst sich entgegen; er hat sich selbst als das wahre feinselige Hindernis seiner selbst zu überwinden; die Entwicklung, die in der Natur ein ruhiges Hervorgehen ist, ist im Geist ein harter unendlicher Kampf gegen sich selbst. Was der Geist will, ist, seinen eigenen Begriff zu erreichen; aber er selbst verdeckt sich denselben, ist stolz und voll von Genuss in dieser Entfremdung seiner selbst*" (76); and "*So erscheint in der Existenz der Fortgang als ein Fortschreiten von dem Unvollkommenen zum Vollkommneren. . . . Das Unvollkommene so als das Gegenteil seiner in ihm selbst ist der Widerspruch, der wohl existiert, aber ebensosehr aufgehoben und gelöst wird*" (78).

19. *Phänomenologie*, 3:19; Eng., p. 7.

20. de Man, *Blindness and Insight*, p. 53.

21. Jameson, *Marxism and Form*, p. 180, is right to see that "the aim of the work is the creation of a typology," where *aim* (*Ziel*) is precisely the correct term, but then precisely wrong when he continues, "of a characteristically Hegelian working out of pure formal possibilities in the chronological unfolding of history itself," for there are, of course, no "pure formal possibilities" worked out for Hegel, in history or any other site of true *Wissenschaft*.

22. I have noted with these references only the places where Lukács uses the term *Sprung;* several other places, where there is further imagery of abysses, unbridgeable gaps, exploding (*sprengen*, related to *Sprung*), and the like, would also be germane.

23. See John Freccero, "Dante's Ulysses: From Epic to Novel," in *Dante: The Poetics of Conversion* (Cambridge, Mass.: Harvard U.P., 1986), pp. 136-51, esp. p. 138.

24. See above. Lukács echoes this phrase in his own "Wenn das Unterschei-

dende zwischen den Menschen zur unüberbrückbaren Kluft geworden ist" (57; 66), just as elsewhere he clearly alludes to Nietzsche's portrait of ancient Greece in *The Birth of Tragedy* (23; 31).

25. Apart from Benjamin's essay "The Storyteller," which is treated in the present study in its own chapter, the best reading of Lukács's end of the novel in his claims about Flaubert's *Éducation sentimentale* is in de Man, *Blindness and Insight*, pp. 55–59.

Chapter 7
BENJAMIN'S THESES "ON THE CONCEPT OF HISTORY"

1. Walter Benjamin, *Gesammelte Schriften*, ed. Rolf Tiedemann and Hermann Schweppenhäuser, 7 vols. (Frankfurt am Main: Suhrkamp, 1972–89), 1:1227, henceforth cited as GS. "Über den Begriff der Geschichte" is popularly known in English as "Theses on the Philosophy of History" (from an earlier German title, "Geschichtsphilosophische Thesen"), as it appeared in the first English collection of Benjamin's writings, *Illuminations*, ed. Hannah Arendt, trans. Harry Zohn (New York: Harcourt, Brace & World, 1968), pp. 253–64. I shall quote occasionally from Zohn's translation without providing page references; otherwise, the translations are my own.

2. Representative of German scholarly and polemical commentary on the theses is the volume *Materialien zu Benjamins Thesen "Über den Begriff der Geschichte": Beiträge und Interpretationen*, ed. Peter Bulthaup (Frankfurt am Main: Suhrkamp, 1975), henceforth cited as M. The present chapter first appeared in an early version as a review article concerned with this volume in *Diacritics* 9 (1979), 2–17; see its initial pages for a further description of the volume's contents. Additionally, see the important essays by Jürgen Habermas, "Bewusstmachende oder rettende Kritik—die Aktualität Walter Benjamins," and Gershom Scholem, "Walter Benjamin und sein Engel," in *Zur Aktualität Walter Benjamins*, ed. Siegfried Unseld (Frankfurt am Main: Suhrkamp, 1972), pp. 173–223 and 87–138, and the most informed commentary in English to date, Irving Wohlfarth, "On the Messianic Structure of Walter Benjamin's Last Reflections," in *Glyph* 3, ed. Samuel Weber and Henry Sussman (Baltimore: Johns Hopkins U.P., 1978), pp. 148–212. There has also appeared a Heidelberg dissertation on the theses, Jeanne-Marie Gagnebin, *Zur Geschichtsphilosophie Walter Benjamins: Die Unabgeschlossenheit des Sinnes* (Erlangen: Palm & Enke, 1978), the findings of which do not, however, advance beyond those of the *Materialien* volume. A capacious discussion of history in Benjamin may be found in the all-too-brief essay by Irving Wohlfarth, "History, Literature, and the Text: The Case of Walter Benjamin," *MLN* 96 (1981), 1002–14. Only after the present manuscript was completed did there come to my attention Stéphane Mosès's "Geschichte und Subjektivität—Zur Konstitution der historischen Zeit bei Walter Benjamin," in *Das Subjekt der Dichtung: Festschrift für Gerhard Kaiser*, ed. Gerhard Buhr, Friedrich A. Kittler, and Horst Turk (Würzburg: Königs-

hausen & Neumann, 1990), pp. 153–78, which encompassing study will have to be taken into account in any future work on Benjamin and history.

3. Bertolt Brecht, *Arbeitsjournal: Erster Band, 1938 bis 1942,* ed. Werner Hecht (Frankfurt am Main: Suhrkamp, 1973), p. 294.

4. Surviving draft notes to the theses include sections titled "Neue Thesen" and lettered B, C, H, and K (see GS, 1:1233–35).

5. "Thesen über Feuerbach," in *Karl Marx, Friedrich Engels: Werke,* ed. Inst. für Marxismus-Leninismus beim ZK d. SED, vol. 3 (Berlin: Dietz, 1969), p. 7.

6. As Marx and Engels represent it in *Die heilige Familie, oder Kritik der kritischen Kritik* (1845), in *Werke,* vol. 2 (Berlin: Dietz, 1957), p. 90: "Already in *Hegel* the absolute spirit of history has its material in the *masses,* and its corresponding expression only in *philosophy.* The philosopher meanwhile appears only as the organ in which the absolute spirit that makes history, after the running out of the movement [*nach Ablauf der Bewegung*], retroactively [*nachträglich*] comes to consciousness. The philosopher's part in history is reduced to this retroactive consciousness of his, for the real movement is achieved *unconsciously* by the absolute spirit. The philosopher thus arrives *post festum.*" The later and briefer version of this in *Das Kapital: Kritik der politischen Ökonomie,* vol. 1 (1883), in Karl Marx and Friedrich Engels, *Gesamtausgabe* (MEGA), ed. Inst. für Marxismus-Leninismus beim ZK d. KPdSU u. Inst. für Marxismus-Leninismus beim ZK d. SED (Berlin: Dietz, 1989), pt. 2, vol. 8, p. 104: "Reflection [*Das Nachdenken*] on the forms of human life and, consequently, also their scholarly and scientific [*wissenschaftlich*] analysis take a course directly opposite to their actual development. It begins *post festum* and therefore with the finished results of the process of development."

7. See Martin Luther, "Ein Sendbrief von Dolmetschen" (1530), in *Die gantze Heilige Schrifft,* ed. Hans Volz et al., 3 vols. (Munich: Deutscher Taschenbuch Verlag, 1974), 3:242*–249* (suppl.).

8. Tiedemann (M, 81) and Wohlfarth ("On the Messianic Structure," p. 154) both associate the image in the ninth thesis with the baroque of Benjamin's *Trauerspiel* book, without going into the structure of the emblem; I discuss emblems and the *Trauerspiel* book below, in chap. 10. Among the considerable literature on Alciati and baroque emblems, see Erwin Panofsky, *Studies in Iconology: Humanistic Themes in the Art of the Renaissance* (New York: Oxford U.P., 1937); Mario Praz, *Studies in Seventeenth Century Imagery,* 2 vols. (London: Studies of the Warburg Institute, 1939–47); R. G. Freeman, *English Emblem Books* (London: Chatto & Windus, 1948); and E. R. Curtius, *European Literature and the Latin Middle Ages,* trans. Willard R. Trask (New York: Pantheon, 1953), pp. 345, 346.

9. The theses are in GS, 1:691–704. Their brevity and familiarity allow me to forgo the awkwardness of citing each quotation by page number.

10. See, e.g., Gerhard Kaiser and Tiedemann (M, 54–56 and 82–86). Klee's *Angelus Novus,* which later came into Scholem's possession, is photographically reproduced in Scholem's "Walter Benjamin und sein Engel."

11. The longest within the theses, that is; more extended critiques of histori-

cism may be found in his *Passagen-Werk*, GS, vol. 5, and in the essay "Eduard Fuchs, der Sammler und der Historiker," GS, 2:465–505. Several passages from the Fuchs essay appear verbatim in the theses.

12. See also, for Benjamin's notes on this topic, GS, 1:1240, 1241, and 1252, and Wohlfarth, "On the Messianic Structure," pp. 170–78.

13. On the relations of heliotropism and tropological structures, see Jacques Derrida, "La Mythologie blanche," in *Marges de la philosophie* (Paris: Minuit, 1972), pp. 257–324.

14. It will remain for subsequent chapters of the present study to examine the extent to which, in Benjamin's understanding, an image *is* "the historical thing itself." That is, what thesis 5 describes as the historical "Bild, das auf Nimmerwiedersehen im Augenblick seiner Erkennbarkeit eben aufblitzt," will be examined in the next chapter in the context of Benjamin's claim that "Das, wovon man weiss, dass man es bald nicht mehr vor sich haben wird, das wird Bild" (GS, 1:590). And the last chapter returns to Benjamin's language of historical imagery "flashing" by.

15. Walter Benjamin, *Briefe*, ed. Gershom Scholem and Theodor W. Adorno, 2 vols. (Frankfurt am Main: Suhrkamp, 1966), 2:528–29.

16. On Benjamin's "constellation," for example, as an epistemological and metaphysical construction, see chap. 10, below.

17. *Passagen-Werk*, MS Konvolut N 3, cited in Rolf Tiedemann, *Studien zur Philosophie Walter Benjamins* (1965), 2d ed. (Frankfurt am Main: Suhrkamp, 1973), p. 130; now in GS, vol. 5. For another formulation of the "knowability" of time fixed in both the object known and the knower, see "Literaturgeschichte und Literaturwissenschaft," GS, 3:290: "Denn es handelt sich ja nicht darum, die Werke des Schrifttums im Zusammenhang ihrer Zeit darzustellen, sondern in der Zeit, da sie entstanden, die Zeit, die sie erkennt—das ist die unsere—zur Darstellung zu bringen."

18. Wohlfarth, "On the Messianic Structure," p. 190.

19. Ibid., p. 164.

20. Paul de Man, *Blindness and Insight: Essays in the Rhetoric of Contemporary Criticism* (New York: Oxford U.P., 1971), p. 165.

21. The Hofmannsthal quotation, the last line of *Der Tor und der Tod*, also appears (without attribution) in Benjamin's "Über das mimetische Vermögen," GS, 2:213.

22. Benjamin to Gretel Adorno, April 1940, cited in GS, 1:1226.

23. Wohlfarth, "On the Messianic Structure," pp. 150ff., 164–65. I cannot, however, agree with his distinction between Hegelian *Erinnerung* and Benjaminian *Eingedenken*, according to which the latter contrasts with the former by an "exteriorization of the self that explodes the confines of its private interiority" (p. 189); as my earlier chapter on the end of the *Phenomenology* demonstrated, Hegel's *Erinnerung* steps back outside itself, and this is precisely the knowing of history as Wissenschaft.

24. This phrase appears in another draft note for the theses as "unwillkürliche Erinnerung" (GS, 1:1233).

25. See Benjamin's recently published *Verzeichnis der gelesenen Schriften*, GS, 7:457.

26. Habermas, "Bewusstmachende oder rettende Kritik," pp. 207, 215.

Chapter 8
BENJAMIN, BAUDELAIRE, AND THE ALLEGORY OF HISTORY

1. G. W. F. Hegel, *Phänomenologie des Geistes*, in *Werke*, ed. Eva Moldenhauer and Karl Markus Michel, 20 vols. (Frankfurt am Main: Suhrkamp, 1969–71), 3:60: "die Meinung erfährt, dass es anders gemeint ist, als sie meinte."

2. I am referring in general to the broadly Marxist versions of Benjamin in such journals as *New German Critique* and *Telos* and specifically to the highly polemical misrepresentation of Benjamin in Terry Eagleton, *Walter Benjamin, or Towards a Revolutionary Criticism* (London: Verso, 1981). The chapter "The Marxist Rabbi: Walter Benjamin" in Eagleton's recent *The Ideology of the Aesthetic* (Oxford: Blackwell, 1990), pp. 316–40, does not improve upon the earlier work. In this Anglophonic context, the publication of Paul de Man's last lecture on Benjamin's "Task of the Translator" essay, "Conclusions," now in de Man, *The Resistance to Theory* (Minneapolis: U. of Minnesota P., 1986), pp. 73–105, offers one of the first opportunities for a genuine engagement with the problem of history in Benjamin.

3. Marcel Raymond, *De Baudelaire au surréalisme* (Paris: José Corti, 1940); Hugo Friedrich, *Die Struktur der modernen Lyrik: Von der Mitte des neunzehnten bis zur Mitte des zwanzigsten Jahrhunderts* (Hamburg: Rowohlt, 1956); Edmund Wilson, *Axel's Castle: A Study in the Imaginative Literature of 1870–1930* (New York: Charles Scribner's Sons, 1931); Monroe K. Spears, *Dionysus and the City: Modernism in Twentieth-Century Poetry* (New York: Oxford U.P., 1970). I do not intend this list to be exhaustive, only representative of what has become a cliché of modern literary history.

4. Bertolt Brecht, *Arbeitsjournal: Erster Band, 1938 bis 1942*, ed. Werner Hecht (Frankfurt am Main: Suhrkamp, 1973), p. 16.

5. "I want to display Baudelaire as he is embedded in the nineteenth century" and "The Baudelaire work will provide a perspectivally structured view into the depths of the nineteenth century" (Benjamin to Scholem, 14 April 1938, in Walter Benjamin, *Briefe*, ed. Gershom Scholem and Theodor W. Adorno, 2 vols. [Frankfurt am Main: Suhrkamp, 1966], 2:748, henceforth cited as Br [also to Horkheimer, 16 April 1938, Br, 2:752]; and Benjamin to Pollock, 4 July 1938, in Walter Benjamin, *Gesammelte Schriften*, ed. Rolf Tiedemann and Hermann Schweppenhauser, 7 vols. [Frankfurt am Main: Suhrkamp, 1972–89], 1:1078, henceforth cited as GS).

6. Benjamin to Horkheimer, 16 April 1938, Br, 2:751.

7. "The commodity is treated as the fulfillment of the allegorical perspective

in Baudelaire. . . . The dispersion of allegorical appearance [*Die Zerstreuung des allegorischen Scheins*] is implied in this fulfillment [*Erfüllung*]" (ibid., p. 752).

8. "It decisively turns its back on the art-theoretical questioning of the first part and undertakes a social-critical interpretation of the poet. This is a presupposition of Marxist criticism, but in itself alone it does not fulfill [*erfüllt*] the latter's concept. This achievement is reserved for the third part, in which form is to come into its own within the material contexts as decisively as it posed itself as a problem in the first part" (ibid., 28 September 1938, Br, 2:774).

9. Adorno to Benjamin, 10 November 1938, Br, 2:782–90.

10. Benjamin to Adorno, 9 December 1938, Br, 2:791–94.

11. Adorno to Benjamin, 10 November 1938, Br, 2:784.

12. This essay does both more and less than Benjamin claimed in his extremely modest remarks about this "revision" of "Der Flaneur." Its thoughts on the loss of experience (*Erfahrung*) and the decay of the "aura" supplement the essays "The Storyteller" and "The Work of Art in the Age of Its Technical Reproducibility"; its remarks on the different modes of remembering indicated by the terms *Erinnerung, Gedächtnis,* and *Eingedenken* overlap with the complex of reflections upon the philosophy of history represented by the Eduard Fuchs essay and the theses on the concept of history. There are also pages on Hugo, Poe, and Hoffmann carried over from "Das Paris des Second Empire." In other words, this is an extremely complex text within the Benjaminian *oeuvre,* having at least three or four main themes and relations in common with his other work. It is not the object of my considerations in the remainder of this chapter.

13. All quotes from Charles Baudelaire, *Ein Lyriker im Zeitalter des Hochkapitalismus* and from the notes and drafts surrounding it are taken from GS, vol. 1, and will be identified in the text by page number; those quotes from the parts titled "Das Paris des Second Empire bei Baudelaire" and "Zentralpark" will be further identified in the text by SE and ZP, respectively.

14. The editor of the recent, two-volume Pléiade edition of Baudelaire's *Oeuvres complètes,* Claude Pichois (Paris: Gallimard, 1975), following Felix Leakey, "The Originality of Baudelaire's *Le Cygne:* Genesis as Structure and Theme," in *Order and Adventure in Post-Romantic French Poetry,* ed. E. M. Beaumont, J. M. Cocking, and J. Cruickshank (Oxford: Blackwell, 1973), pp. 38–55, juxtaposes with "Le Cygne" this passage on Constantin Guys from Baudelaire's contemporary *Le Peintre de la vie moderne:* "Ainsi, dans l'exécution de M.G. se montrent deux choses: l'une, une contention de mémoire résurrectionniste, évocatrice, une mémoire qui dit à chaque chose: 'Lazare, lève-toi!'; l'autre, un feu, une ivresse de crayon, de pinceau, ressemblant presque à une fureur. *C'est la peur de n'aller pas assez vite, de laisser échapper le fantôme avant que la synthèse n'en soit extraite et saisie*" (my emphasis; cited in 1:1006). It is possible that Benjamin's "What one knows that one will soon no longer have before one—this is what becomes an image" echoes the line from *Le Peintre de la vie moderne,* a text Benjamin demonstrably knew. Cf. also Benjamin's remark in his "Short History of Photography" that for early photographic models, the prolonged procedure caused them "not to live out from the instant, but to live their way into it [*nicht aus dem Augenblick heraus, sondern in ihn hinein zu leben*]"; during their extended exposure to the apparatus, they "grew, as it were, into

the image" (GS, 2:373). In notes to an unfinished introduction to "Das Paris des Second Empire bei Baudelaire," Benjamin also compares an image in Baudelaire with a photographic image (see GS, 1:1164–66).

15. Cited in Baudelaire, *Oeuvres complètes*, 1:1007.

16. Hans Robert Jauss, "Zur Frage der Struktureinheit älterer und moderner Lyrik," *Germanisch-Romanische Monatsschrift* 41 (1960), now in Jauss, *Ästhetische Erfahrung und literarische Hermeneutik*, vol. 1 (Munich: W. Fink, 1977), pp. 295–342.

17. Wolfgang Fietkau, *Schwanengesang auf 1848—Ein Rendezvous am Louvre: Baudelaire, Marx, Proudhon und Victor Hugo* (Hamburg: Rowohlt, 1978), pp. 28–123, 223–40, 368–73, 455.

18. The best of these is Paul de Man's discussion of Baudelaire's "Spleen II" in his introduction to Hans Robert Jauss, *Toward an Aesthetic of Reception*, trans. Timothy Bahti (Minneapolis: U. of Minnesota P., 1983), pp. xv–xxv. See also Hans-Jost Frey, "Über die Erinnerung bei Baudelaire," *Symposium* 33, no. 4 (1979), 312–30, with 322–30 specifically on "Le Cygne"; although he nowhere refers to Benjamin's studies, his own seems clearly informed by a knowledge of them. The several collections of essays that have followed the 1982 publication of the *Passagen-Werk* as volume 5 of Benjamin's *Gesammelte Schriften* have not, for their part, made any significant contribution to an ongoing reassessment of Benjamin's work on Baudelaire. For my part, I have separated altogether a consideration of the *Passagen-Werk* from the present chapters on Benjamin and history; the mass and density of its pages, together with the uncertainty of its editing, have dictated such a decision. For a fine first consideration in English, see Alexander Gelley, "History and Actualization in Walter Benjamin's *Arcades Project*," in *The States of Theory*, ed. David Carroll (New York: Columbia U.P., forthcoming).

19. Baudelaire, *Oeuvres complètes*, 1:85–87. The familiarity of the poem will allow me to avoid the awkwardness of citing line numbers.

20. Cf. Fietkau, *Schwanengesang*, pp. 53–54, 372, on the meanings of the words in question; and Benjamin, GS, 1:742: "l'oeuvre de Haussmann . . . constitue un terrible memento mori à l'intention et au coeur de Paris même" (Benjamin's French).

21. Baudelaire's letter to Hugo of 7 December 1859, which included this poem, echoes the line in question: "Ce qui était important pour moi, c'était de dire vite tout ce qu'un accident, une image, peut contenir de suggestions, et comment la vue d'un animal souffrant pousse l'esprit vers . . . tous ceux qui sont privés de quelque chose d'irretrouvable" (cited in *Oeuvres complètes*, 1:1007). Whether Benjamin's sentence "What one knows that one will soon no longer have before one—this is what becomes an image" also echoes this passage from Baudelaire's correspondence is uncertain.

22. Hannah Arendt, introduction to Benjamin, *Illuminations*, ed. Arendt, trans. Harry Zohn (New York: Harcourt, Brace & World, 1968), pp. 13–14.

23. Jonathan Culler, "Apostrophe," *Diacritics* 7, no. 4 (1977), 64–65.

24. The retrospective effect of reading "ruisseau sans eau" as *ruiss*- without *-eau* is yielded not only by the exposure of the *son* (sound) of *eau* within the

phrase "son beau lac natal" (an exposure assisted by the swan's "utterance" of "Eau" immediately thereafter). The effect is also yielded by reading *eau vide*—empty or absent water—within the phrase "tombeau vide," which later effect is itself set up by the line-ending of "Ovide," pronounced "eau vide." On signs canceling the substantiality of what they appear to announce, see Benjamin's remark on allegory at the end of his *Ursprung des deutschen Trauerspiels* (1928), in GS, 1:406: "Leer aus geht die Allegorie. Das schlechthin Böse, das als bleibende Tiefe sie hegte, existiert nur in ihr, ist einzig und allein Allegorie, bedeutet etwas anderes als es ist. Und zwar bedeutet es genau das Nichtsein dessen, was es vorstellt." I interpret these sentences in chap. 10, below.

25. See Fietkau, *Schwanengesang*, pp. 44–45, 56–62, and Baudelaire, *Oeuvres complètes*, 1:1004.

26. Benjamin, GS, 4:29.

27. Baudelaire, *Oeuvres complètes*, 1:651.

28. Fietkau, *Schwanengesang*, p. 75, where he refers to Racine's *Andromaque*, vv. 292–293.

29. I owe this homophony to a lecture by Yves Bonnefoy, delivered at Wesleyan University in April 1973. To my knowledge, the lecture has remained unpublished.

30. The triad of terms *Erinnerung, Andenken*, and *Gedächtnis* is used and contrasted by Benjamin (in, for example, the essay "On Some Motifs in Baudelaire" and, as we shall see in the next chapter, his "Storyteller" essay), but they are of Hegelian heritage. On the opposition in Hegel between the interiorization of *Erinnerung* and the thought of *Denken* and *Gedächtnis*, see Paul de Man, "Sign and Symbol in Hegel's *Aesthetics*," *Critical Inquiry* 8 (Summer 1982), 761–75, esp. 770–74. The conflation of allegory and irony here is of course justified by Baudelaire's poem, with the allegorical swan beneath "le ciel ironique et cruellement bleu," but I refer also to de Man's argument in "The Rhetoric of Temporality," in *Interpretation: Theory and Practice*, ed. Charles S. Singleton (Baltimore: Johns Hopkins U.P., 1969), pp. 206–7, for the "fundamental structure of allegory" as "the tendency of the language toward narrative," the structure of irony as "the reversed mirror-image of this form," and the "dialectical interplay between the two modes" as "mak[ing] up what is called literary history."

Chapter 9
BENJAMIN'S "THE STORYTELLER"

1. Walter Benjamin, *Gesammelte Schriften*, ed. Rolf Tiedemann and Hermann Schweppenhäuser, 7 vols. (Frankfurt am Main: Suhrkamp, 1972–89), 2:448; quotations from "Der Erzähler" and the draft versions and notes surrounding it are henceforth cited as GS. The Valéry quote is from "Les Broderies de Marie Monnier" (1924), in *Oeuvres*, ed. Jean Hytier, 2 vols. (Paris: Gallimard, 1960), 2:1244.

2. "Haschisch in Marseilles," GS, 4:416.

3. GS, 2:1285; also 4:1012.

4. See "Über den Begriff der Geschichte," thesis 16: "Auf den Begriff einer Gegenwart, die nicht Übergang ist sondern in der die Zeit einsteht und zum Stillstand gekommen ist, kann der historische Materialist nicht verzichten" (GS, 1:702).

5. R. G. Collingwood, "Question and Answer," in *An Autobiography* (Oxford: Oxford U.P., 1939), pp. 29-43; Hans-Georg Gadamer, *Wahrheit und Methode: Grundzüge einer philosophischen Hermeneutik*, 3d ed. (Tübingen: J. C. B. Mohr, 1972), pp. 351-60.

6. "Erfahrung, die von Mund zu Mund geht, ist die Quelle, aus der alle Erzähler geschöpft haben" (GS, 2:440); "Was den Roman von der Erzählung (und vom Epischen im engeren Sinne) trennt, ist sein wesentliches Angewiesensein auf das Buch. Die Ausbreitung des Romans wird erst mit Erfindung der Buchdruckerkunst möglich. Das mündlich Tradierbare, das Gut der Epik, ist von anderer Beschaffenheit als das, was den Bestand des Romans ausmacht. Es hebt den Roman gegen alle übrigen Formen der Prosadichtung—Märchen, Sage, ja selbst Novelle—ab, dass er aus mündlicher Tradition weder kommt noch in sie eingeht. Vor allem aber gegen das Erzählen" (GS, 2:442).

7. "Das Kunstwerk im Zeitalter seiner technischen Reproduzierbarkeit," 2d version, GS, 1:475, 477.

8. G. W. F. Hegel, *Phänomenologie der Geistes*, in *Werke*, ed. Eva Moldenhauer and Karl Markus Michel, 20 vols. (Frankfurt am Main: Suhrkamp, 1969-71), 3:18-19: "Aber wie beim Kinde nach lange stiller Ernährung der erste Atemzug jene Allmählichkeit des nur vermehrenden Fortgangs abbricht—ein qualitativer Sprung—und jetzt das Kind geboren ist, so reift der sich bildende Geist langsam und stille der neuen Gestalt entgegen. . . . Dies allmähliche Zerbröckeln, das die Physiognomie des Ganzen nicht veränderte, wird durch den Aufgang unterbrochen, der, ein Blitz, in einem Male das Gebilde der neuen Welt hinstellt."

9. "Über den Begriff der Geschichte," thesis 9, GS, 1:698.

10. Ibid., thesis 16, GS, 1:702.

11. Ibid.: "Der Historismus stellt das 'ewige' Bild der Vergangenheit, der historische Materialist eine Erfahrung mit ihr, die einzig dasteht."

12. "Das Kunstwerk im Zeitalter," GS, 1:477-78.

13. Cf. the pages near the end of Benjamin's *Ursprung des deutschen Trauerspiels* on "Die Leiche als Emblem," GS, 1:390-93.

14. The predominance that death assumes in Benjamin's essay may be judged by comparing it with a draft version, where additional reasons for the decline of communicability are given, including the centrality of money, the increasing disrepute of sexual relations, and the rise of neuroses (GS, 2:1285).

15. For a more explicitly allegorical version of the fateful undoing of the *Netz* of storytelling, see the draft version: "So unfasslich es ist: nichts 'Ewiges' im Menschen bleibt, sieht man näher zu, so absolut und unbedingt wie es zuerst sich anlässt. Wie zart ist nicht im Grunde das Netz gewoben, in welchem diese

wunderbare Gabe, das Erzählen ruht und wie lösen nicht unauffällig aber unwiderruflich sich alle Ecken und Enden!" (GS, 2:1284).

16. The first mentions in literature of mechanical clocks are found in Jean de Meun's *Roman de la rose* and Dante's *Paradiso*. Clocks with mechanically moving processions are even later.

17. In "Über den Begriff der Geschichte," thesis 15, GS, 1:701-2, Benjamin distinguishes between calendars, which memorially mark time, and clocks, which run emptily onward; here, I am making a parallel distinction between clocks that mark time and those that do not.

18. On the relation of histories to stories in Benjamin's essay, see the following passage: "Jedwede Untersuchung einer bestimmten epischen Form hat es mit dem Verhältnis zu tun, in dem diese Form zur Geschichtsschreibung steht. Ja, man darf weitergehen und sich die Frage vorlegen, ob die Geschichtsschreibung nicht den Punkt schöpferischer Indifferenz zwischen allen Formen der Epik darstellt. Dann würde die geschriebene Geschichte sich zu den epischen Formen verhalten wie das weisse Lichte zu den Spektralfarben. Wie dem auch sei, unter allen Formen der Epik gibt es nicht eine, deren Vorkommen in dem reinen, farblosen Licht der geschriebenen Geschichte zweifelsfreier ist als die Chronik. Und im breiten Farbband der Chronik stufen die Arten, in denen erzählt werden kann, sich wie Schattierungen ein und derselben Farben ab. Der Chronist ist der Geschichts-Erzähler" (GS, 2:451).

19. For an antecedent transcendental and theological usage of "the unforgettable" in Benjamin, see his "Die Aufgabe des Übersetzers" (1923): "gewisse Relationsbegriffe ihren guten, ja vielleicht besten Sinn behalten, wenn sie nicht von vorne herein ausschliesslich auf den Menschen bezogen werden. So dürfte von einem unvergesslichen Leben oder Augenblick gesprochen werden, auch wenn alle Menschen sie vergessen hätten. Wenn nämlich deren Wesen es forderte, nicht vergessen zu werden, so würde jenes Prädikat nichts Falsches, sondern nur eine Forderung, der Menschen nicht entsprechen, und zugleich auch wohl den Verweis auf einen Bereich enthalten, in dem ihr entsprochen wäre: auf ein Gedenken Gottes" (GS, 4:10).

20. In a draft version, Benjamin combines a historical claim with a regret for the loss of the allegorical (the "exemplary") dimension to underscore this point about the solitary nature of the novel reader: "Die [innerste] Geburtskammer des Romans ist—geschichtlich gesehen—die Einsamkeit des [unberatenen] Individuums, das sich über seine wichtigsten Anliegen nicht mehr exemplarisch aussprechen kann, selbst unberaten ist und keinen Rat geben kann" (GS, 2:1281).

21. Harry Zohn's translation in *Illuminations* (New York: Harcourt, Brace & World, 1968), which I have had occasion to criticize in an earlier chapter, is exact here.

22. Benjamin's use of *darstellen* here supports his argument about truth being articulated here (see the "Erkenntniskritische Vorrede" to the *Ursprung des deutschen Trauerspiels*, GS, 1:207-12).

23. *Ursprung des deutschen Trauerspiels*, GS, 1:406.

24. Here, Benjamin avoids any use of *darstellen* (see n. 22). This is as good a

place as any to quote Benjamin, in a draft version of this essay, cautioning against excessive pathos in the face of the death of storytelling's reception of death: "Der Unfug des Sterbens. Nun dann ist eben auch das Erzählen ein Unfug. Dann stirbt vielleicht, vorerst einmal, das pour commencer, die ganze Aura von Trost, Weisheit, Feierlichkeit, mit welcher wir den Tod umgeben haben, ab? Tant mieux. Nicht weinen. Der Unsinn der kritischen Prognosen. Film statt Erzählung. Die ewig lebenspendende Nüance" (GS, 2:1282).

25. "Das Gedächtnis ist das epische Vermögen vor allen anderen. Nur dank eines umfassenden Gedächtnisses kann die Epik einerseits den Lauf der Dinge sich zu eigen, andererseits mit deren Hinschwinden, mit der gewalt des Todes ihren Frieden machen" (GS, 2:453).

26. "Das verewigende Gedächtnis des Romanciers [steht] im Gegensatz zu dem kurzweiligen des Erzählers. Das erste ist dem *einem* Helden geweiht, der *einen* Irrfahrt oder dem *einen* Kampf; das zweite den *vielen* zerstreuten Begebenheiten. Es ist, mit anderen Worten, das *Eingedenken*, das als das Musische des Romans dem Gedächtnis, dem Musischen der Erzählung, zur Seite tritt, nachdem sich mit dem Zerfall des Epos die Einheit ihres Ursprungs in der Erinnerung geschieden hatte" (GS, 2:454).

27. Where Benjamin speaks of "wisdom" and "counsel" in this essay, he could still speak of *truth* in a draft version: "Eine Wahrheit erweist sich in einer Erzählung. Eine Erzählung mündet in eine Weisheit. Der Erzähler ist immer auch einer der Rat weiss. . . . Heute beginnen solche Worte schon sehr altmodisch zu klingen" (GS, 2:1283–84).

28. For an anticipation of this notion of "profane happiness" as an escape from mythic nature, see Benjamin's early essay "Schicksal und Charackter," GS, 2:171–79; for a critical interpretation of aspects of his argument, see my "Theories of Knowledge: Fate and Forgetting in the Early Works of Walter Benjamin," in *Benjamin's Ground: New Readings of Walter Benjamin*, ed. Rainer Nägele (Detroit: Wayne State U.P., 1988), 61–82.

29. Compare Benjamin's remark elsewhere in the essay similarly equating the "higher" salvationary and "lower" natural-historical perspectives: "Ob der Weltlauf ein heilsgeschichtlich bedingter oder ein natürlicher ist, das macht keinen Unterschied" (GS, 2:452).

30. See GS, 2:461–62, and also Benjamin's use of related terms for allegory (*überschlagen, umspringen, umschlagen*) in his *Ursprung des deutschen Trauerspiels*, GS, 1:405–6.

31. Cf. Benjamin in a draft version of this essay: "Und die Erzählung muss, für jetzt, in den Abgrund zurück. Sie ist neuer Weisheit zu leer und vor allem alter zu voll, um uns dienen zu können" (GS, 2:1284).

32. See GS, 2:464: "Die Rolle der Hand in der Produktion ist bescheidener geworden und der Platz, den sie beim Erzählen ausgefüllt hat, ist verödet. . . . Sprichwörter, so könnte man sagen, sind Trümmer, die am Platz von alten Geschichten stehen." On the allegorical significance of such imagery according to Benjamin, see the section "Die Ruine" in his *Ursprung des deutschen Trauerspiels*, GS, 1:353–58.

Chapter 10
BENJAMIN'S *URSPRUNG DES DEUTCHEN TRAUERSPIELS*

1. "Ursprung ist das Ziel," quoted in "Über den Begriff der Geschichte," thesis 16, *Gesammelte Schriften*, ed. Rolf Tiedemann and Hermann Schweppenhäuser, 7 vols. (Frankfurt am Main: Suhrkamp, 1972–89), 1:701.

2. The first such work of his might have been his dissertation, for letters written during its inception indicate that he was thinking of choosing Kant and the philosophy of history as his topic (see Walter Benjamin, *Briefe*, ed. Gershom Scholem and Theodor W. Adorno, 2 vols. [Frankfurt am Main: Suhrkamp, 1966], 1:137–38, 151–52, 159, 161, 176).

3. My unpacking can begin by clarifying some of its linguistic tags. The title *Ursprung des deutschen Trauerspiels* will be abbreviated in the text as *Ursprung*. Benjamin's term and concept *Ursprung*—the German word itself—will be rendered as "origin," always within quotation marks. *Trauerspeil* (literally "mourning play") will be left in German. I have profited from John Osborne's redoubtable translation (*The Origin of German Tragic Drama* [London: New Left Books, 1977]) but have been obliged to modify its version at many turns.

4. The best secondary literature on Benjamin's book is in two comprehensive German studies of his work: Rolf Tiedemann, *Studien zur Philosophie Walter Benjamins* (1965), 2d ed. (Frankfurt am Main: Suhrkamp, 1973), and Winfried Menninghaus, *Walter Benjamins Theorie der Sprachmagie* (Frankfurt: Suhrkamp, 1980). See also, on the prologue, Fred Lönker, "Benjamins Darstellungstheorie: Zur 'Erkenntniskritischen Vorrede' zum 'Ursprung des deutschen Trauerspiels,'" in *Urszenen: Literaturwissenschaften als Diskursanalyse und Diskurskritik*, ed. Friedrich Kittler and Horst Turk (Frankfurt am Main: Suhrkamp, 1977), pp. 293–322. In English, Bainard Cowan's "Walter Benjamin's Theory of Allegory," *New German Critique* 22 (1981), 109–22, is an accomplished first presentation of some of the book's leading themes, and Charles Rosen's two-part review article, "The Ruins of Walter Benjamin" and "The Origins of Walter Benjamin," *New York Review of Books*, 27 October 1977, 31–40, and 10 November 1977, 30–38, is learned and insightful, but other representations of this work in book-length English-language studies of Benjamin and the Frankfurt School are unreliable. Some of the best students of Benjamin in America, however—Rainer Nägele, Samuel Weber, Irving Wohlfarth—are now writing on the *Ursprung* and will help correct the regrettable state of the American reception of this masterwork.

5. Quotations from Benjamin's *Ursprung* and from notes and letters surrounding its composition are from his *Gesammelte Schriften*, vol. 1, and are cited in this text by page numbers alone.

6. One such distinction, Benjamin says, is that his "philosophical" treatment presupposes unity, while literary-historical treatments are obliged to demonstrate multiplicity (218).

7. "Die Phänomene gehen aber nicht integral in ihrem rohen empirischen Bestande, dem der Schein sich beimischt, sondern in ihren Elementen allein, gerettet, in das Reich der Ideen ein . . . Begriffen . . . sind es, welche an den

Dingen die Lösung in die Elemente vollziehen. . . . Durch ihre Vermittlerrolle leihen die Begriffe den Phänomen Anteil am Sein der Ideen" (213-14).

8. "Im Wesen der Wahrheit [ist] die Einheit durchaus unvermittelt und direkte Bestimmung" (210).

9. For Benjamin's original employment of the pair of terms *Sachgehalt* and *Wahrheitsgehalt*, see his essay "Goethes Wahlverwandtschaften," *Gesammelte Schriften*, 1:125-26.

10. It is possible that Benjamin alludes here to Hölderlin's fragment, "Werden und Vergehen," given that title by Ludwig von Pigenot and Friedrich Seebass, the final editors of the first critical edition begun by Norbert von Hellingrath and completed in 1923, that is, just as Benjamin is preparing this text.

11. It is this misunderstanding that some "reception historians" would convey, rendering "posthistory" as, in effect, historical reception (see Hans Robert Jauss, *Toward an Aesthetic of Reception*, trans. Timothy Bahti [Minneapolis: U. of Minnesota P., 1982], p. 95).

12. Although this reference to "the dialectic" invites speculation, it is still undecided how much Hegel Benjamin at this point—or ever—really knew. The two mentions of Hegel in the prologue are very general, and the body of the book cites his *Ästhetik* only twice. Benjamin's specific use of "dialectic" here appears to lack Hegel's distinctive feature, namely, that of determinate negation.

13. After the first sentence of this passage, Benjamin footnotes his own preface to his Baudelaire translation, "Die Aufgabe des Überstezters"; the note apparently refers to the passage that begins: "Dass eine Übersetzung niemals, so gut sie auch sei, etwas für das Original zu bedeuten vermag, leuchtet ein. Dennoch steht sie mit diesem Kraft seiner Übersetzbarkeit im nächsten Zusammenhang. Ja, dieser Zusammenhang ist um so inniger, als es für das Original selbst nichts mehr bedeutet. Er darf ein natürlicher genannt werden und zwar genauer ein Zusammenhang des Lebens. So wie die Äusserungen des Lebens innigst mit dem Lebendigen zusammenhängen, ohne ihm etwas zu bedeuten, geht die Übersetzung aus dem Original hervor. Zwar nicht aus seinem Leben so sehr denn aus seinem 'Überleben'" (*Gesammelte Schriften*, 4:10).

14. "Criticism is the mortification of works" echoes Benjamin's sentence from his contemporary book *Einbahnstrasse*, "The work is the death-mask of its conception" (*Gesammelte Schriften*, 4:107).

15. Osborne's translation, p. 66, misunderstands Benjamin's negative in the first sentence and thus mistranslates it as "The baroque knows no eschatology; and for that very reason it possesses no mechanism. . . ."

16. See p. 275 for Benjamin's remarks on the primacy of the image of the second hand on the clock face for this era's sense of "repeatable time without quality [*qualitätslosen wiederholbaren Zeit*]."

17. The apparent synonymity in this sentence's use of the terms "mourning" and "melancholy" suggests either that Benjamin had not read Freud's essay "Mourning and Melancholia," the publication of which in 1918 (*Zeitschrift für Psychoanalyse* 4 [1916-18]) precedes Benjamin's work on the *Ursprung*, or that he ignored it if he had read it. But the following continuation of Benjamin's

argument on mourning nonetheless approximates Freud's thesis on melancholy as an obsessive unwillingness to give up a dead or departed love-object: "Wenn für das Trauerspiel im Herzen der Trauer die Gesetze, entfaltet teils, teils unentfaltet, sich finden, so ist es weder der Gefühlszustand des Dichters noch des Publikums, dem ihre Darstellung sich widmet, vielmehr ein vom empirischen Subjekt gelöstes und innig an die Fülle eines Gegenstands gebundenes Fühlen. . . . Bestimmt wird er durch die erstaunliche Beharrlichkeit der Intention, die unter den Gefühlen ausser diesem vielleicht—und das nicht spielweis—nur der Liebe eignet. Denn während im Bereiche der Affektivität nicht selten Anziehung mit der Entfremdung in dem Verhältnis einer Intention zum Gegenstande alterniert, ist Trauer zur besondern Steigerung, kontinuierlichen Vertiefung ihrer Intention befähigt" (318).

18. Benjamin's language here implies, I believe, the contrasting pair in German *sinnlich* ("sensorial" or "sensuous") and *sinnvoll* ("meaningful").

19. See his "The Rhetoric of Temporality," in *Interpretation: Theory and Practice*, ed. Charles S. Singleton (Baltimore: Johns Hopkins U.P., 1969), 173–209, on the first page of which he cites Benjamin's text—perhaps the first employment of Benjamin in English-language literary theory.

20. On this line, see my "Ambiguity and Indeterminacy: The Juncture," *Comparative Literature* 38, no. 3 (1986), 209–23.

21. Osborne's translation of this sentence, "In the allegorical construction of the baroque *Trauerspiel* such ruins have always stood out clearly as formal elements of the preserved work of art" (182), misses Benjamin's strong sense of "ruined forms of the saved."

22. See above, chap. 9.

23. This image echoes the penultimate image of Benjamin's essay "Aufgabe des Übersetzers," composed a year or two earlier; referring to Hölderlin's translations of Sophocles, he wrote that "In ihnen stürzt der Sinn von Abgrund zu Abgrund, bis er droht in bodenlosen Sprachtiefen sich zu verlieren. Aber es gibt ein Halten" (*Gesammelte Schriften*, 4:21). The echo may be deliberate, for in his *Ursprung*, p. 365, Benjamin recalls these translations in endorsing von Hellingrath's characterization of them as stemming from Hölderlin's "baroque" period.

24. Despite its promising title and several interesting readings, Howard Stern's *Gegenbild, Reihenfolge, Sprung: An Essay on Related Figures of Argument in Walter Benjamin* (Bern: Peter Lang, 1982) disappointingly never discusses the figure *Sprung* in the context of the *Ursprung*.

25. See also p. 341, where Benjamin quotes Creuzer: "The difference between the two modes is to be located in the momentary, which allegory lacks. . . . There [in the symbol] there is momentary totality; here there is progression in a series of moments."

26. "Denn mitten in jener wissentlichen Entwürdigung des Gegenstandes bewahrt ja die melancholische Intention auf unvergleichliche Art seinem Dingsein die Treue" (398).

27. For the insistence on the separation of the fulfillment of meaning from its

allegorical locus, see also p. 398: "Dem allegorisch Bedeutenden ist es durch Schuld versagt, seine Sinnerfüllung in sich selbst zu finden."

28. On allegories of reading and their unreadability, see Paul de Man, *Allegories of Reading: Figural Language in Rousseau, Nietzsche, Rilke, and Proust* (New Haven: Yale U.P., 1979), p. 205 and passim, and Carol Jacobs, "Allegories of Reading Paul de Man," in *Reading de Man Reading*, ed. Lindsay Waters and Wlad Godzich (Minneapolis: U. of Minnesota P., 1989), pp. 105–20.

Index

333

Designed by Gerard A. Valerio

Composed by Graphic Composition, Inc., in Plantin text and display

Printed on 50-lb. Glatfelter B 16 and bound in Joanna Arrestox cloth by Thomson-Shore, Inc.